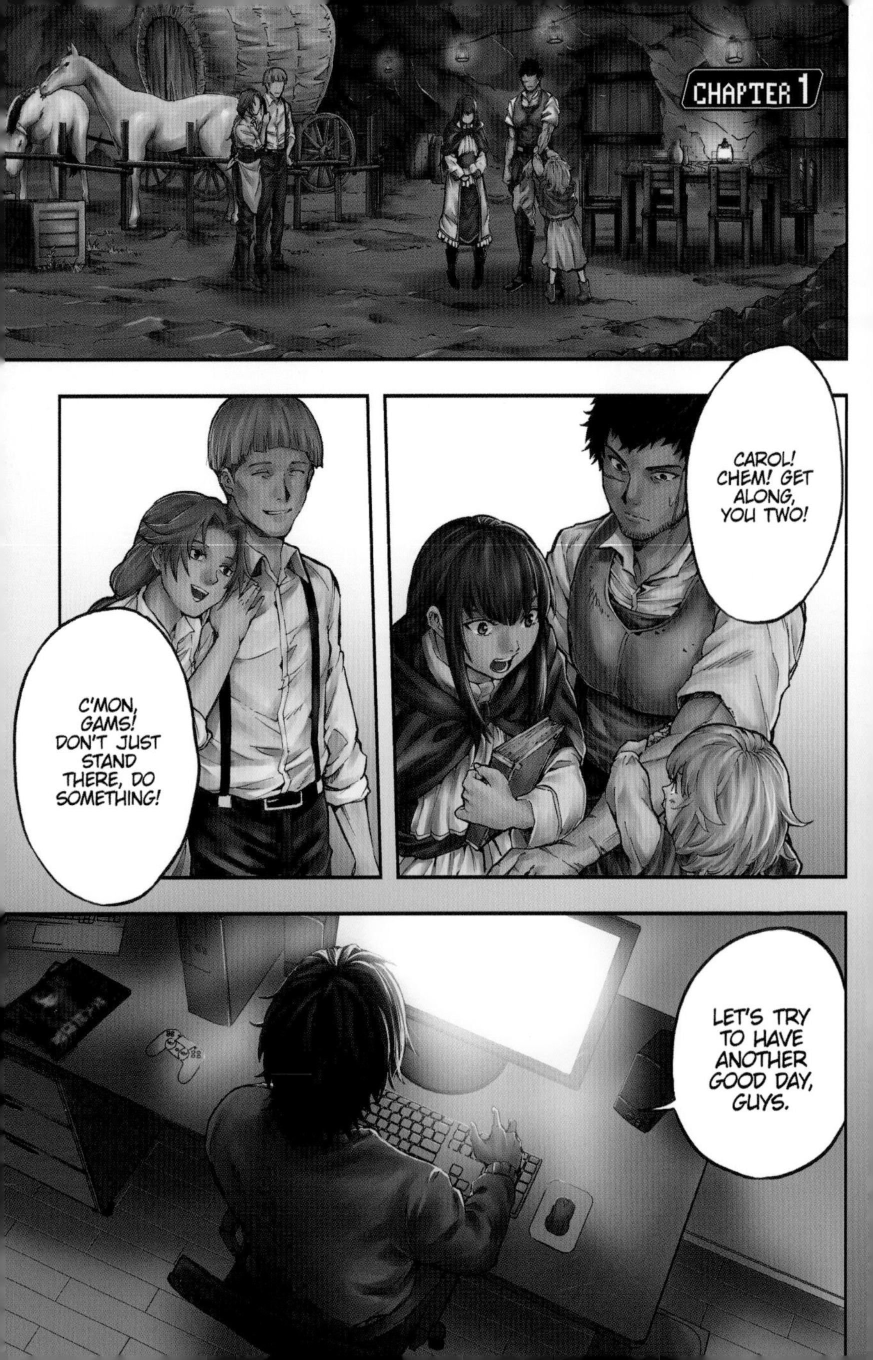
CHAPTER 1
CAROL! CHEM! GET ALONG, YOU TWO!
C'MON, GAMS! DON'T JUST STAND THERE, DO SOMETHING!
LET'S TRY TO HAVE ANOTHER GOOD DAY, GUYS.

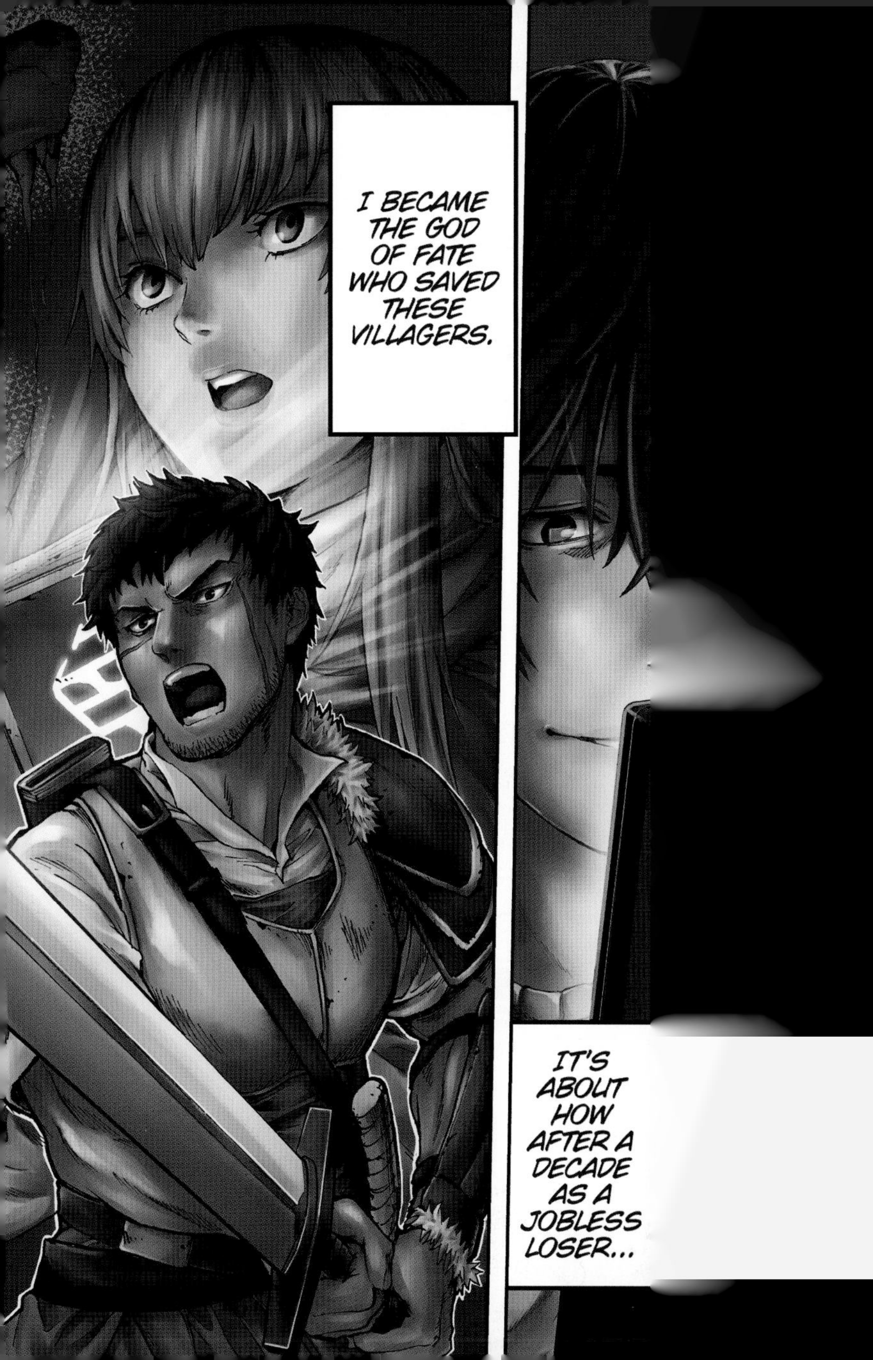
IT'S ABOUT HOW AFTER A DECADE AS A JOBLESS LOSER...
I BECAME THE GOD OF FATE WHO SAVED THESE VILLAGERS.

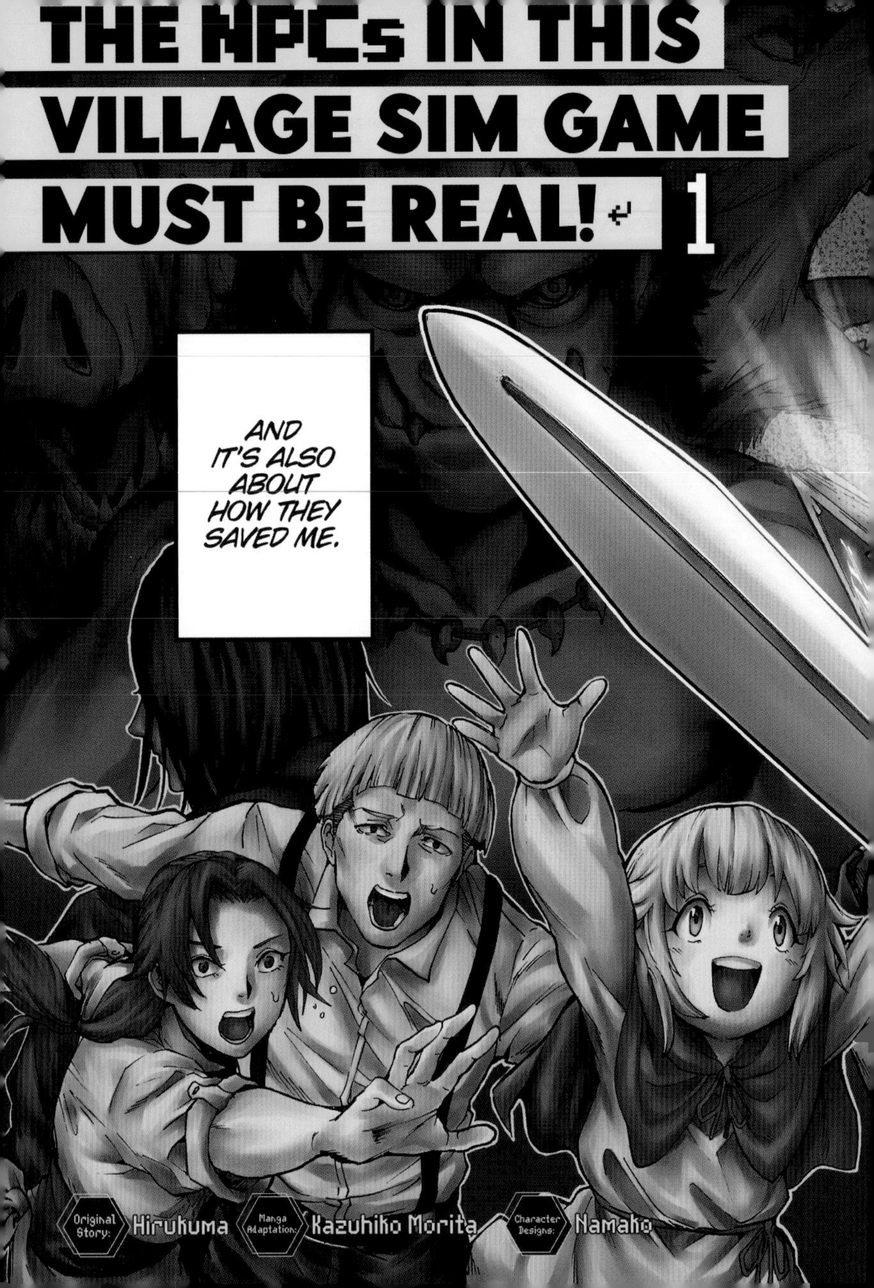
THE NPCs IN THIS VILLAGE SIM GAME MUST BE REAL! 1
AND IT'S ALSO ABOUT HOW THEY SAVED ME.
Original Story: Hirukuma
Manga Adaptation: Kazuhiko Morita
Character Designs: Namako

THE NPCs IN THIS VILLAGE SIM GAME MUST BE REAL! ↵

1

CONTENTS

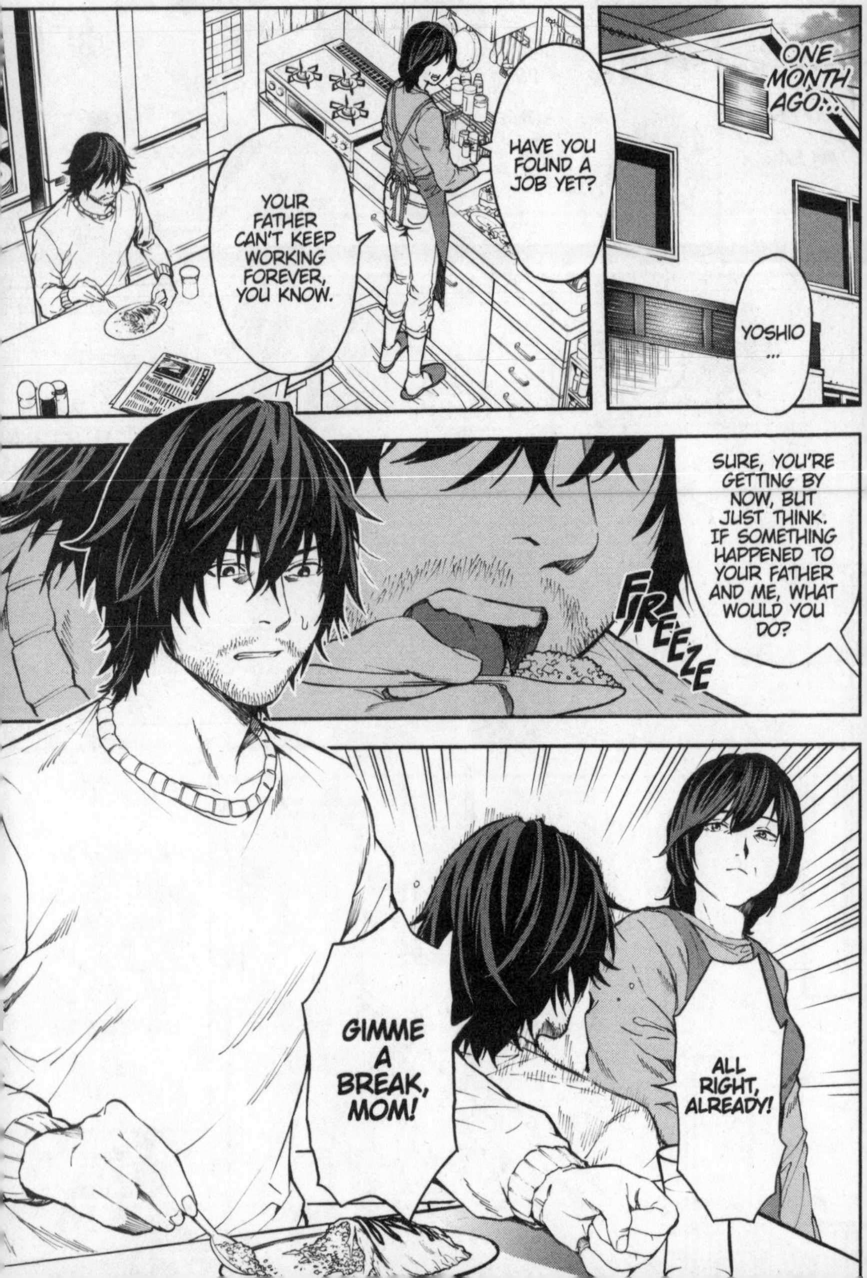
ONE MONTH AGO...
YOSHIO ...
HAVE YOU FOUND A JOB YET?
YOUR FATHER CAN'T KEEP WORKING FOREVER, YOU KNOW.
SURE, YOU'RE GETTING BY NOW, BUT JUST THINK. IF SOMETHING HAPPENED TO YOUR FATHER AND ME, WHAT WOULD YOU DO?
FREEZE
ALL RIGHT, ALREADY!
GIMME A BREAK, MOM!

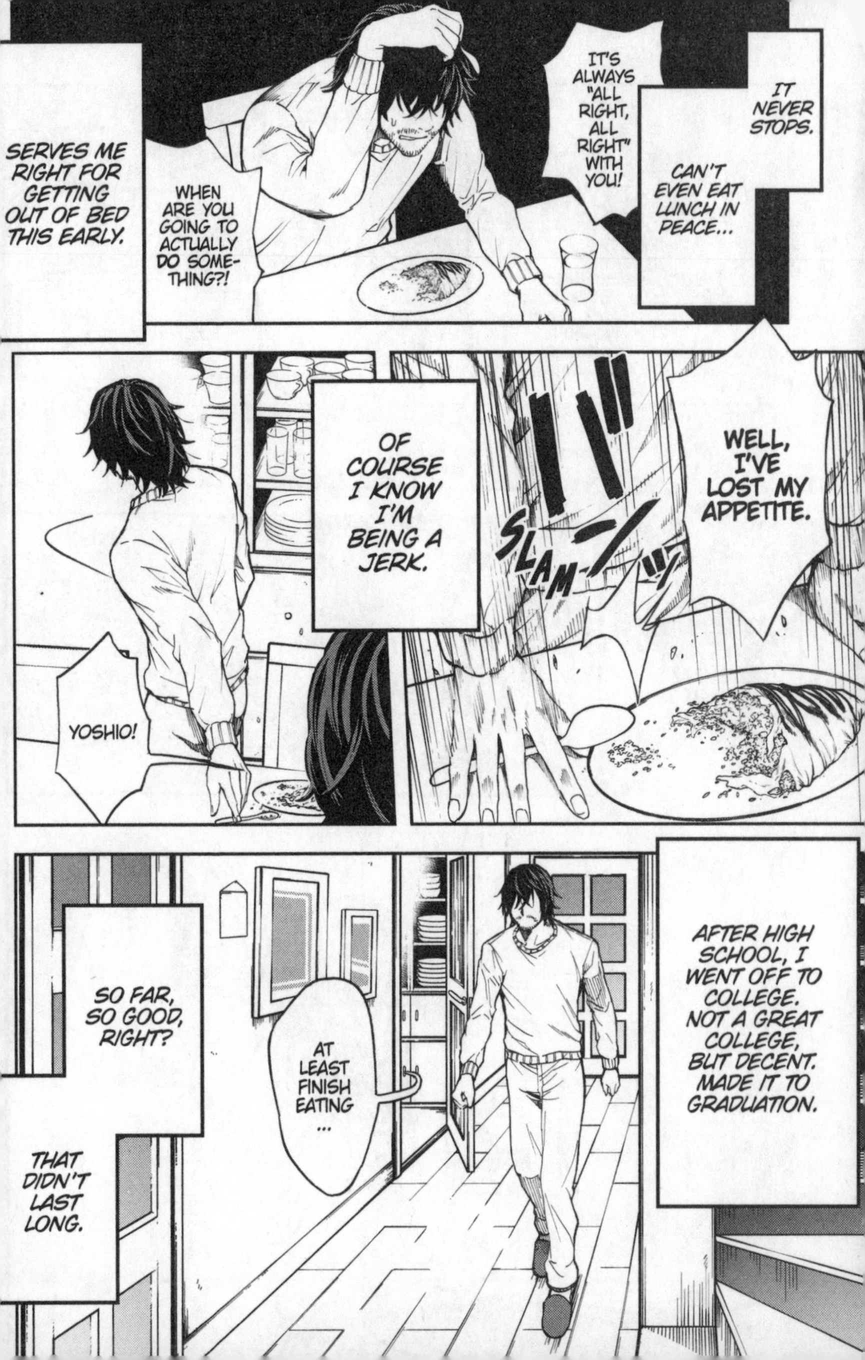
IT NEVER STOPS.
CAN'T EVEN EAT LUNCH IN PEACE...
IT'S ALWAYS "ALL RIGHT, ALL RIGHT" WITH YOU!
WHEN ARE YOU GOING TO ACTUALLY DO SOME-THING?!
SERVES ME RIGHT FOR GETTING OUT OF BED THIS EARLY.
WELL, I'VE LOST MY APPETITE.
SLAM-!!
OF COURSE I KNOW I'M BEING A JERK.
YOSHIO!
AFTER HIGH SCHOOL, I WENT OFF TO COLLEGE. NOT A GREAT COLLEGE, BUT DECENT. MADE IT TO GRADUATION.
AT LEAST FINISH EATING ...
SO FAR, SO GOOD, RIGHT?
THAT DIDN'T LAST LONG.

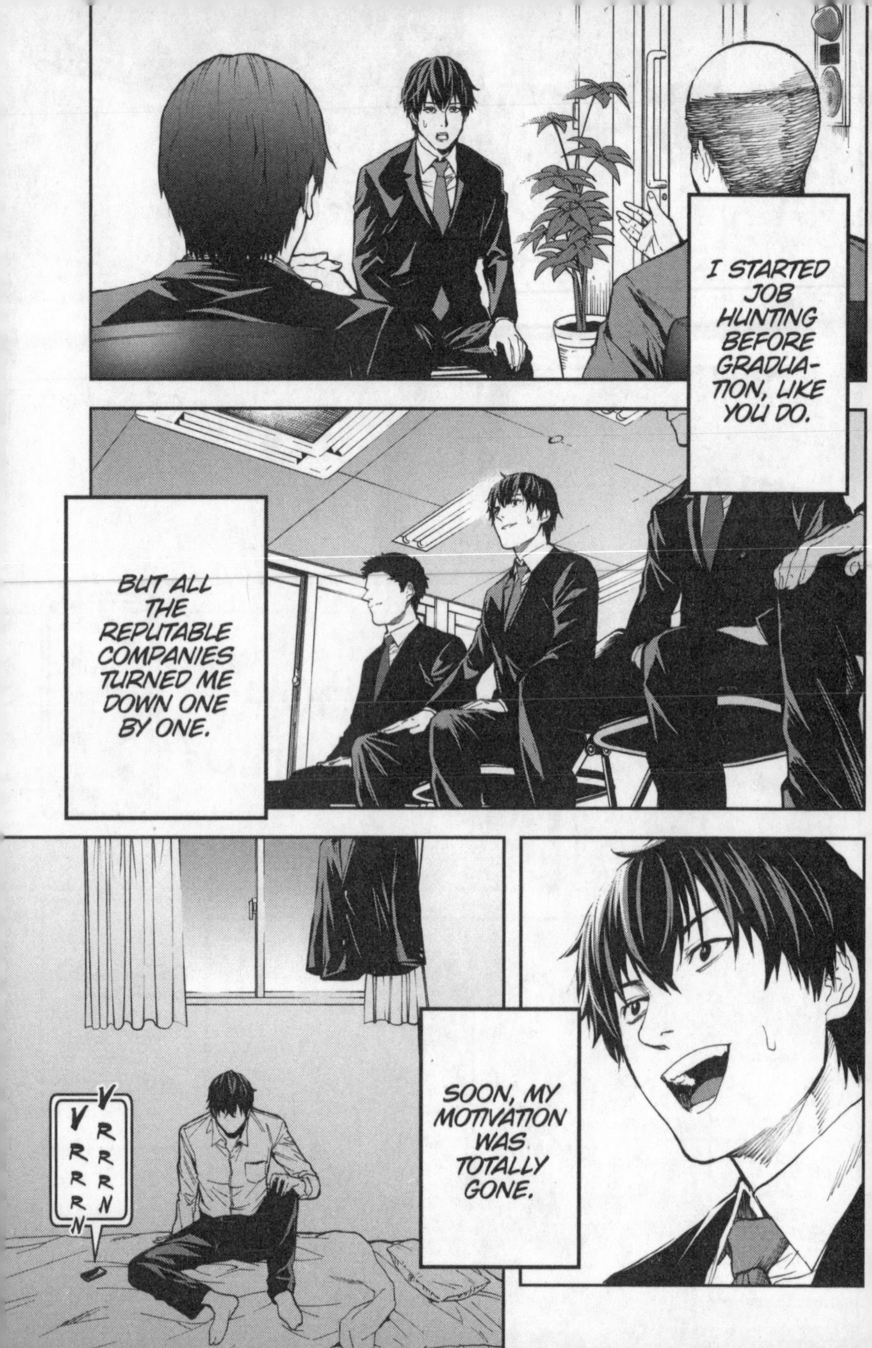
I STARTED JOB HUNTING BEFORE GRADUATION, LIKE YOU DO.
BUT ALL THE REPUTABLE COMPANIES TURNED ME DOWN ONE BY ONE.
SOON, MY MOTIVATION WAS TOTALLY GONE.
VRRRN
VRRRN

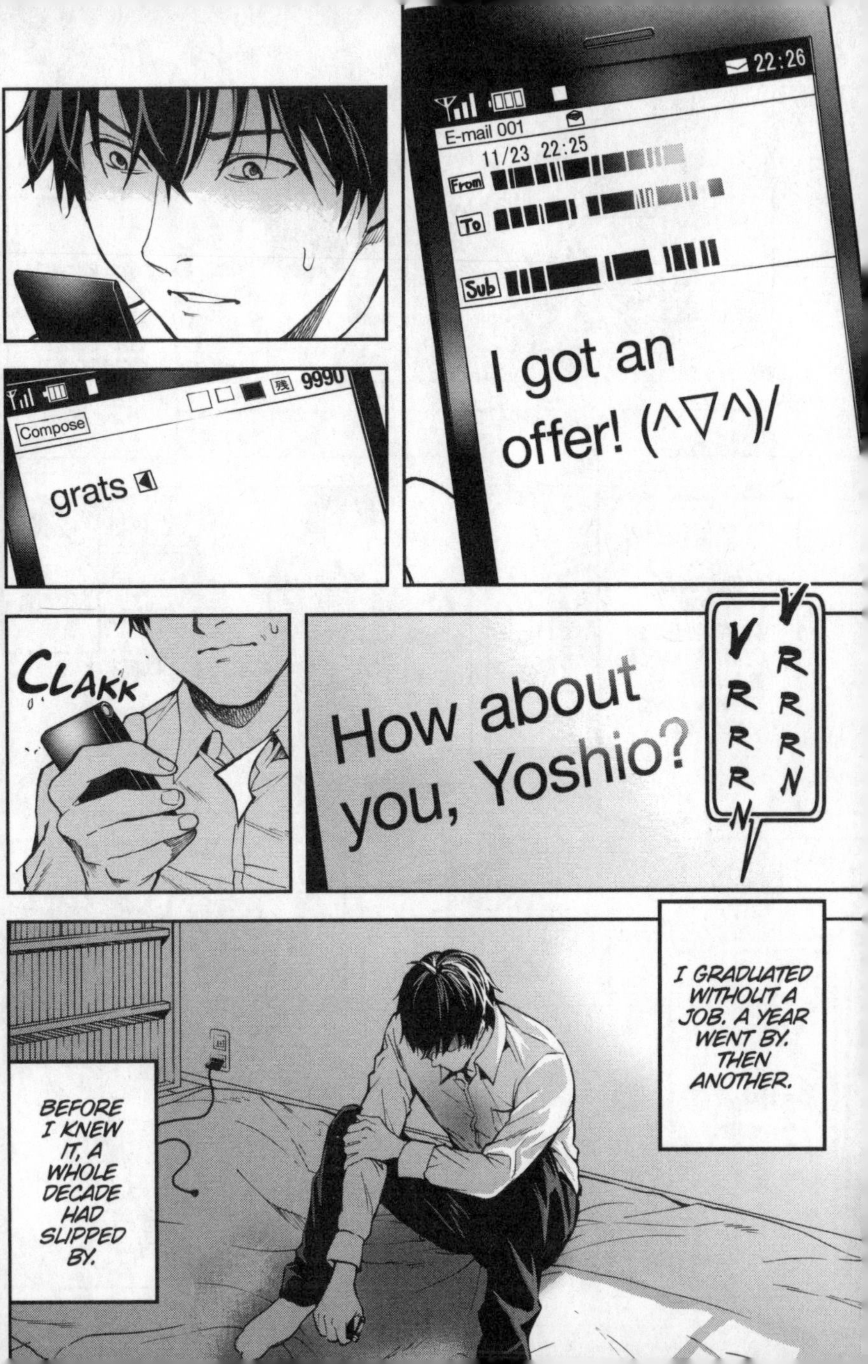
22:26
E-mail 001
11/23 22:25
From [redacted]
To [redacted]
Sub [redacted]
I got an offer! (^▽^)/
残 9990
Compose
grats
VRRRN VRRRN
How about you, Yoshio?
CLAKK
I GRADUATED WITHOUT A JOB. A YEAR WENT BY. THEN ANOTHER.
BEFORE I KNEW IT, A WHOLE DECADE HAD SLIPPED BY.

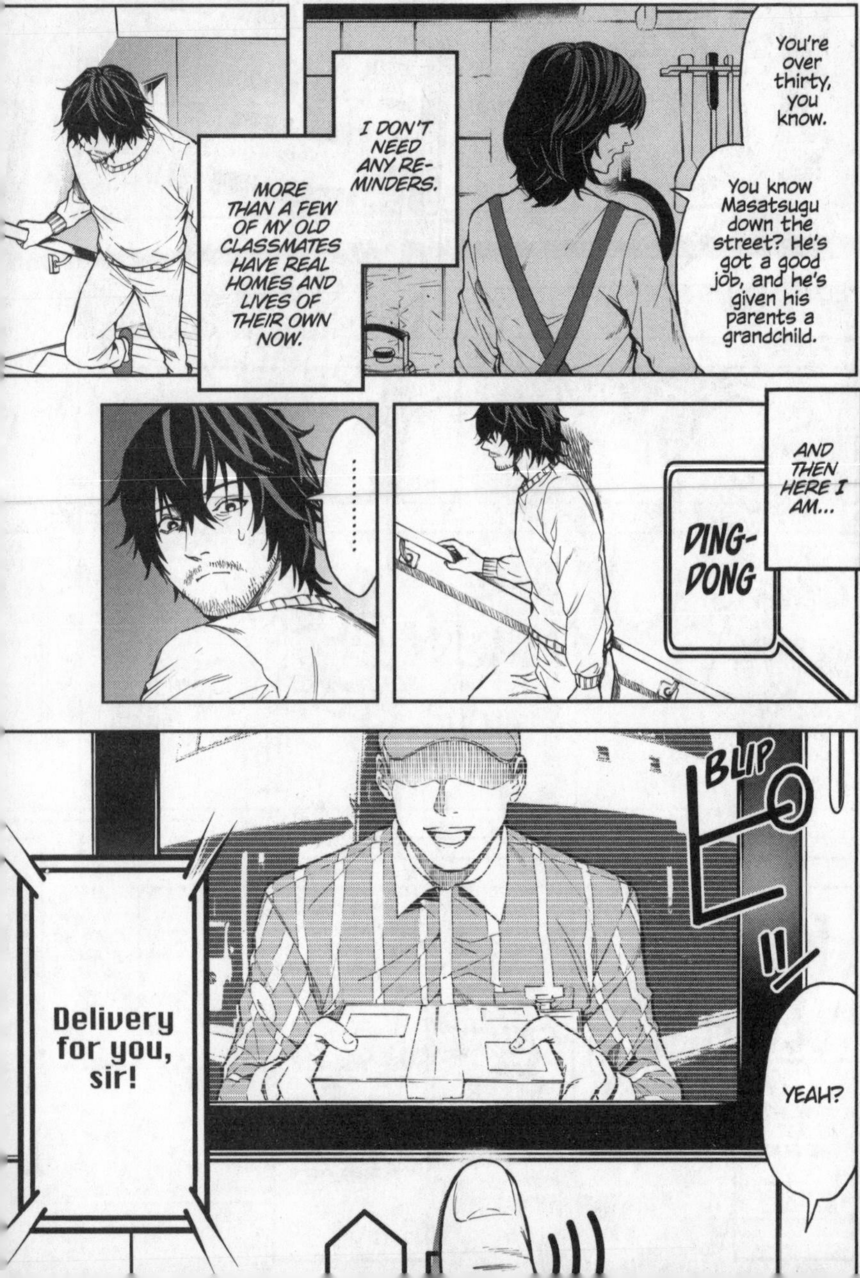
You're over thirty, you know.
You know Masatsugu down the street? He's got a good job, and he's given his parents a grandchild.
I DON'T NEED ANY RE-MINDERS.
MORE THAN A FEW OF MY OLD CLASSMATES HAVE REAL HOMES AND LIVES OF THEIR OWN NOW.
AND THEN HERE I AM...
DING-DONG
......
BLIP
YEAH?
Delivery for you, sir!

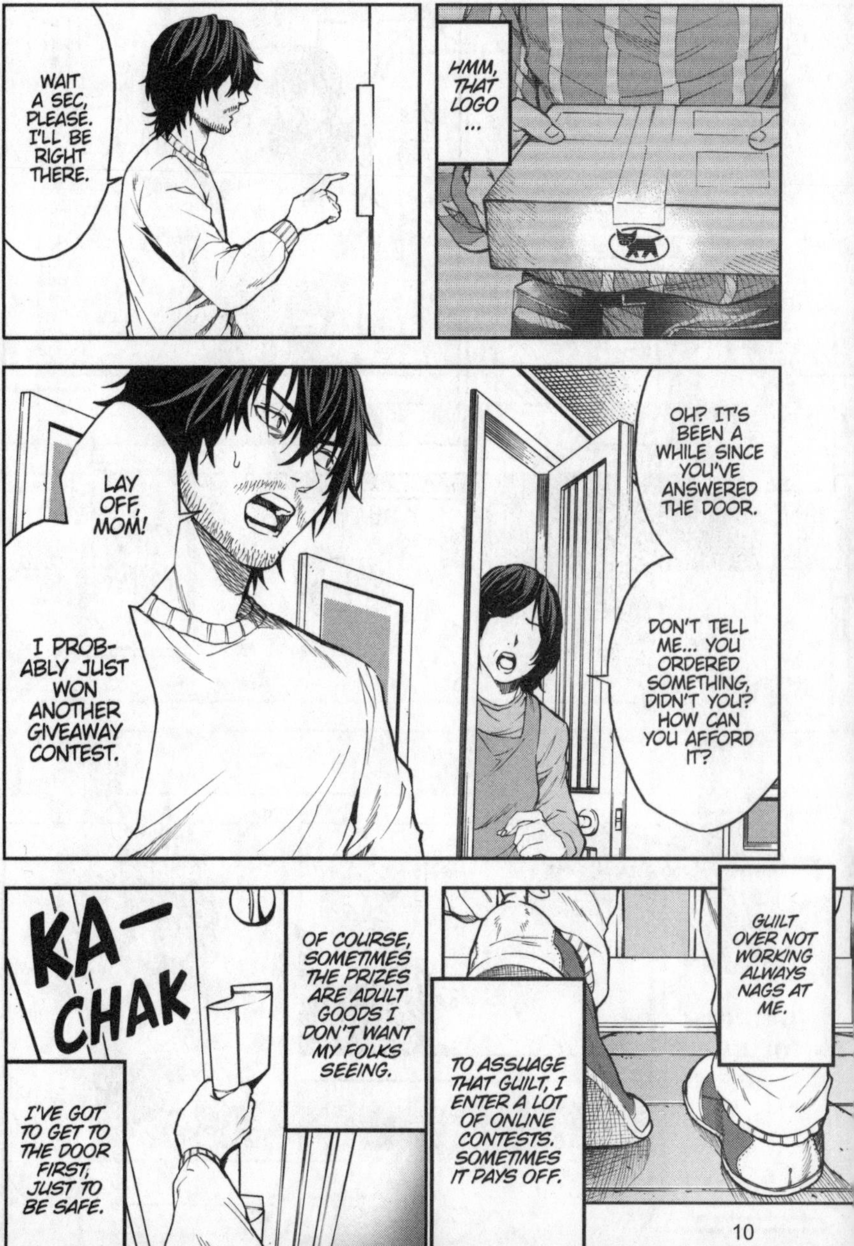
HMM, THAT LOGO ...
WAIT A SEC, PLEASE. I'LL BE RIGHT THERE.
OH? IT'S BEEN A WHILE SINCE YOU'VE ANSWERED THE DOOR.
LAY OFF, MOM!
DON'T TELL ME... YOU ORDERED SOMETHING, DIDN'T YOU? HOW CAN YOU AFFORD IT?
I PROB-ABLY JUST WON ANOTHER GIVEAWAY CONTEST.
GUILT OVER NOT WORKING ALWAYS NAGS AT ME.
TO ASSUAGE THAT GUILT, I ENTER A LOT OF ONLINE CONTESTS. SOMETIMES IT PAYS OFF.
OF COURSE, SOMETIMES THE PRIZES ARE ADULT GOODS I DON'T WANT MY FOLKS SEEING.
KA-CHAK
I'VE GOT TO GET TO THE DOOR FIRST, JUST TO BE SAFE.

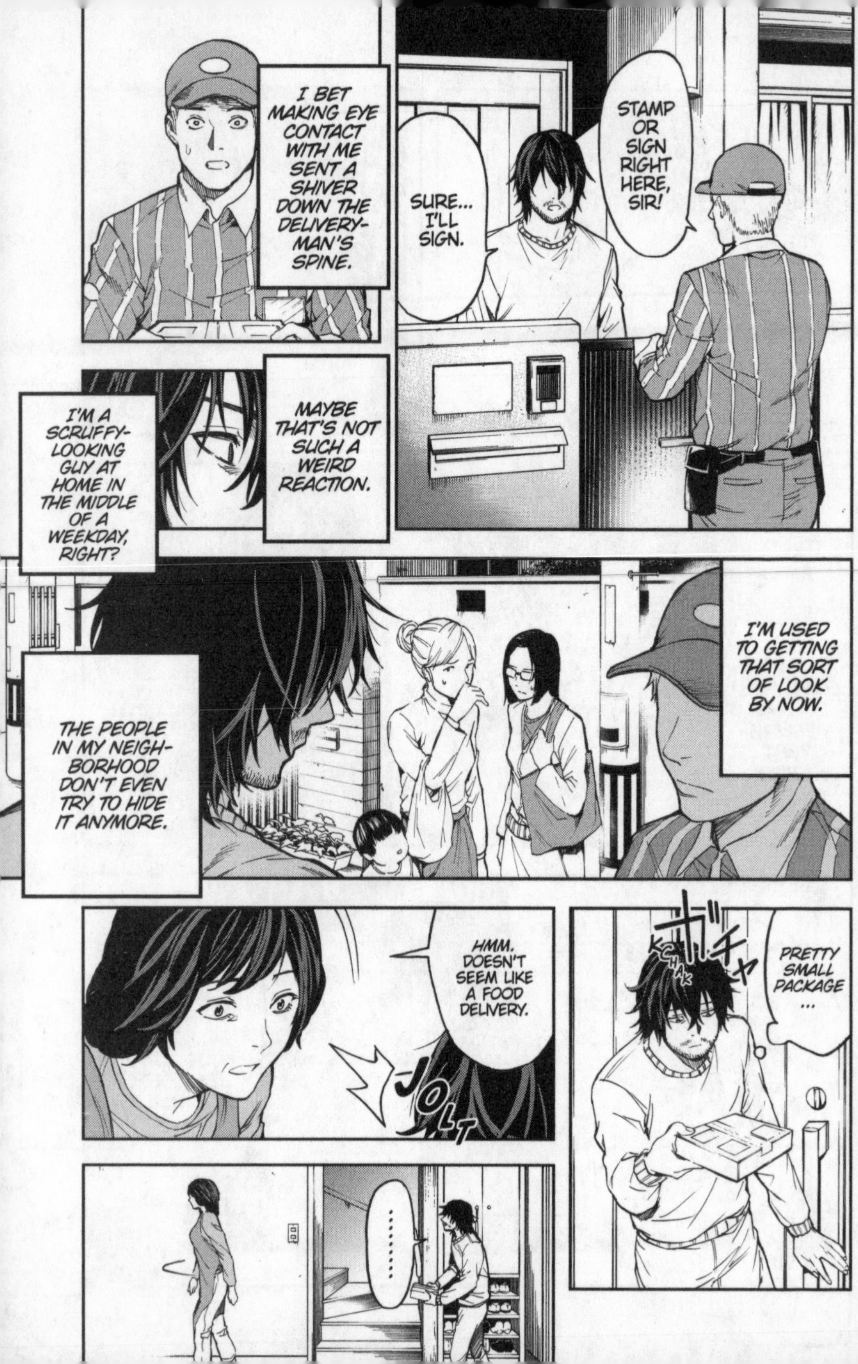
STAMP OR SIGN RIGHT HERE, SIR!
SURE... I'LL SIGN.
I BET MAKING EYE CONTACT WITH ME SENT A SHIVER DOWN THE DELIVERY-MAN'S SPINE.
MAYBE THAT'S NOT SUCH A WEIRD REACTION.
I'M A SCRUFFY-LOOKING GUY AT HOME IN THE MIDDLE OF A WEEKDAY, RIGHT?
I'M USED TO GETTING THAT SORT OF LOOK BY NOW.
THE PEOPLE IN MY NEIGH-BORHOOD DON'T EVEN TRY TO HIDE IT ANYMORE.
ガチャ
KCHAK
PRETTY SMALL PACKAGE ...
HMM. DOESN'T SEEM LIKE A FOOD DELIVERY.
JOLT
......

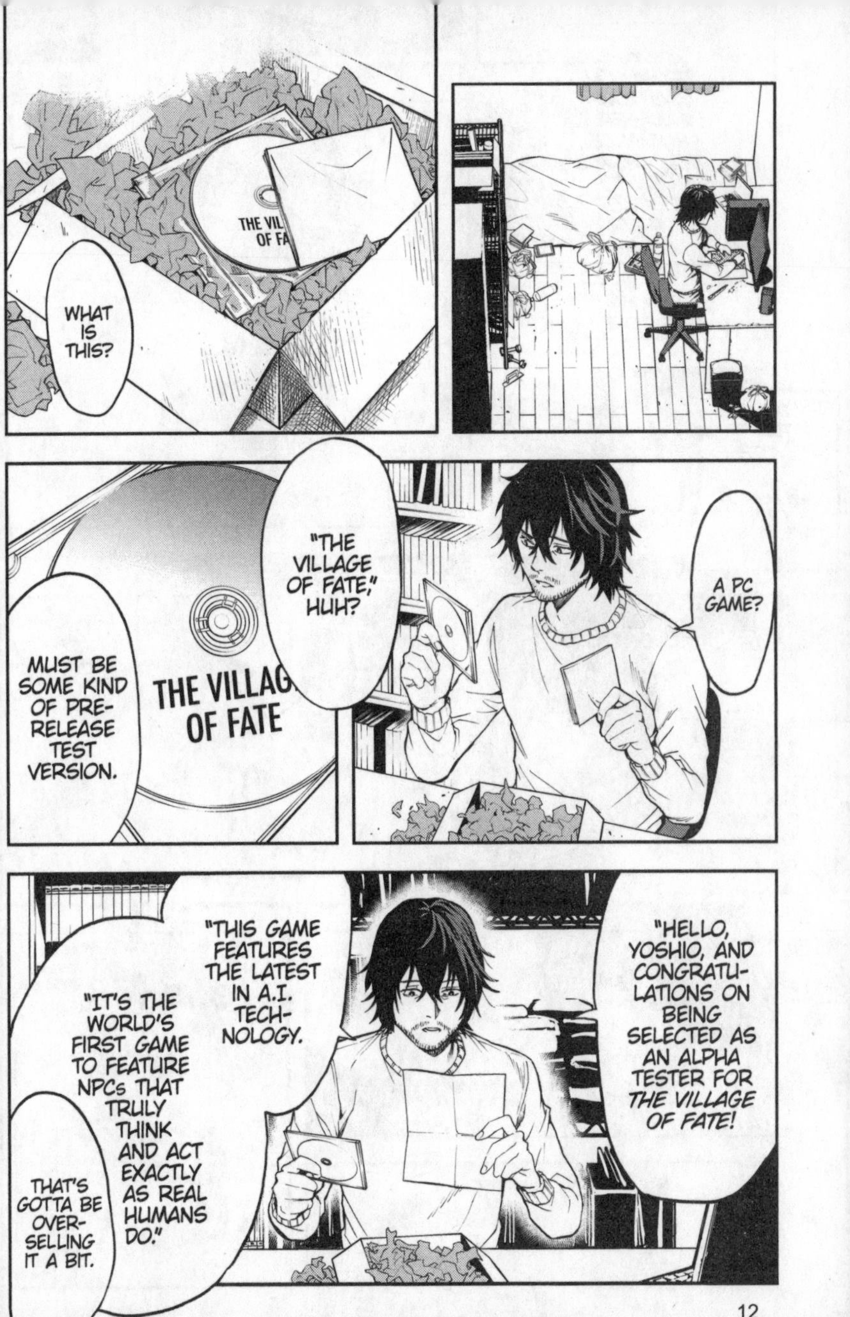
THE VIL
OF FA
WHAT IS THIS?
A PC GAME?
"THE VILLAGE OF FATE," HUH?
THE VILLAG
OF FATE
MUST BE SOME KIND OF PRE-RELEASE TEST VERSION.
"HELLO, YOSHIO, AND CONGRATULATIONS ON BEING SELECTED AS AN ALPHA TESTER FOR *THE VILLAGE OF FATE!*
"THIS GAME FEATURES THE LATEST IN A.I. TECHNOLOGY.
"IT'S THE WORLD'S FIRST GAME TO FEATURE NPCs THAT TRULY THINK AND ACT EXACTLY AS REAL HUMANS DO."
THAT'S GOTTA BE OVERSELLING IT A BIT.

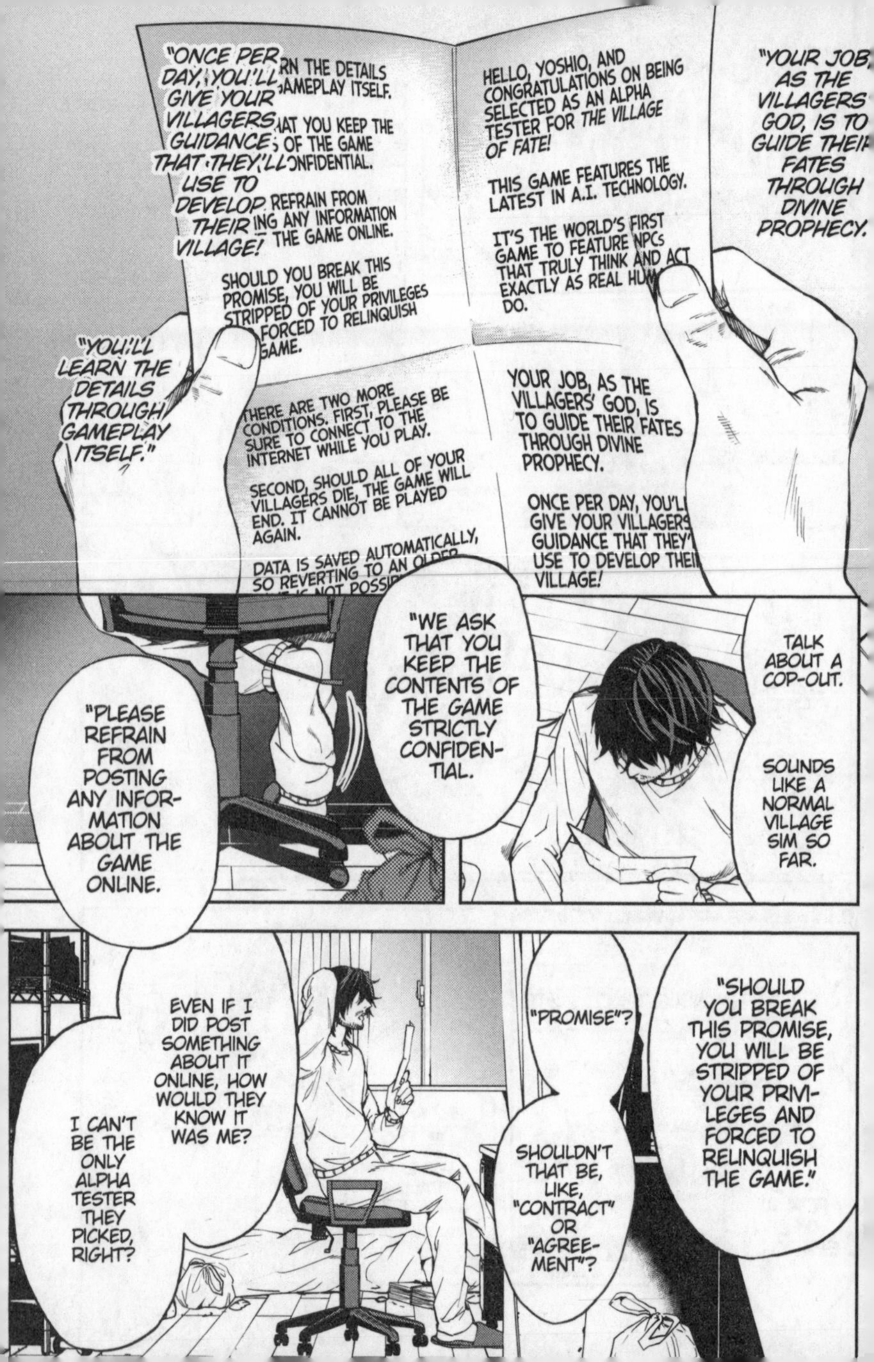
"YOUR JOB, AS THE VILLAGERS' GOD, IS TO GUIDE THEIR FATES THROUGH DIVINE PROPHECY.
HELLO, YOSHIO, AND CONGRATULATIONS ON BEING SELECTED AS AN ALPHA TESTER FOR THE VILLAGE OF FATE!
THIS GAME FEATURES THE LATEST IN A.I. TECHNOLOGY.
IT'S THE WORLD'S FIRST GAME TO FEATURE NPCs THAT TRULY THINK AND ACT
YOUR JOB, AS THE VILLAGERS' GOD, IS TO GUIDE THEIR FATES THROUGH DIVINE PROPHECY.
VILLAGE!
"ONCE PER DAY, YOU'LL GIVE YOUR VILLAGERS GUIDANCE THAT THEY'LL USE TO DEVELOP THEIR VILLAGE!
SHOULD YOU BREAK THIS PROMISE, YOU WILL BE STRIPPED OF YOUR PRIVILEGES
THERE ARE TWO MORE CONDITIONS. FIRST, PLEASE BE SURE TO CONNECT TO THE INTERNET WHILE YOU PLAY.
SECOND, SHOULD ALL OF YOUR VILLAGERS DIE, THE GAME WILL END. IT CANNOT BE PLAYED AGAIN.
DATA IS SAVED AUTOMATICALLY,
"YOU'LL LEARN THE DETAILS THROUGH GAMEPLAY ITSELF."
TALK ABOUT A COP-OUT.
SOUNDS LIKE A NORMAL VILLAGE SIM SO FAR.
"WE ASK THAT YOU KEEP THE CONTENTS OF THE GAME STRICTLY CONFIDEN-TIAL.
"PLEASE REFRAIN FROM POSTING ANY INFOR-MATION ABOUT THE GAME ONLINE.
"SHOULD YOU BREAK THIS PROMISE, YOU WILL BE STRIPPED OF YOUR PRIVI-LEGES AND FORCED TO RELINQUISH THE GAME."
"PROMISE"?
SHOULDN'T THAT BE, LIKE, "CONTRACT" OR "AGREE-MENT"?
EVEN IF I DID POST SOMETHING ABOUT IT ONLINE, HOW WOULD THEY KNOW IT WAS ME?
I CAN'T BE THE ONLY ALPHA TESTER THEY PICKED, RIGHT?

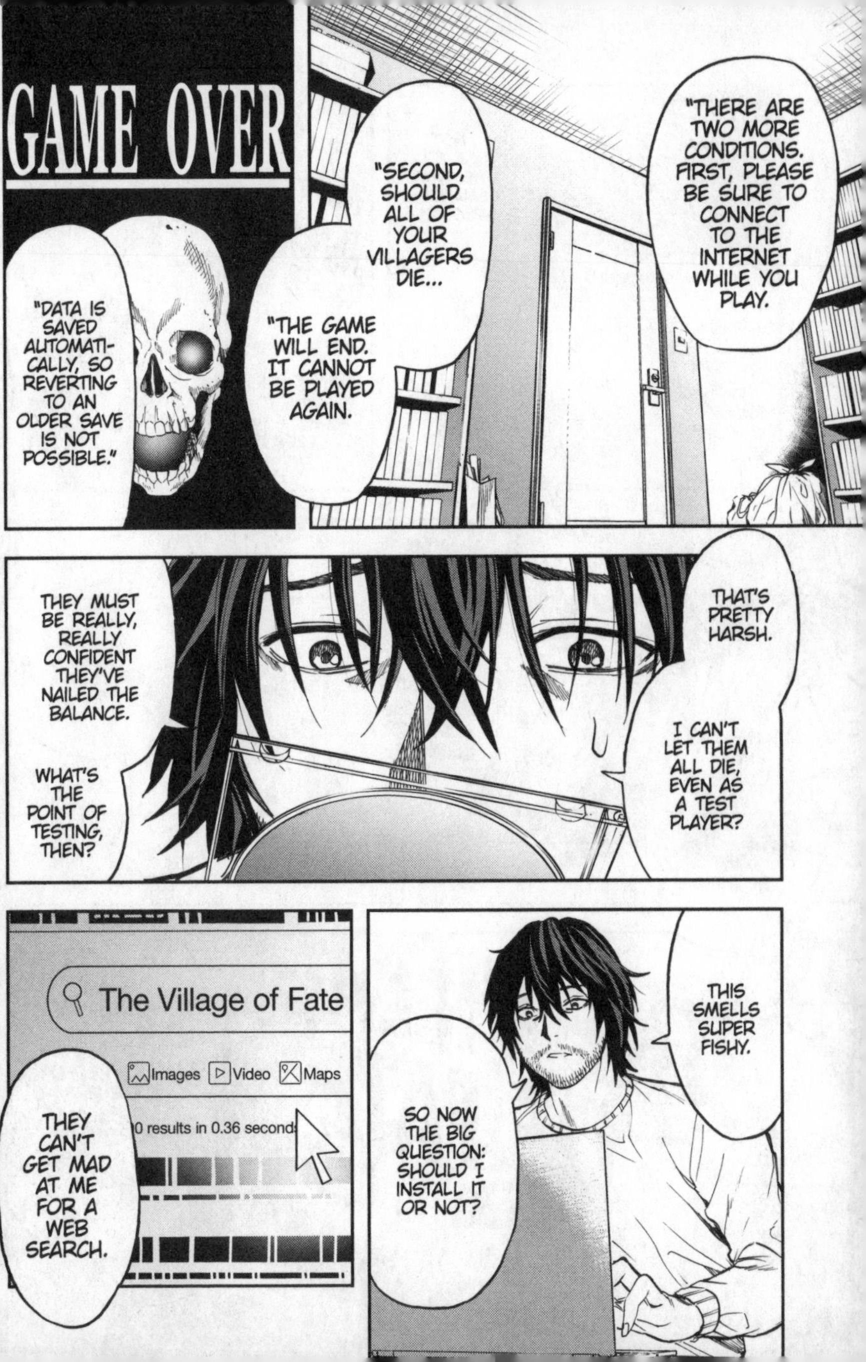
"THERE ARE TWO MORE CONDITIONS. FIRST, PLEASE BE SURE TO CONNECT TO THE INTERNET WHILE YOU PLAY.
"SECOND, SHOULD ALL OF YOUR VILLAGERS DIE...
"THE GAME WILL END. IT CANNOT BE PLAYED AGAIN.
GAME OVER
"DATA IS SAVED AUTOMATICALLY, SO REVERTING TO AN OLDER SAVE IS NOT POSSIBLE."
THAT'S PRETTY HARSH.
I CAN'T LET THEM ALL DIE, EVEN AS A TEST PLAYER?
THEY MUST BE REALLY, REALLY CONFIDENT THEY'VE NAILED THE BALANCE.
WHAT'S THE POINT OF TESTING, THEN?
THIS SMELLS SUPER FISHY.
SO NOW THE BIG QUESTION: SHOULD I INSTALL IT OR NOT?
The Village of Fate
Images
Video
Maps
0 results in 0.36 second
THEY CAN'T GET MAD AT ME FOR A WEB SEARCH.

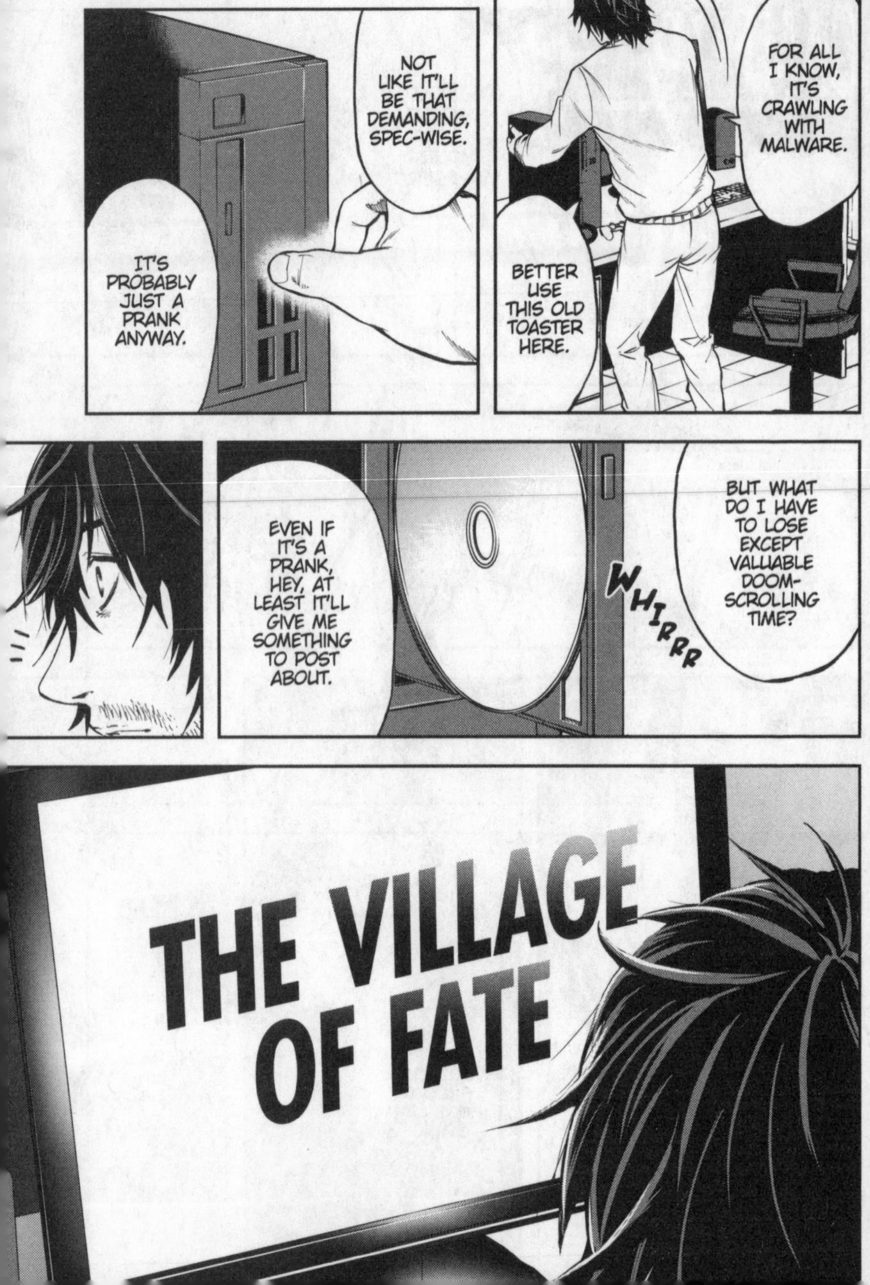
FOR ALL I KNOW, IT'S CRAWLING WITH MALWARE.
BETTER USE THIS OLD TOASTER HERE.
NOT LIKE IT'LL BE THAT DEMANDING, SPEC-WISE.
IT'S PROBABLY JUST A PRANK ANYWAY.
BUT WHAT DO I HAVE TO LOSE EXCEPT VALUABLE DOOM-SCROLLING TIME?
WHIRRR
EVEN IF IT'S A PRANK, HEY, AT LEAST IT'LL GIVE ME SOMETHING TO POST ABOUT.
THE VILLAGE OF FATE

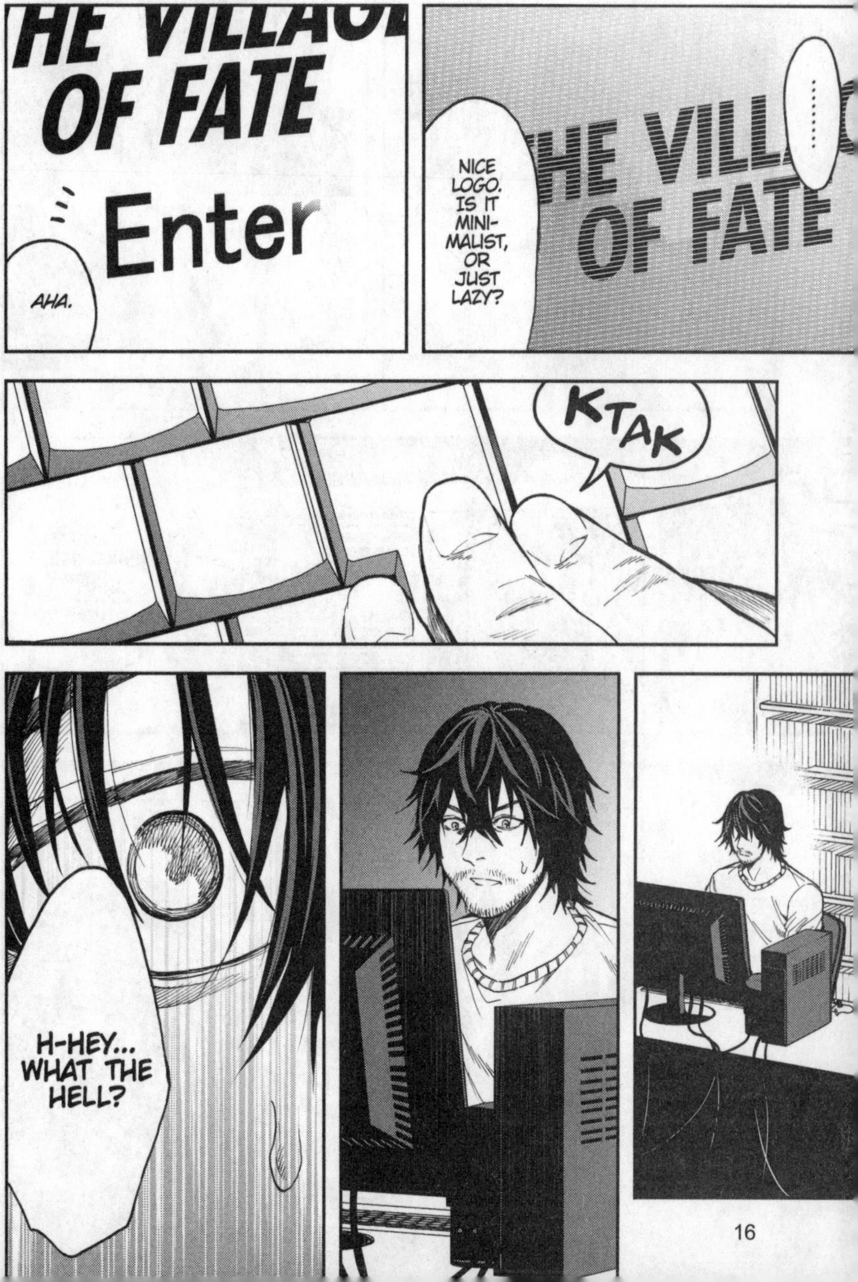
......
HE VILL
OF FATE
NICE LOGO. IS IT MINI-MALIST, OR JUST LAZY?
HE VILLAG
OF FATE
Enter
AHA.
KTAK
H-HEY... WHAT THE HELL?

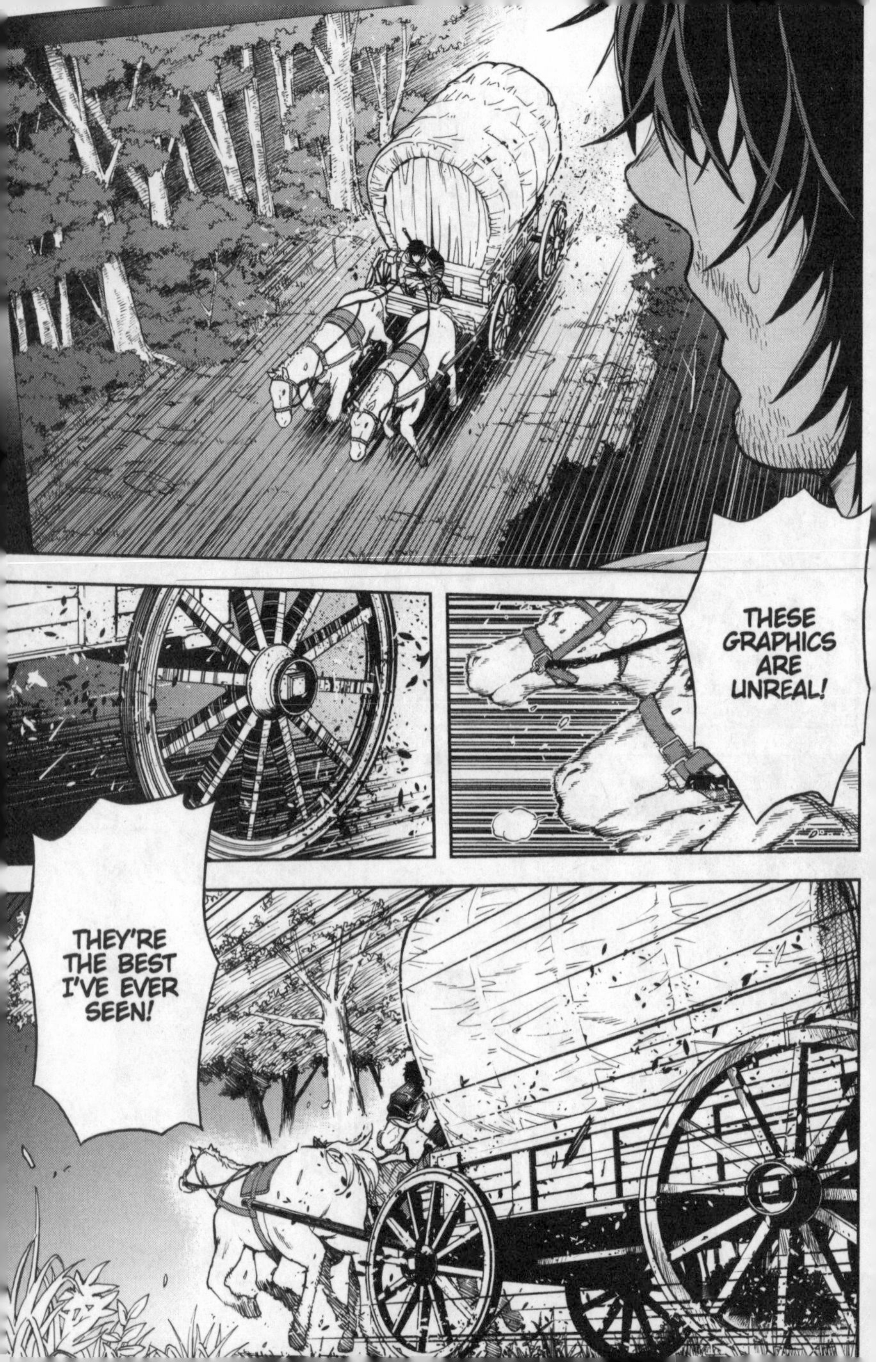
THESE GRAPHICS ARE UNREAL!
THEY'RE THE BEST I'VE EVER SEEN!

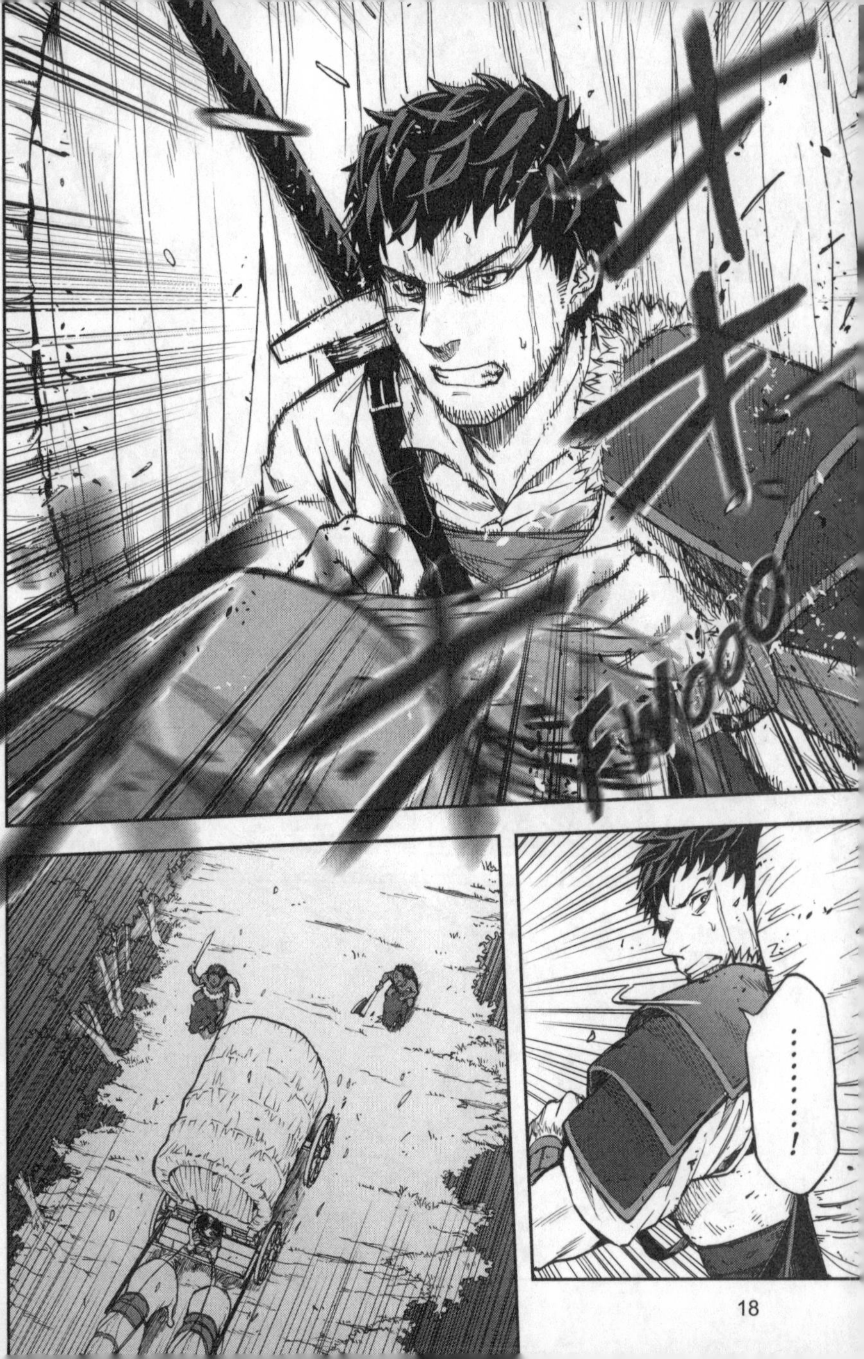
Fwoooo
......!

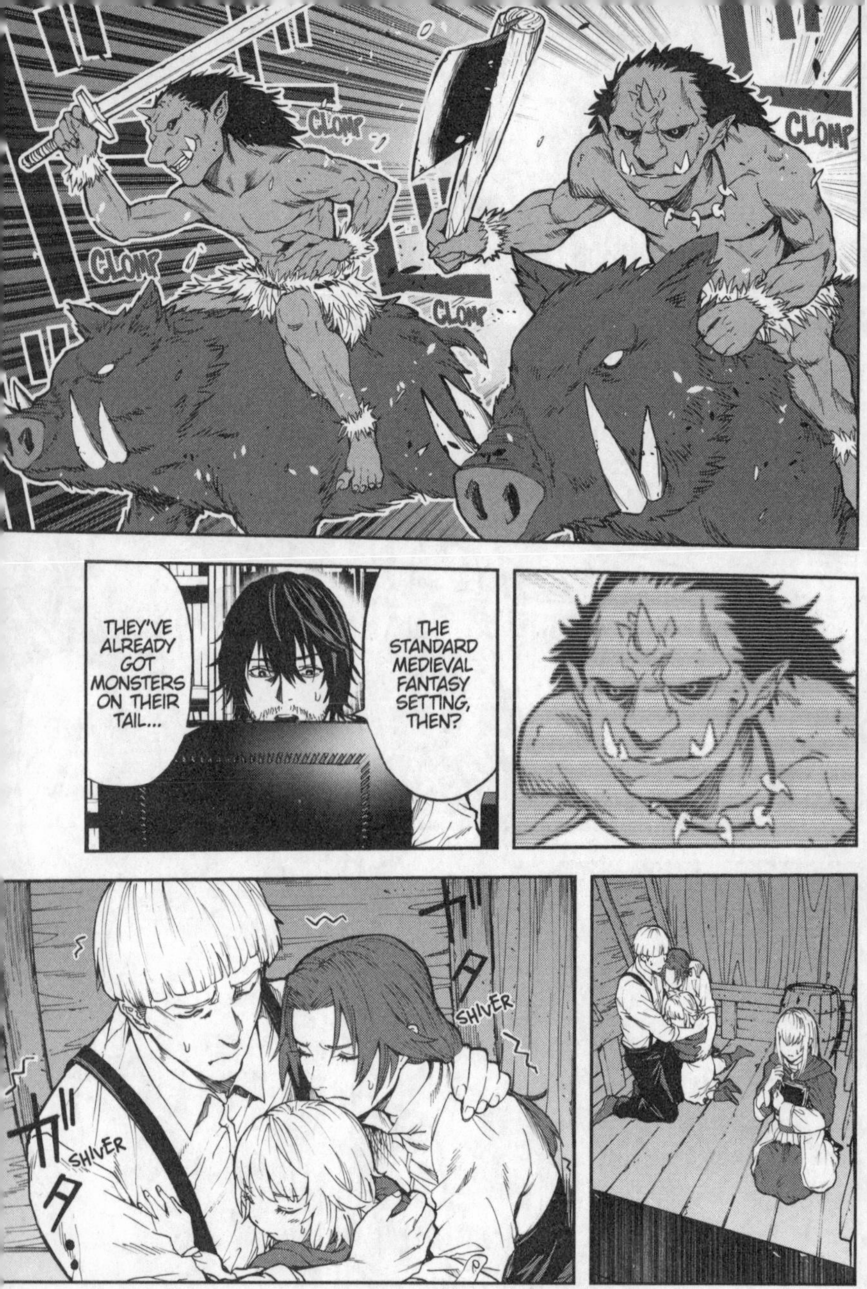
CLOMP
CLOMP
CLOMP
CLOMP
THE STANDARD MEDIEVAL FANTASY SETTING, THEN?
THEY'VE ALREADY GOT MONSTERS ON THEIR TAIL...
ガタ
SHIVER
ガタ
SHIVER

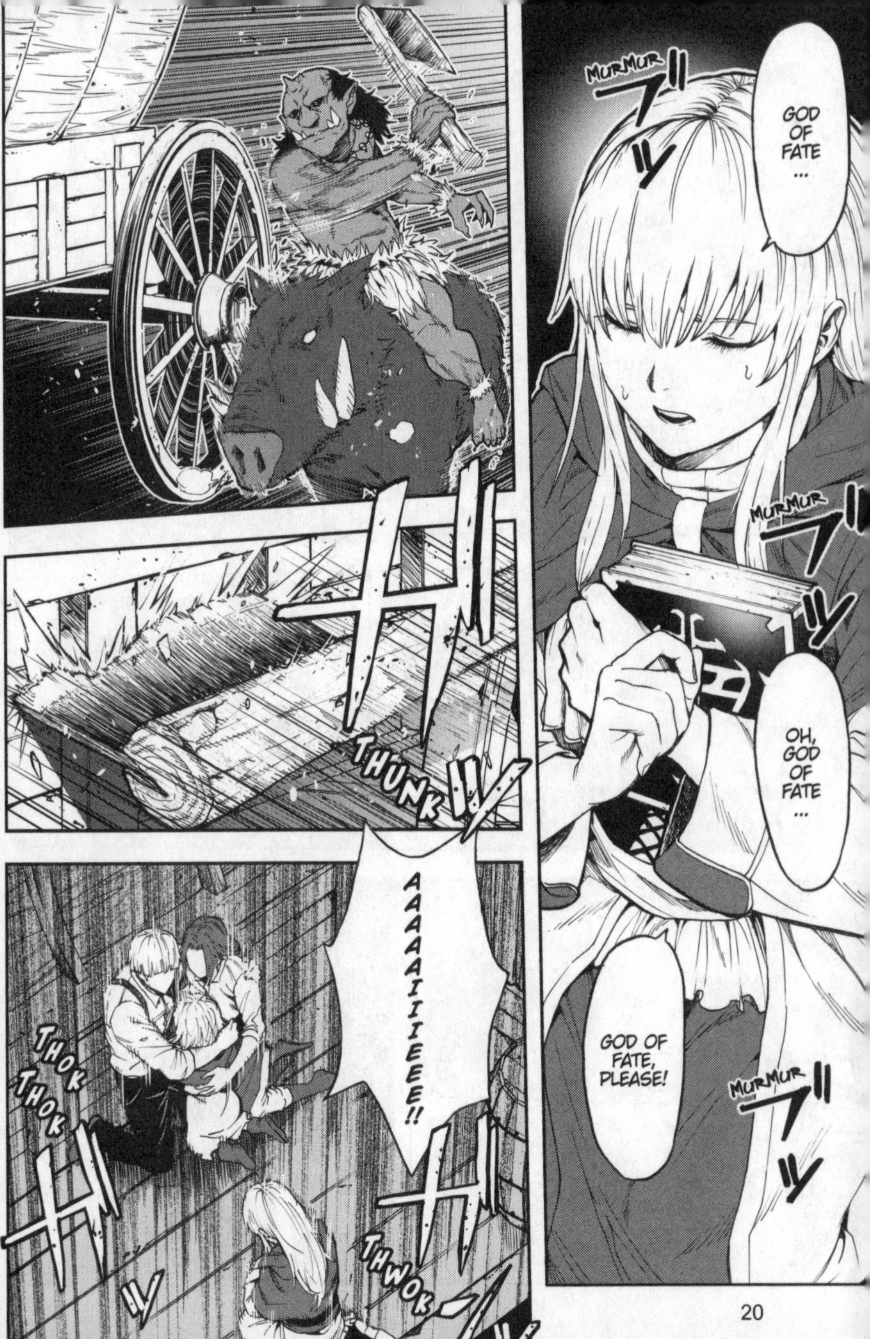
MURMUR
GOD OF FATE ...
MURMUR
OH, GOD OF FATE ...
GOD OF FATE, PLEASE!
MURMUR
THUNK!!
AAAAAIIIEEEE!!
THOK THOK
THWOK!!

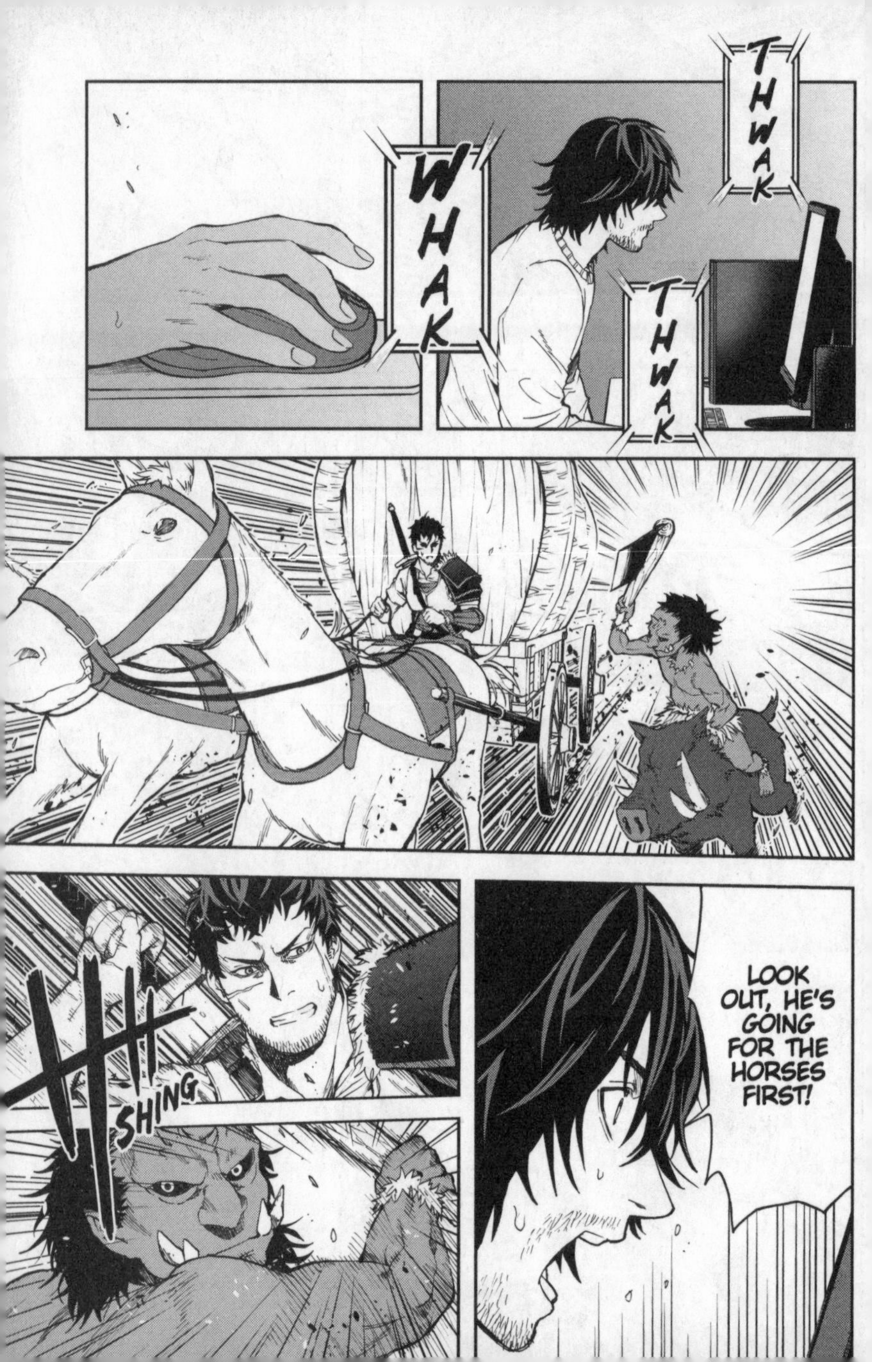
THWAK
THWAK
WHAK
LOOK OUT, HE'S GOING FOR THE HORSES FIRST!
SHING

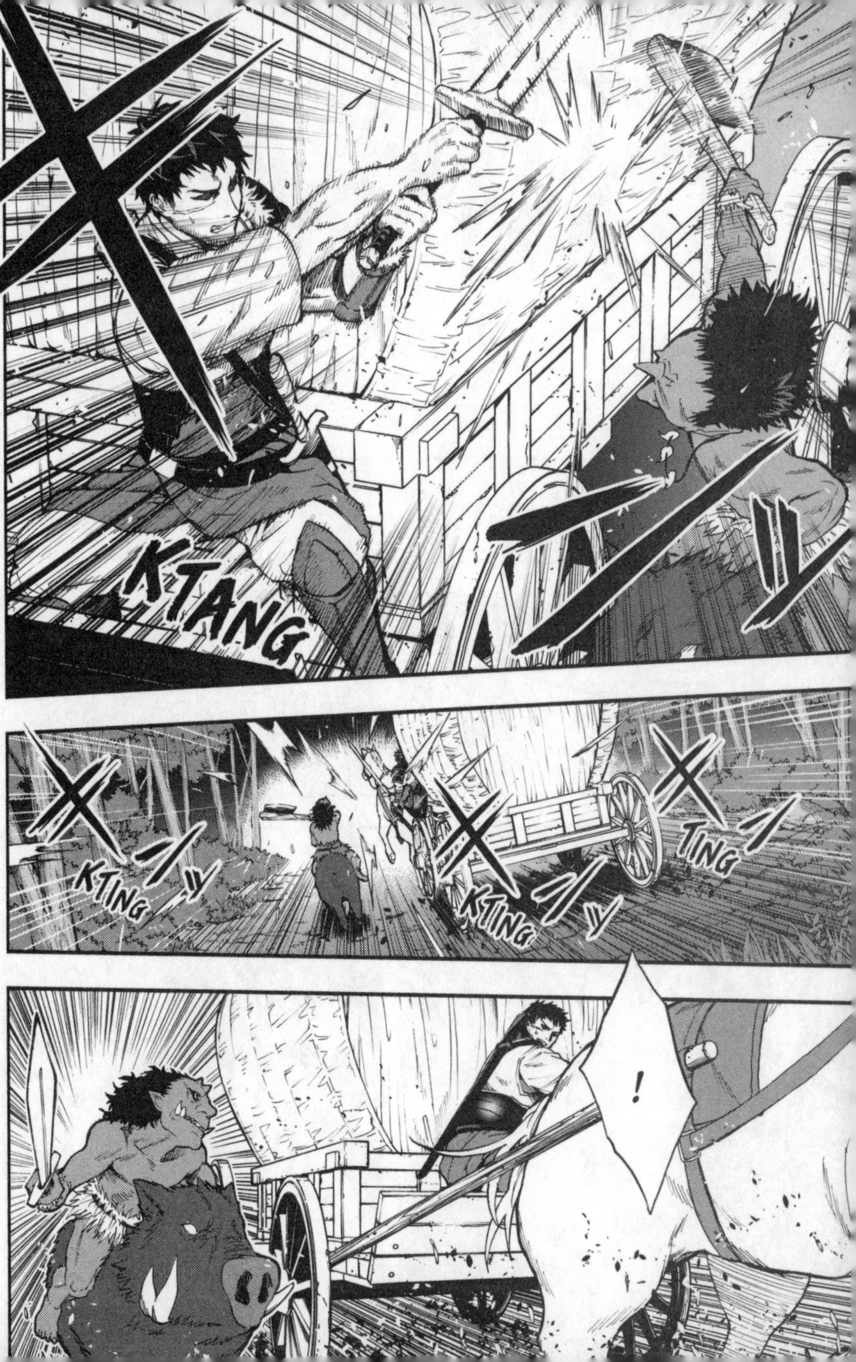
KTANG
TING
KTING
KTING
!

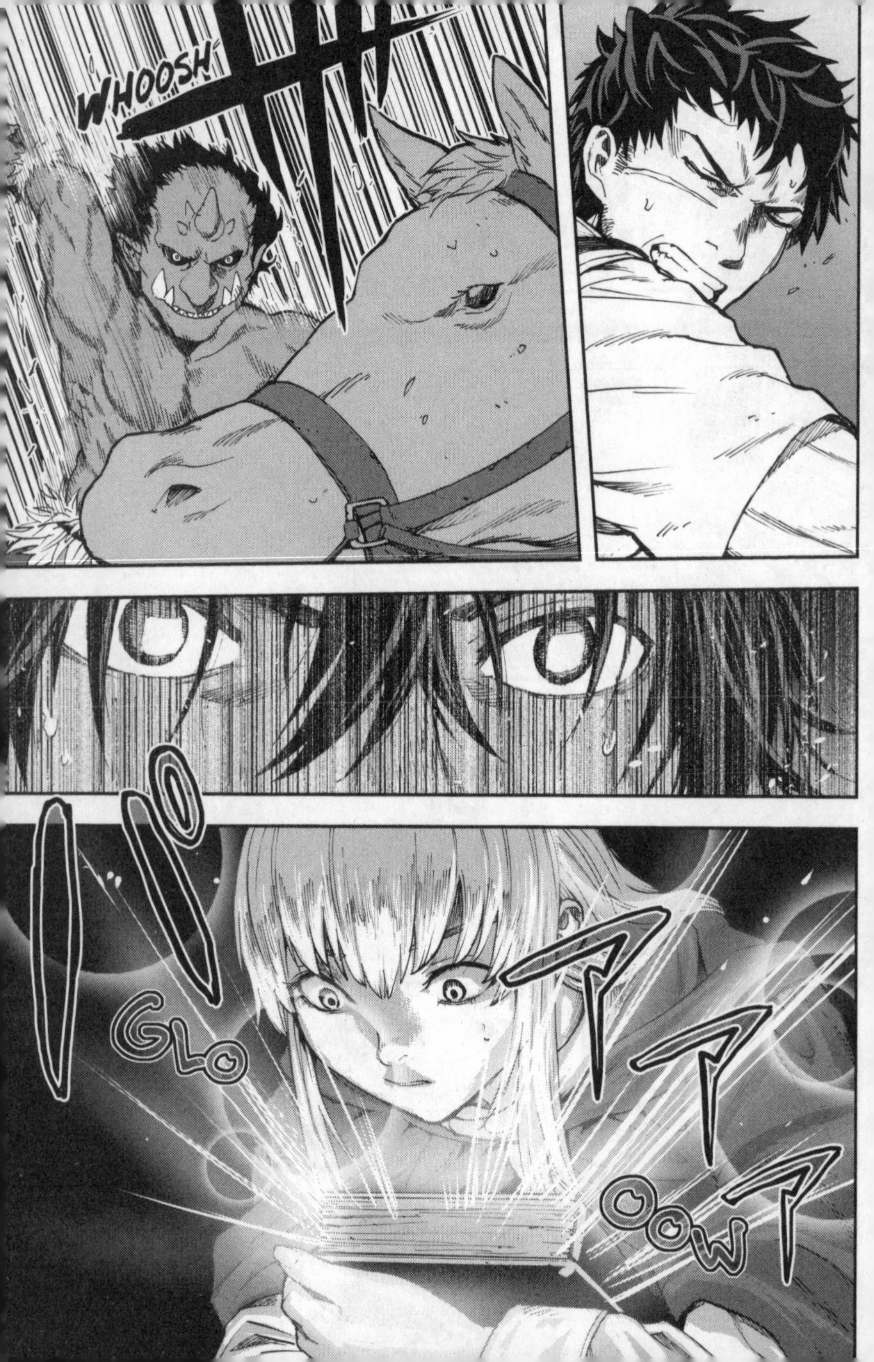
WHOOSH
GLO
OOW

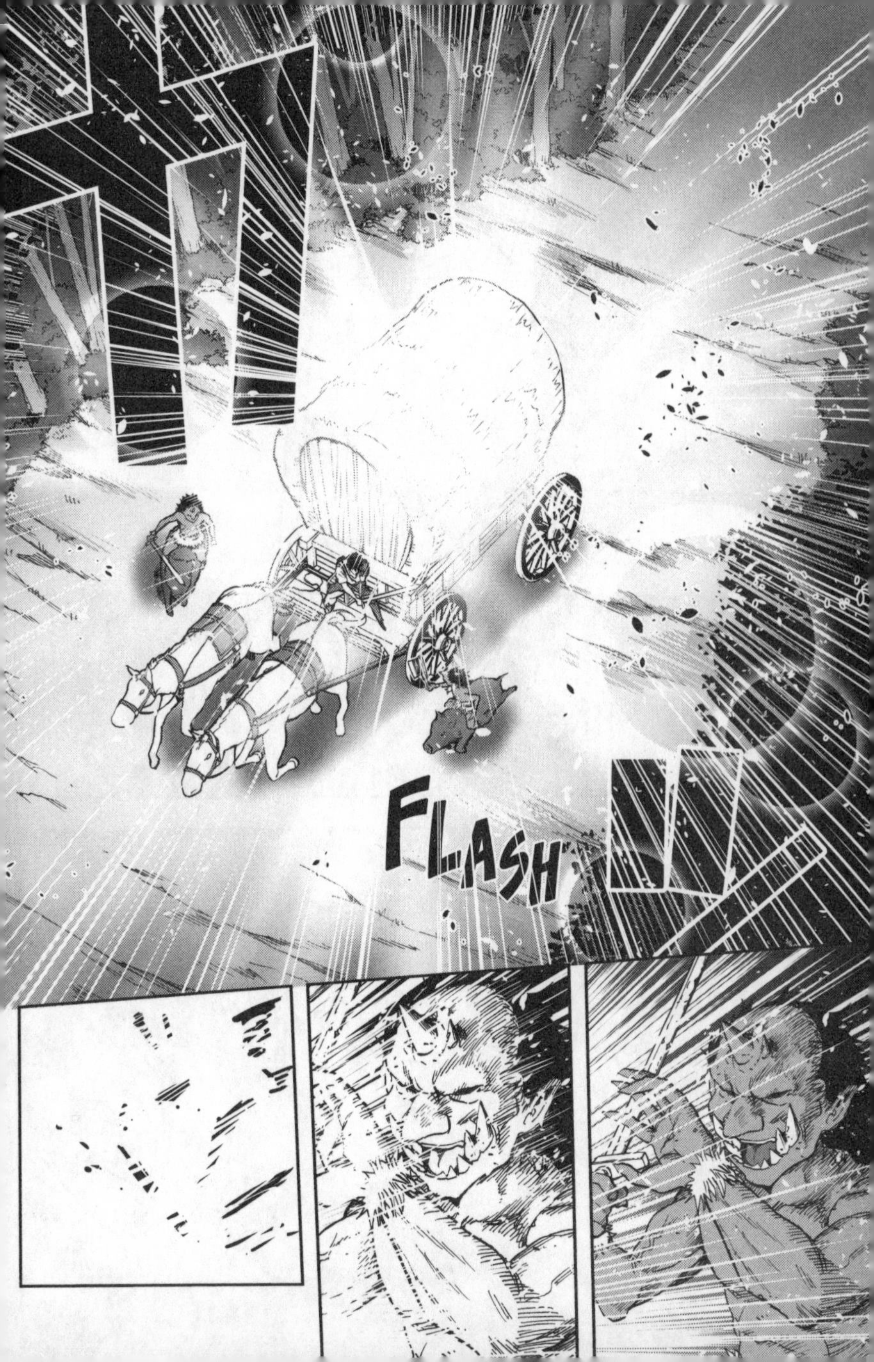
FLASH

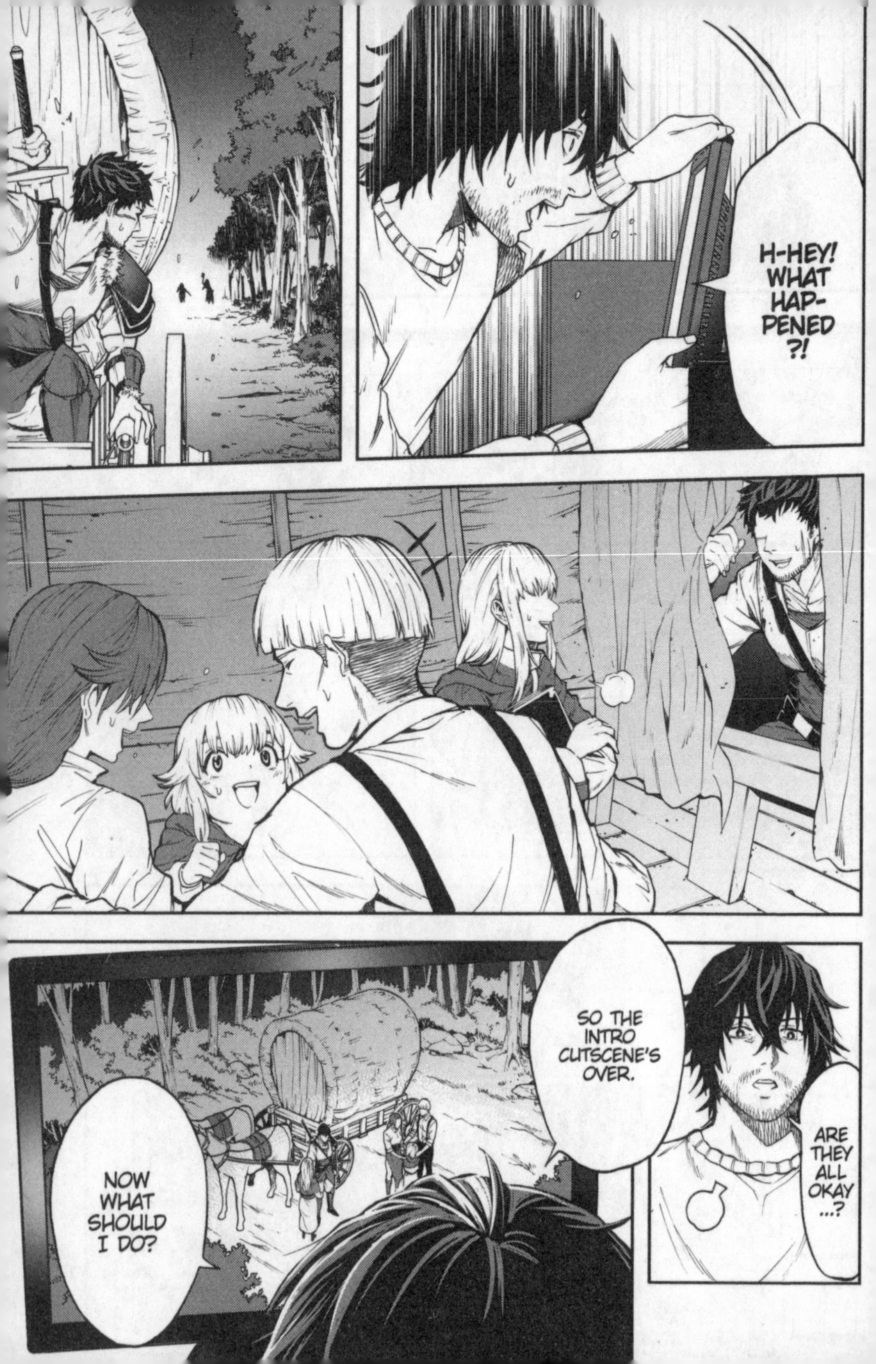
H-HEY! WHAT HAP-PENED?!
ARE THEY ALL OKAY ...?
SO THE INTRO CUTSCENE'S OVER.
NOW WHAT SHOULD I DO?

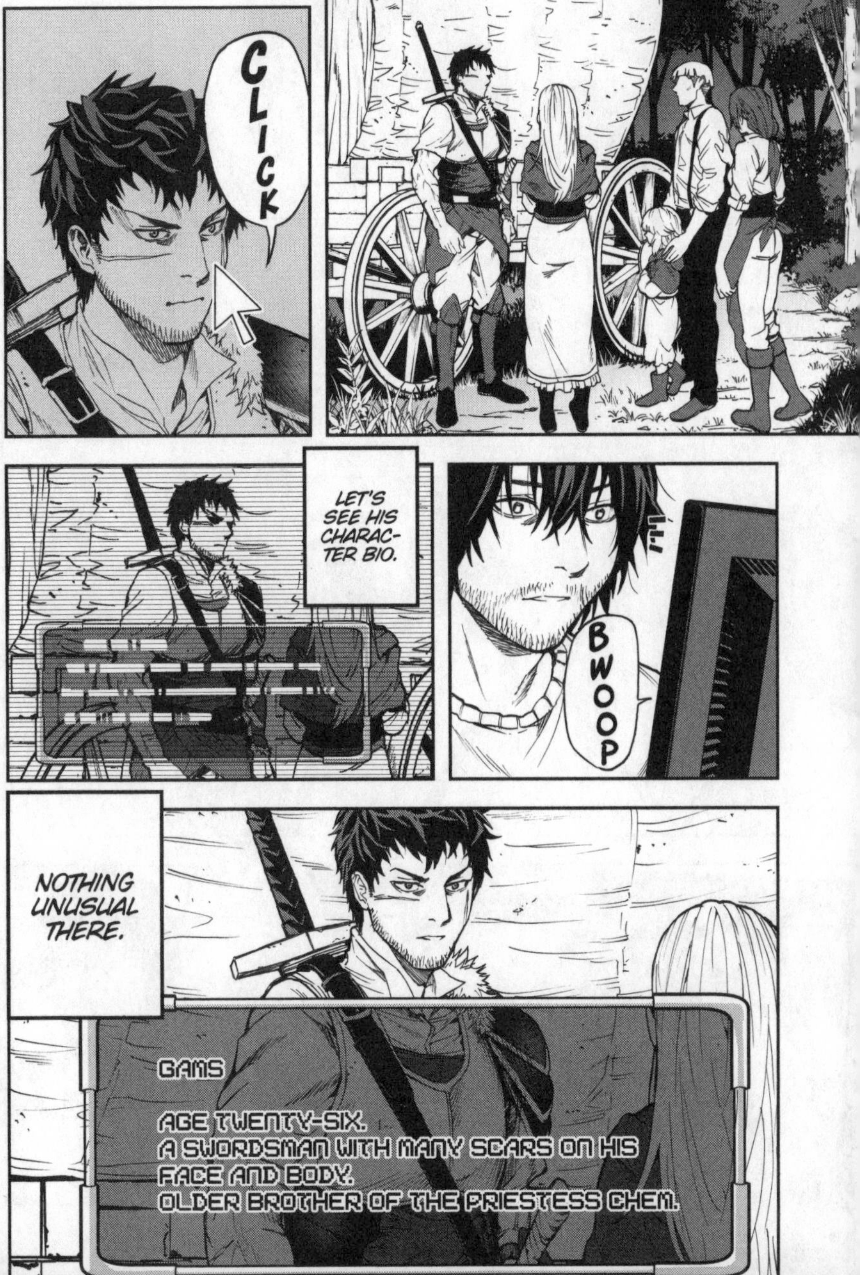
CLICK
LET'S SEE HIS CHARACTER BIO.
BWOOP
NOTHING UNUSUAL THERE.
GAMS
AGE TWENTY-SIX.
A SWORDSMAN WITH MANY SCARS ON HIS FACE AND BODY.
OLDER BROTHER OF THE PRIESTESS CHEM.

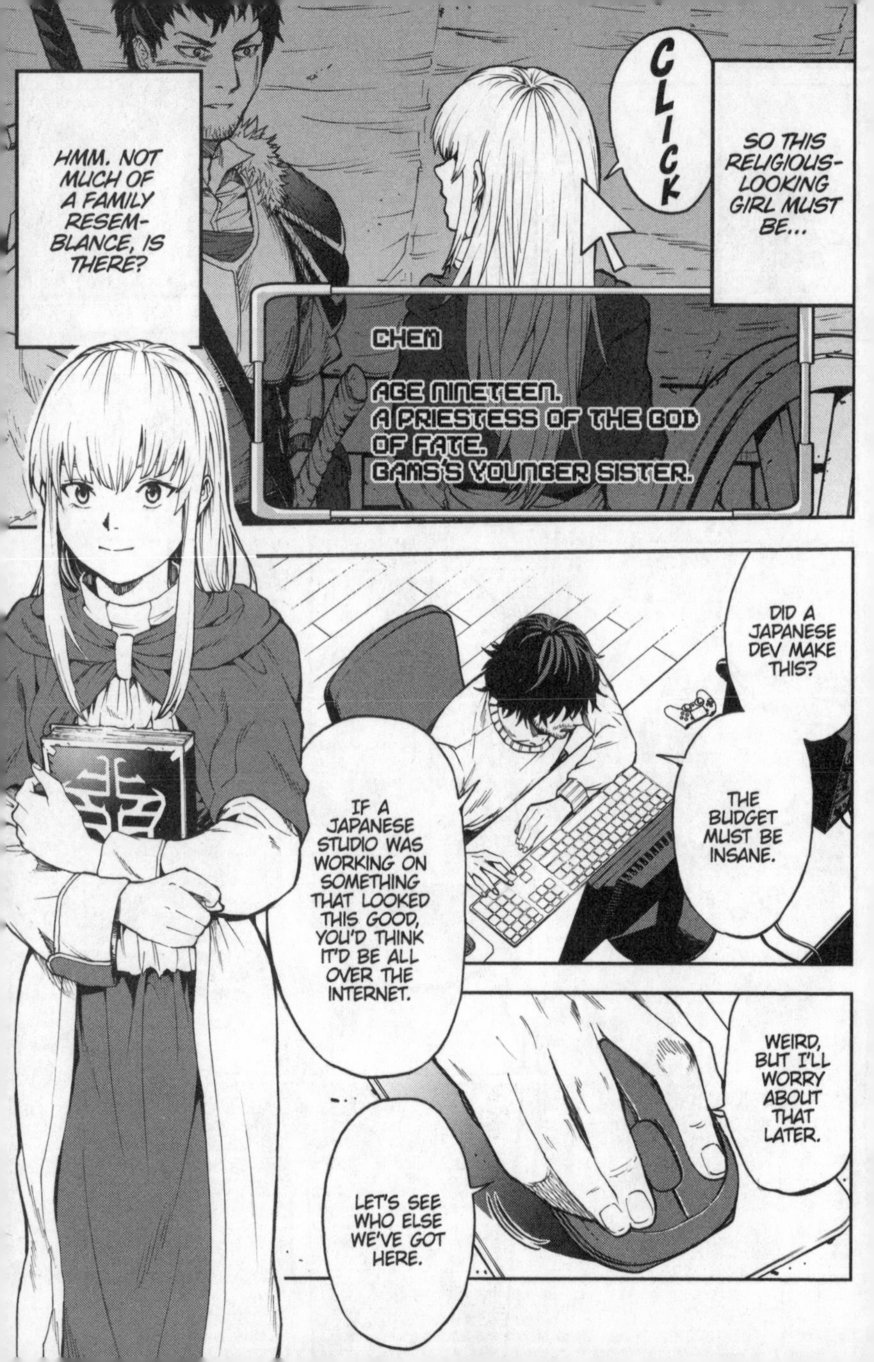

CLICK
SO THIS RELIGIOUS-LOOKING GIRL MUST BE...
CHEM
AGE NINETEEN.
A PRIESTESS OF THE GOD OF FATE.
BAMS'S YOUNGER SISTER.
HMM. NOT MUCH OF A FAMILY RESEM-BLANCE, IS THERE?
DID A JAPANESE DEV MAKE THIS?
THE BUDGET MUST BE INSANE.
IF A JAPANESE STUDIO WAS WORKING ON SOMETHING THAT LOOKED THIS GOOD, YOU'D THINK IT'D BE ALL OVER THE INTERNET.
WEIRD, BUT I'LL WORRY ABOUT THAT LATER.
LET'S SEE WHO ELSE WE'VE GOT HERE.

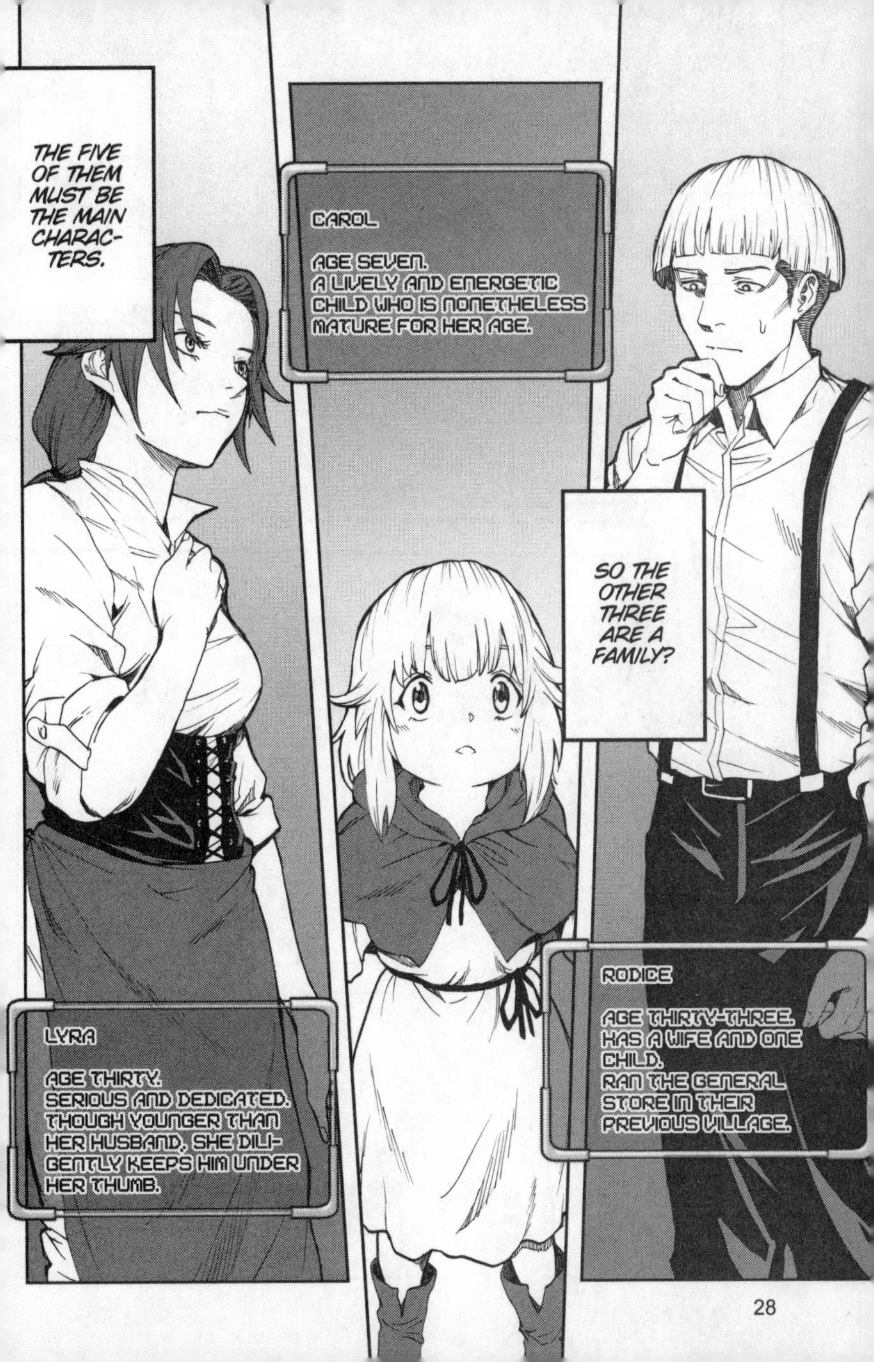

THE FIVE OF THEM MUST BE THE MAIN CHARAC-TERS.
CAROL
AGE SEVEN.
A LIVELY AND ENERGETIC CHILD WHO IS NONETHELESS MATURE FOR HER AGE.
SO THE OTHER THREE ARE A FAMILY?
RODICE
AGE THIRTY-THREE.
HAS A WIFE AND ONE CHILD.
RAN THE GENERAL STORE IN THEIR PREVIOUS VILLAGE.
LYRA
AGE THIRTY.
SERIOUS AND DEDICATED. THOUGH YOUNGER THAN HER HUSBAND, SHE DILI-GENTLY KEEPS HIM UNDER HER THUMB.

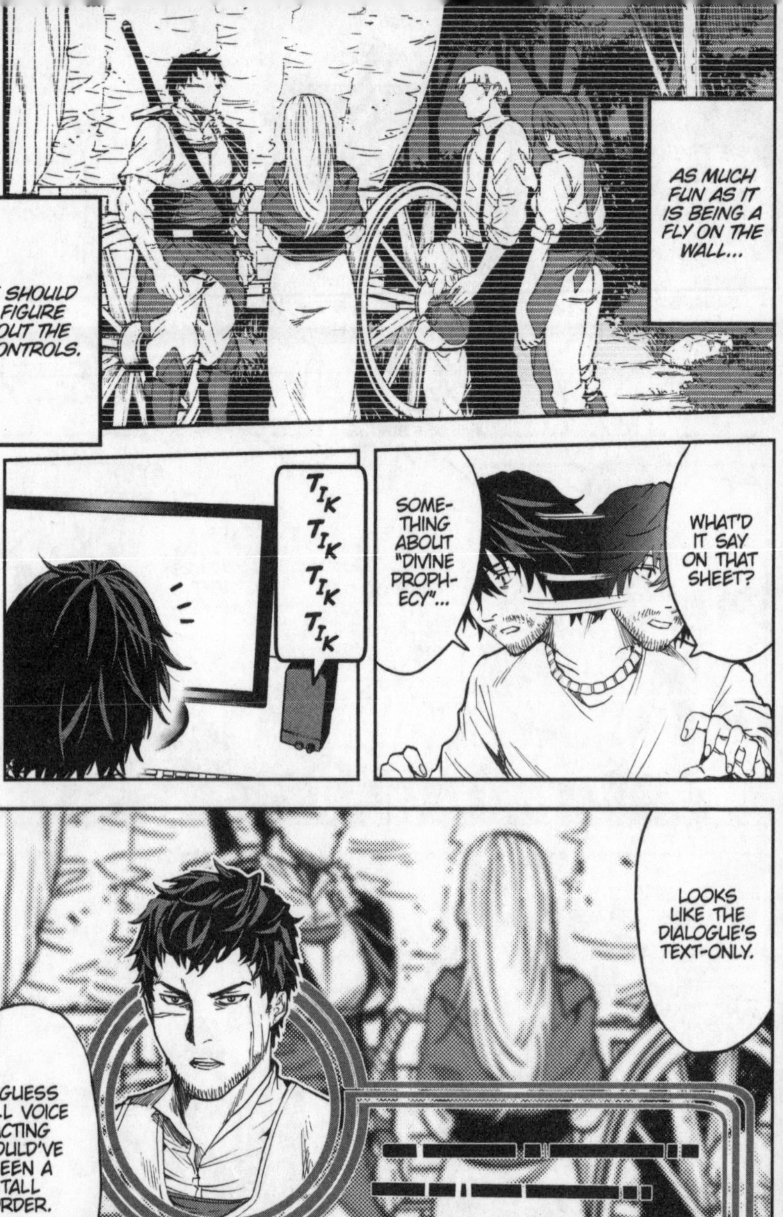
AS MUCH FUN AS IT IS BEING A FLY ON THE WALL...
I SHOULD FIGURE OUT THE CONTROLS.
WHAT'D IT SAY ON THAT SHEET?
SOME-THING ABOUT "DIVINE PROPH-ECY"...
TIK TIK TIK TIK
LOOKS LIKE THE DIALOGUE'S TEXT-ONLY.
I GUESS FULL VOICE ACTING WOULD'VE BEEN A TALL ORDER.

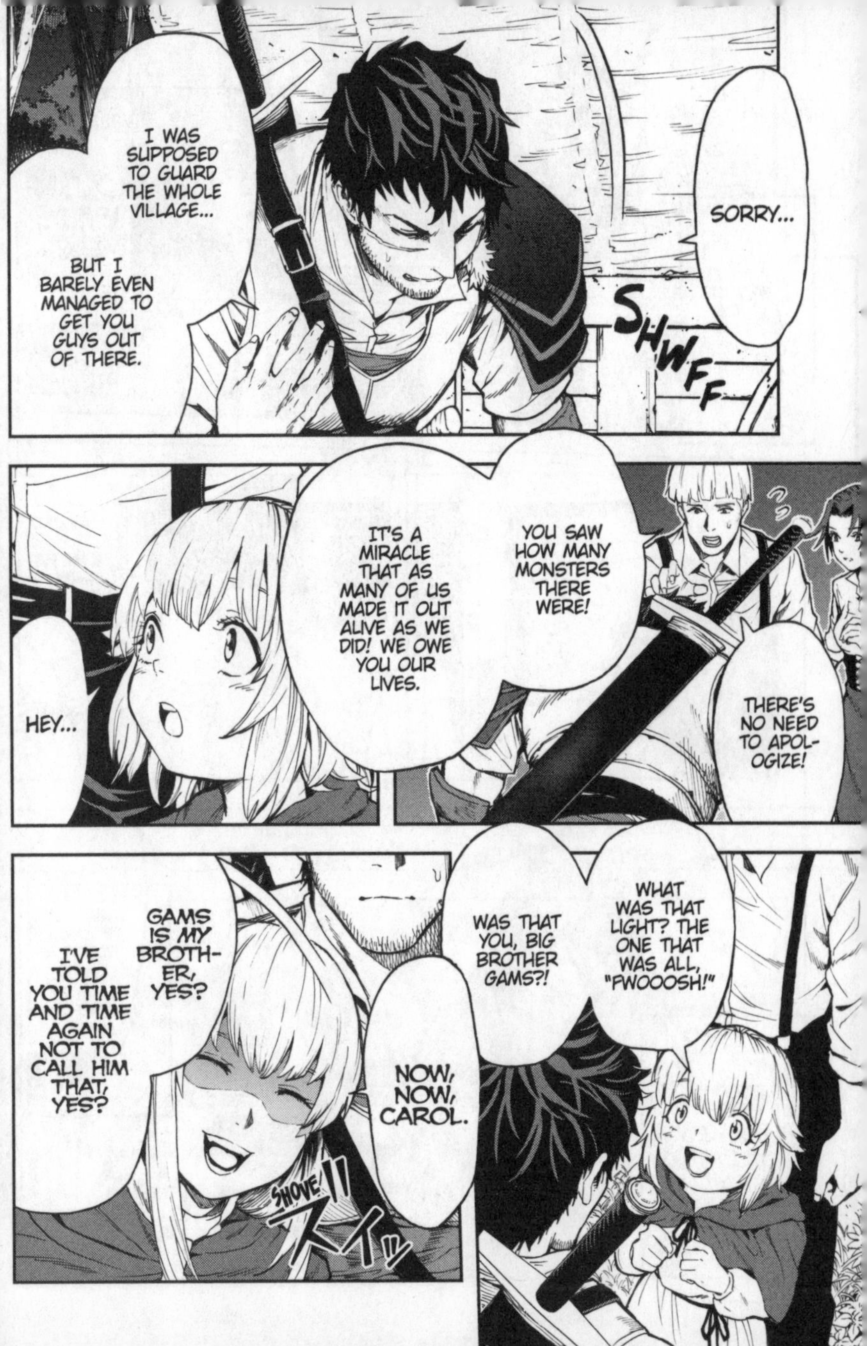
SORRY...
SHWFF
I WAS SUPPOSED TO GUARD THE WHOLE VILLAGE...
BUT I BARELY EVEN MANAGED TO GET YOU GUYS OUT OF THERE.
THERE'S NO NEED TO APOLOGIZE!
YOU SAW HOW MANY MONSTERS THERE WERE!
IT'S A MIRACLE THAT AS MANY OF US MADE IT OUT ALIVE AS WE DID! WE OWE YOU OUR LIVES.
HEY...
WHAT WAS THAT LIGHT? THE ONE THAT WAS ALL, "FWOOOSH!"
WAS THAT YOU, BIG BROTHER GAMS?!
NOW, NOW, CAROL.
GAMS IS MY BROTH-ER, YES?
I'VE TOLD YOU TIME AND TIME AGAIN NOT TO CALL HIM THAT, YES?
SHOVE

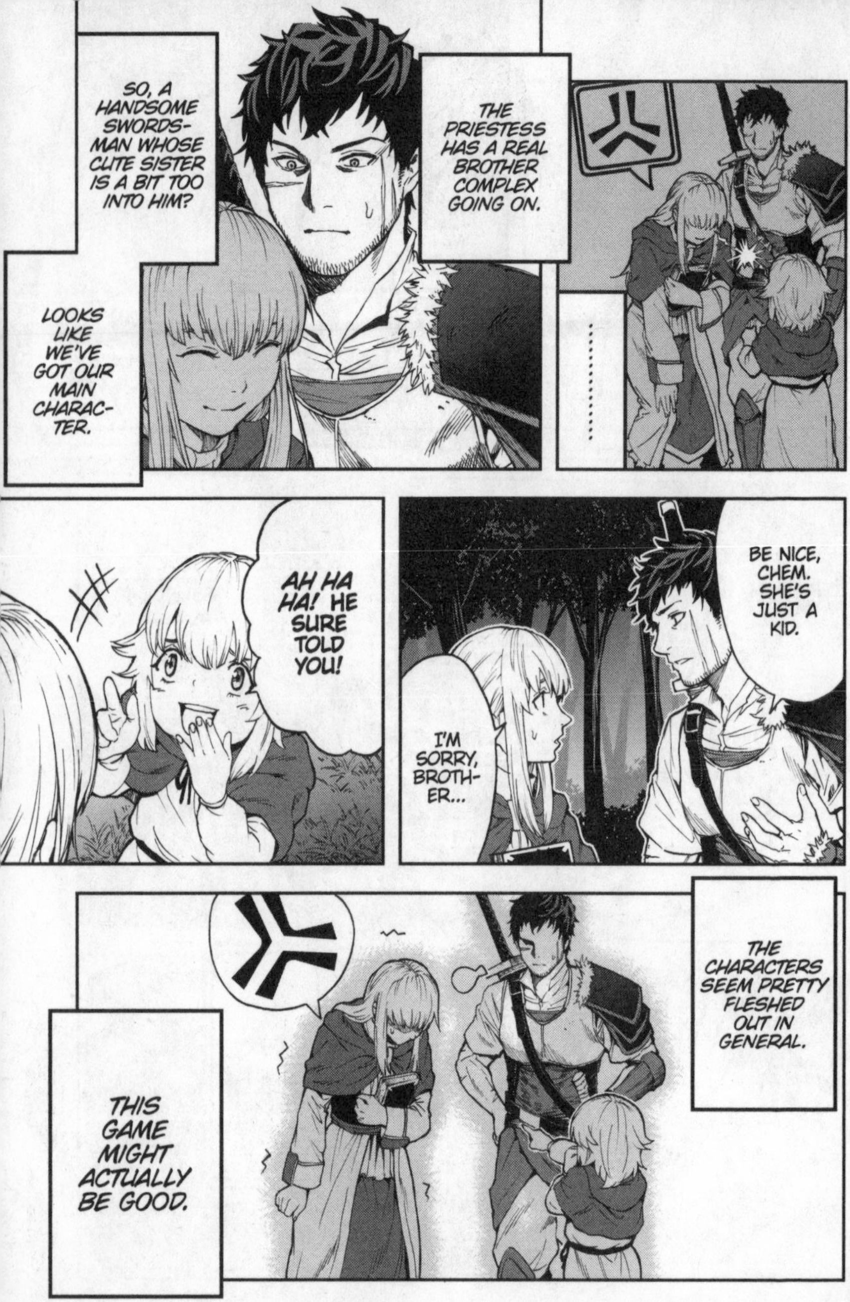
......
THE PRIESTESS HAS A REAL BROTHER COMPLEX GOING ON.
SO, A HANDSOME SWORDSMAN WHOSE CUTE SISTER IS A BIT TOO INTO HIM?
LOOKS LIKE WE'VE GOT OUR MAIN CHARACTER.
BE NICE, CHEM. SHE'S JUST A KID.
I'M SORRY, BROTHER...
AH HA HA! HE SURE TOLD YOU!
THE CHARACTERS SEEM PRETTY FLESHED OUT IN GENERAL.
THIS GAME MIGHT ACTUALLY BE GOOD.

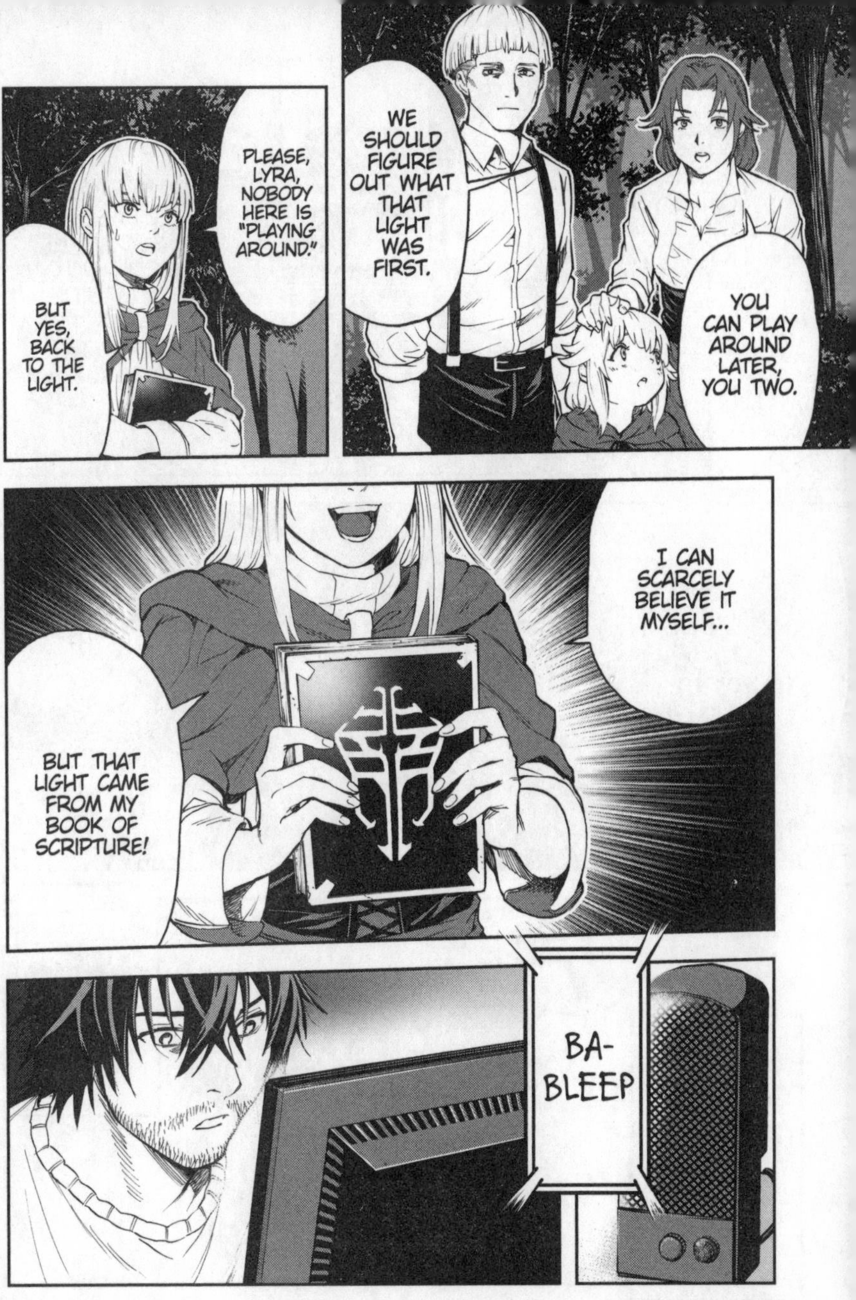
YOU CAN PLAY AROUND LATER, YOU TWO.
WE SHOULD FIGURE OUT WHAT THAT LIGHT WAS FIRST.
PLEASE, LYRA, NOBODY HERE IS "PLAYING AROUND."
BUT YES, BACK TO THE LIGHT.
I CAN SCARCELY BELIEVE IT MYSELF...
BUT THAT LIGHT CAME FROM MY BOOK OF SCRIPTURE!
BA-BLEEP

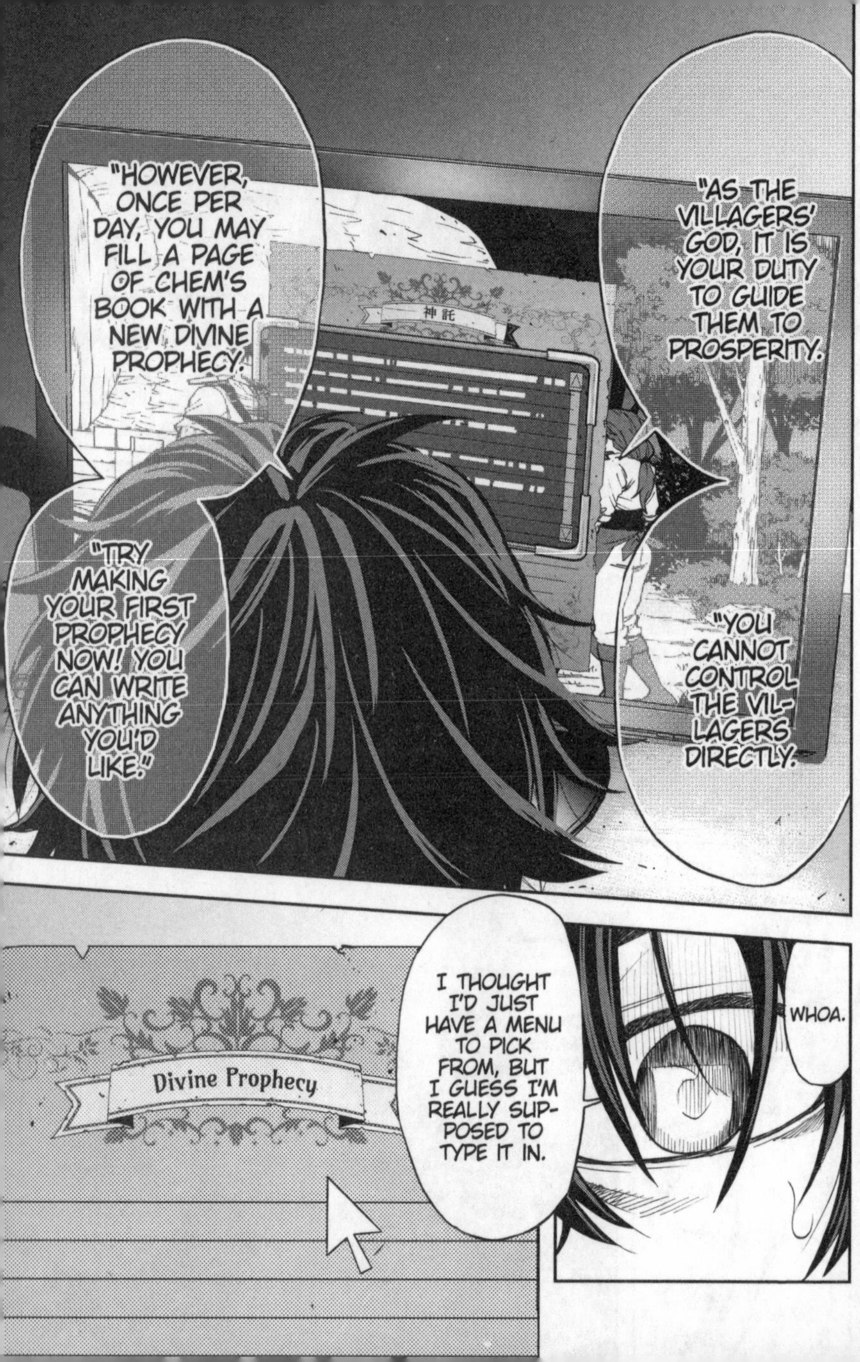
"AS THE VILLAGERS' GOD, IT IS YOUR DUTY TO GUIDE THEM TO PROSPERITY.
"YOU CANNOT CONTROL THE VIL-LAGERS DIRECTLY.
"HOWEVER, ONCE PER DAY, YOU MAY FILL A PAGE OF CHEM'S BOOK WITH A NEW DIVINE PROPHECY.
神託
"TRY MAKING YOUR FIRST PROPHECY NOW! YOU CAN WRITE ANYTHING YOU'D LIKE."
WHOA.
I THOUGHT I'D JUST HAVE A MENU TO PICK FROM, BUT I GUESS I'M REALLY SUP-POSED TO TYPE IT IN.
Divine Prophecy

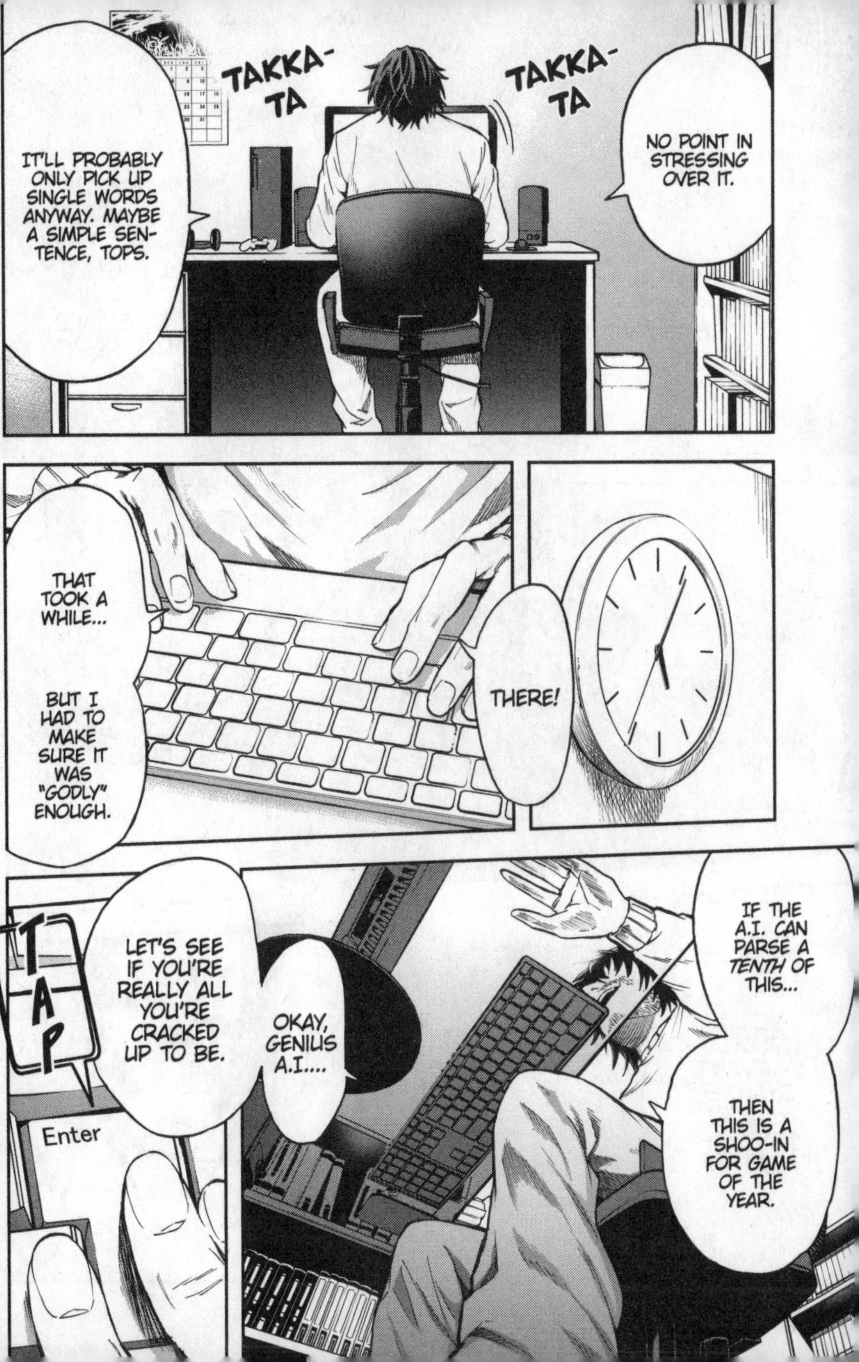
TAKKA-TA
TAKKA-TA
NO POINT IN STRESSING OVER IT.
IT'LL PROBABLY ONLY PICK UP SINGLE WORDS ANYWAY. MAYBE A SIMPLE SEN-TENCE, TOPS.
THERE!
THAT TOOK A WHILE...
BUT I HAD TO MAKE SURE IT WAS "GODLY" ENOUGH.
IF THE A.I. CAN PARSE A *TENTH* OF THIS...
THEN THIS IS A SHOO-IN FOR GAME OF THE YEAR.
OKAY, GENIUS A.I....
LET'S SEE IF YOU'RE REALLY ALL YOU'RE CRACKED UP TO BE.
TAP
Enter

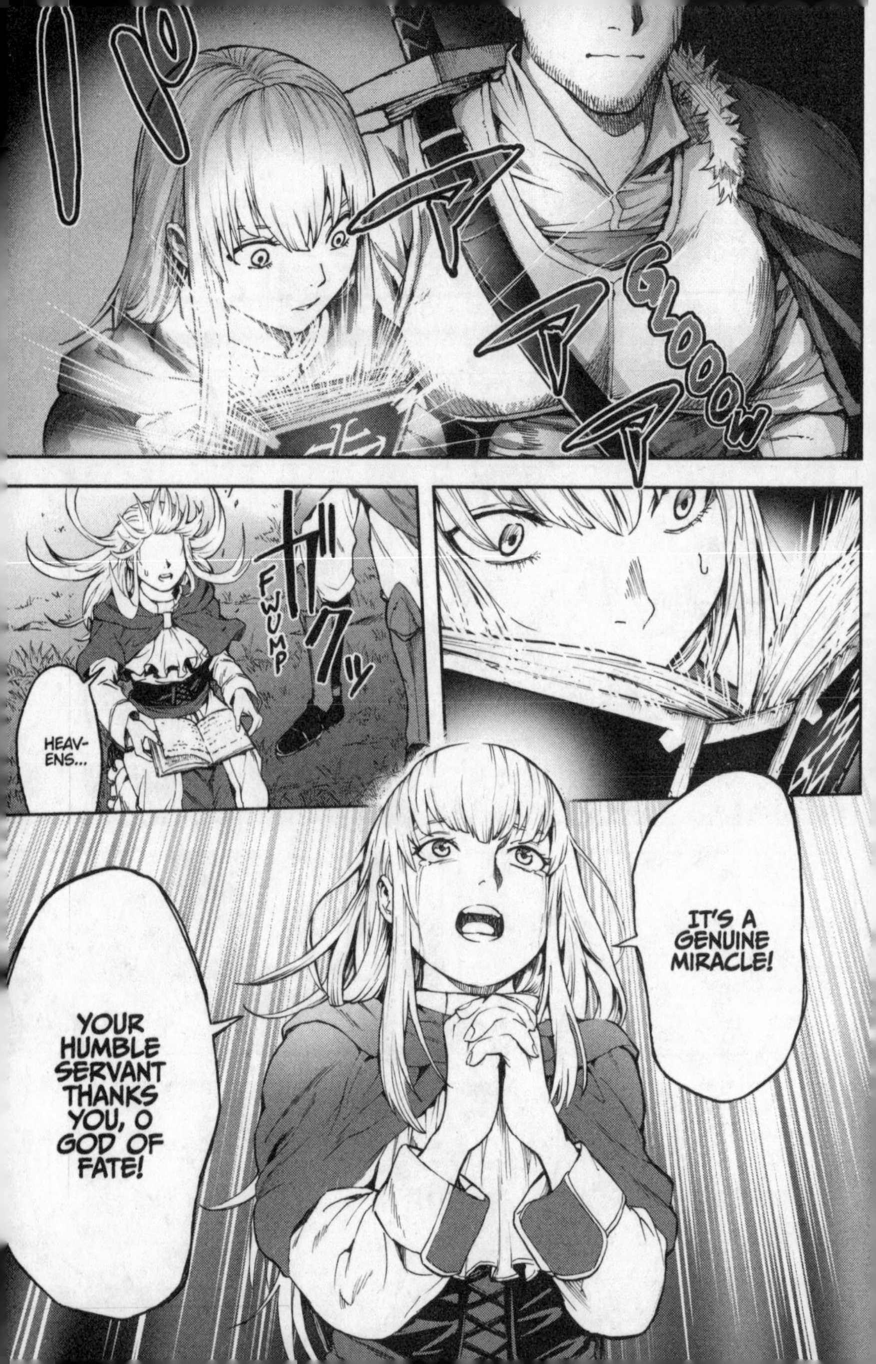

GLOOOW
FWUMP
HEAV-ENS...
IT'S A GENUINE MIRACLE!
YOUR HUMBLE SERVANT THANKS YOU, O GOD OF FATE!

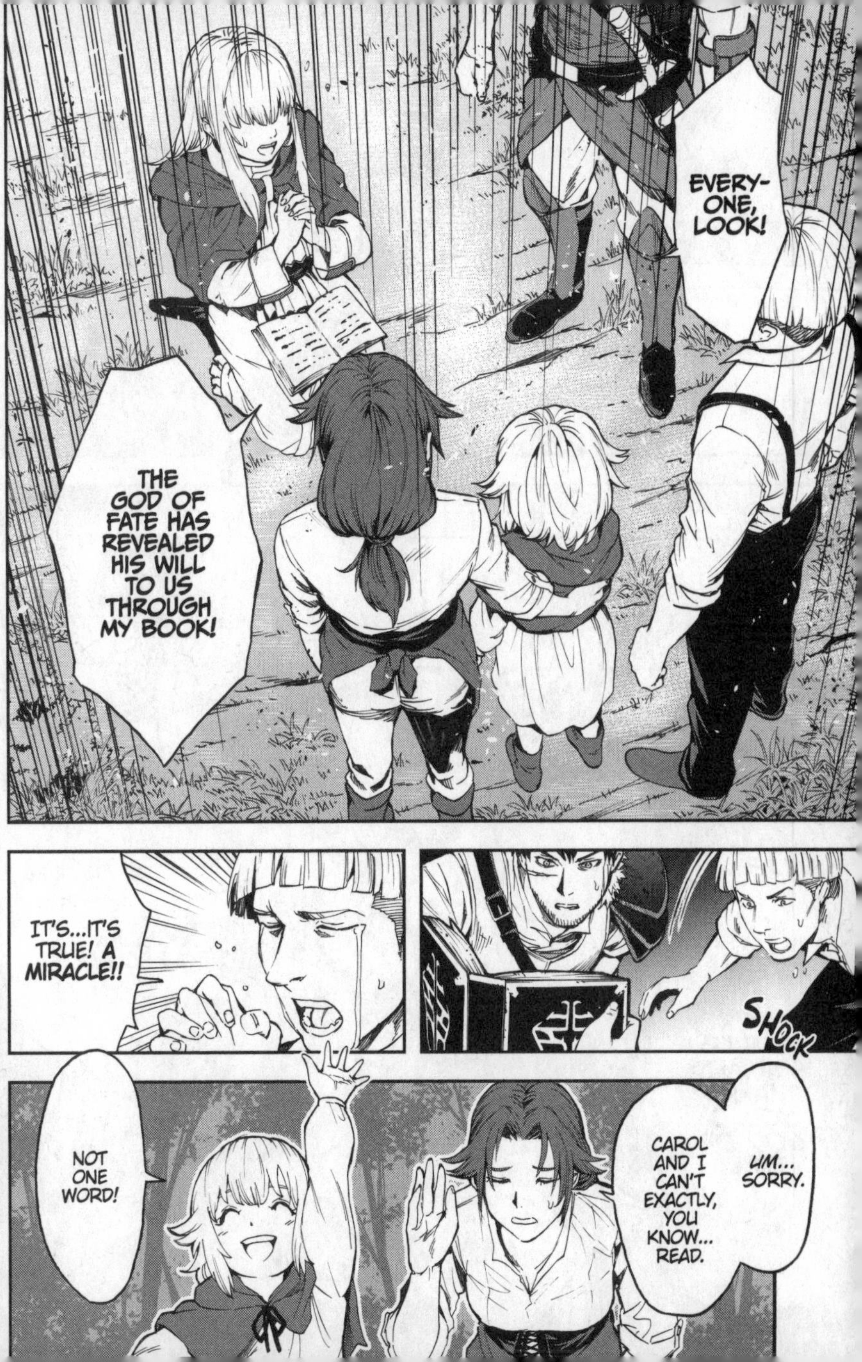
EVERY-ONE, LOOK!
THE GOD OF FATE HAS REVEALED HIS WILL TO US THROUGH MY BOOK!
SHOCK
IT'S...IT'S TRUE! A MIRACLE!!
UM... SORRY.
CAROL AND I CAN'T EXACTLY, YOU KNOW... READ.
NOT ONE WORD!

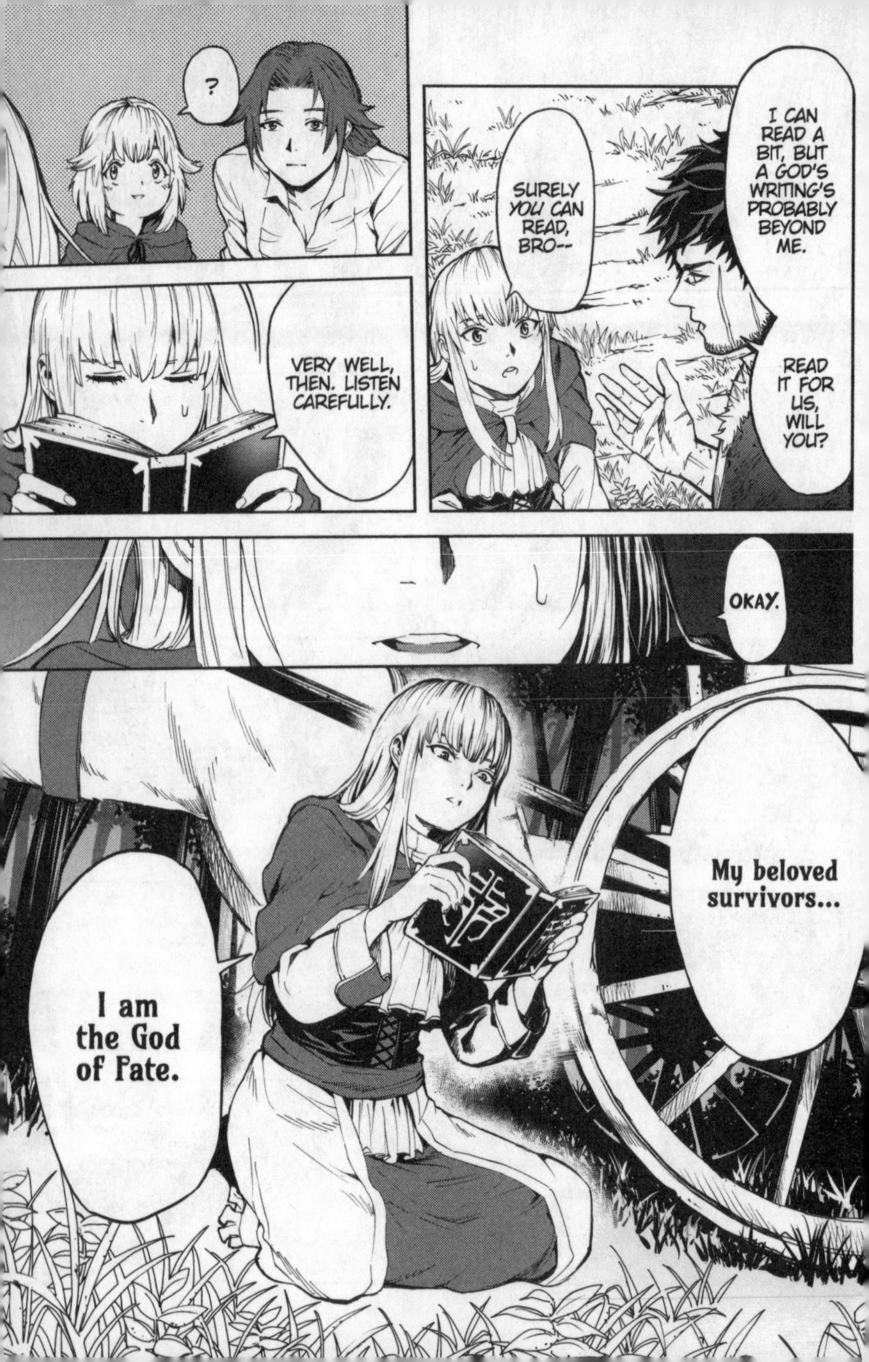
SURELY YOU CAN READ, BRO--
I CAN READ A BIT, BUT A GOD'S WRITING'S PROBABLY BEYOND ME.
READ IT FOR US, WILL YOU?
?
VERY WELL, THEN. LISTEN CAREFULLY.
OKAY.
My beloved survivors...
I am the God of Fate.

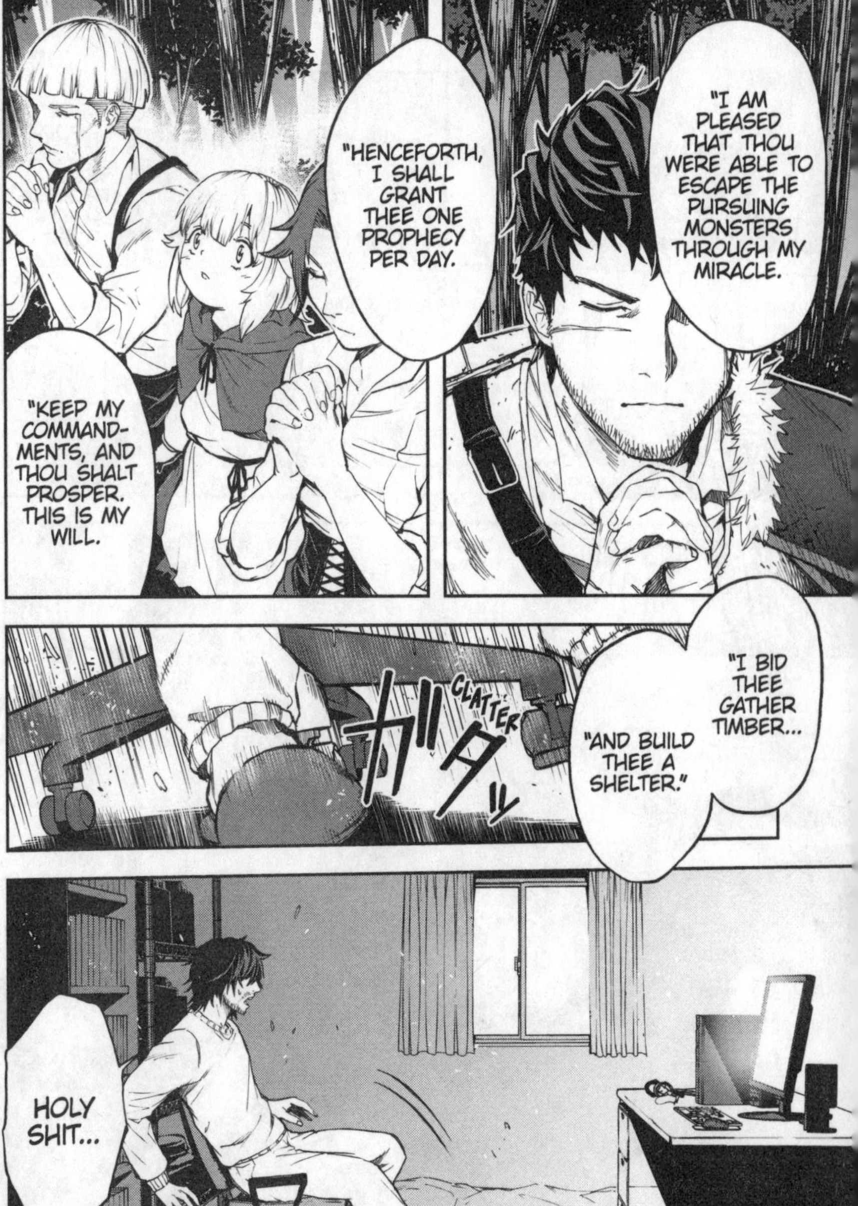
"I AM PLEASED THAT THOU WERE ABLE TO ESCAPE THE PURSUING MONSTERS THROUGH MY MIRACLE.
"HENCEFORTH, I SHALL GRANT THEE ONE PROPHECY PER DAY.
"KEEP MY COMMAND-MENTS, AND THOU SHALT PROSPER. THIS IS MY WILL.
"I BID THEE GATHER TIMBER...
"AND BUILD THEE A SHELTER."
CLATTER
ガタッ
HOLY SHIT...

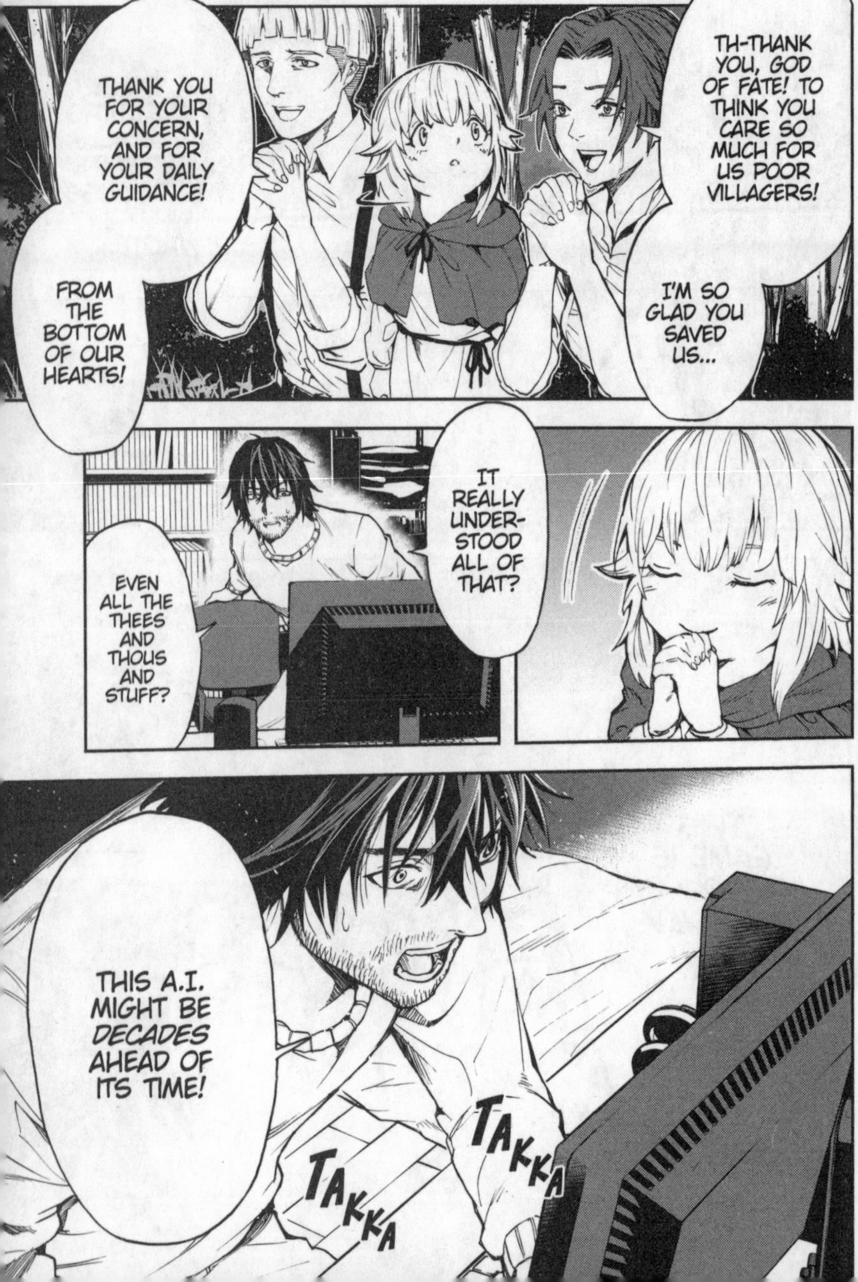
TH-THANK YOU, GOD OF FATE! TO THINK YOU CARE SO MUCH FOR US POOR VILLAGERS!
I'M SO GLAD YOU SAVED US...
THANK YOU FOR YOUR CONCERN, AND FOR YOUR DAILY GUIDANCE!
FROM THE BOTTOM OF OUR HEARTS!
IT REALLY UNDER-STOOD ALL OF THAT?
EVEN ALL THE THEES AND THOUS AND STUFF?
THIS A.I. MIGHT BE *DECADES* AHEAD OF ITS TIME!
TAKKA
TAKKA

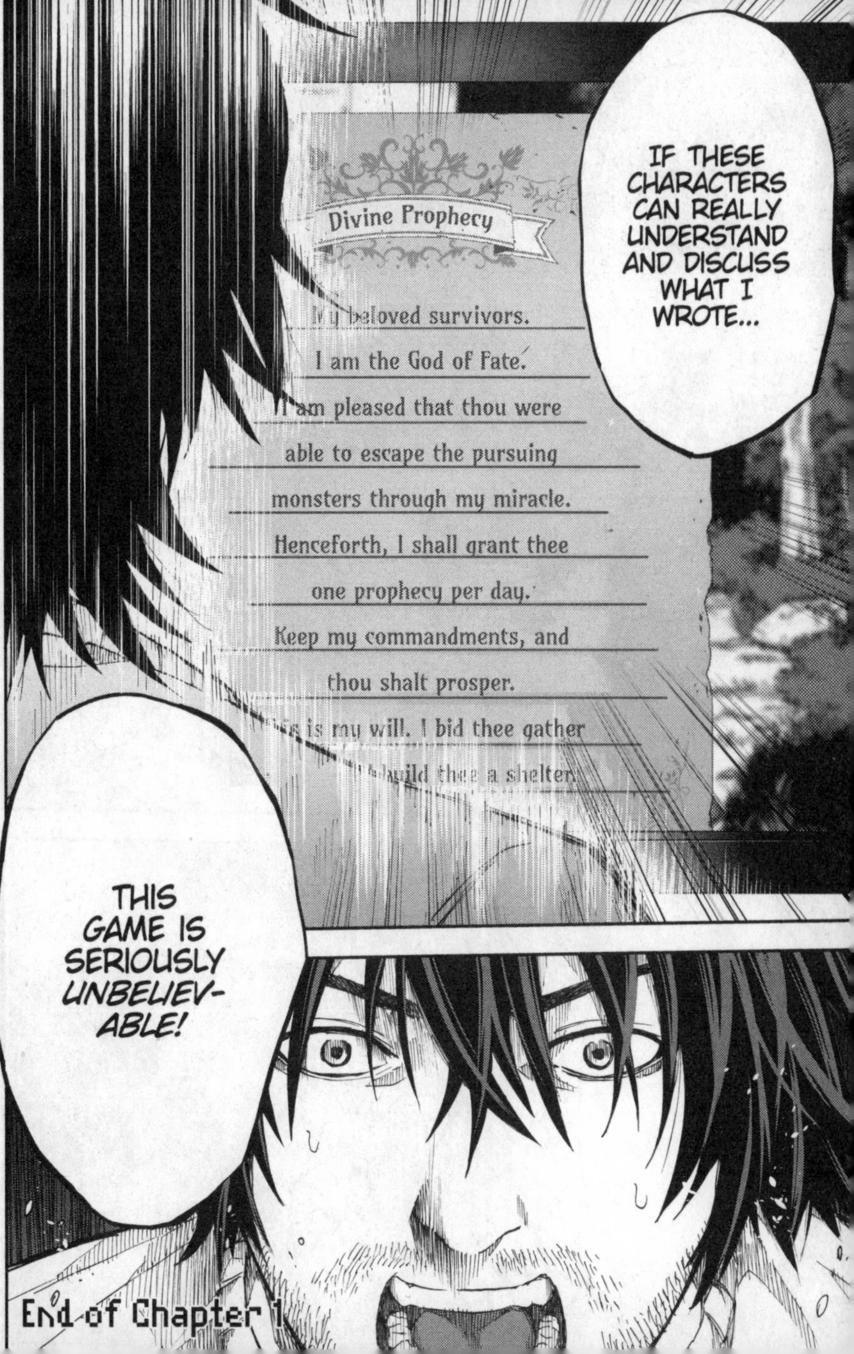
IF THESE CHARACTERS CAN REALLY UNDERSTAND AND DISCUSS WHAT I WROTE...
Divine Prophecy
beloved survivors.
I am the God of Fate.
I am pleased that thou were
able to escape the pursuing
monsters through my miracle.
Henceforth, I shall grant thee
one prophecy per day.
Keep my commandments, and
thou shalt prosper.
is my will. I bid thee gather
build thee a shelter.
THIS GAME IS SERIOUSLY UNBELIEV-ABLE!
End of Chapter 1

Character

Yoshio

▶ Gender: Male

  Class: None → God of Fate

E : Sweatshirt

E : Sweatpants

E : The shame of disappointing
    his parents

THE NPCs IN THIS VILLAGE SIM GAME MUST BE REAL!

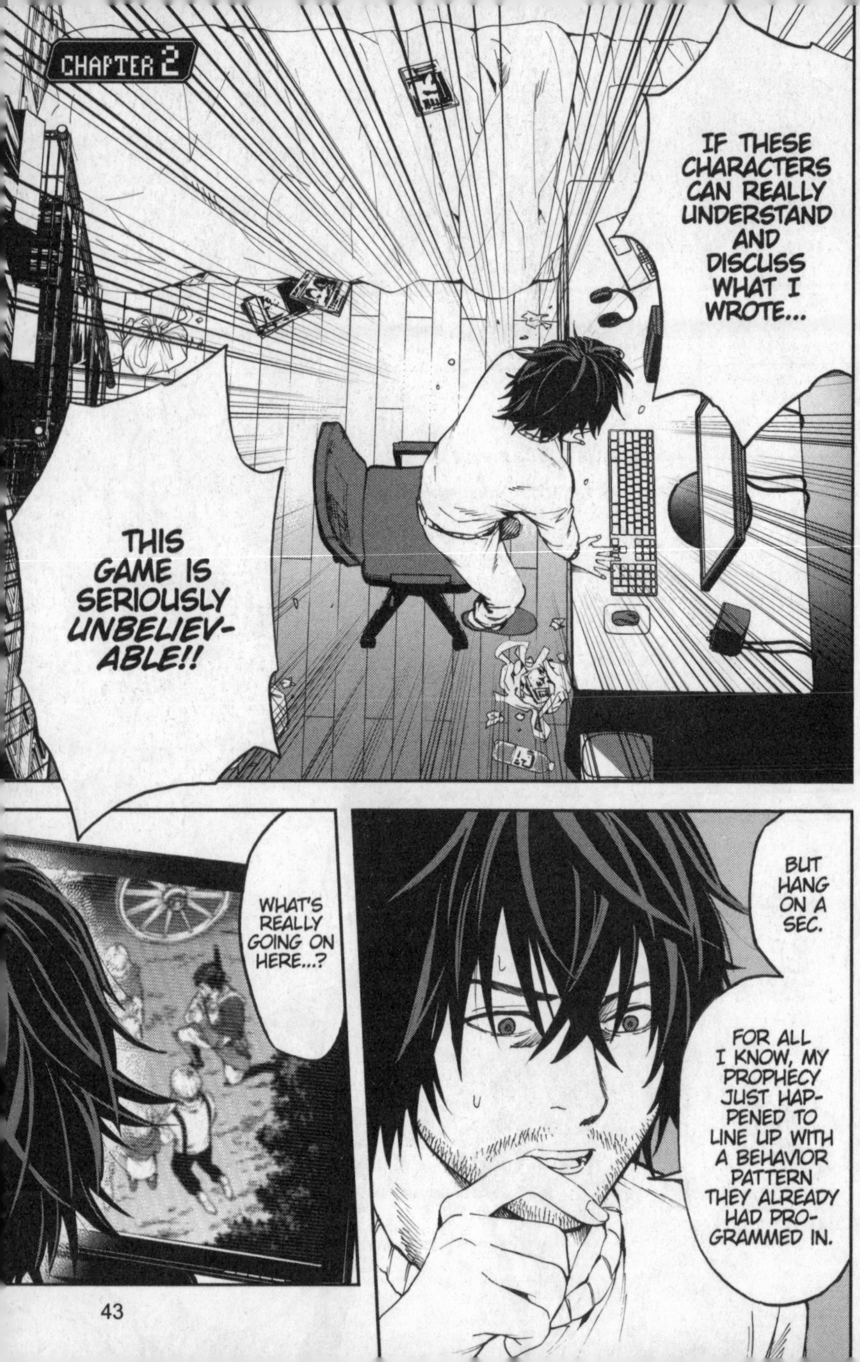
CHAPTER 2
IF THESE CHARACTERS CAN REALLY UNDERSTAND AND DISCUSS WHAT I WROTE...
THIS GAME IS SERIOUSLY UNBELIEVABLE!!
BUT HANG ON A SEC.
FOR ALL I KNOW, MY PROPHECY JUST HAPPENED TO LINE UP WITH A BEHAVIOR PATTERN THEY ALREADY HAD PROGRAMMED IN.
WHAT'S REALLY GOING ON HERE...?

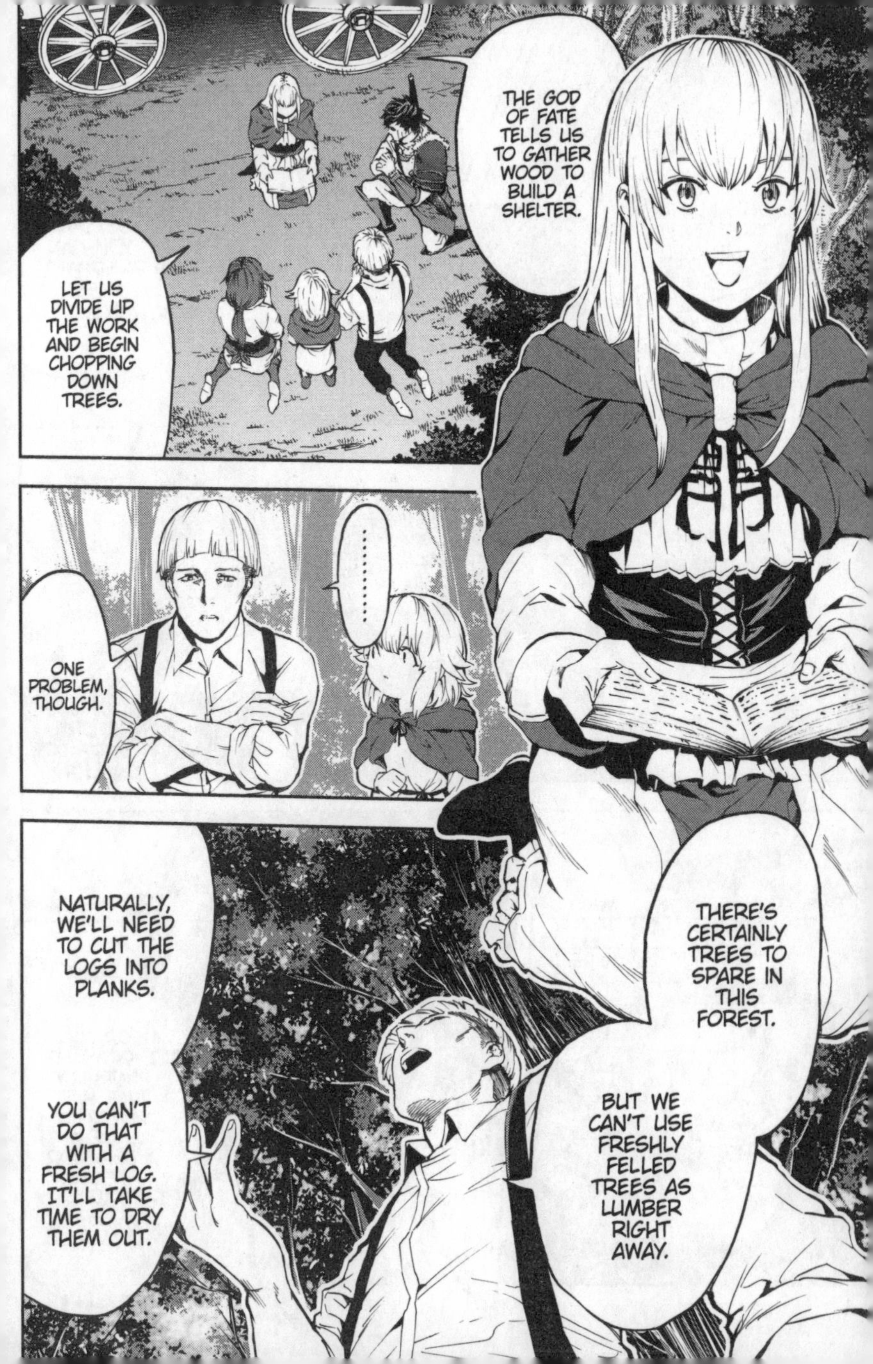
THE GOD OF FATE TELLS US TO GATHER WOOD TO BUILD A SHELTER.
LET US DIVIDE UP THE WORK AND BEGIN CHOPPING DOWN TREES.
......
ONE PROBLEM, THOUGH.
THERE'S CERTAINLY TREES TO SPARE IN THIS FOREST.
BUT WE CAN'T USE FRESHLY FELLED TREES AS LUMBER RIGHT AWAY.
NATURALLY, WE'LL NEED TO CUT THE LOGS INTO PLANKS.
YOU CAN'T DO THAT WITH A FRESH LOG. IT'LL TAKE TIME TO DRY THEM OUT.

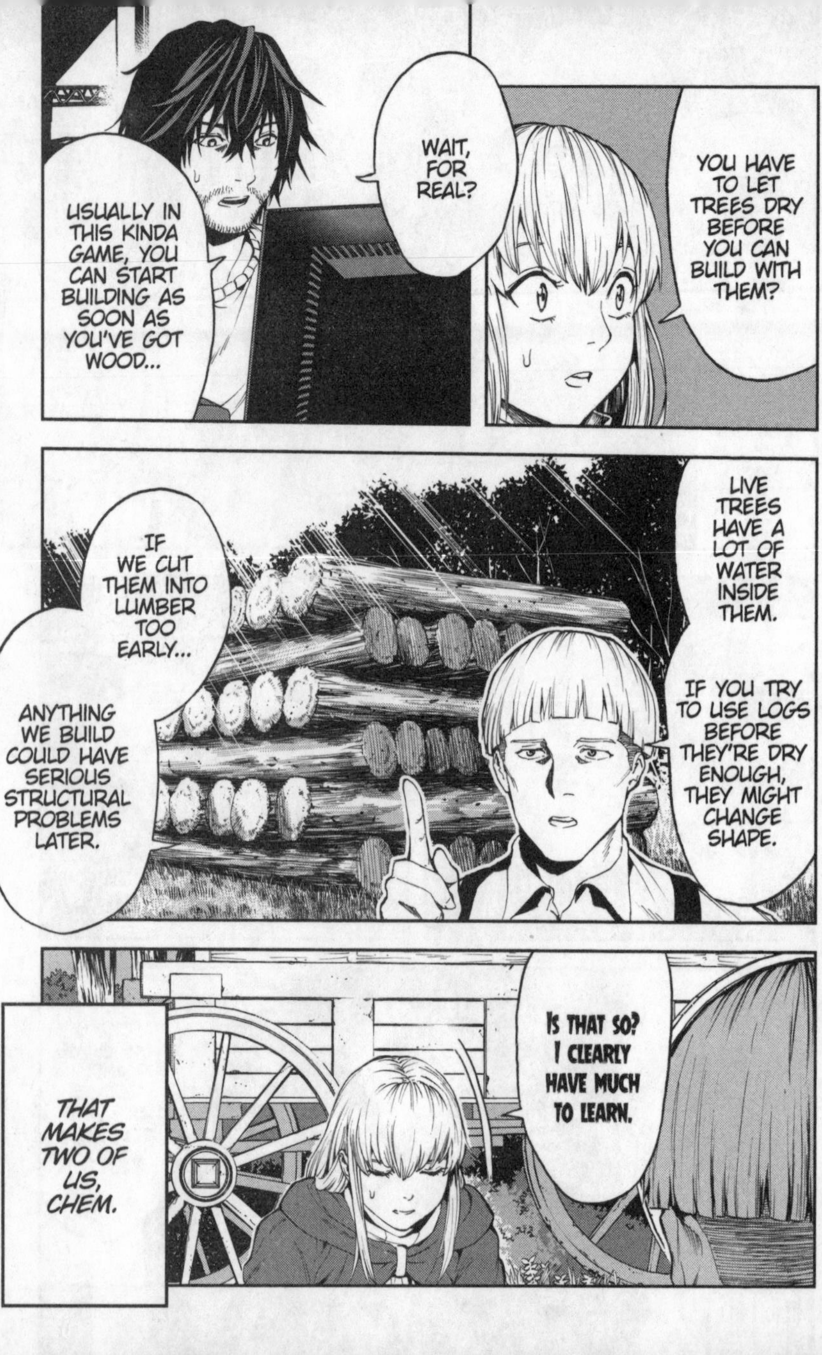
YOU HAVE TO LET TREES DRY BEFORE YOU CAN BUILD WITH THEM?
WAIT, FOR REAL?
USUALLY IN THIS KINDA GAME, YOU CAN START BUILDING AS SOON AS YOU'VE GOT WOOD...
LIVE TREES HAVE A LOT OF WATER INSIDE THEM.
IF YOU TRY TO USE LOGS BEFORE THEY'RE DRY ENOUGH, THEY MIGHT CHANGE SHAPE.
IF WE CUT THEM INTO LUMBER TOO EARLY...
ANYTHING WE BUILD COULD HAVE SERIOUS STRUCTURAL PROBLEMS LATER.
IS THAT SO? I CLEARLY HAVE MUCH TO LEARN.
THAT MAKES TWO OF US, CHEM.

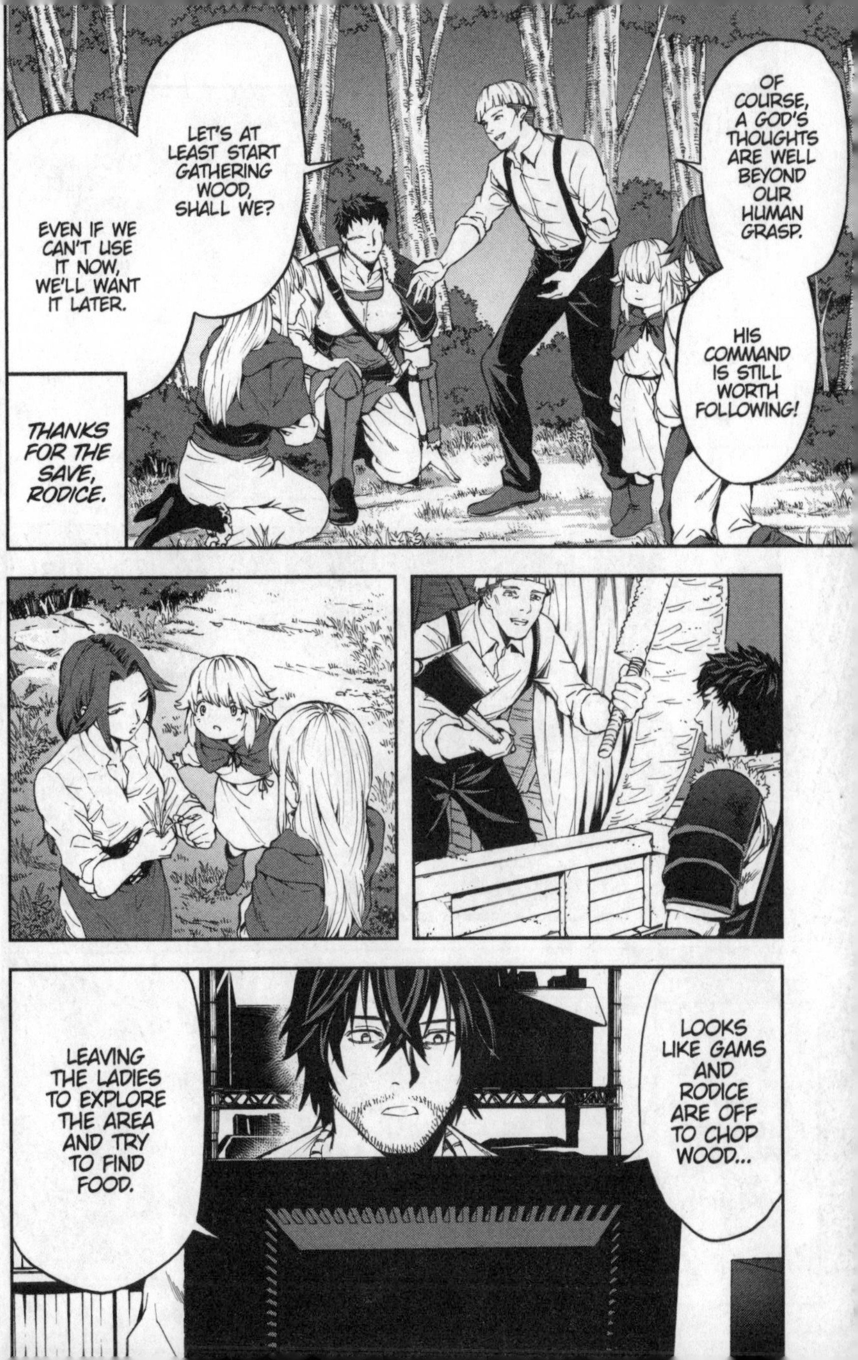
OF COURSE, A GOD'S THOUGHTS ARE WELL BEYOND OUR HUMAN GRASP.
HIS COMMAND IS STILL WORTH FOLLOWING!
LET'S AT LEAST START GATHERING WOOD, SHALL WE?
EVEN IF WE CAN'T USE IT NOW, WE'LL WANT IT LATER.
THANKS FOR THE SAVE, RODICE.
LOOKS LIKE GAMS AND RODICE ARE OFF TO CHOP WOOD...
LEAVING THE LADIES TO EXPLORE THE AREA AND TRY TO FIND FOOD.

IF I SPIN THE MOUSE WHEEL...

I CAN ZOOM OUT QUITE A BIT.

LET'S GET A LOOK AT THEIR SURROUNDINGS.

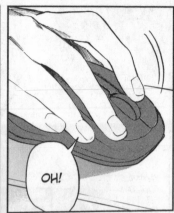

OH!

VWOOM

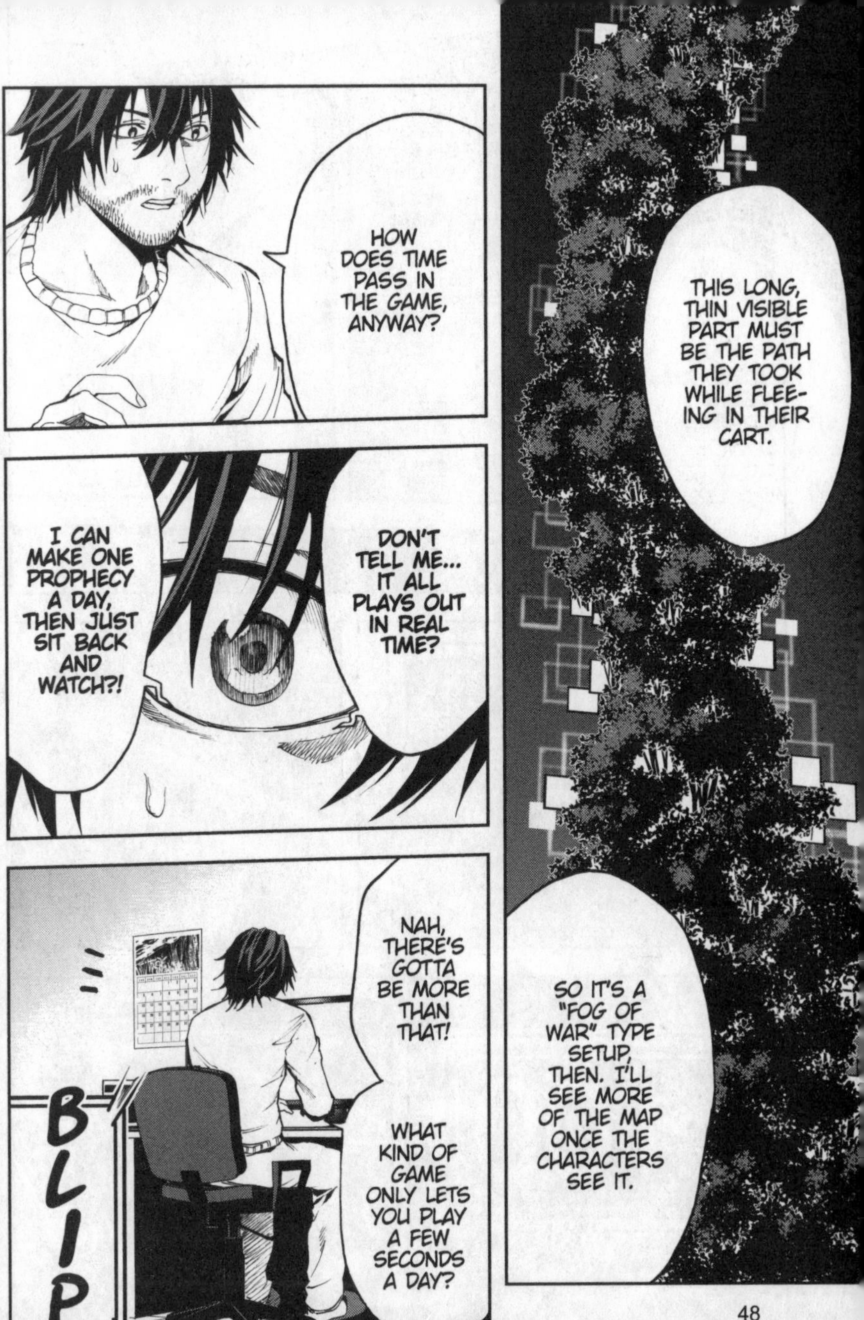
THIS LONG, THIN VISIBLE PART MUST BE THE PATH THEY TOOK WHILE FLEE-ING IN THEIR CART.
SO IT'S A "FOG OF WAR" TYPE SETUP, THEN. I'LL SEE MORE OF THE MAP ONCE THE CHARACTERS SEE IT.
HOW DOES TIME PASS IN THE GAME, ANYWAY?
DON'T TELL ME... IT ALL PLAYS OUT IN REAL TIME?
I CAN MAKE ONE PROPHECY A DAY, THEN JUST SIT BACK AND WATCH?!
NAH, THERE'S GOTTA BE MORE THAN THAT!
WHAT KIND OF GAME ONLY LETS YOU PLAY A FEW SECONDS A DAY?
BLIP

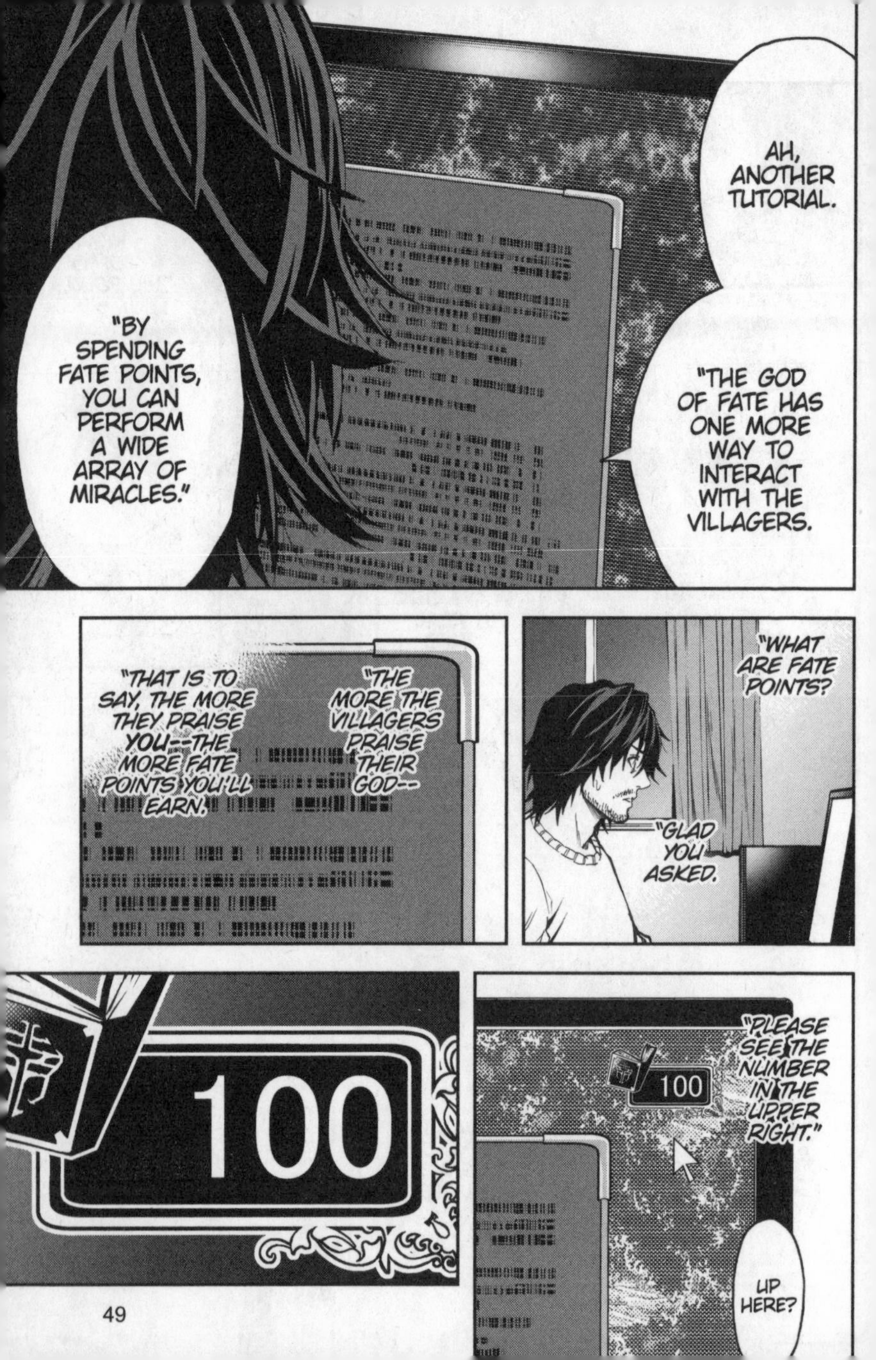
AH, ANOTHER TUTORIAL.
"THE GOD OF FATE HAS ONE MORE WAY TO INTERACT WITH THE VILLAGERS.
"BY SPENDING FATE POINTS, YOU CAN PERFORM A WIDE ARRAY OF MIRACLES."
"WHAT ARE FATE POINTS?
"GLAD YOU ASKED.
"THE MORE THE VILLAGERS PRAISE THEIR GOD--
"THAT IS TO SAY, THE MORE THEY PRAISE YOU--THE MORE FATE POINTS YOU'LL EARN.
"PLEASE SEE THE NUMBER IN THE UPPER RIGHT."
100
UP HERE?
100

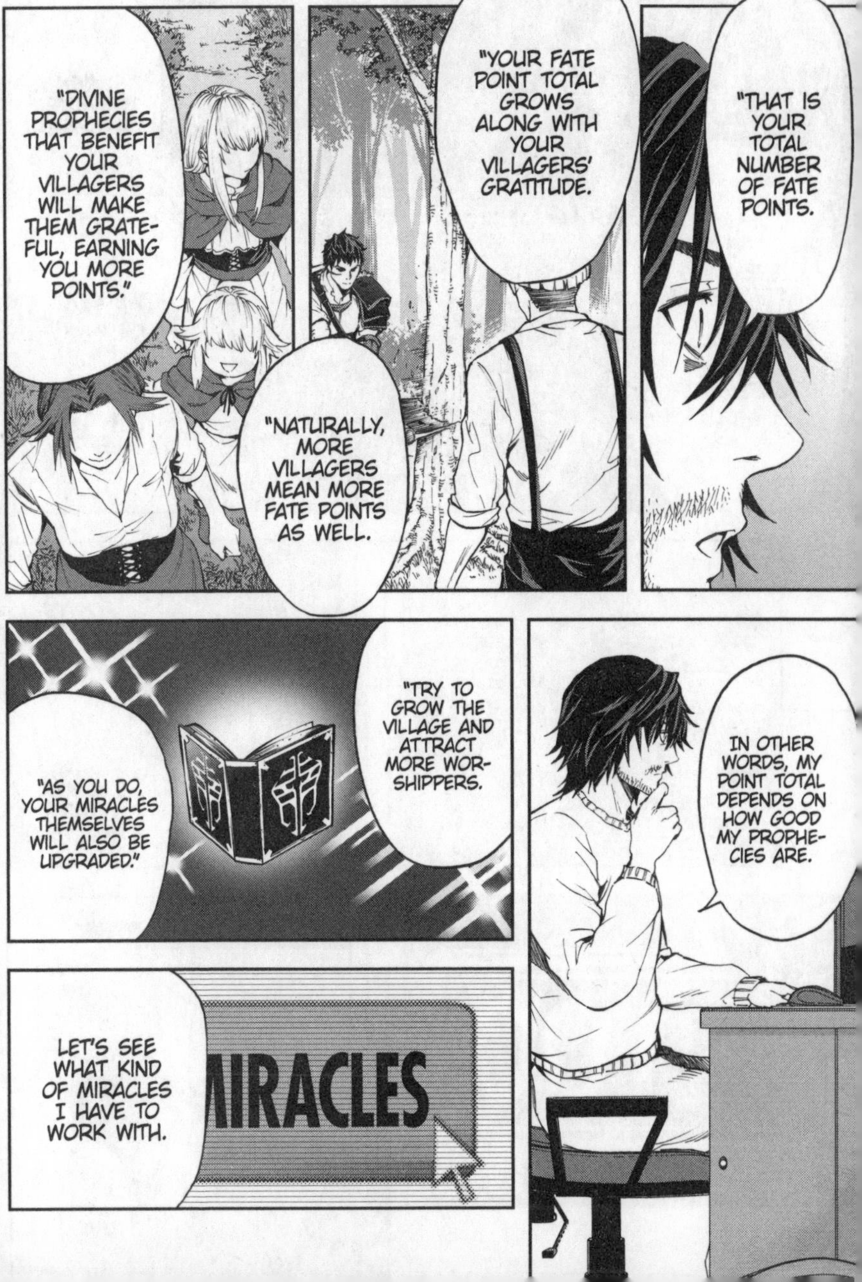
"THAT IS YOUR TOTAL NUMBER OF FATE POINTS.
"YOUR FATE POINT TOTAL GROWS ALONG WITH YOUR VILLAGERS' GRATITUDE.
"NATURALLY, MORE VILLAGERS MEAN MORE FATE POINTS AS WELL.
"DIVINE PROPHECIES THAT BENEFIT YOUR VILLAGERS WILL MAKE THEM GRATE-FUL, EARNING YOU MORE POINTS."
IN OTHER WORDS, MY POINT TOTAL DEPENDS ON HOW GOOD MY PROPHE-CIES ARE.
"TRY TO GROW THE VILLAGE AND ATTRACT MORE WOR-SHIPPERS.
"AS YOU DO, YOUR MIRACLES THEMSELVES WILL ALSO BE UPGRADED."
MIRACLES
LET'S SEE WHAT KIND OF MIRACLES I HAVE TO WORK WITH.

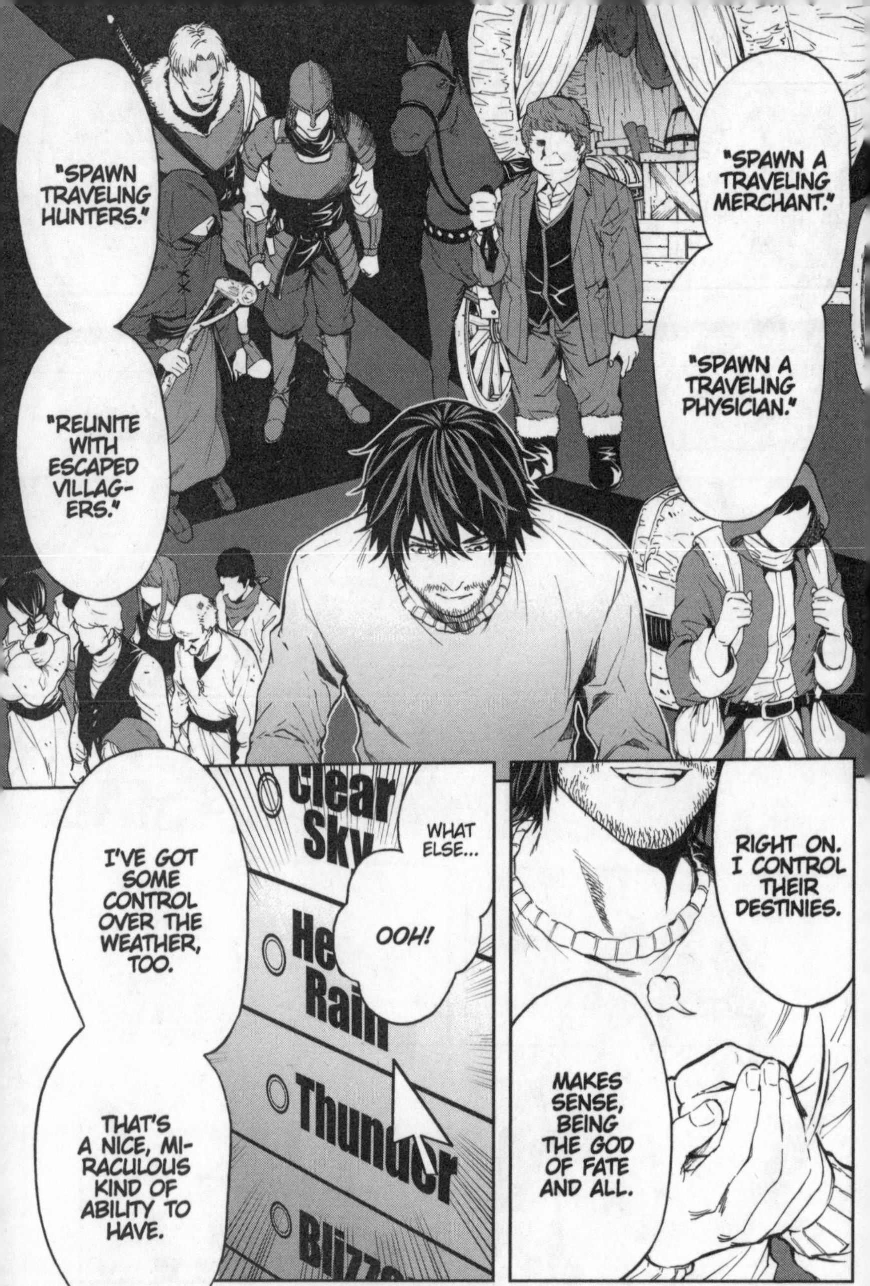
"SPAWN A TRAVELING MERCHANT."
"SPAWN A TRAVELING PHYSICIAN."
"SPAWN TRAVELING HUNTERS."
"REUNITE WITH ESCAPED VILLAGERS."
RIGHT ON. I CONTROL THEIR DESTINIES.
MAKES SENSE, BEING THE GOD OF FATE AND ALL.
WHAT ELSE...
I'VE GOT SOME CONTROL OVER THE WEATHER, TOO.
OOH!
THAT'S A NICE, MIRACULOUS KIND OF ABILITY TO HAVE.
Clear Sky
Thunder

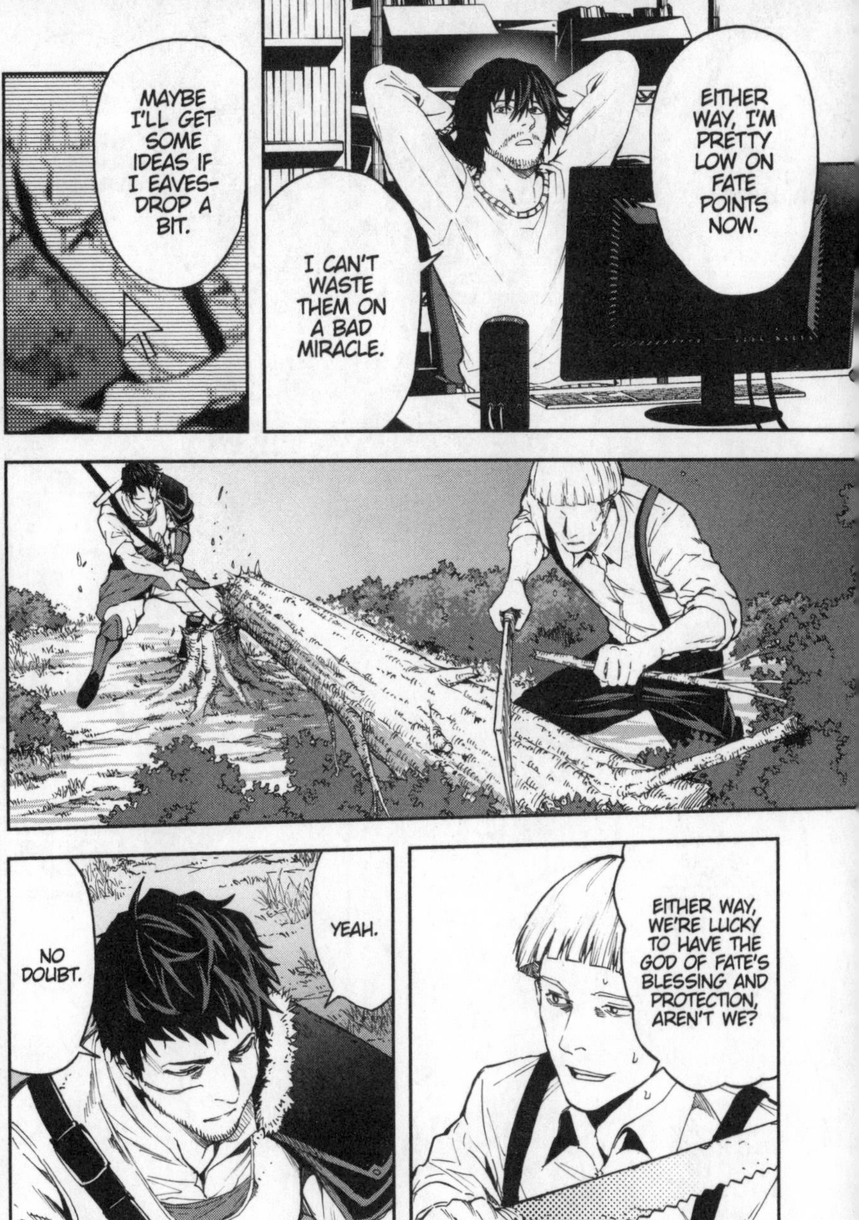
EITHER WAY, I'M PRETTY LOW ON FATE POINTS NOW.
I CAN'T WASTE THEM ON A BAD MIRACLE.
MAYBE I'LL GET SOME IDEAS IF I EAVES-DROP A BIT.
EITHER WAY, WE'RE LUCKY TO HAVE THE GOD OF FATE'S BLESSING AND PROTECTION, AREN'T WE?
YEAH.
NO DOUBT.

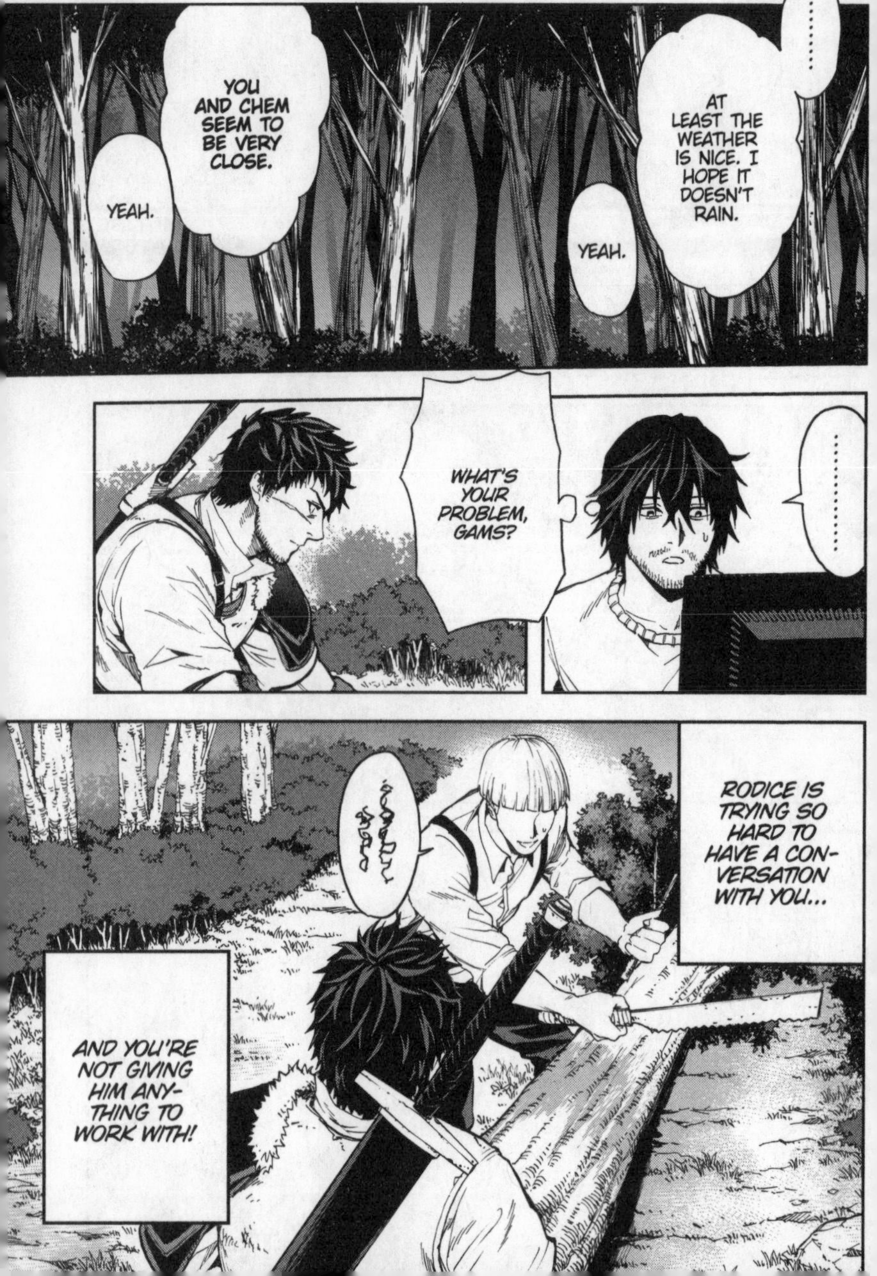
......
AT LEAST THE WEATHER IS NICE. I HOPE IT DOESN'T RAIN.
YEAH.
YOU AND CHEM SEEM TO BE VERY CLOSE.
YEAH.
......
WHAT'S YOUR PROBLEM, GAMS?
RODICE IS TRYING SO HARD TO HAVE A CON-VERSATION WITH YOU...
AND YOU'RE NOT GIVING HIM ANY-THING TO WORK WITH!

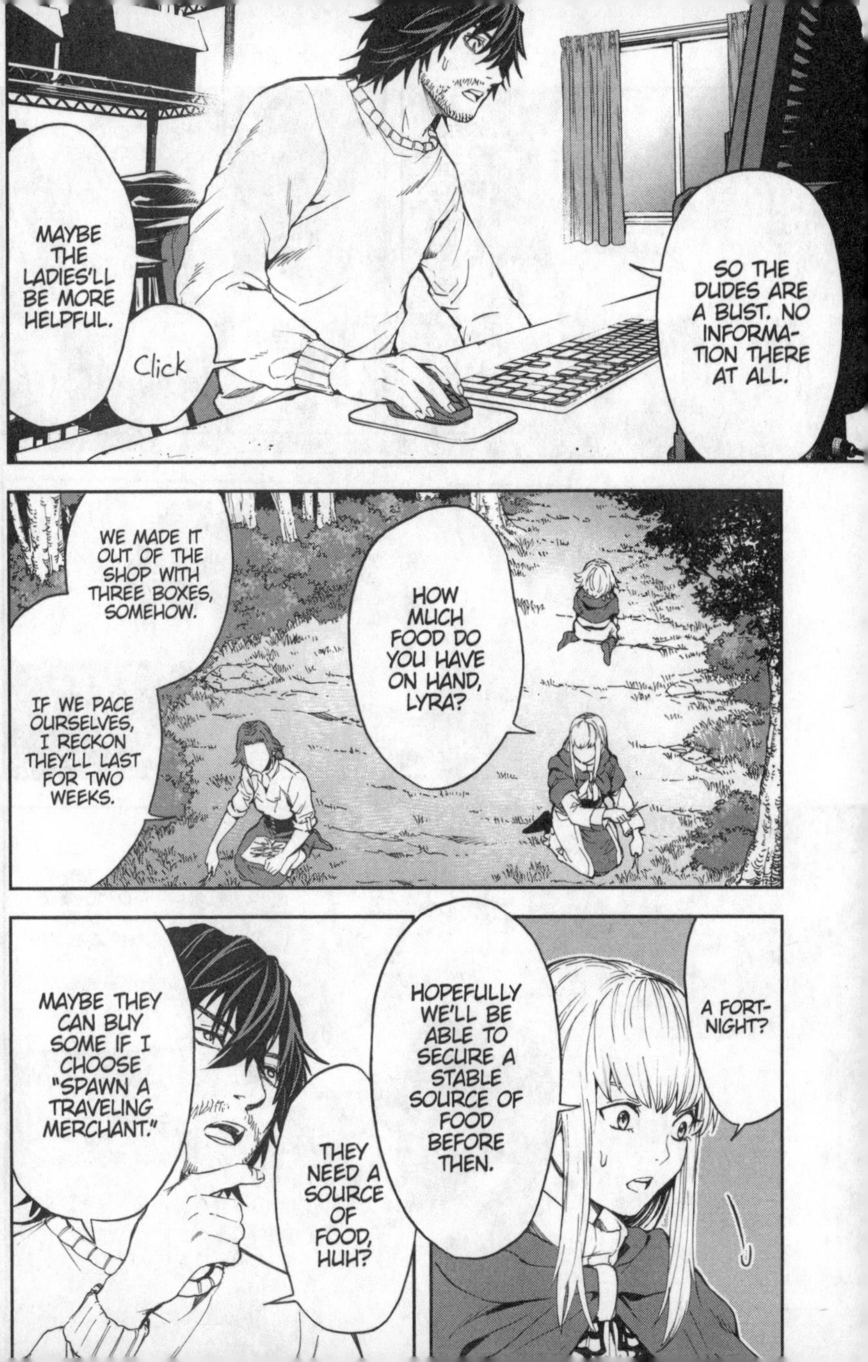
SO THE DUDES ARE A BUST. NO INFORMATION THERE AT ALL.
Click
MAYBE THE LADIES'LL BE MORE HELPFUL.
HOW MUCH FOOD DO YOU HAVE ON HAND, LYRA?
WE MADE IT OUT OF THE SHOP WITH THREE BOXES, SOMEHOW.
IF WE PACE OURSELVES, I RECKON THEY'LL LAST FOR TWO WEEKS.
A FORTNIGHT?
HOPEFULLY WE'LL BE ABLE TO SECURE A STABLE SOURCE OF FOOD BEFORE THEN.
THEY NEED A SOURCE OF FOOD, HUH?
MAYBE THEY CAN BUY SOME IF I CHOOSE "SPAWN A TRAVELING MERCHANT."

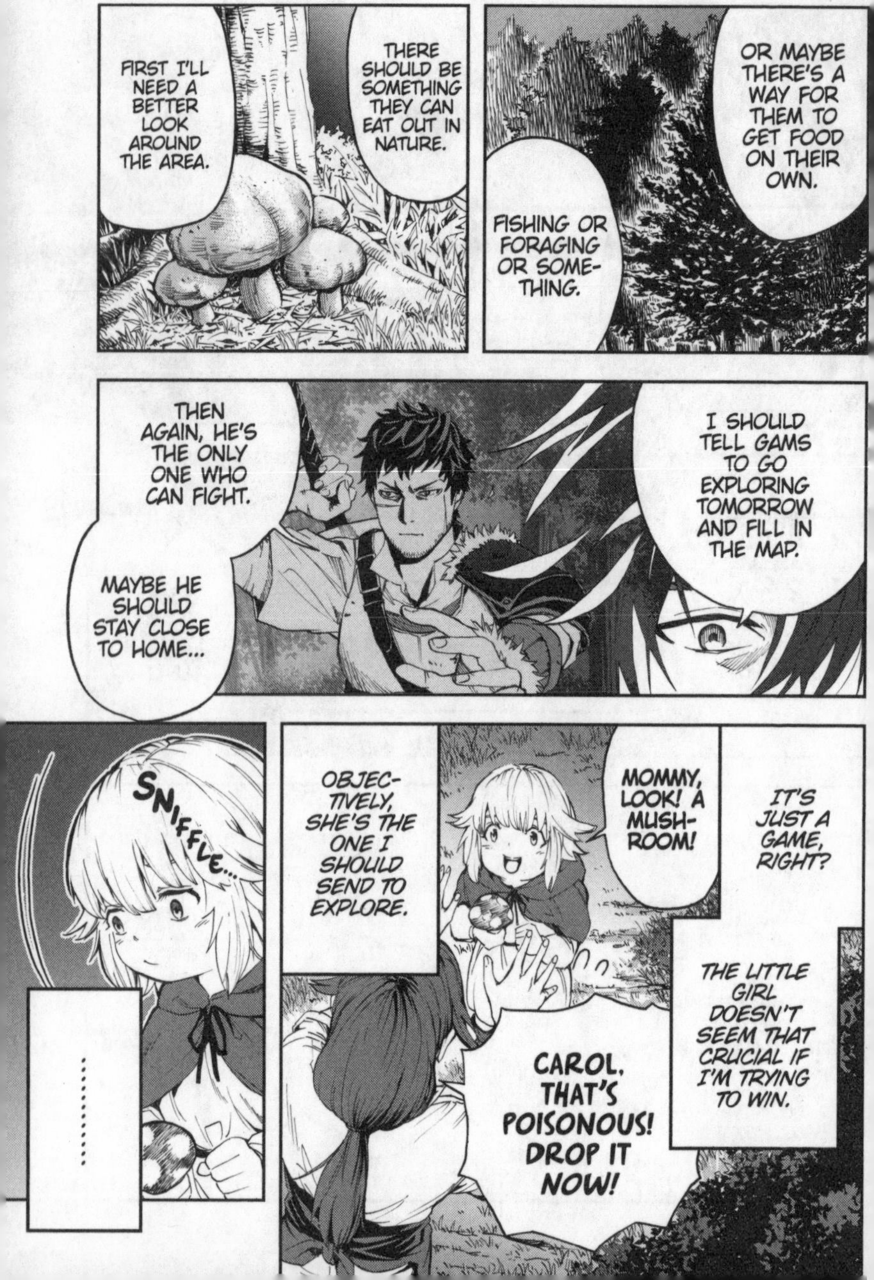
OR MAYBE THERE'S A WAY FOR THEM TO GET FOOD ON THEIR OWN.
FISHING OR FORAGING OR SOME-THING.
THERE SHOULD BE SOMETHING THEY CAN EAT OUT IN NATURE.
FIRST I'LL NEED A BETTER LOOK AROUND THE AREA.
I SHOULD TELL GAMS TO GO EXPLORING TOMORROW AND FILL IN THE MAP.
THEN AGAIN, HE'S THE ONLY ONE WHO CAN FIGHT.
MAYBE HE SHOULD STAY CLOSE TO HOME...
IT'S JUST A GAME, RIGHT?
MOMMY, LOOK! A MUSH-ROOM!
OBJEC-TIVELY, SHE'S THE ONE I SHOULD SEND TO EXPLORE.
THE LITTLE GIRL DOESN'T SEEM THAT CRUCIAL IF I'M TRYING TO WIN.
CAROL. THAT'S POISONOUS! DROP IT NOW!
SNIFFLE...
......

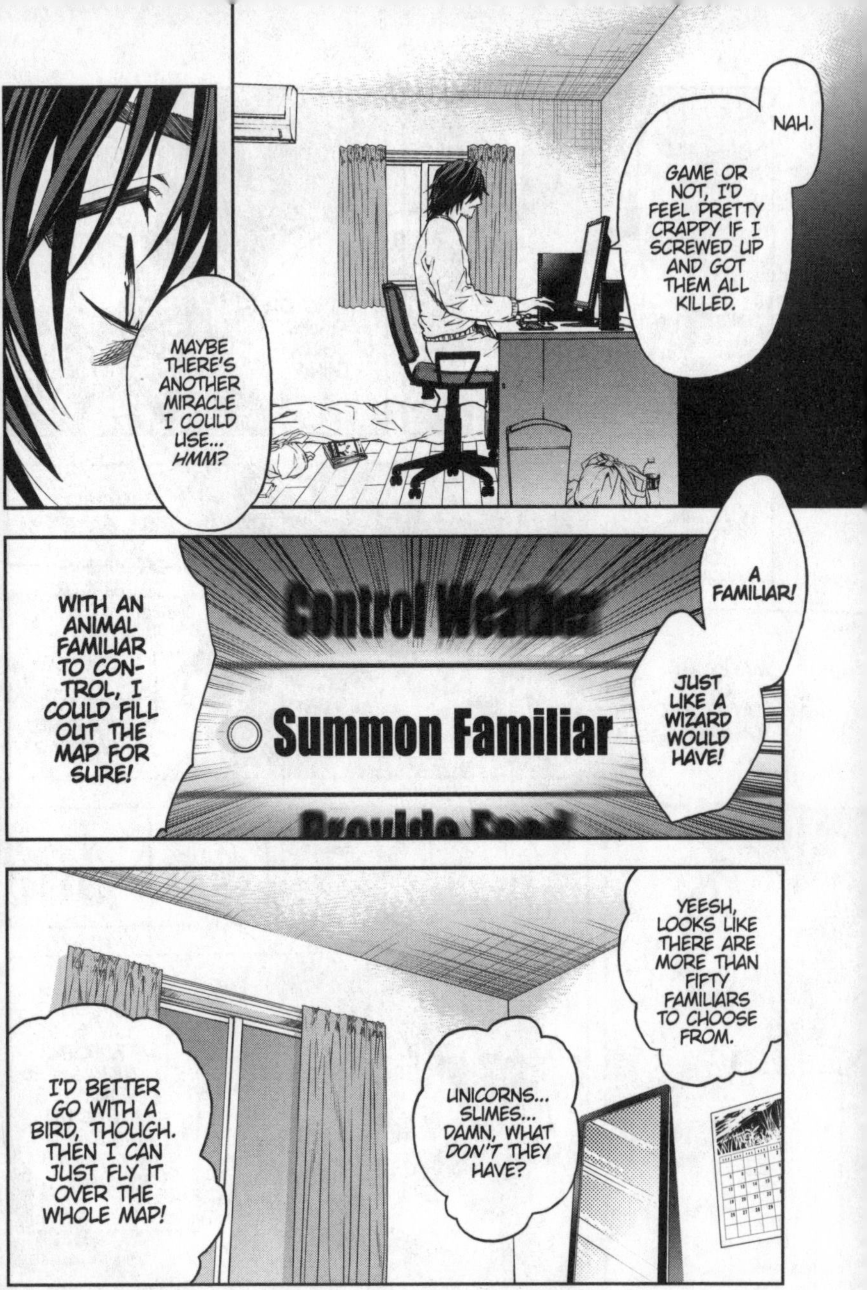
NAH.
GAME OR NOT, I'D FEEL PRETTY CRAPPY IF I SCREWED UP AND GOT THEM ALL KILLED.
MAYBE THERE'S ANOTHER MIRACLE I COULD USE... *HMM?*
A FAMILIAR!
JUST LIKE A WIZARD WOULD HAVE!
Control Weather
Summon Familiar
WITH AN ANIMAL FAMILIAR TO CON-TROL, I COULD FILL OUT THE MAP FOR SURE!
YEESH, LOOKS LIKE THERE ARE MORE THAN FIFTY FAMILIARS TO CHOOSE FROM.
UNICORNS... SLIMES... DAMN, WHAT *DON'T* THEY HAVE?
I'D BETTER GO WITH A BIRD, THOUGH. THEN I CAN JUST FLY IT OVER THE WHOLE MAP!

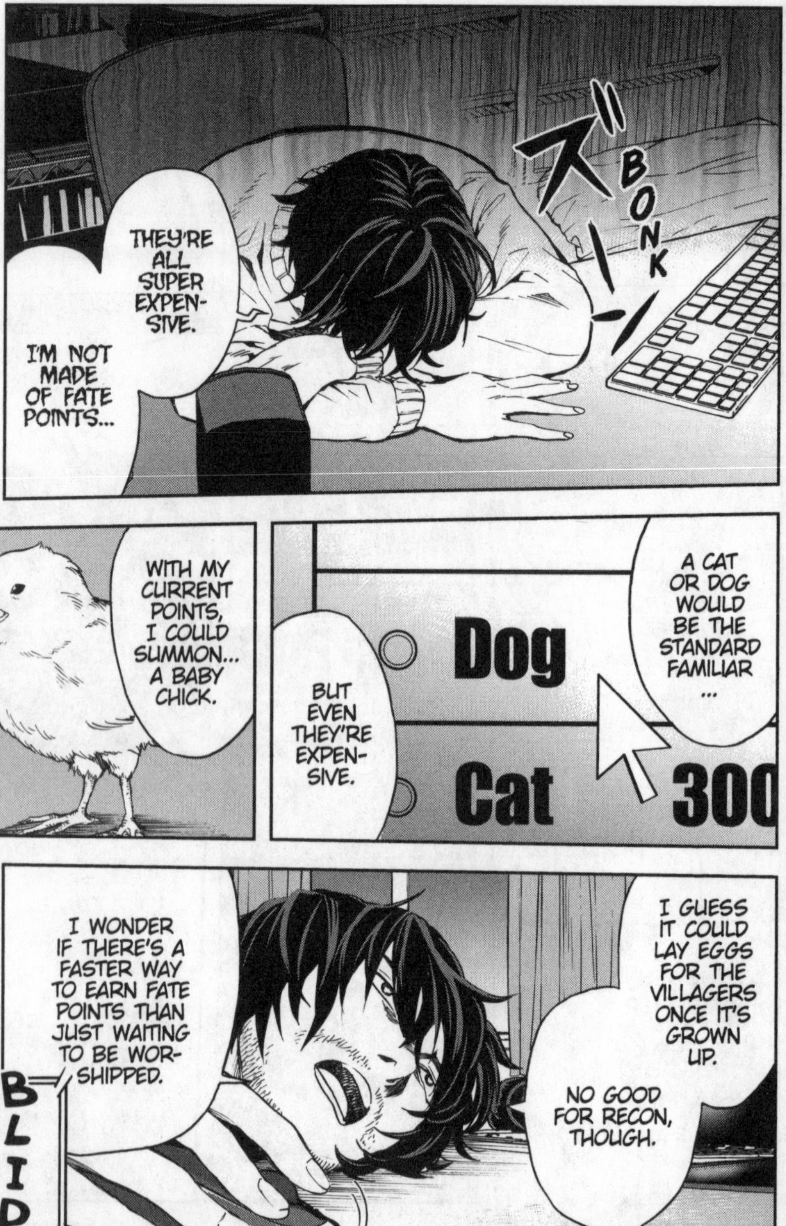
BONK
THEY'RE ALL SUPER EXPEN-SIVE.
I'M NOT MADE OF FATE POINTS...
A CAT OR DOG WOULD BE THE STANDARD FAMILIAR ...
Dog
Cat
300
BUT EVEN THEY'RE EXPEN-SIVE.
WITH MY CURRENT POINTS, I COULD SUMMON... A BABY CHICK.
I GUESS IT COULD LAY EGGS FOR THE VILLAGERS ONCE IT'S GROWN UP.
NO GOOD FOR RECON, THOUGH.
I WONDER IF THERE'S A FASTER WAY TO EARN FATE POINTS THAN JUST WAITING TO BE WOR-SHIPPED.
BLIP

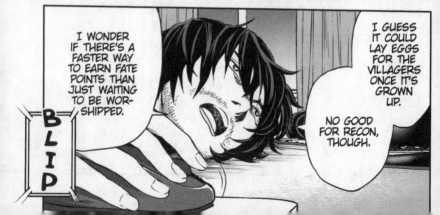

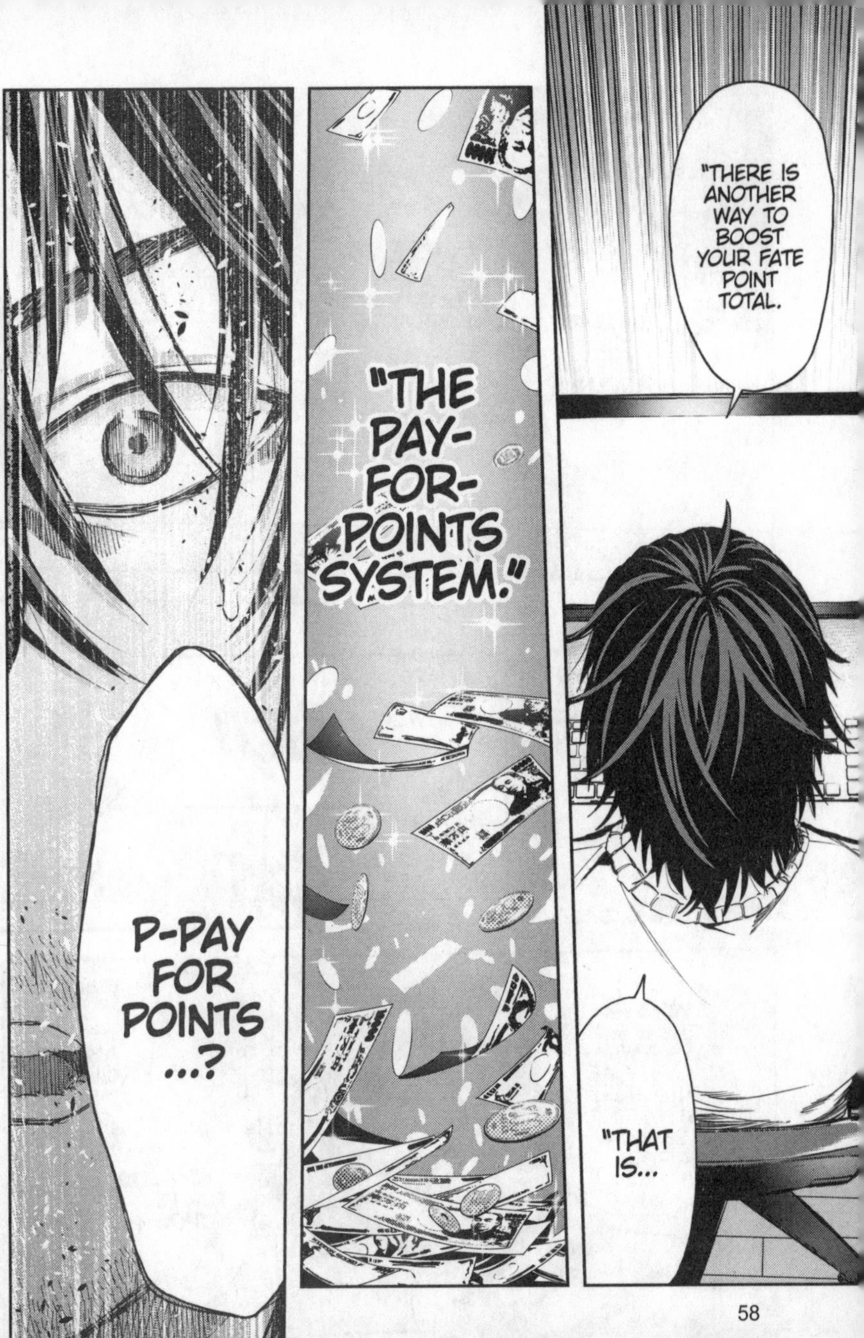
"THERE IS ANOTHER WAY TO BOOST YOUR FATE POINT TOTAL.
"THAT IS...
"THE PAY-FOR-POINTS SYSTEM."
P-PAY FOR POINTS ...?

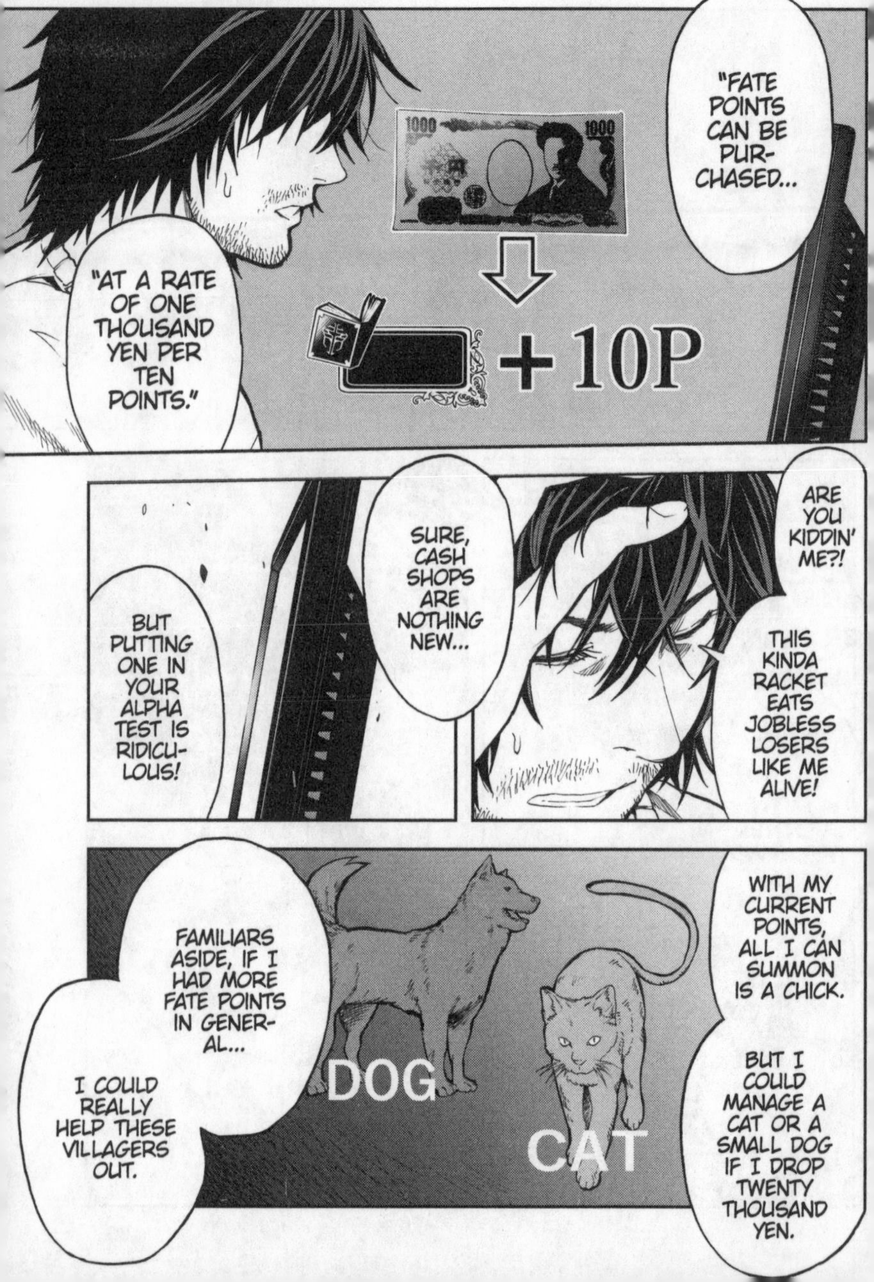
"FATE POINTS CAN BE PUR-CHASED...
1000
+10P
"AT A RATE OF ONE THOUSAND YEN PER TEN POINTS."
ARE YOU KIDDIN' ME?!
THIS KINDA RACKET EATS JOBLESS LOSERS LIKE ME ALIVE!
SURE, CASH SHOPS ARE NOTHING NEW...
BUT PUTTING ONE IN YOUR ALPHA TEST IS RIDICU-LOUS!
WITH MY CURRENT POINTS, ALL I CAN SUMMON IS A CHICK.
BUT I COULD MANAGE A CAT OR A SMALL DOG IF I DROP TWENTY THOUSAND YEN.
DOG
CAT
FAMILIARS ASIDE, IF I HAD MORE FATE POINTS IN GENER-AL...
I COULD REALLY HELP THESE VILLAGERS OUT.

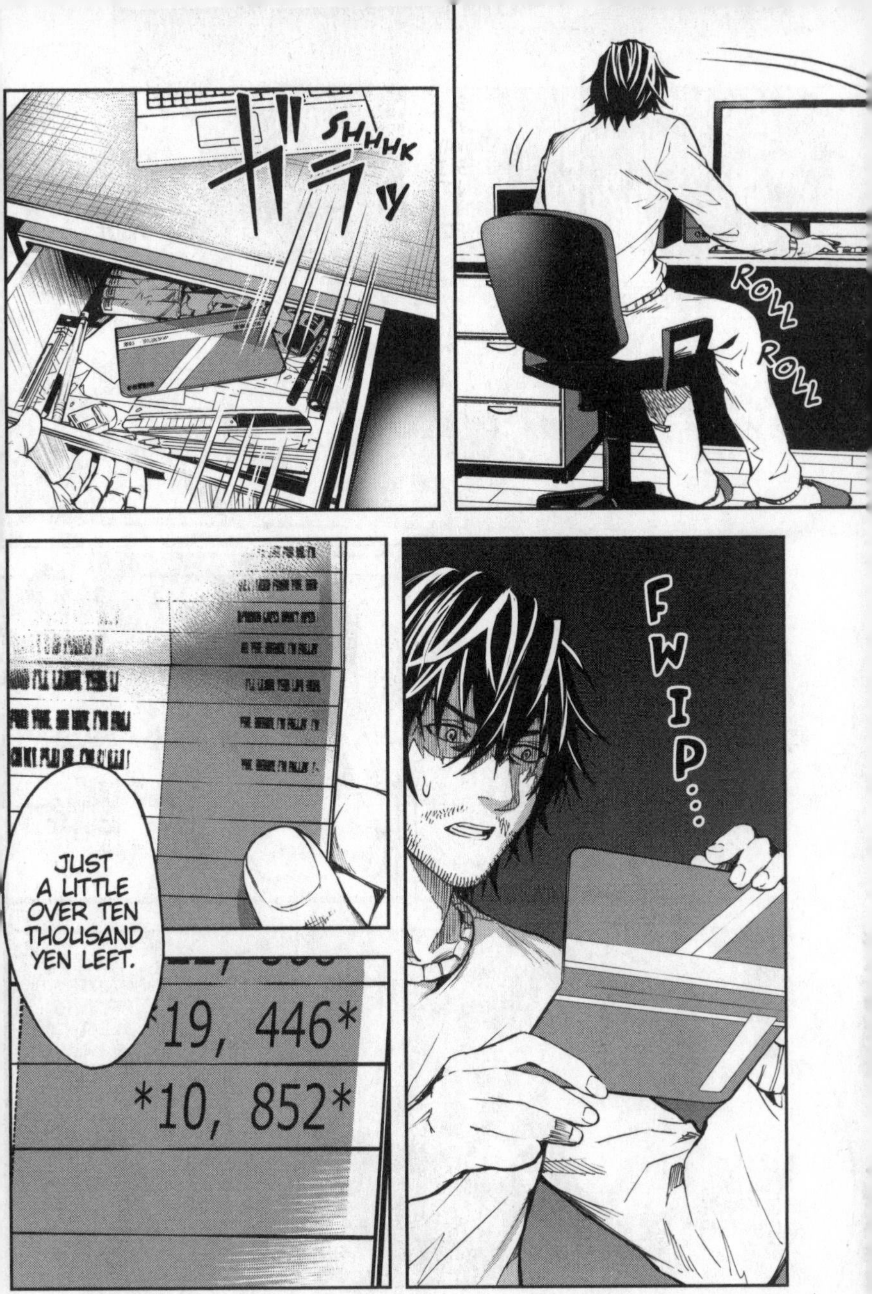
ROLL ROLL
ガラッ
SHHHK
FWIP...
19, 446
10, 852
JUST A LITTLE OVER TEN THOUSAND YEN LEFT.

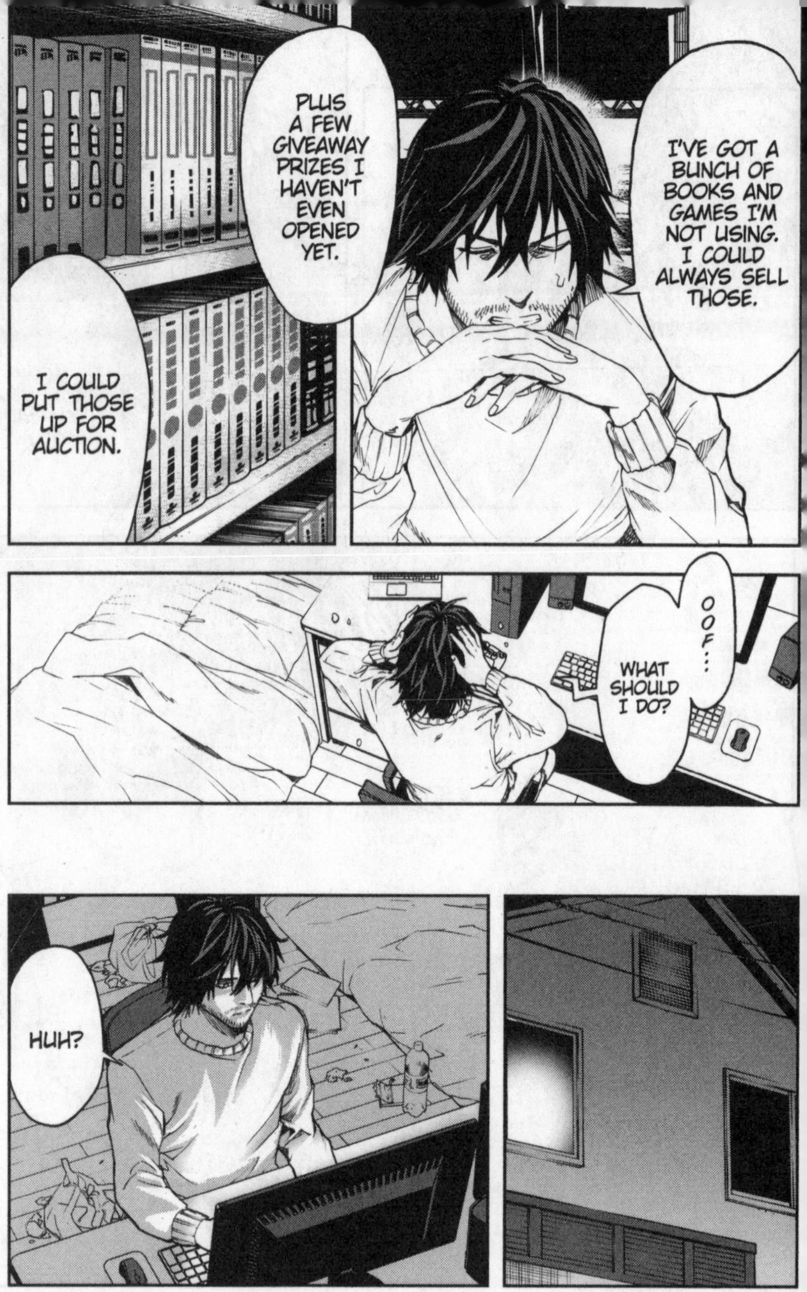
I'VE GOT A BUNCH OF BOOKS AND GAMES I'M NOT USING. I COULD ALWAYS SELL THOSE.
PLUS A FEW GIVEAWAY PRIZES I HAVEN'T EVEN OPENED YET.
I COULD PUT THOSE UP FOR AUCTION.
OOF...
WHAT SHOULD I DO?
HUH?

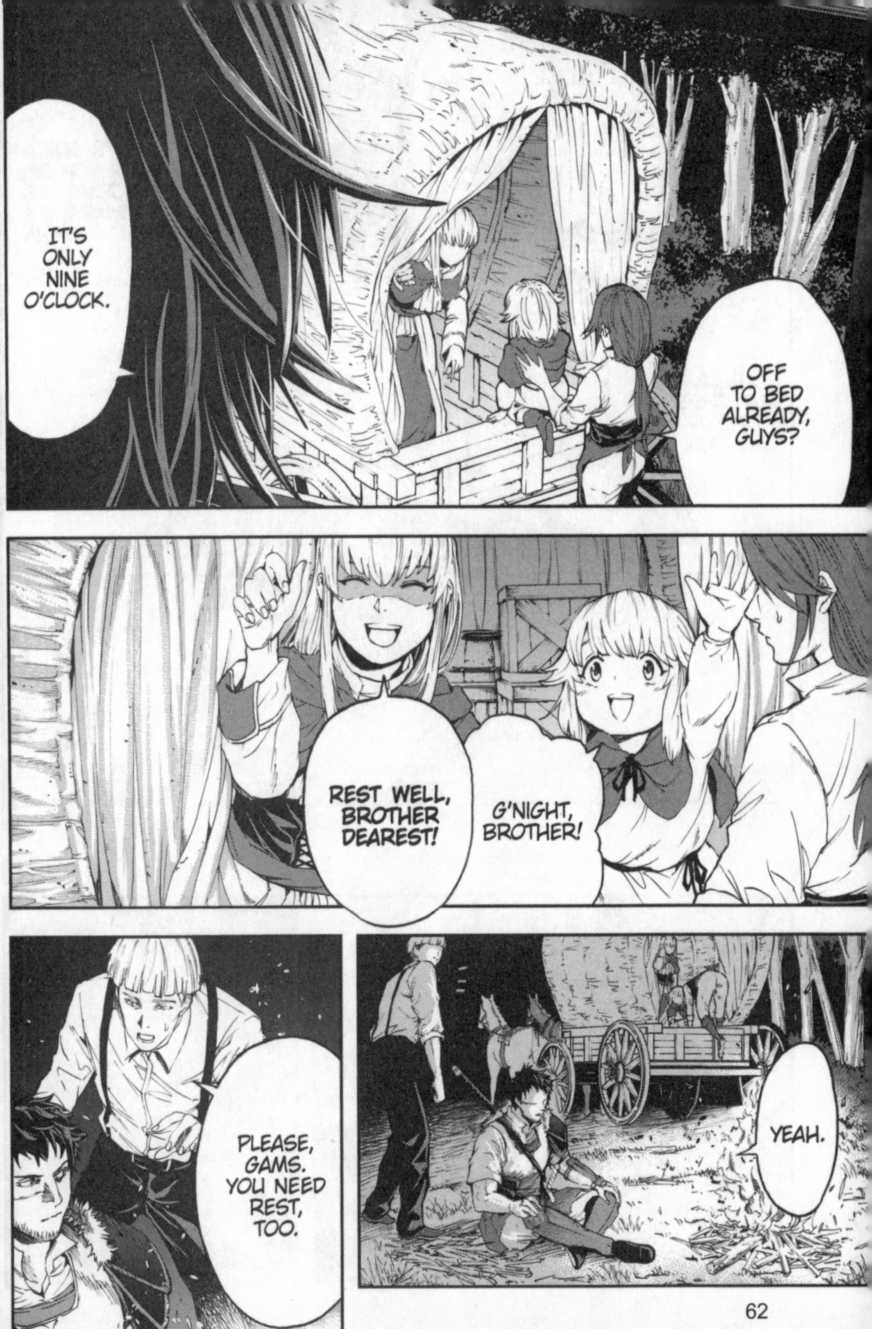
IT'S ONLY NINE O'CLOCK.
OFF TO BED ALREADY, GUYS?
REST WELL, BROTHER DEAREST!
G'NIGHT, BROTHER!
PLEASE, GAMS. YOU NEED REST, TOO.
YEAH.

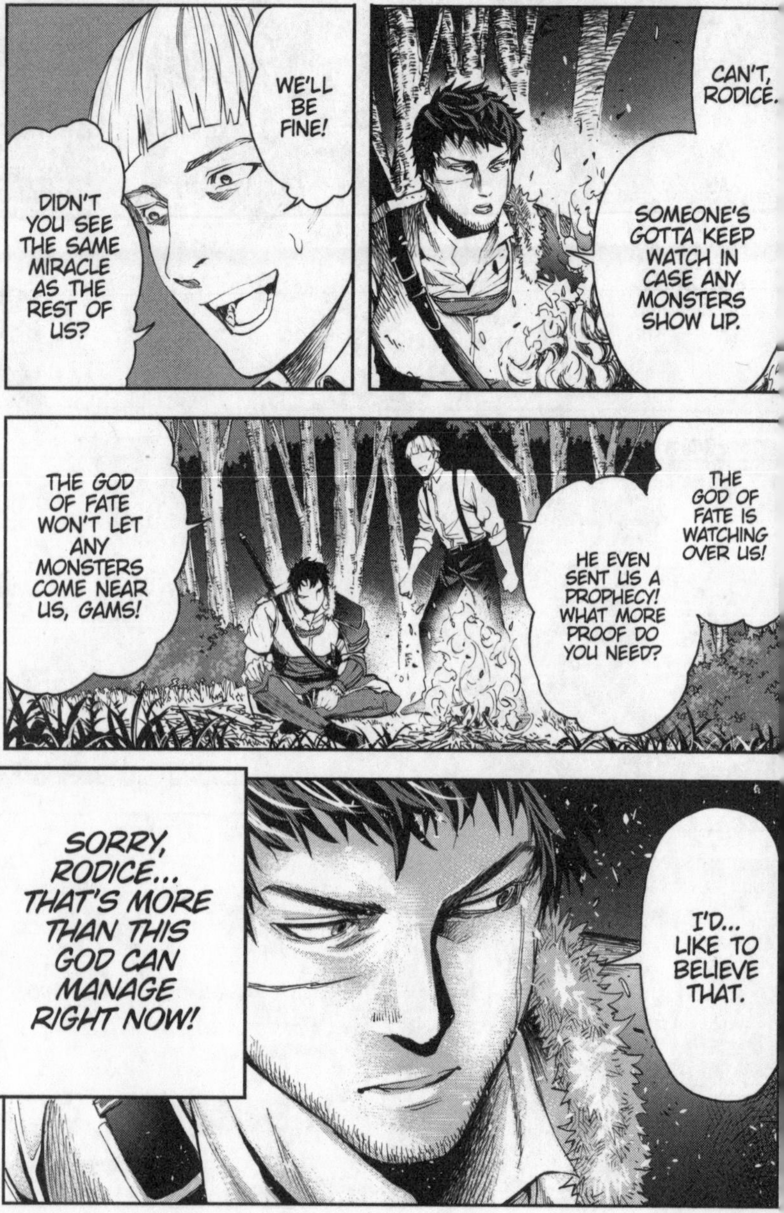
CAN'T, RODICE.
SOMEONE'S GOTTA KEEP WATCH IN CASE ANY MONSTERS SHOW UP.
WE'LL BE FINE!
DIDN'T YOU SEE THE SAME MIRACLE AS THE REST OF US?
THE GOD OF FATE IS WATCHING OVER US!
HE EVEN SENT US A PROPHECY! WHAT MORE PROOF DO YOU NEED?
THE GOD OF FATE WON'T LET ANY MONSTERS COME NEAR US, GAMS!
I'D... LIKE TO BELIEVE THAT.
SORRY, RODICE... THAT'S MORE THAN THIS GOD CAN MANAGE RIGHT NOW!

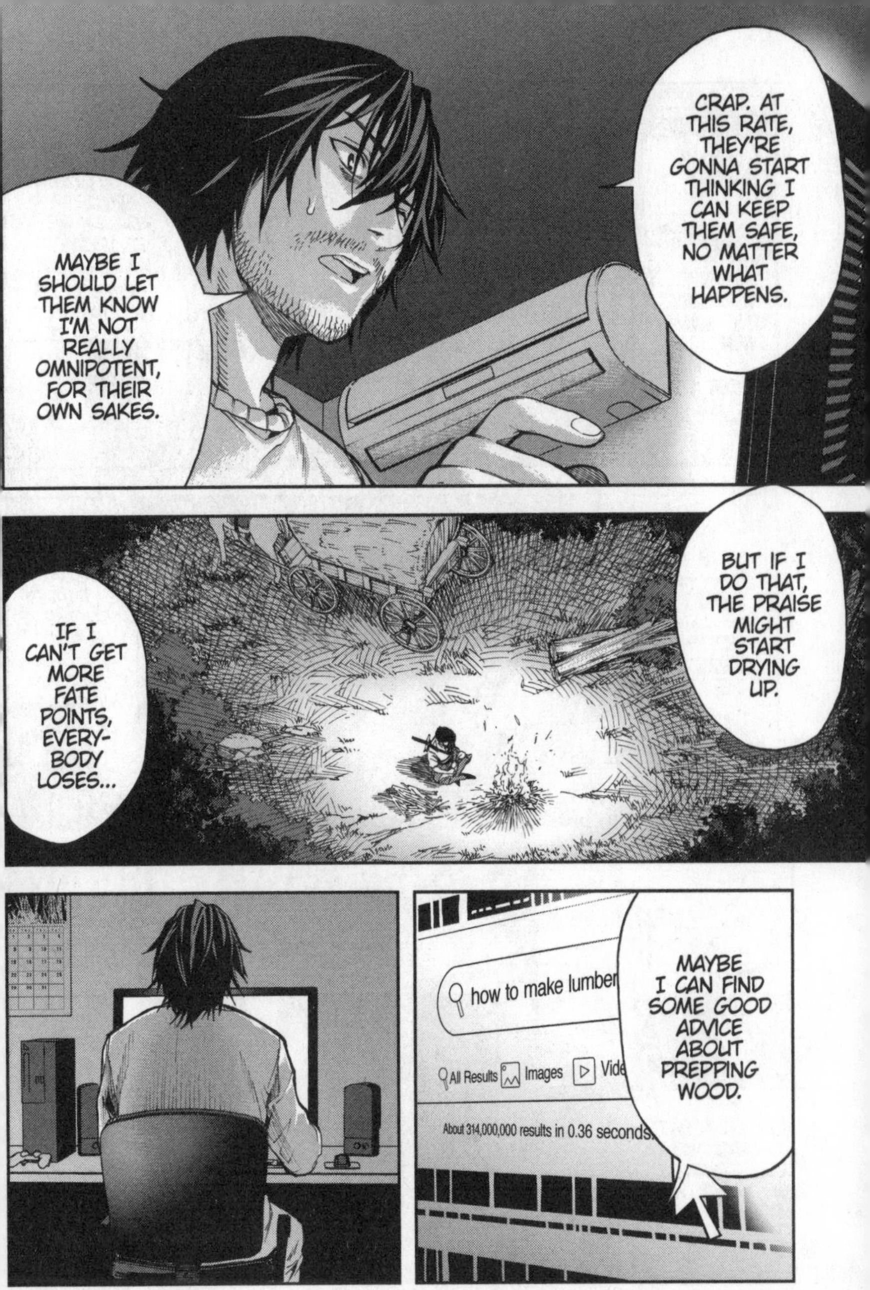
CRAP. AT THIS RATE, THEY'RE GONNA START THINKING I CAN KEEP THEM SAFE, NO MATTER WHAT HAPPENS.
MAYBE I SHOULD LET THEM KNOW I'M NOT REALLY OMNIPOTENT, FOR THEIR OWN SAKES.
BUT IF I DO THAT, THE PRAISE MIGHT START DRYING UP.
IF I CAN'T GET MORE FATE POINTS, EVERY-BODY LOSES...
how to make lumber
All Results
Images
Vide
About 314,000,000 results in 0.36 seconds
MAYBE I CAN FIND SOME GOOD ADVICE ABOUT PREPPING WOOD.

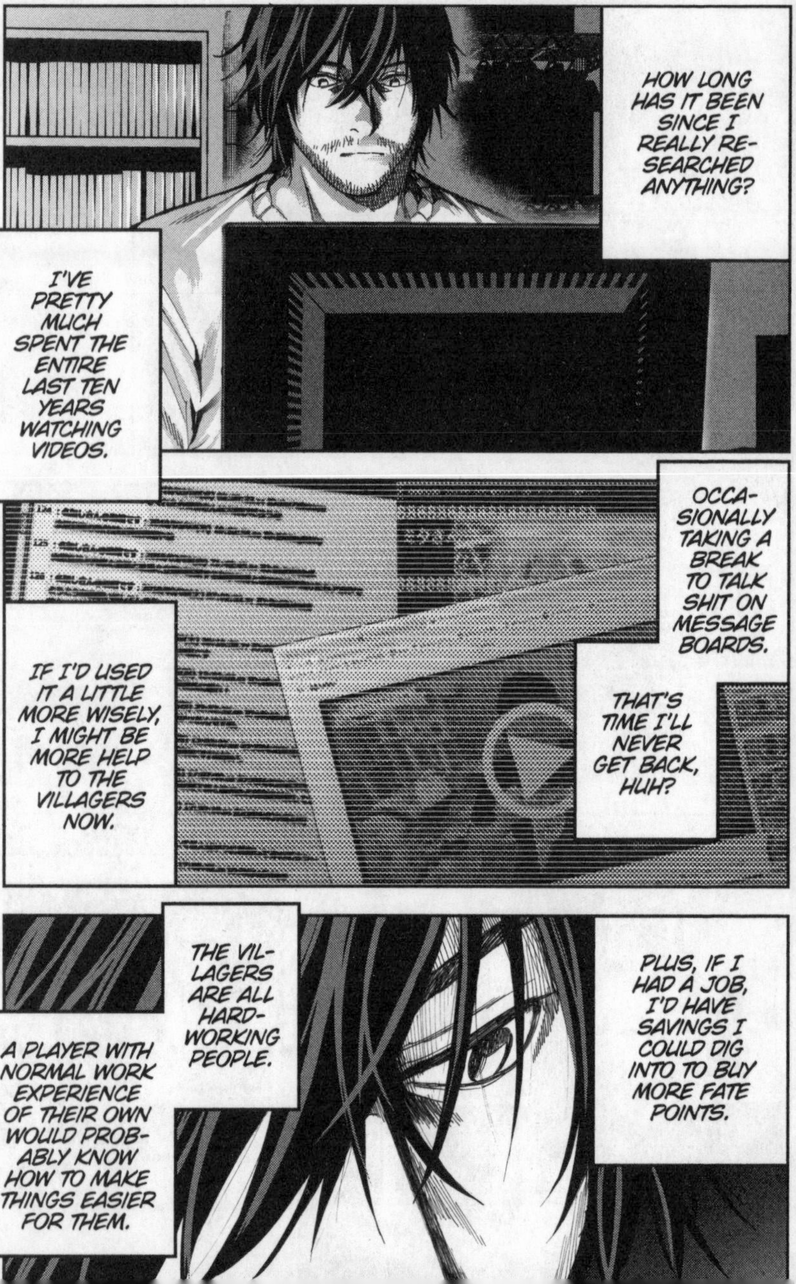

HOW LONG HAS IT BEEN SINCE I REALLY RESEARCHED ANYTHING?
I'VE PRETTY MUCH SPENT THE ENTIRE LAST TEN YEARS WATCHING VIDEOS.
OCCASIONALLY TAKING A BREAK TO TALK SHIT ON MESSAGE BOARDS.
THAT'S TIME I'LL NEVER GET BACK, HUH?
IF I'D USED IT A LITTLE MORE WISELY, I MIGHT BE MORE HELP TO THE VILLAGERS NOW.
PLUS, IF I HAD A JOB, I'D HAVE SAVINGS I COULD DIG INTO TO BUY MORE FATE POINTS.
THE VILLAGERS ARE ALL HARD-WORKING PEOPLE.
A PLAYER WITH NORMAL WORK EXPERIENCE OF THEIR OWN WOULD PROBABLY KNOW HOW TO MAKE THINGS EASIER FOR THEM.

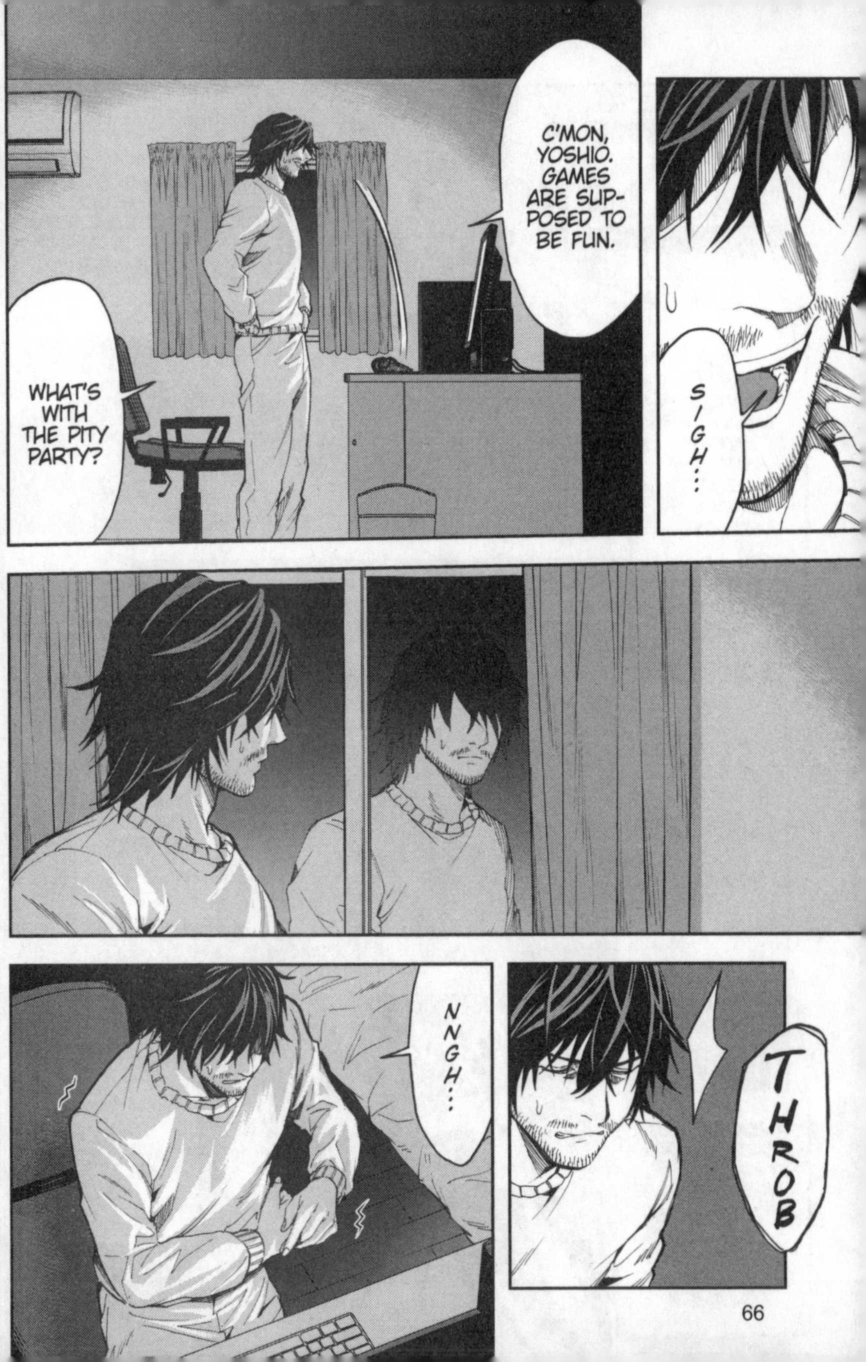
SIGH...
C'MON, YOSHIO. GAMES ARE SUP-POSED TO BE FUN.
WHAT'S WITH THE PITY PARTY?
THROB
NNGH...

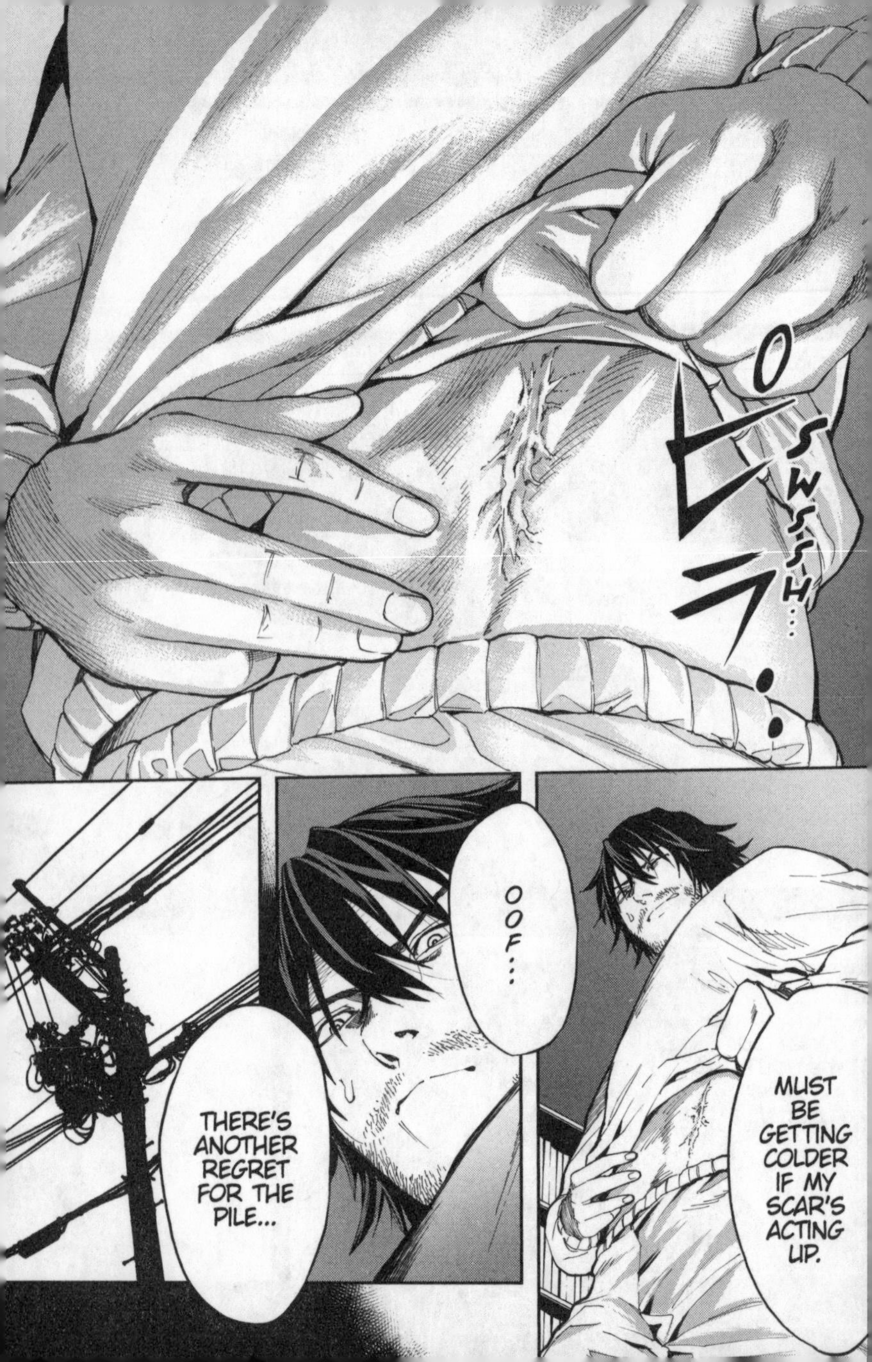
SWSSSH...
MUST BE GETTING COLDER IF MY SCAR'S ACTING UP.
OOF...
THERE'S ANOTHER REGRET FOR THE PILE...

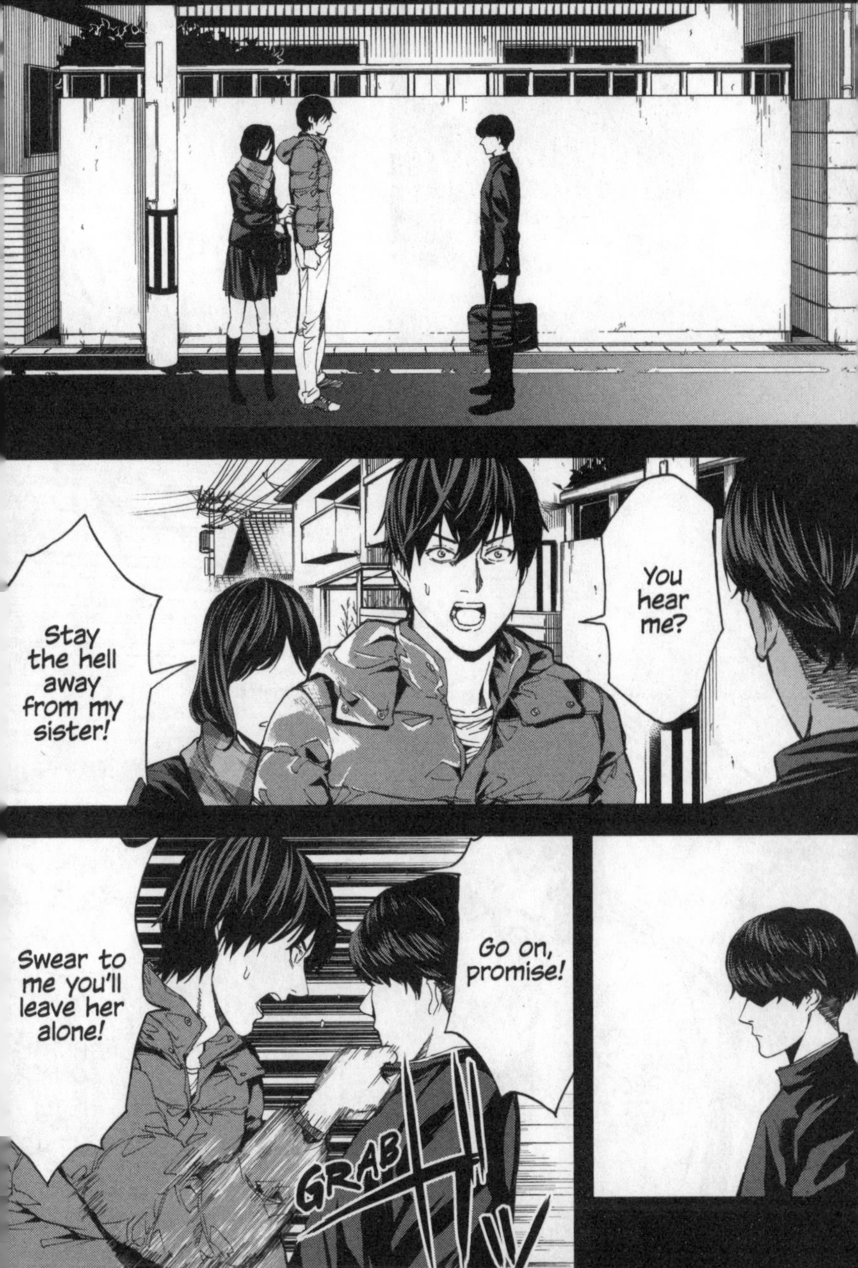
Stay the hell away from my sister!
You hear me?
Swear to me you'll leave her alone!
Go on, promise!
GRAB

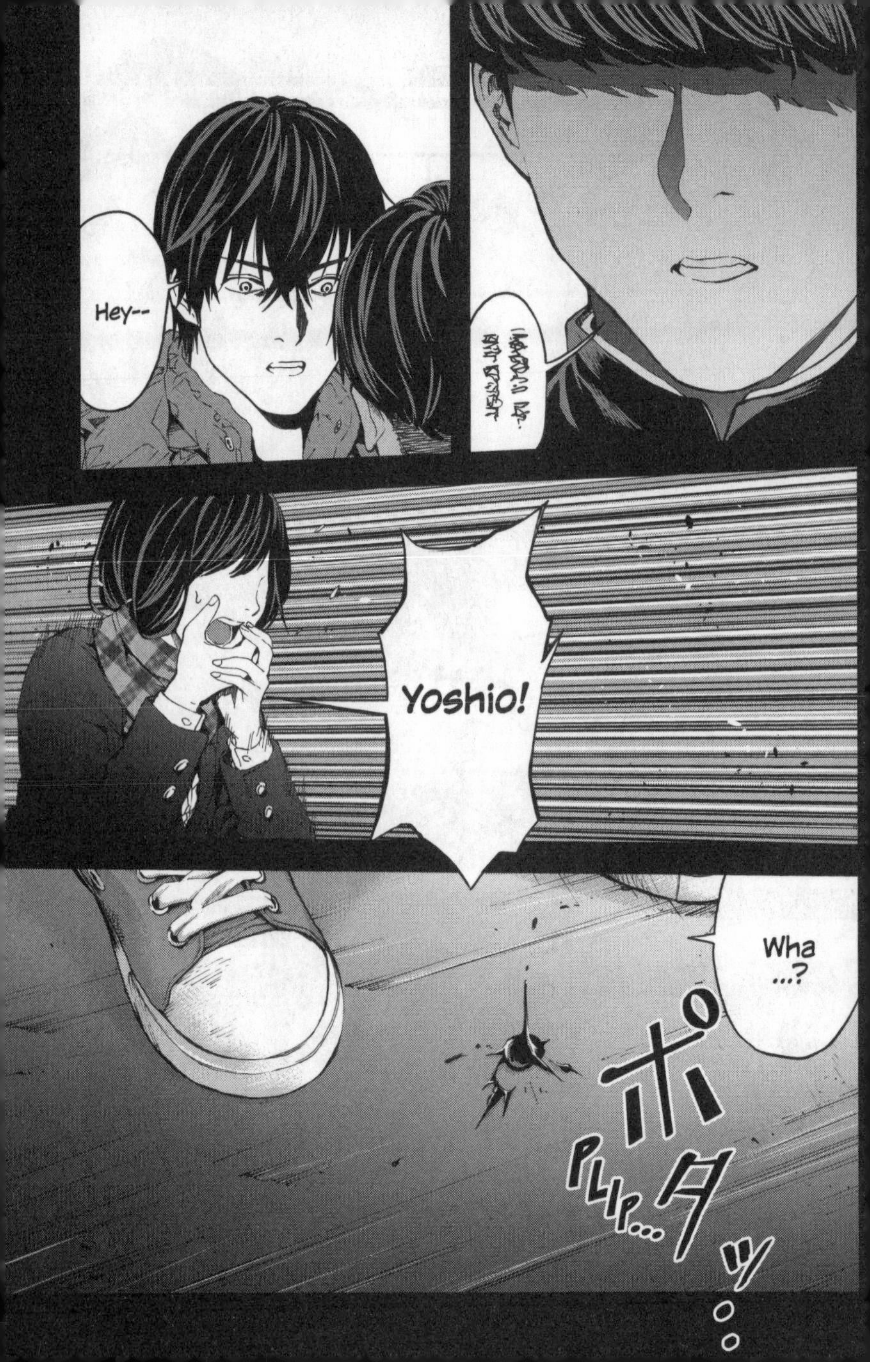
Hey--
Yoshio!
Wha ...?
ポタッ
PLIP...

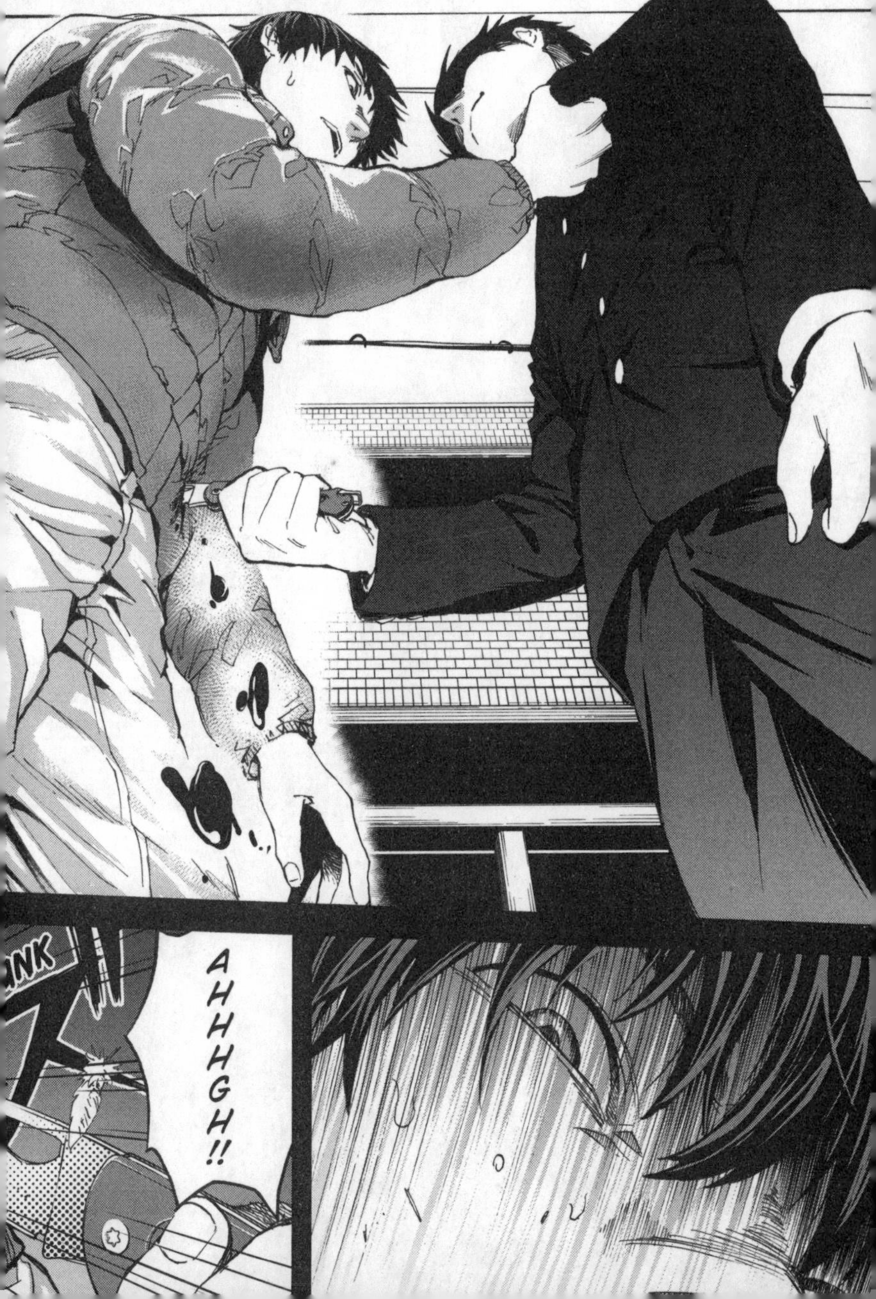
AHHHGH!!

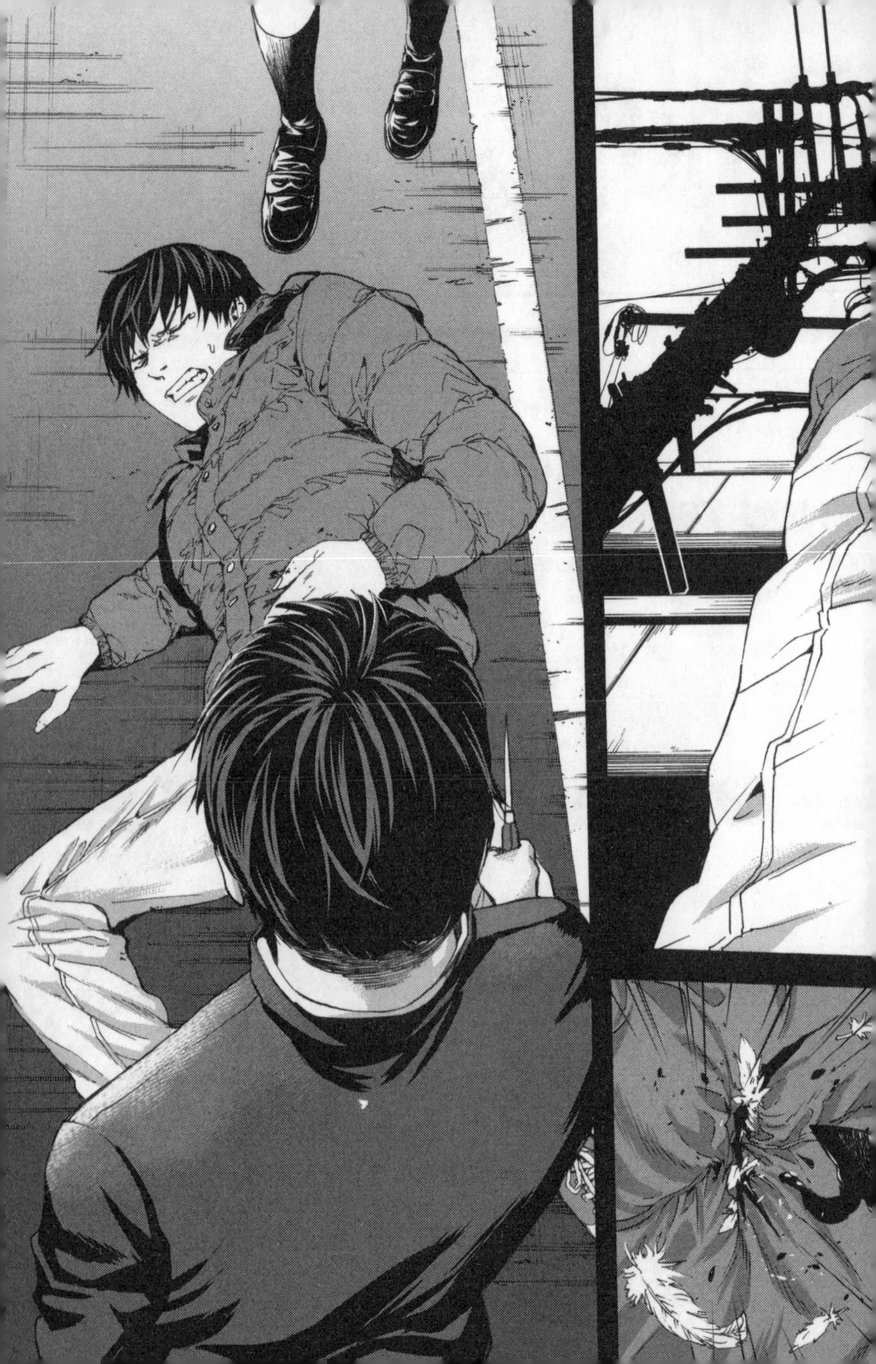

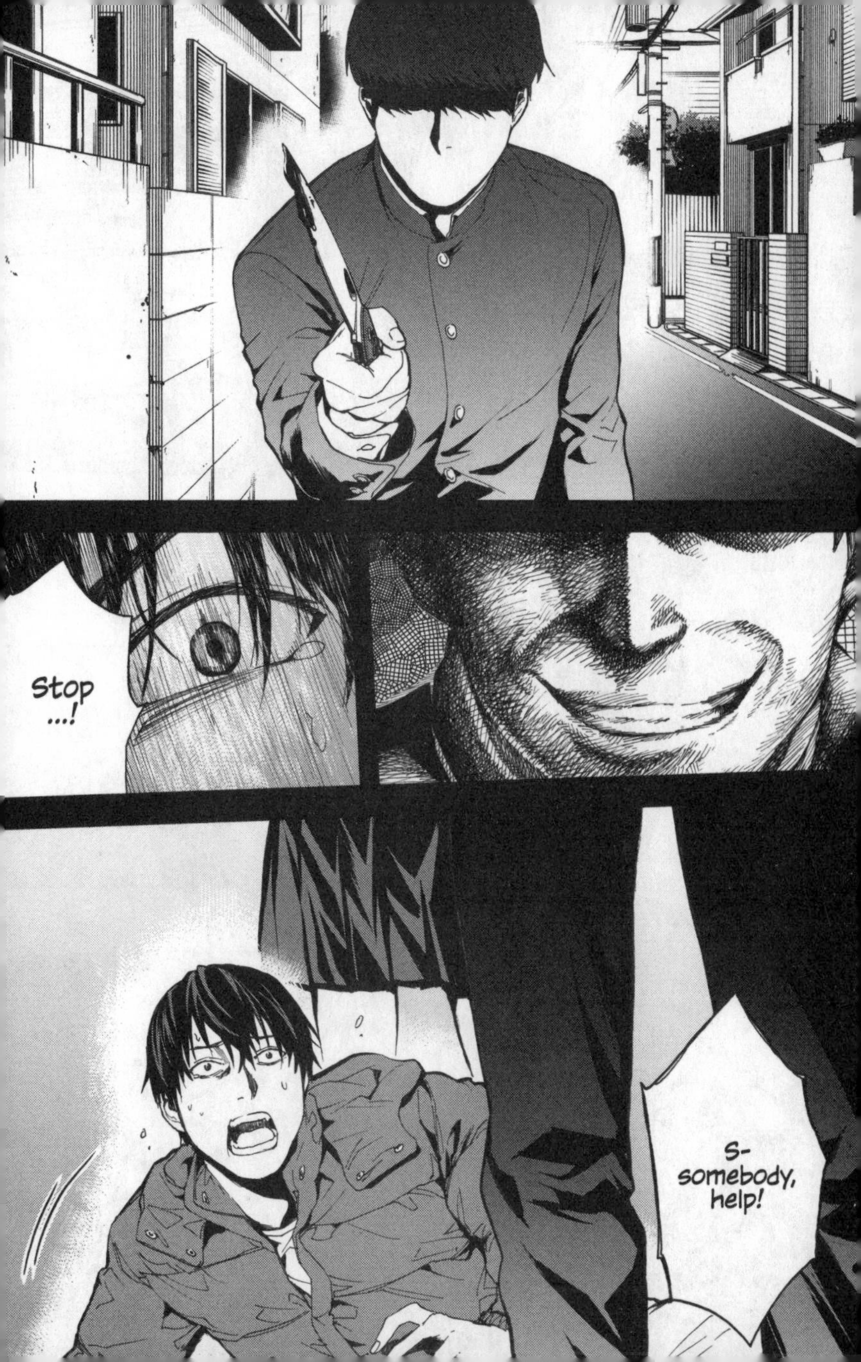
Stop ...!
S- somebody, help!

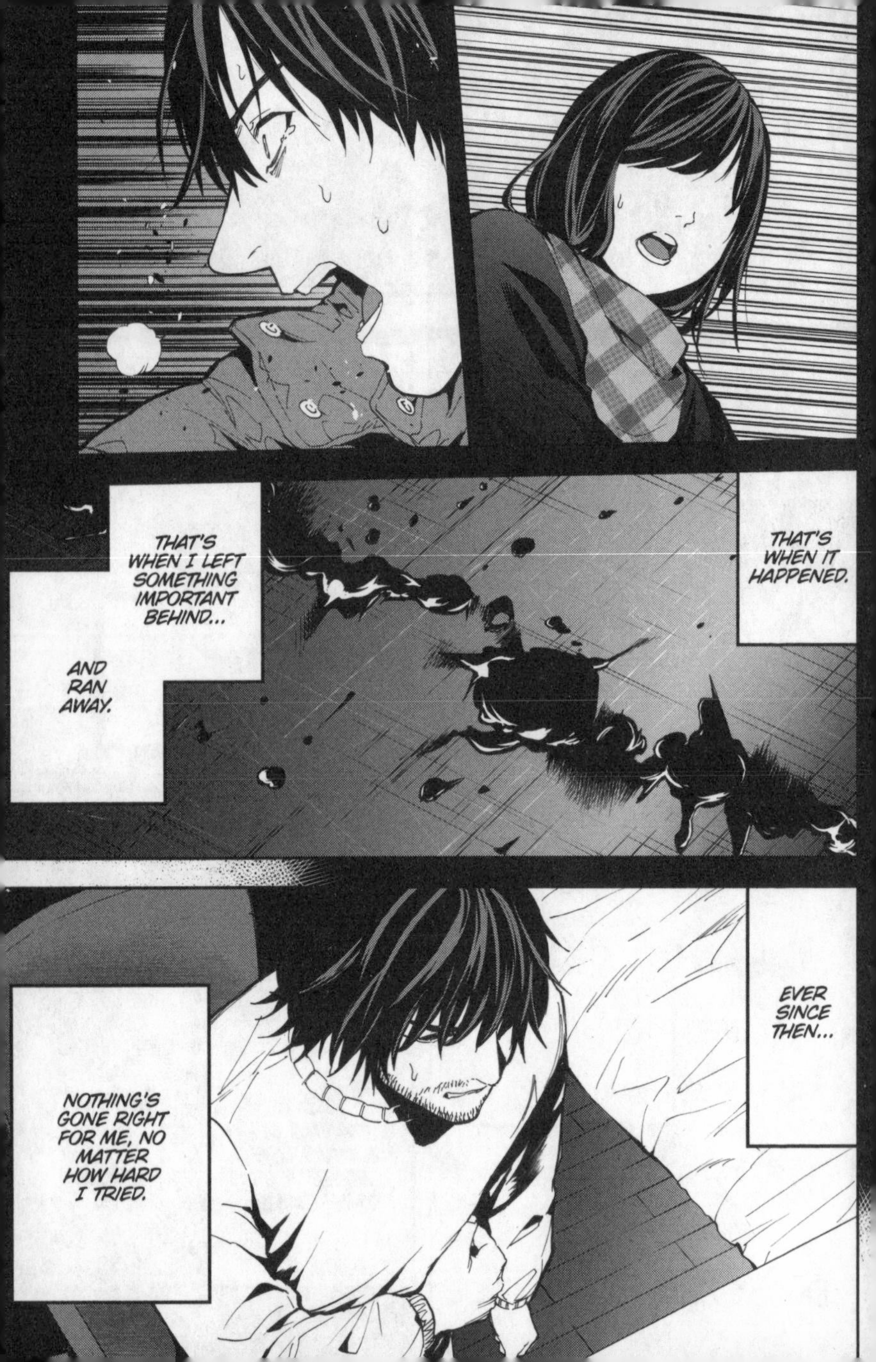
THAT'S WHEN IT HAPPENED.
THAT'S WHEN I LEFT SOMETHING IMPORTANT BEHIND...
AND RAN AWAY.
EVER SINCE THEN...
NOTHING'S GONE RIGHT FOR ME, NO MATTER HOW HARD I TRIED.

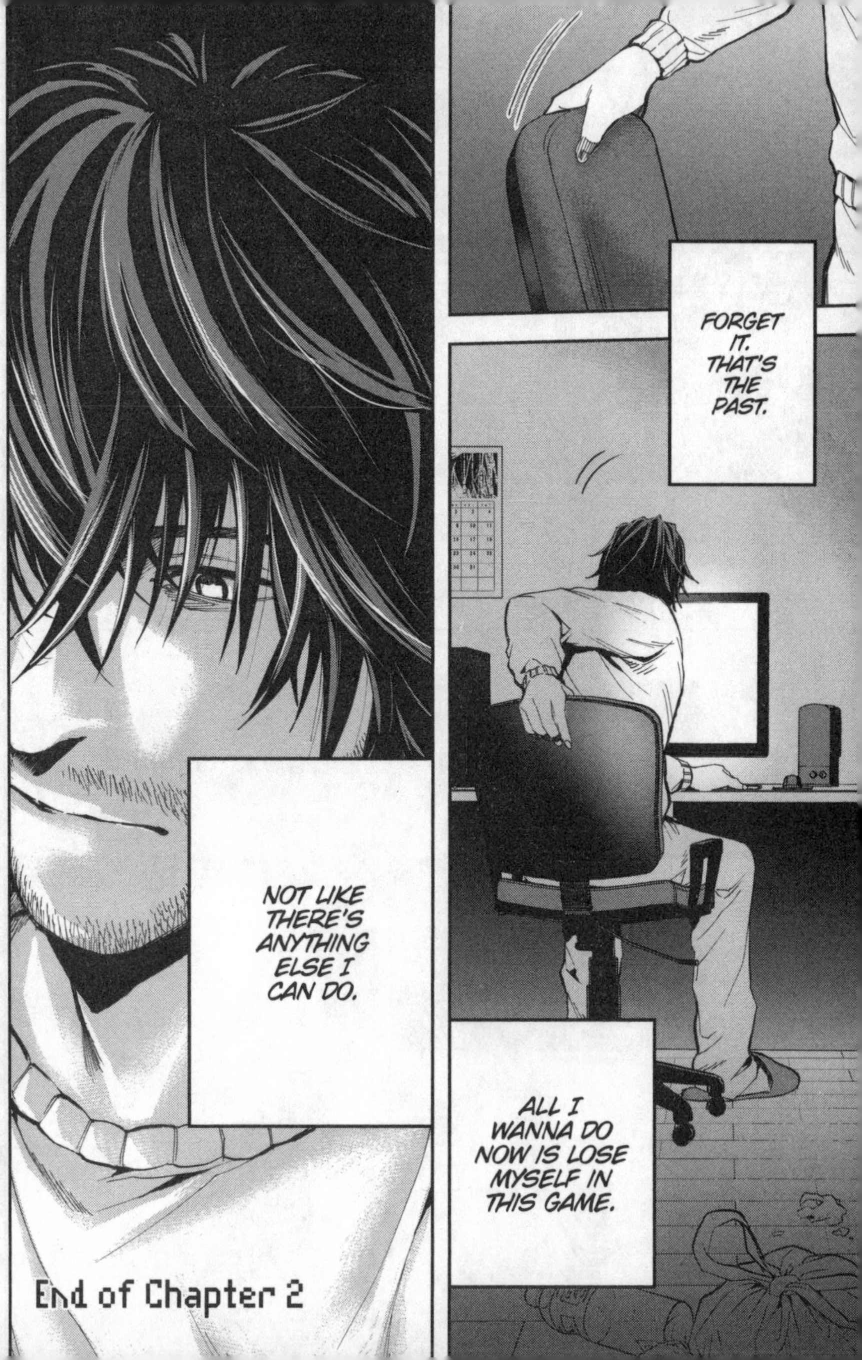
FORGET IT. THAT'S THE PAST.
ALL I WANNA DO NOW IS LOSE MYSELF IN THIS GAME.
NOT LIKE THERE'S ANYTHING ELSE I CAN DO.
End of Chapter 2

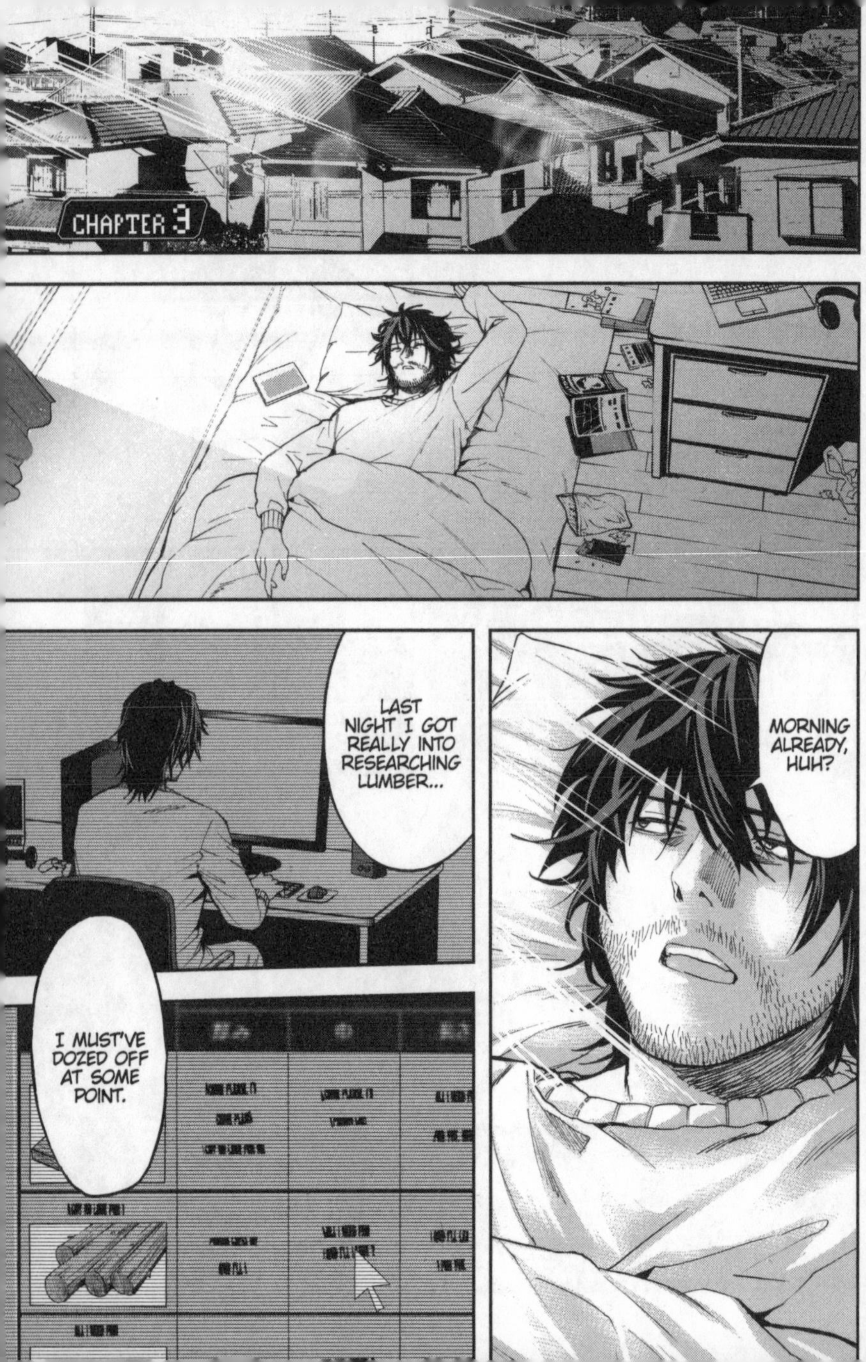
CHAPTER 3
MORNING ALREADY, HUH?
LAST NIGHT I GOT REALLY INTO RESEARCHING LUMBER...
I MUST'VE DOZED OFF AT SOME POINT.

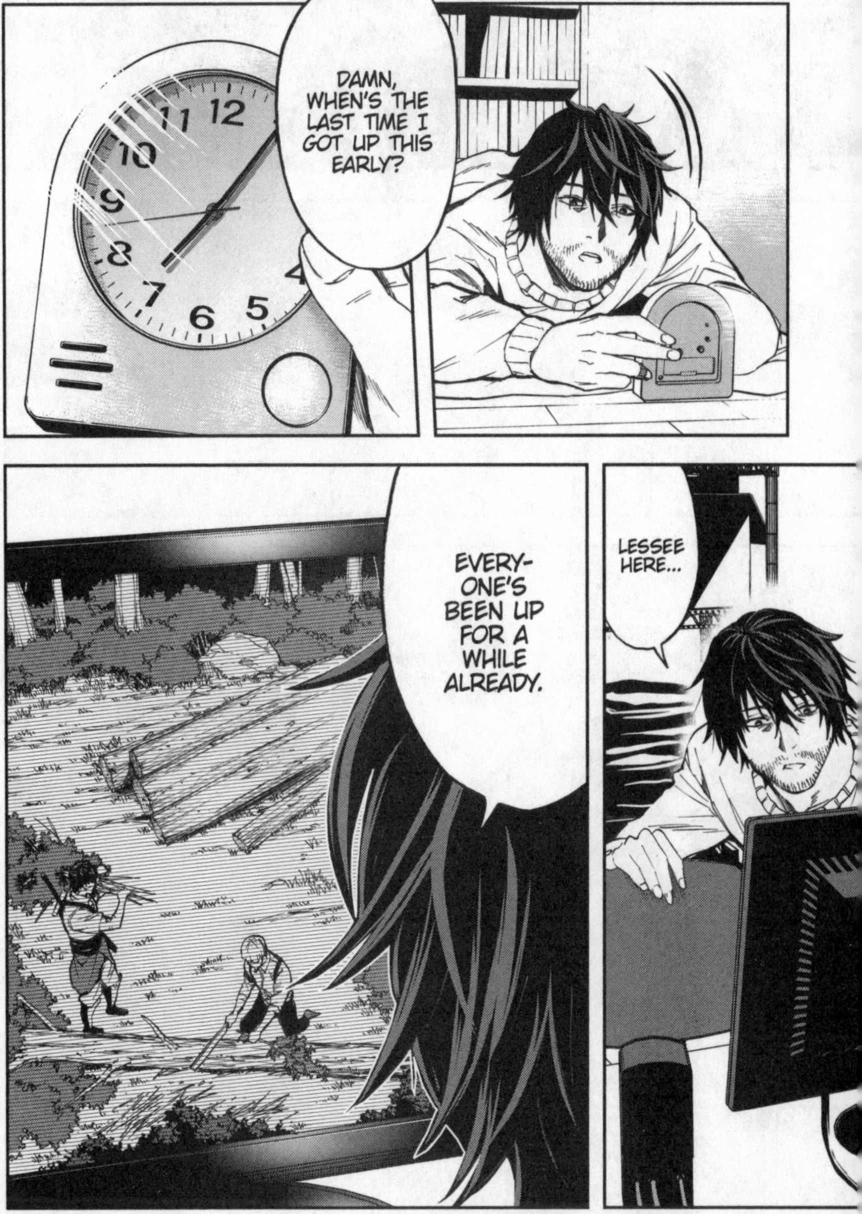
DAMN, WHEN'S THE LAST TIME I GOT UP THIS EARLY?
LESSEE HERE...
EVERY-ONE'S BEEN UP FOR A WHILE ALREADY.

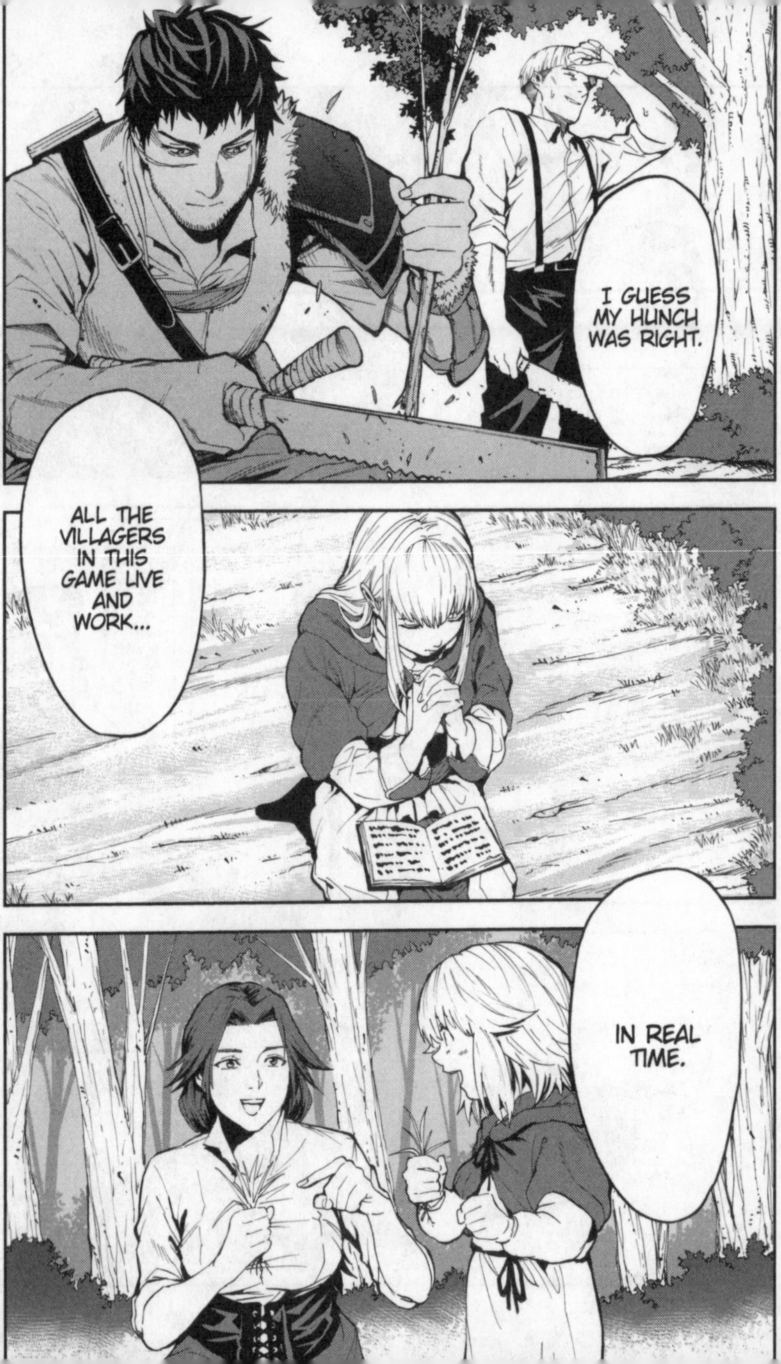
I GUESS MY HUNCH WAS RIGHT.
ALL THE VILLAGERS IN THIS GAME LIVE AND WORK...
IN REAL TIME.

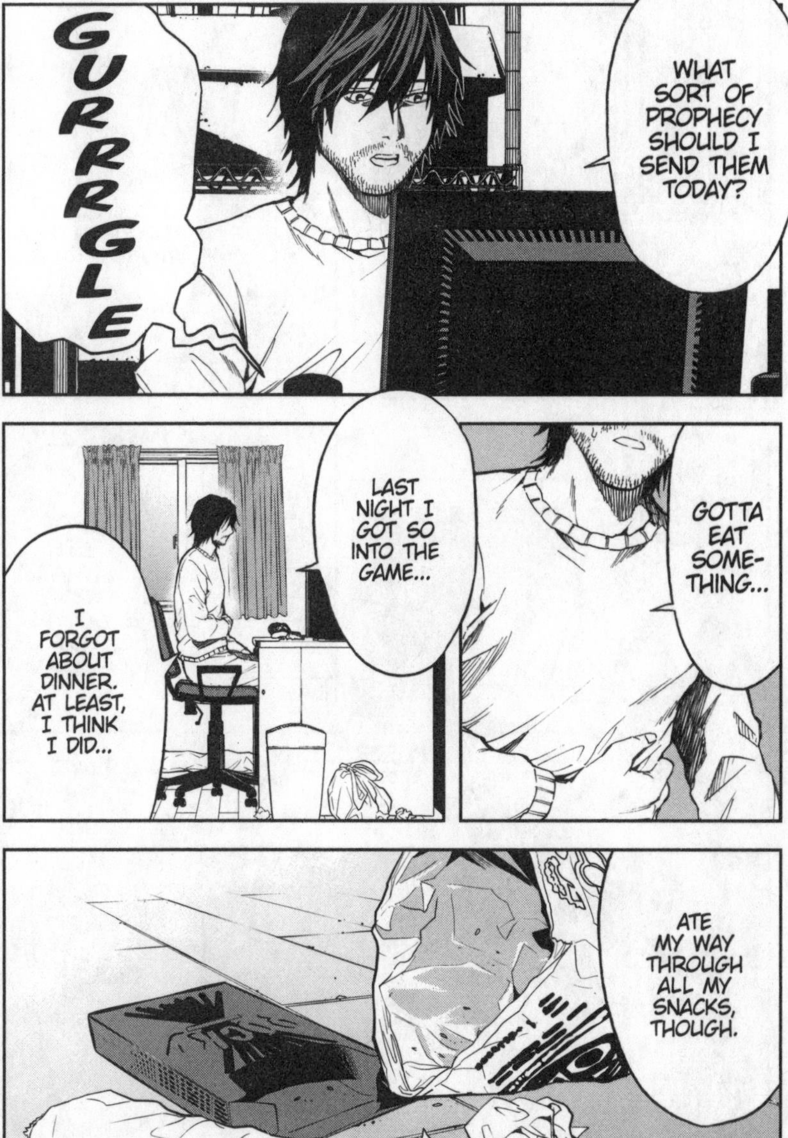
WHAT SORT OF PROPHECY SHOULD I SEND THEM TODAY?
GURRRGLE
GOTTA EAT SOME-THING...
LAST NIGHT I GOT SO INTO THE GAME...
I FORGOT ABOUT DINNER. AT LEAST, I THINK I DID...
ATE MY WAY THROUGH ALL MY SNACKS, THOUGH.

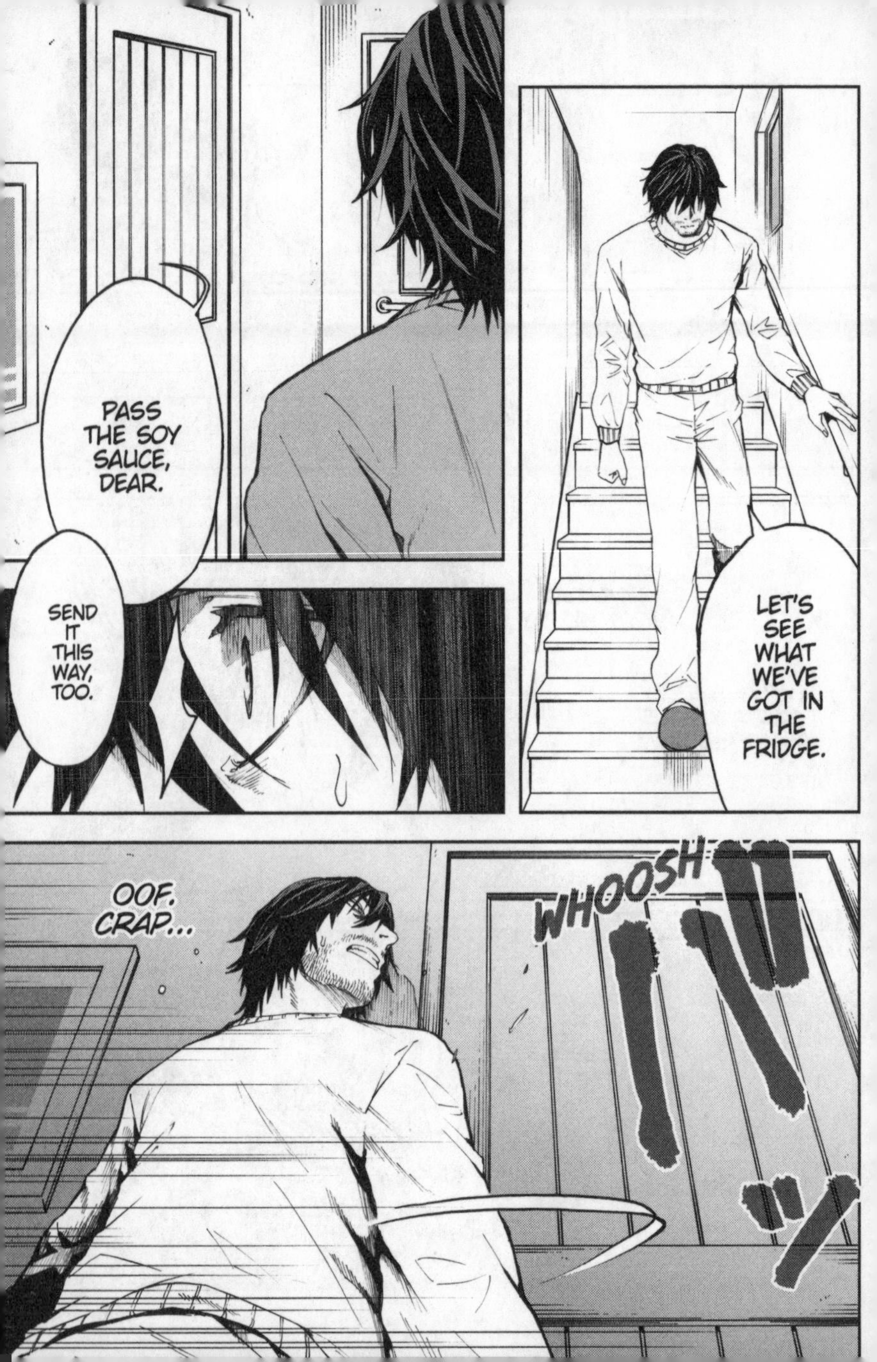
LET'S SEE WHAT WE'VE GOT IN THE FRIDGE.
PASS THE SOY SAUCE, DEAR.
SEND IT THIS WAY, TOO.
WHOOSH
OOF. CRAP...

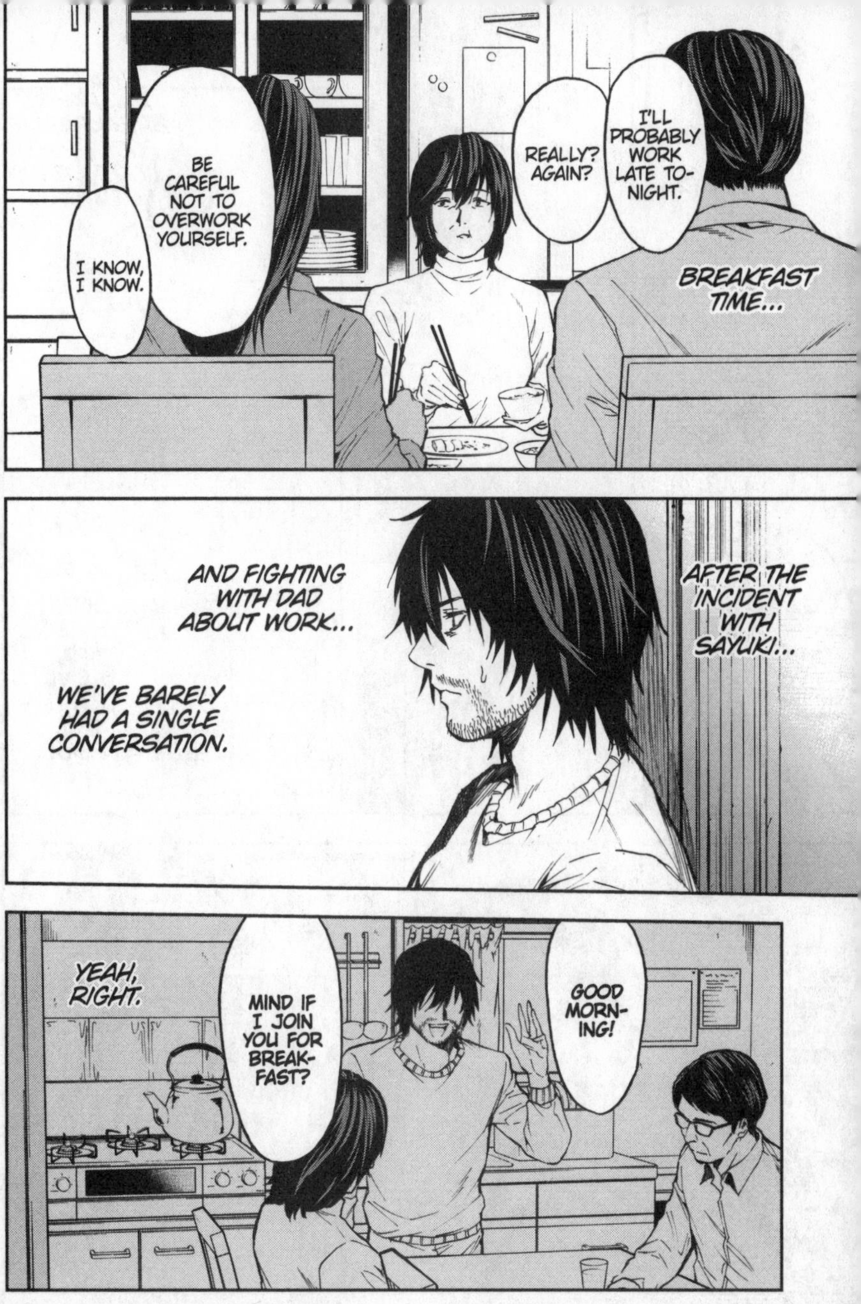
I'LL PROBABLY WORK LATE TO-NIGHT.
REALLY? AGAIN?
BE CAREFUL NOT TO OVERWORK YOURSELF.
I KNOW, I KNOW.
BREAKFAST TIME...
AFTER THE INCIDENT WITH SAYUKI...
AND FIGHTING WITH DAD ABOUT WORK...
WE'VE BARELY HAD A SINGLE CONVERSATION.
GOOD MORN-ING!
MIND IF I JOIN YOU FOR BREAK-FAST?
YEAH, RIGHT.

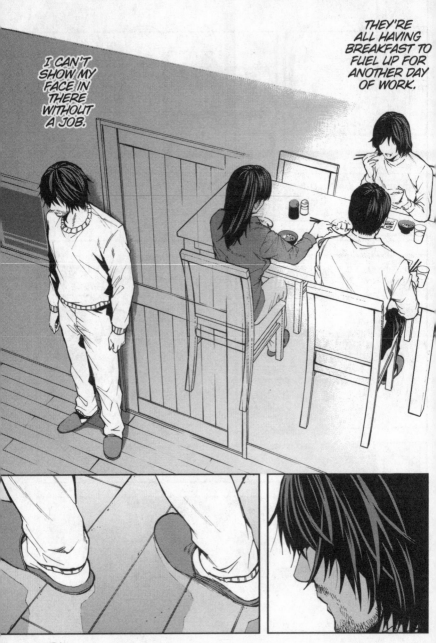

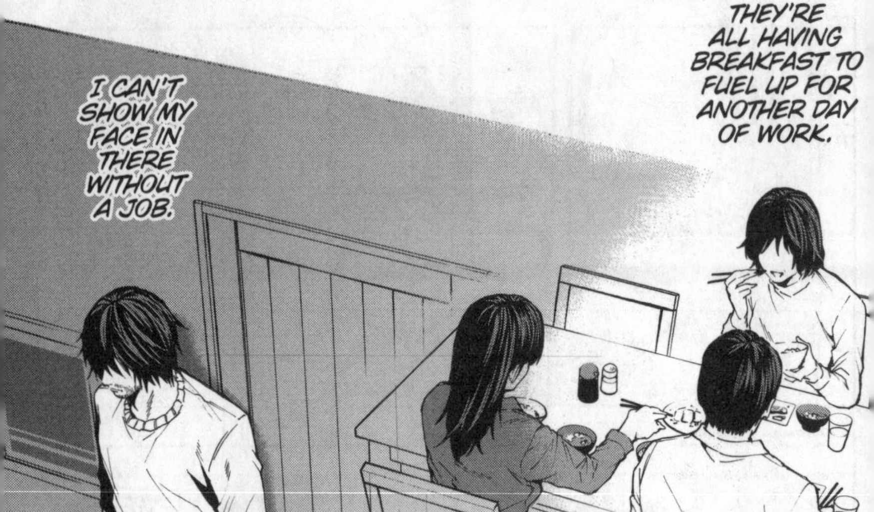
THEY'RE ALL HAVING BREAKFAST TO FUEL UP FOR ANOTHER DAY OF WORK.
I CAN'T SHOW MY FACE IN THERE WITHOUT A JOB.
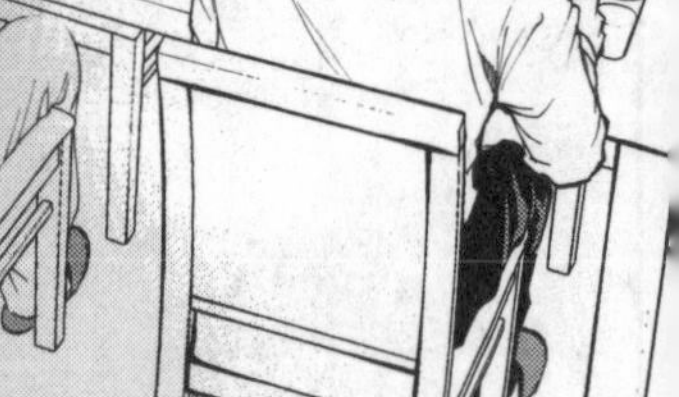
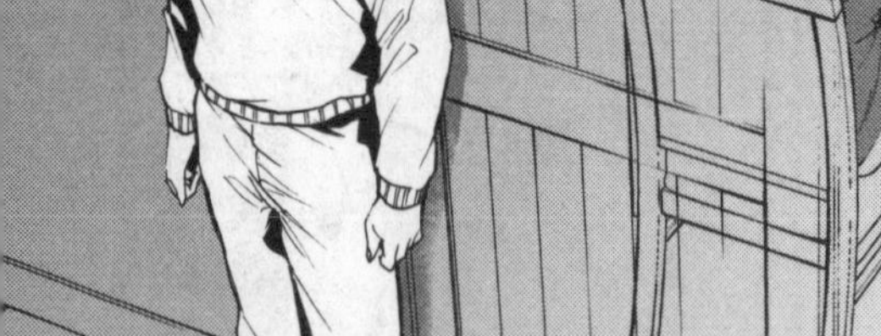

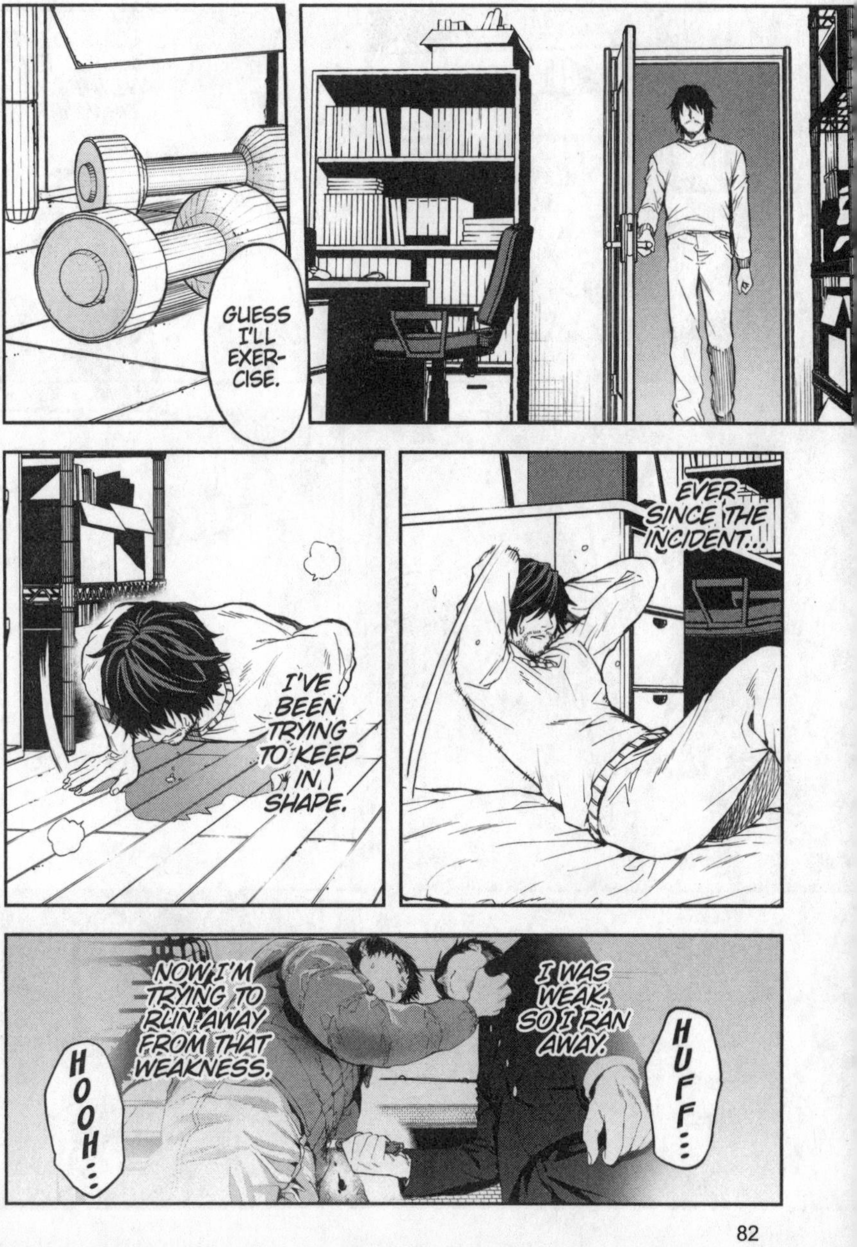
GUESS I'LL EXER-CISE.
EVER SINCE THE INCIDENT...
I'VE BEEN TRYING TO KEEP IN SHAPE.
HUFF...
I WAS WEAK, SO I RAN AWAY.
NOW I'M TRYING TO RUN AWAY FROM THAT WEAKNESS.
HOOH...

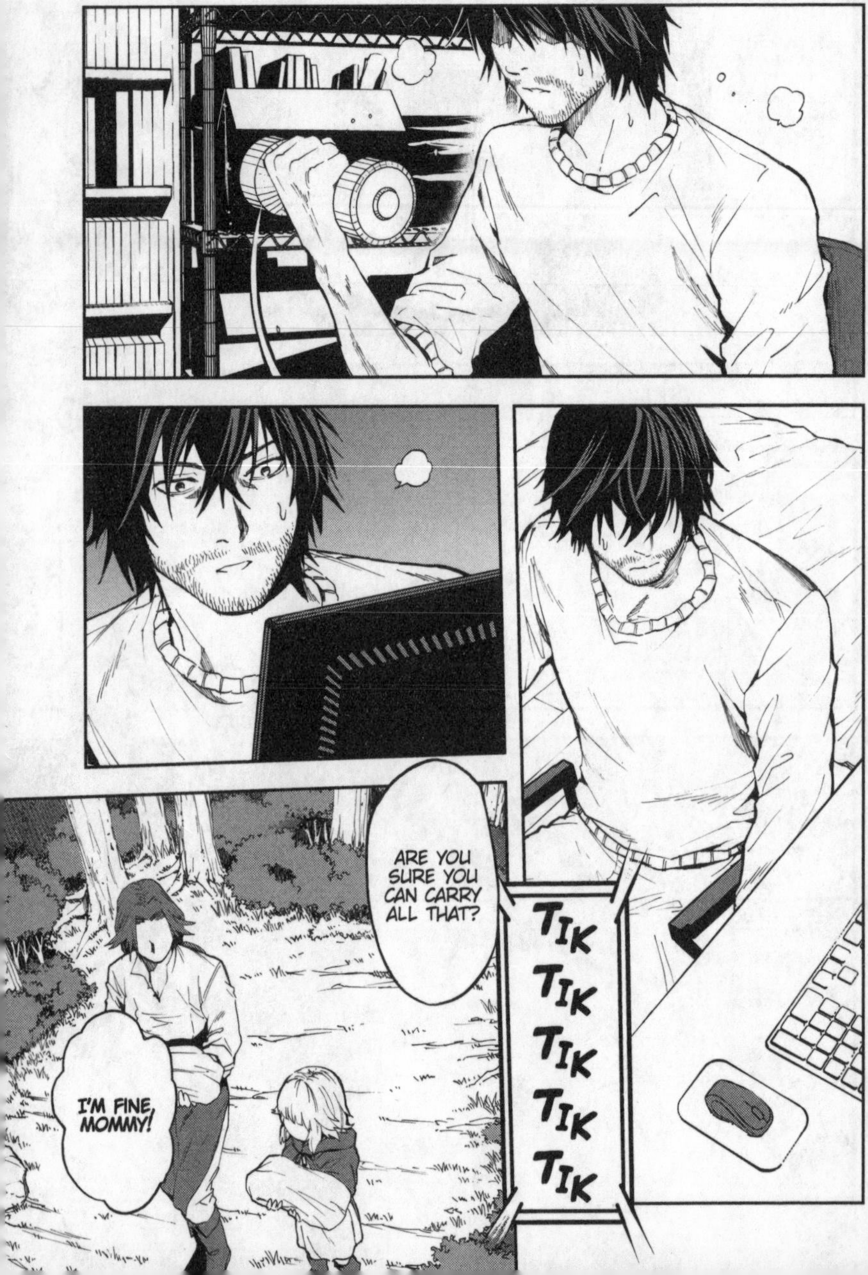
TIK TIK TIK TIK TIK
ARE YOU SURE YOU CAN CARRY ALL THAT?
I'M FINE, MOMMY!

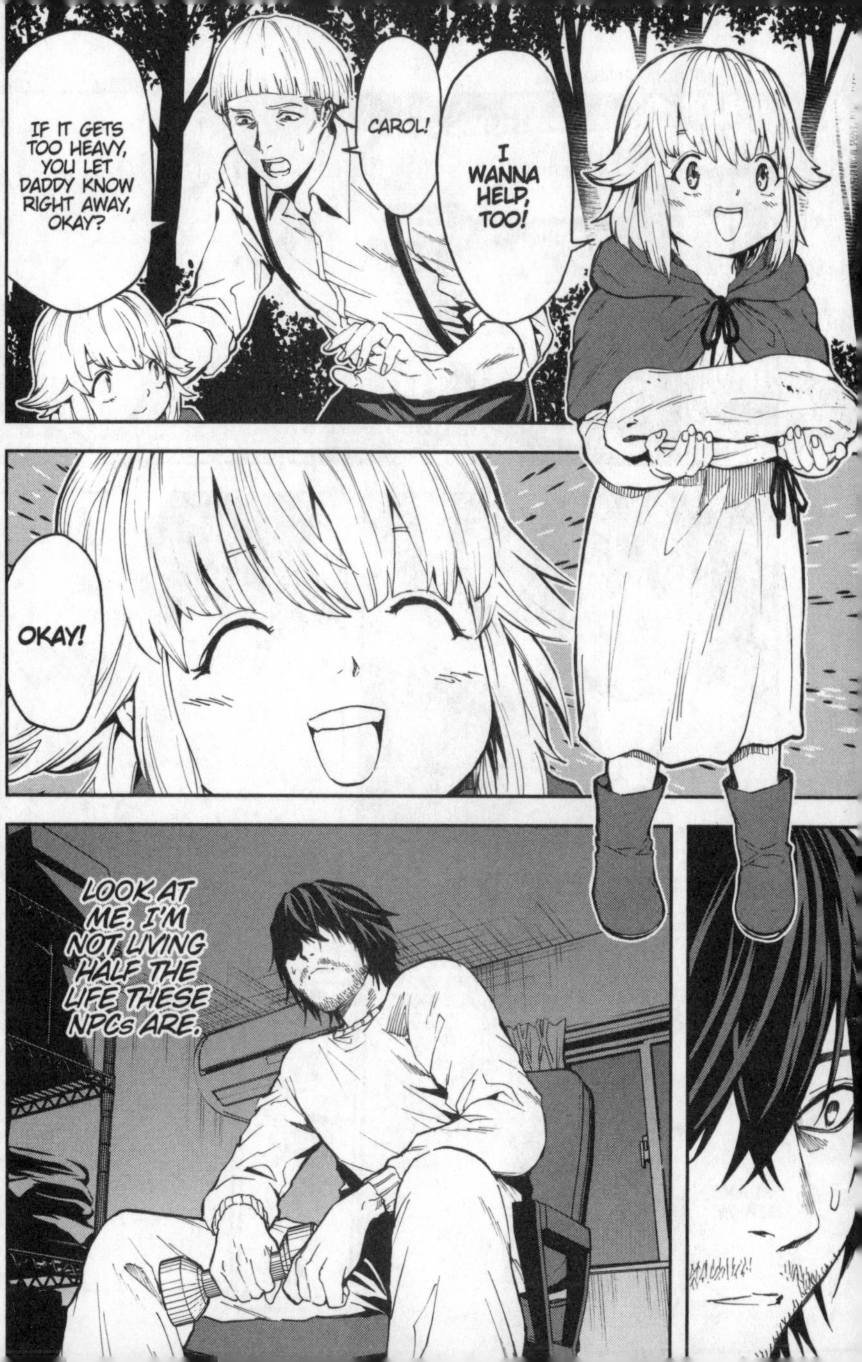
I WANNA HELP, TOO!
CAROL!
IF IT GETS TOO HEAVY, YOU LET DADDY KNOW RIGHT AWAY, OKAY?
OKAY!
LOOK AT ME. I'M NOT LIVING HALF THE LIFE THESE NPCs ARE.

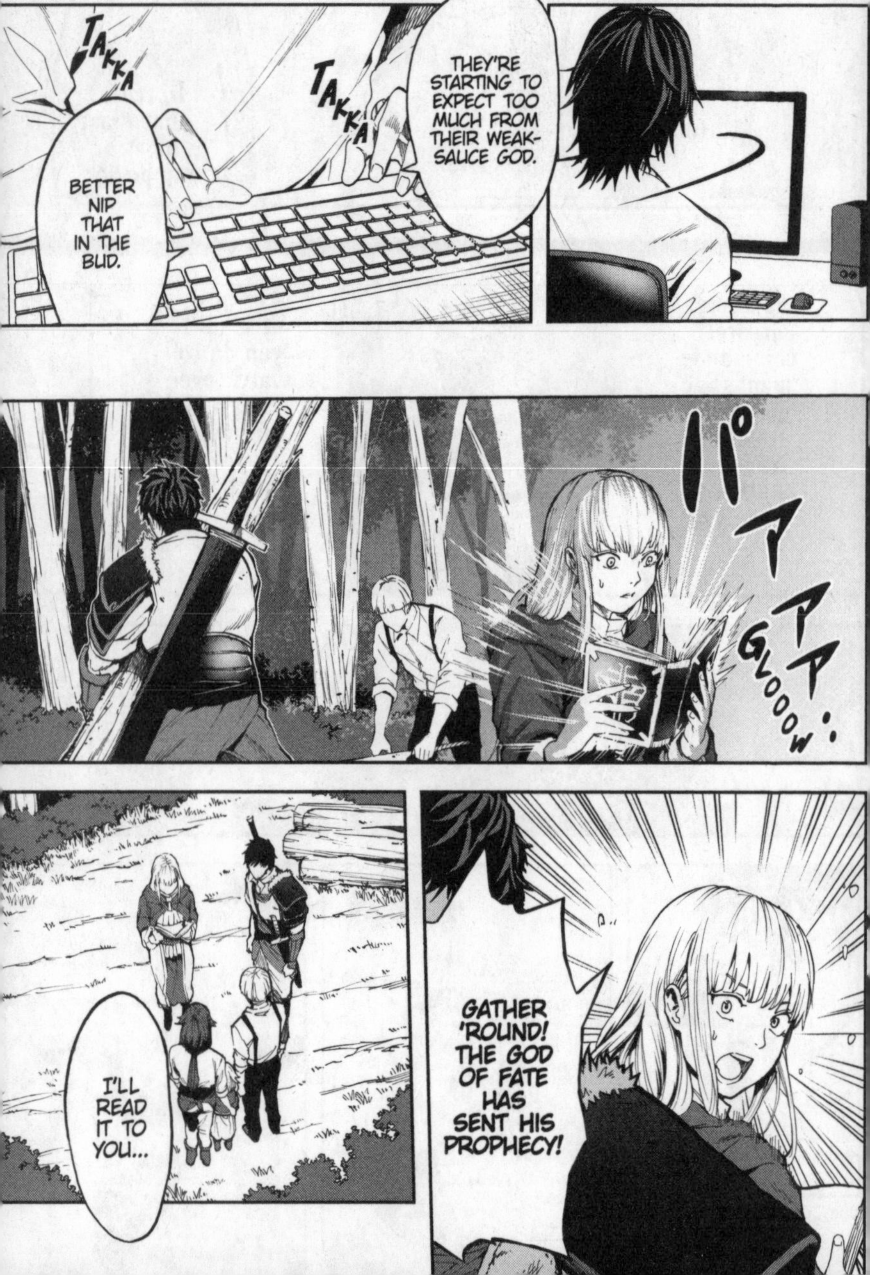
THEY'RE STARTING TO EXPECT TOO MUCH FROM THEIR WEAK-SAUCE GOD.
TAKKA
TAKKA
BETTER NIP THAT IN THE BUD.
パァァ..
GLOOOOW
GATHER 'ROUND! THE GOD OF FATE HAS SENT HIS PROPHECY!
I'LL READ IT TO YOU...

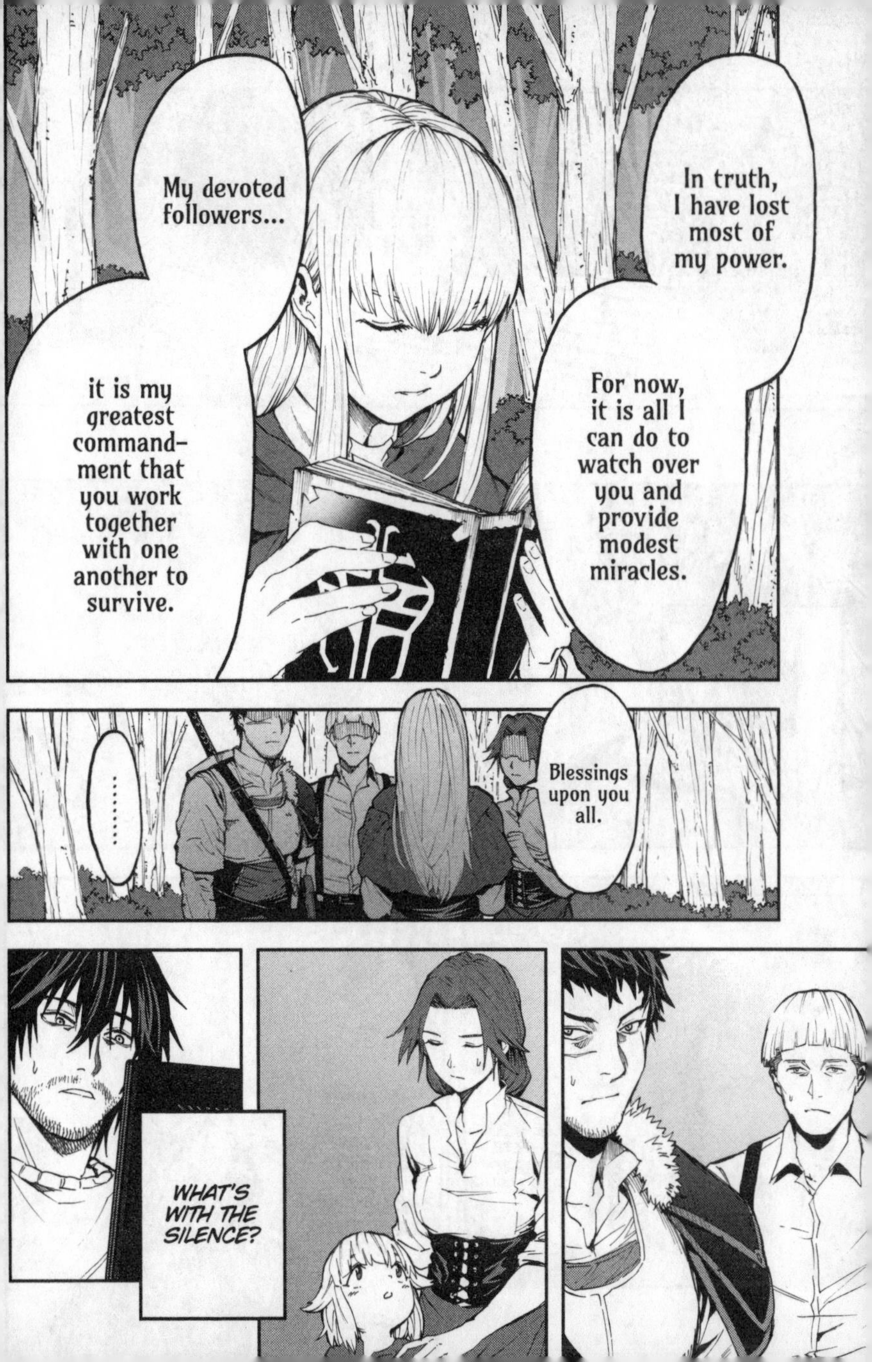
In truth, I have lost most of my power.
For now, it is all I can do to watch over you and provide modest miracles.
My devoted followers...
it is my greatest command-ment that you work together with one another to survive.
Blessings upon you all.
......
WHAT'S WITH THE SILENCE?

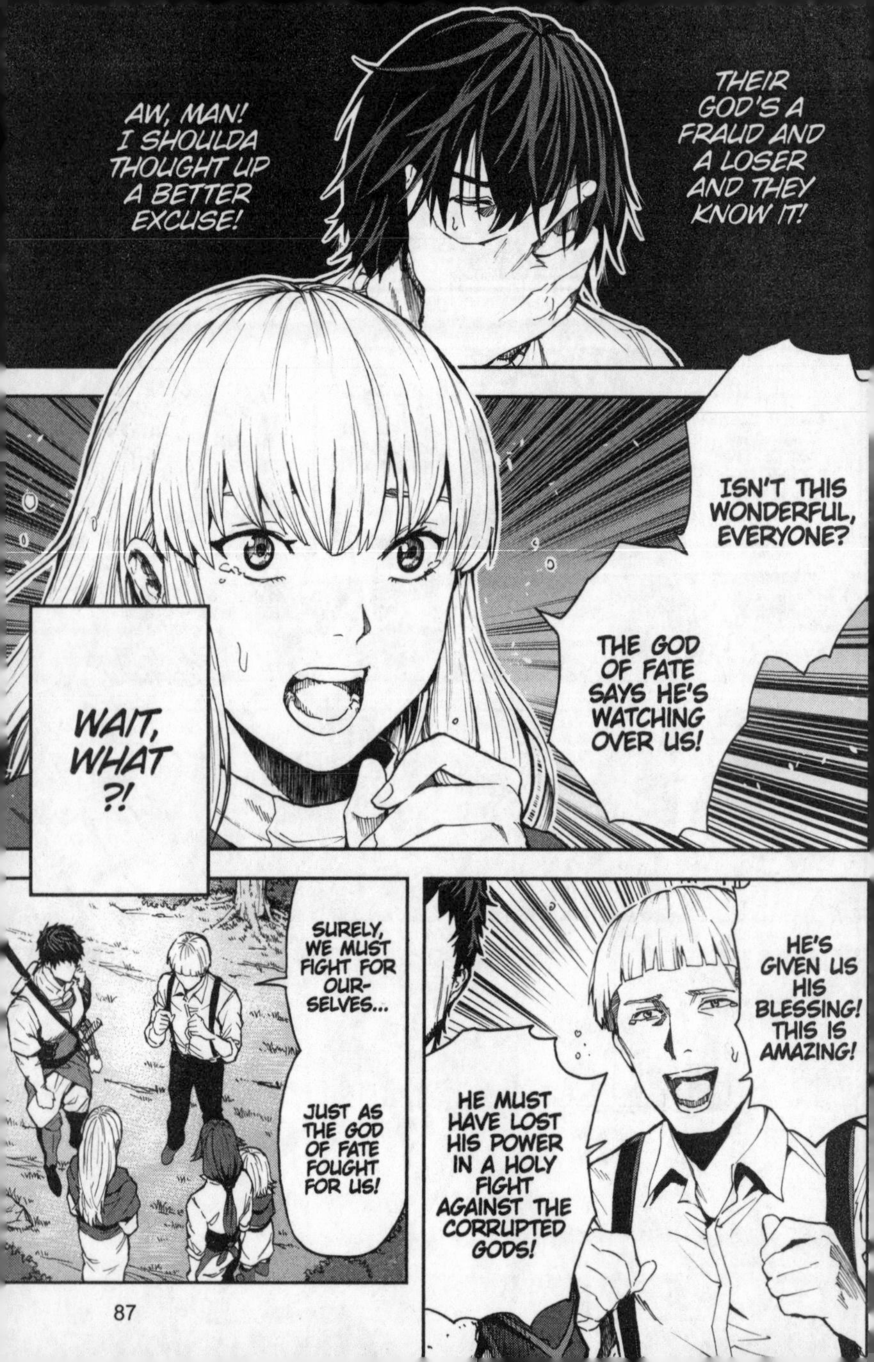
THEIR GOD'S A FRAUD AND A LOSER AND THEY KNOW IT!
AW, MAN! I SHOULDA THOUGHT UP A BETTER EXCUSE!
ISN'T THIS WONDERFUL, EVERYONE?
THE GOD OF FATE SAYS HE'S WATCHING OVER US!
WAIT, WHAT?!
HE'S GIVEN US HIS BLESSING! THIS IS AMAZING!
HE MUST HAVE LOST HIS POWER IN A HOLY FIGHT AGAINST THE CORRUPTED GODS!
SURELY, WE MUST FIGHT FOR OUR-SELVES...
JUST AS THE GOD OF FATE FOUGHT FOR US!

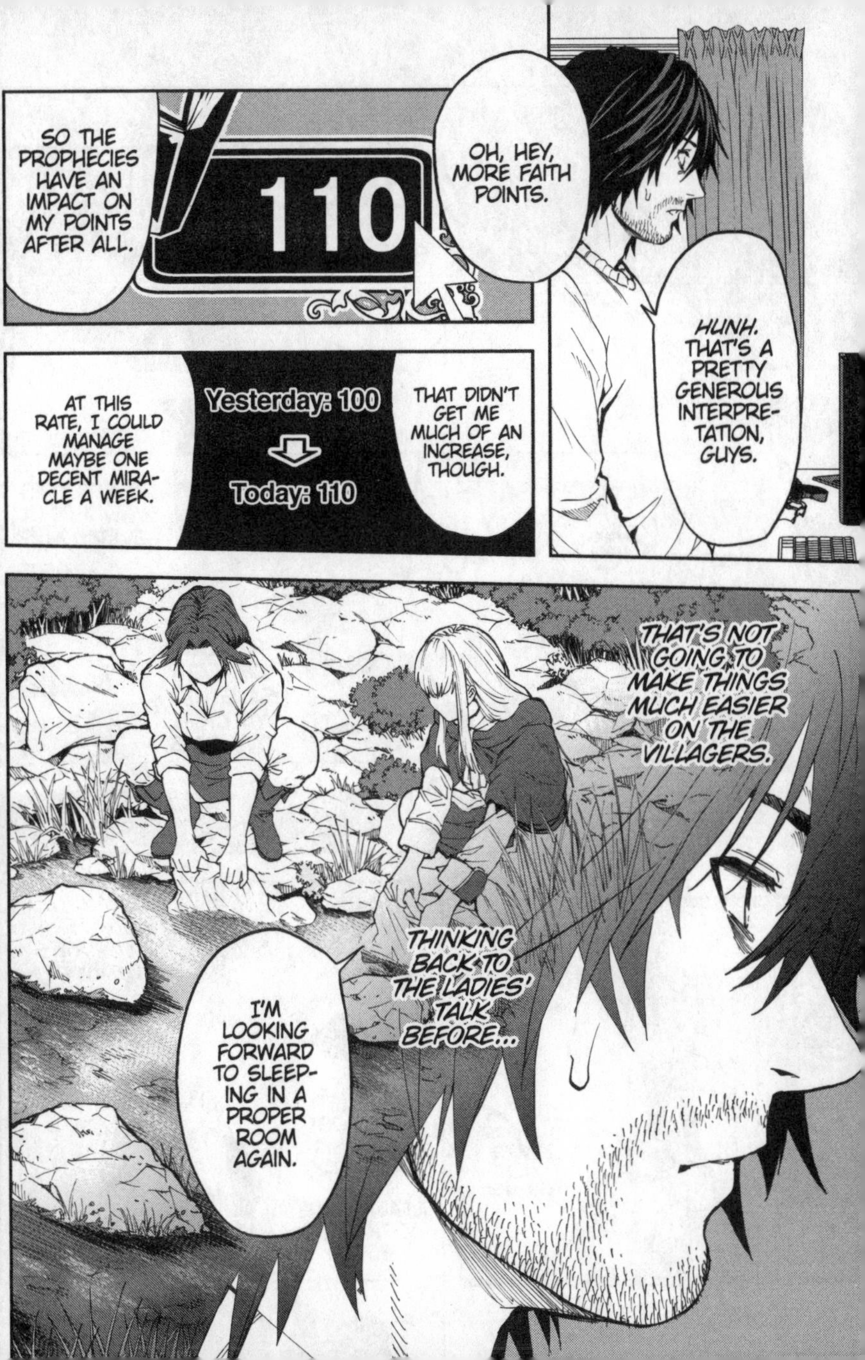
OH, HEY, MORE FAITH POINTS.
HUNH. THAT'S A PRETTY GENEROUS INTERPRETATION, GUYS.
110
SO THE PROPHECIES HAVE AN IMPACT ON MY POINTS AFTER ALL.
THAT DIDN'T GET ME MUCH OF AN INCREASE, THOUGH.
Yesterday: 100
Today: 110
AT THIS RATE, I COULD MANAGE MAYBE ONE DECENT MIRACLE A WEEK.
THAT'S NOT GOING TO MAKE THINGS MUCH EASIER ON THE VILLAGERS.
THINKING BACK TO THE LADIES' TALK BEFORE...
I'M LOOKING FORWARD TO SLEEPING IN A PROPER ROOM AGAIN.

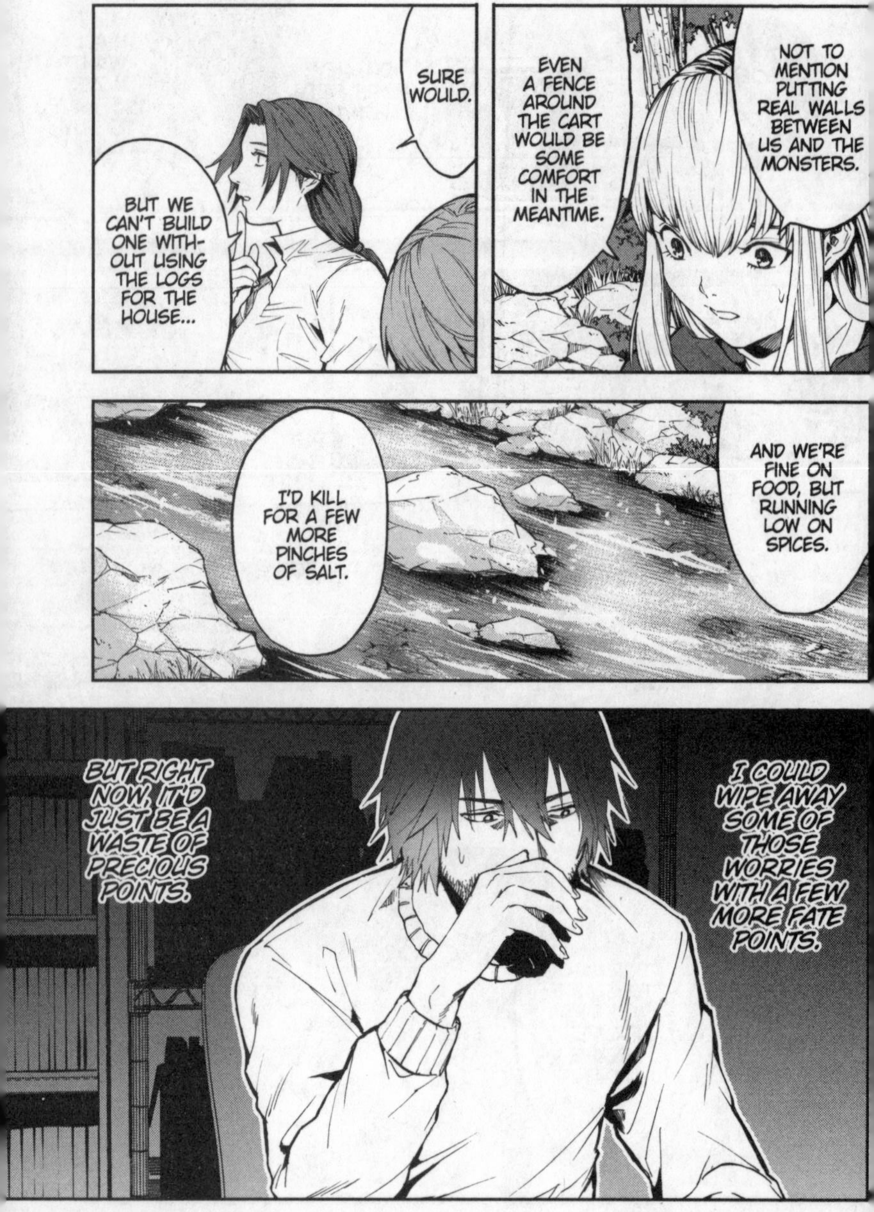
NOT TO MENTION PUTTING REAL WALLS BETWEEN US AND THE MONSTERS.
EVEN A FENCE AROUND THE CART WOULD BE SOME COMFORT IN THE MEANTIME.
SURE WOULD.
BUT WE CAN'T BUILD ONE WITH-OUT USING THE LOGS FOR THE HOUSE...
AND WE'RE FINE ON FOOD, BUT RUNNING LOW ON SPICES.
I'D KILL FOR A FEW MORE PINCHES OF SALT.
I COULD WIPE AWAY SOME OF THOSE WORRIES WITH A FEW MORE FATE POINTS.
BUT RIGHT NOW, IT'D JUST BE A WASTE OF PRECIOUS POINTS.

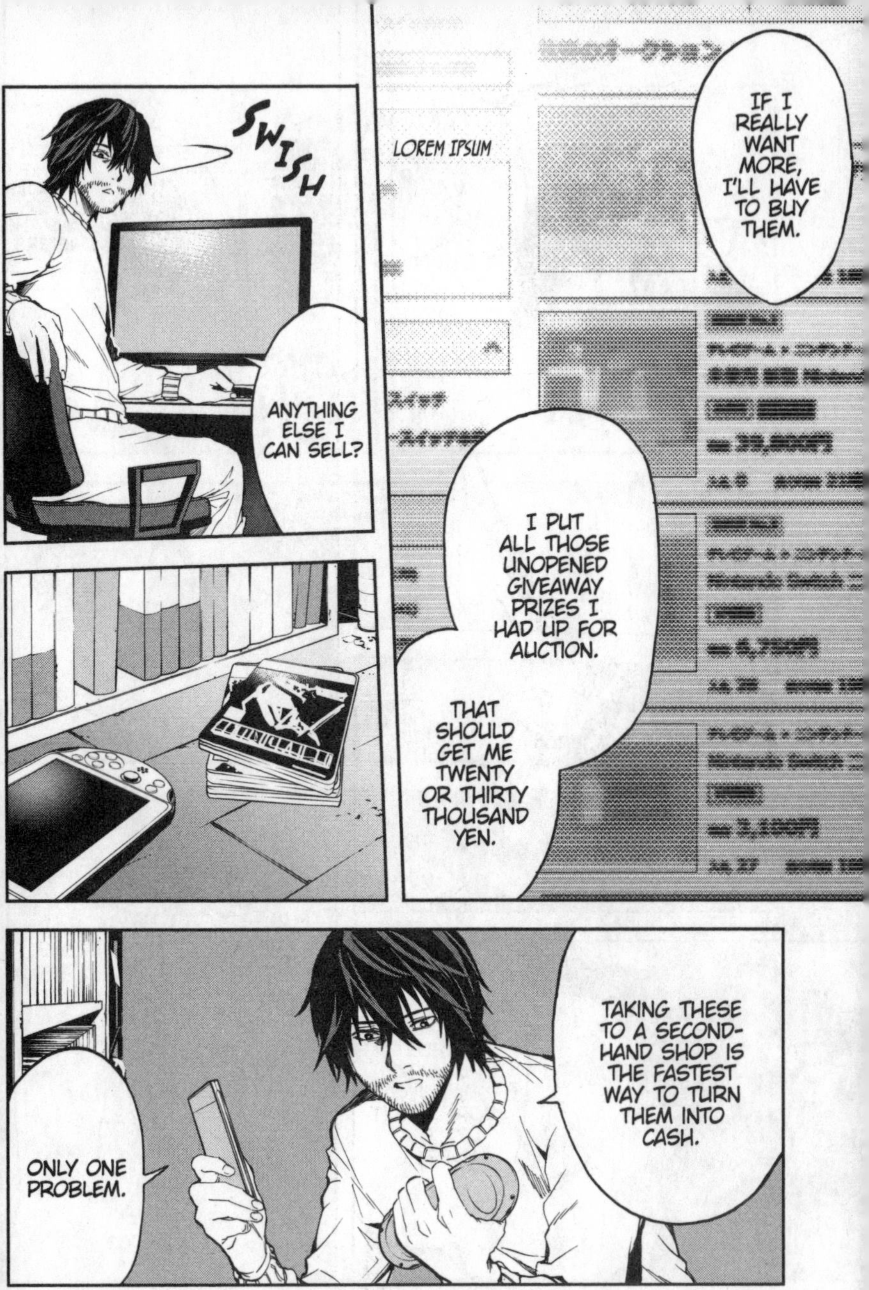
IF I REALLY WANT MORE, I'LL HAVE TO BUY THEM.
LOREM IPSUM
I PUT ALL THOSE UNOPENED GIVEAWAY PRIZES I HAD UP FOR AUCTION.
THAT SHOULD GET ME TWENTY OR THIRTY THOUSAND YEN.
SWISH
ANYTHING ELSE I CAN SELL?
TAKING THESE TO A SECOND-HAND SHOP IS THE FASTEST WAY TO TURN THEM INTO CASH.
ONLY ONE PROBLEM.

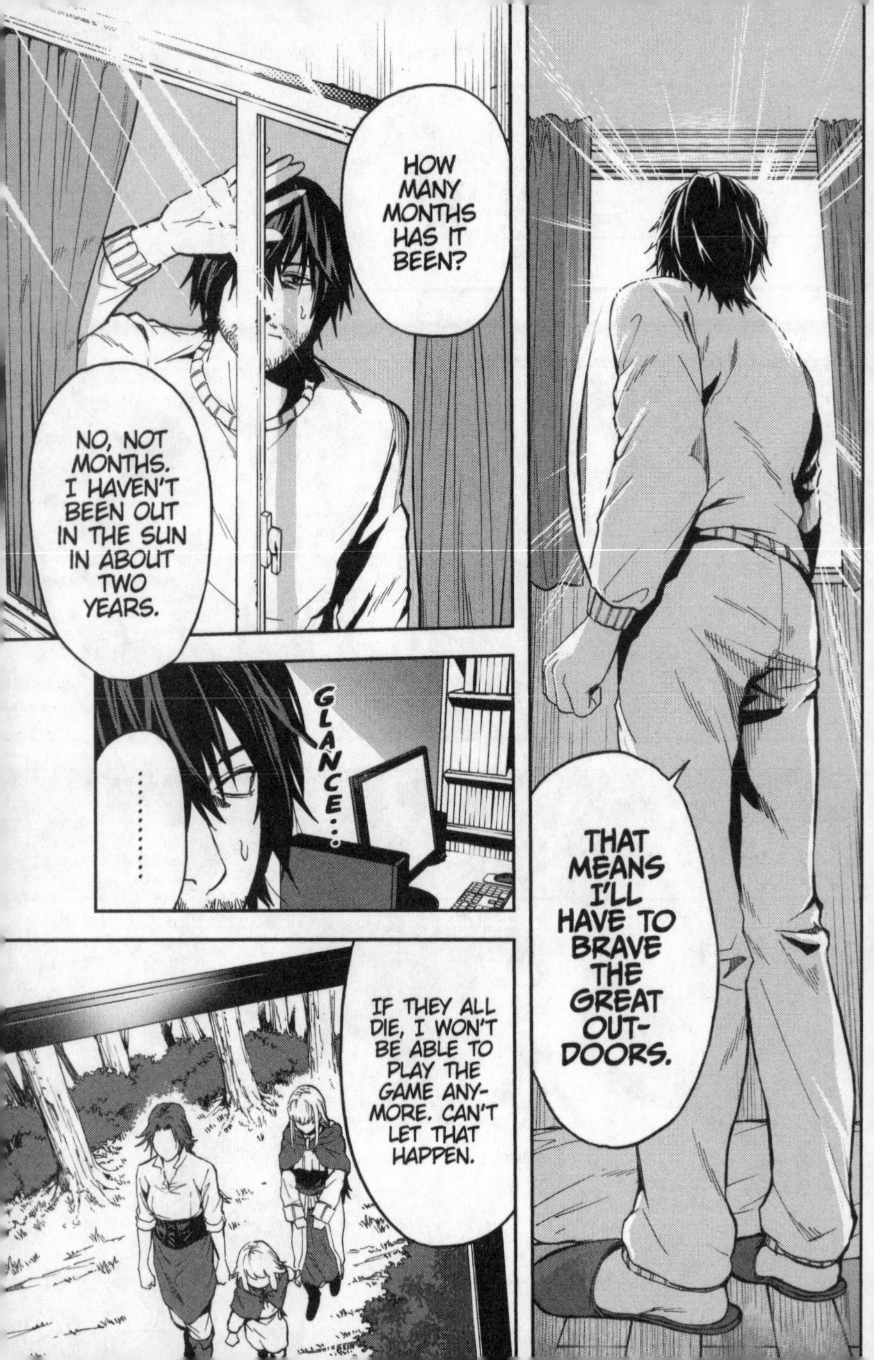
HOW MANY MONTHS HAS IT BEEN?
NO, NOT MONTHS. I HAVEN'T BEEN OUT IN THE SUN IN ABOUT TWO YEARS.
GLANCE...
......
IF THEY ALL DIE, I WON'T BE ABLE TO PLAY THE GAME ANY-MORE. CAN'T LET THAT HAPPEN.
THAT MEANS I'LL HAVE TO BRAVE THE GREAT OUT-DOORS.

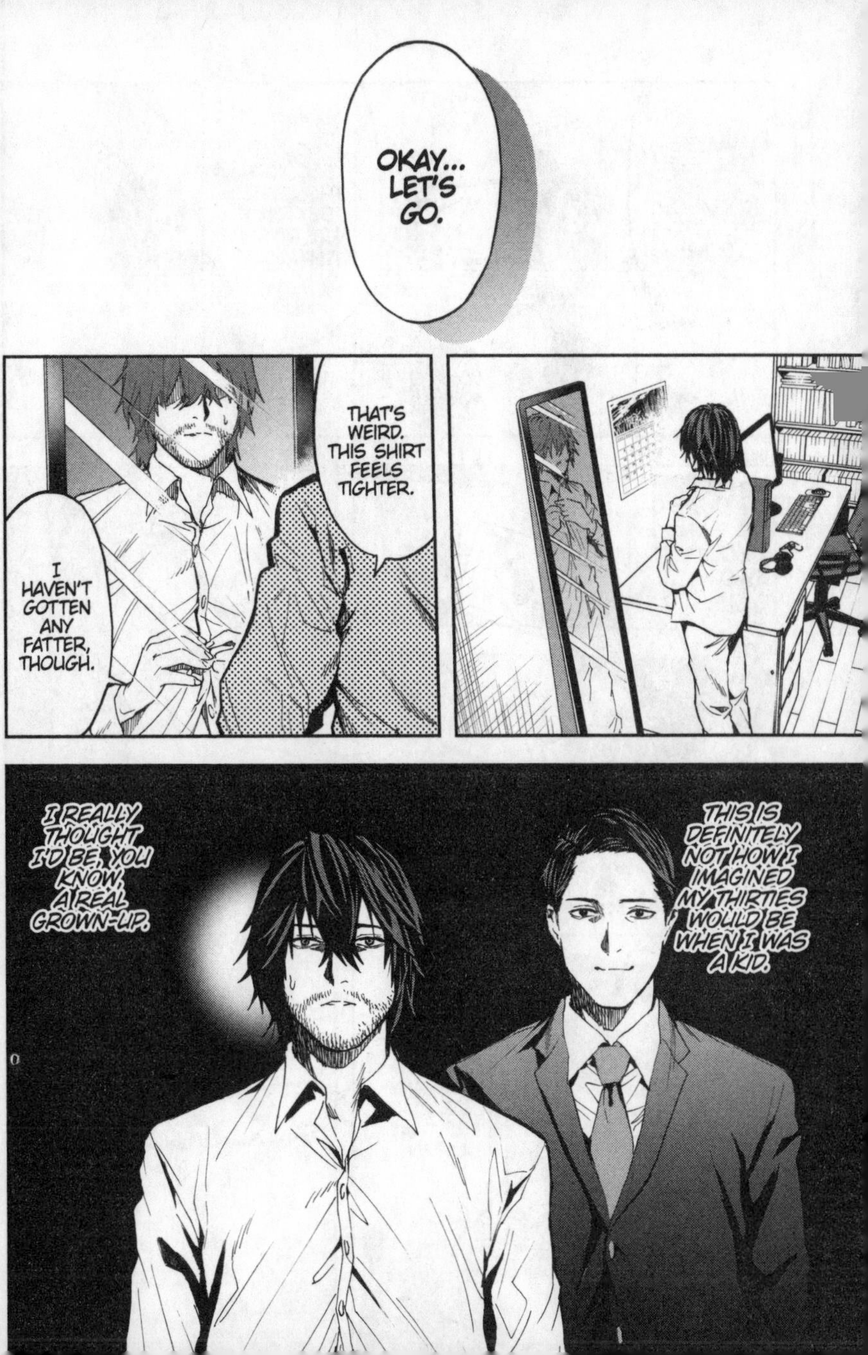
OKAY... LET'S GO.
THAT'S WEIRD. THIS SHIRT FEELS TIGHTER.
I HAVEN'T GOTTEN ANY FATTER, THOUGH.
THIS IS DEFINITELY NOT HOW I IMAGINED MY THIRTIES WOULD BE WHEN I WAS A KID.
I REALLY THOUGHT I'D BE, YOU KNOW, A REAL GROWN-UP.

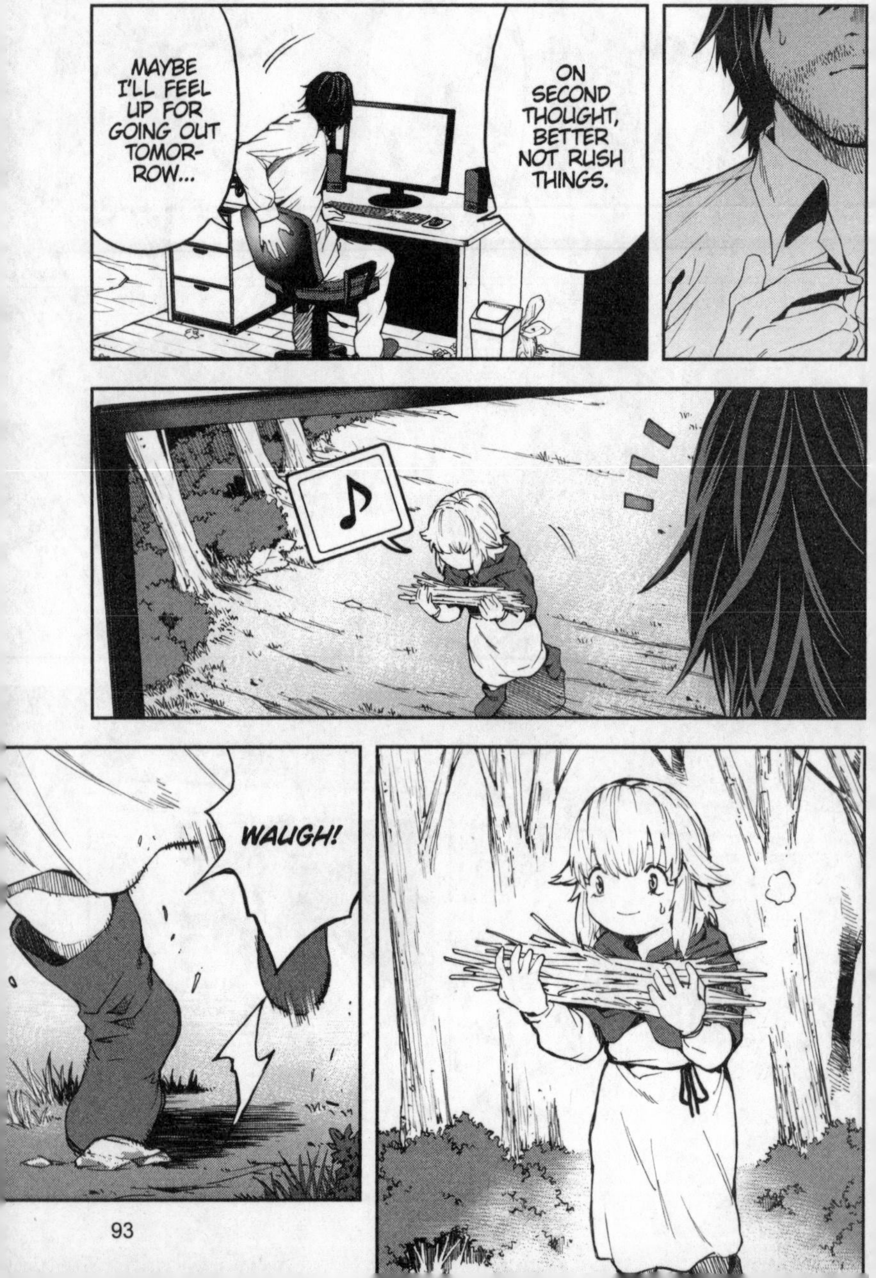
ON SECOND THOUGHT, BETTER NOT RUSH THINGS.
MAYBE I'LL FEEL UP FOR GOING OUT TOMOR-ROW...
♪
WAUGH!

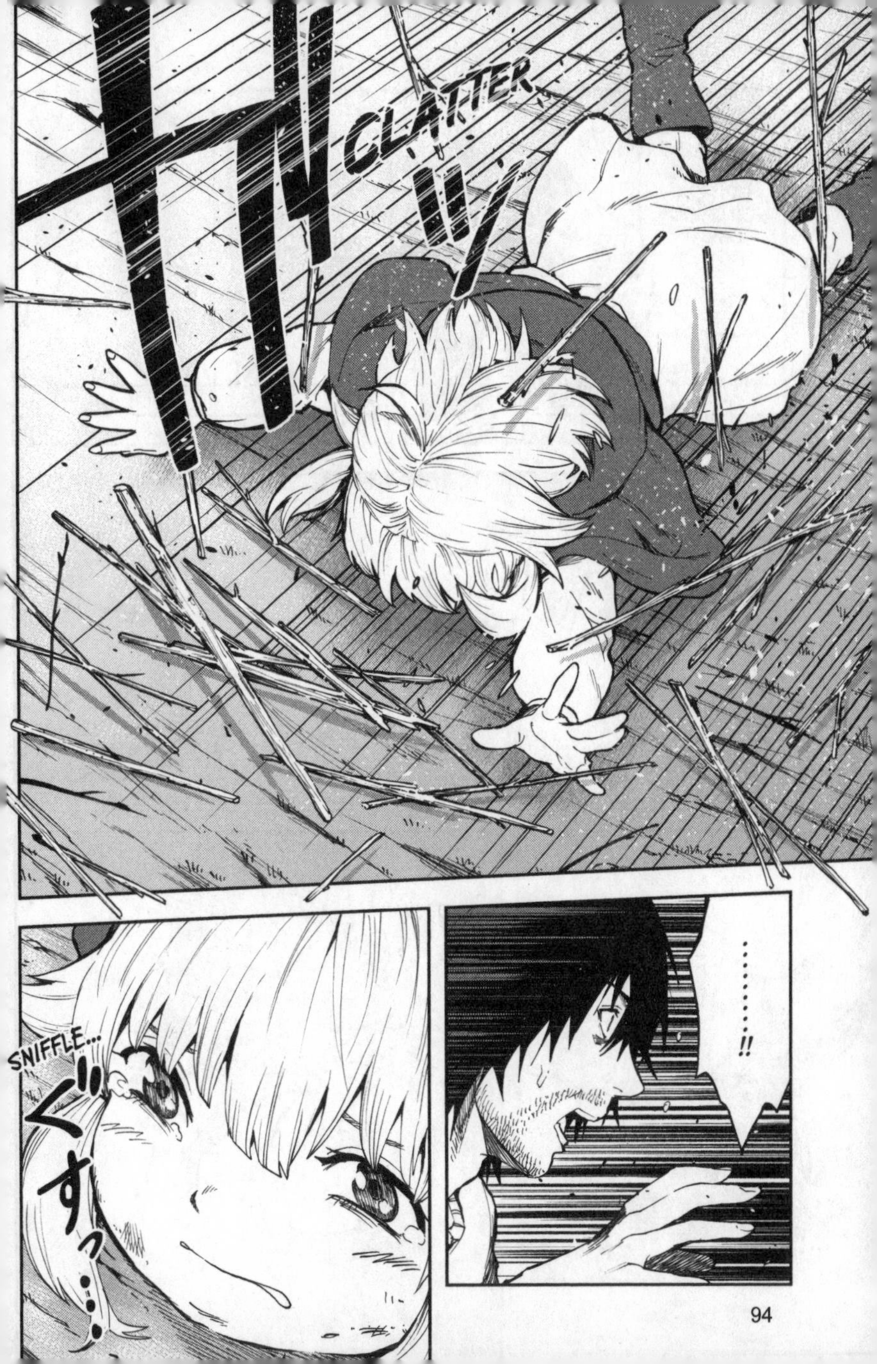
CLATTER
……!!
SNIFFLE...
ぐすっ…

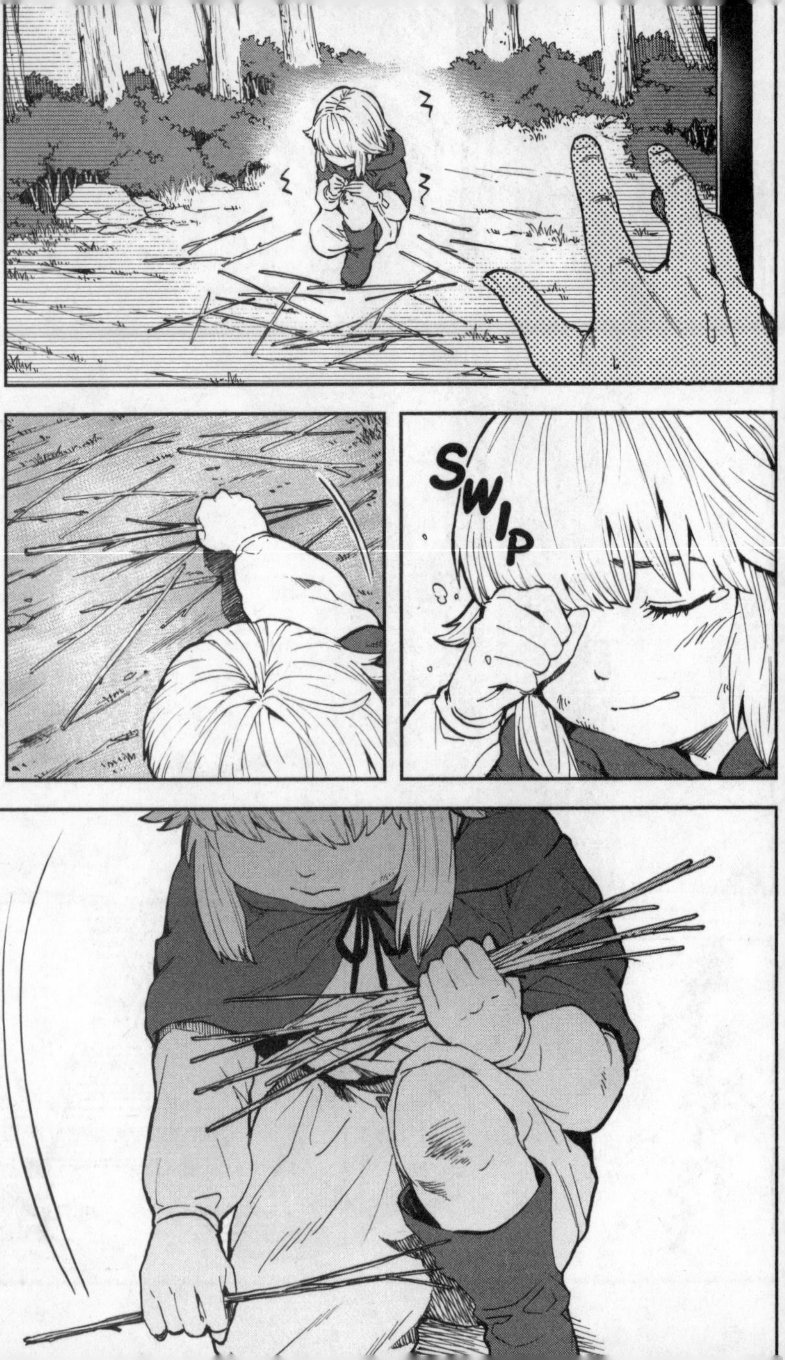
SWIP

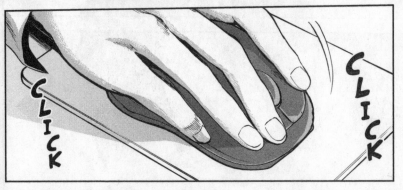

CLICK

CLICK

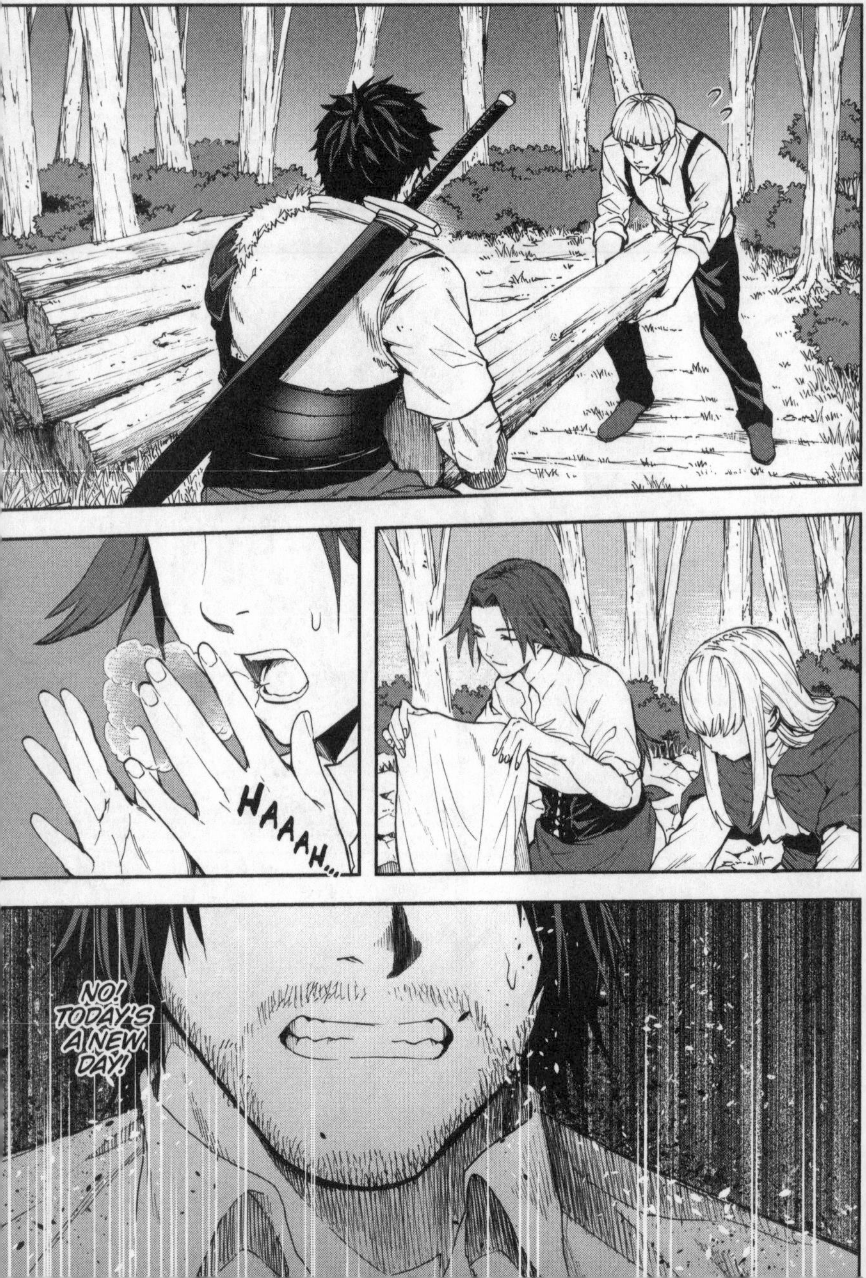
HAAAH...
NO! TODAY'S A NEW DAY!

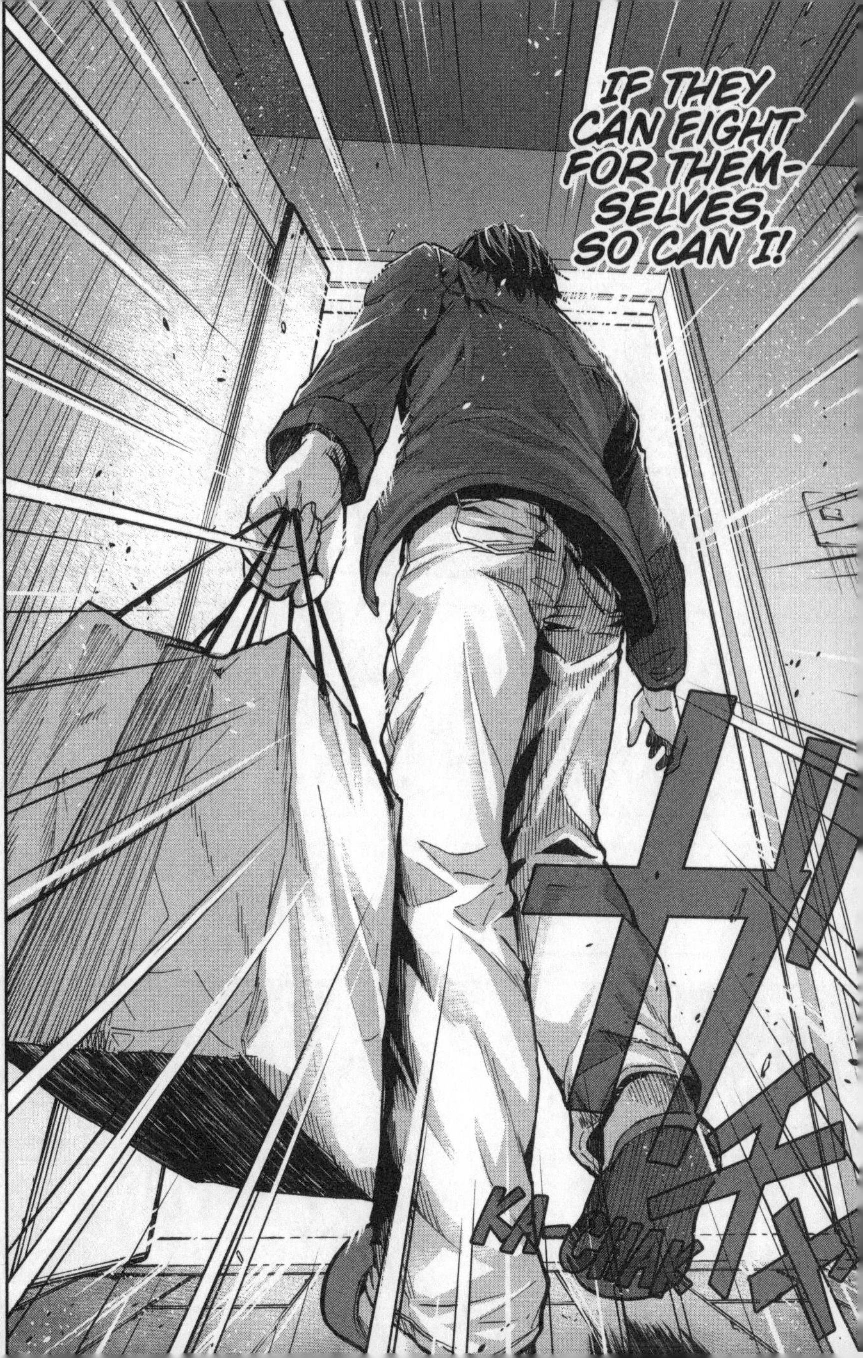
IF THEY CAN FIGHT FOR THEM-SELVES, SO CAN I!
KA-CHAK

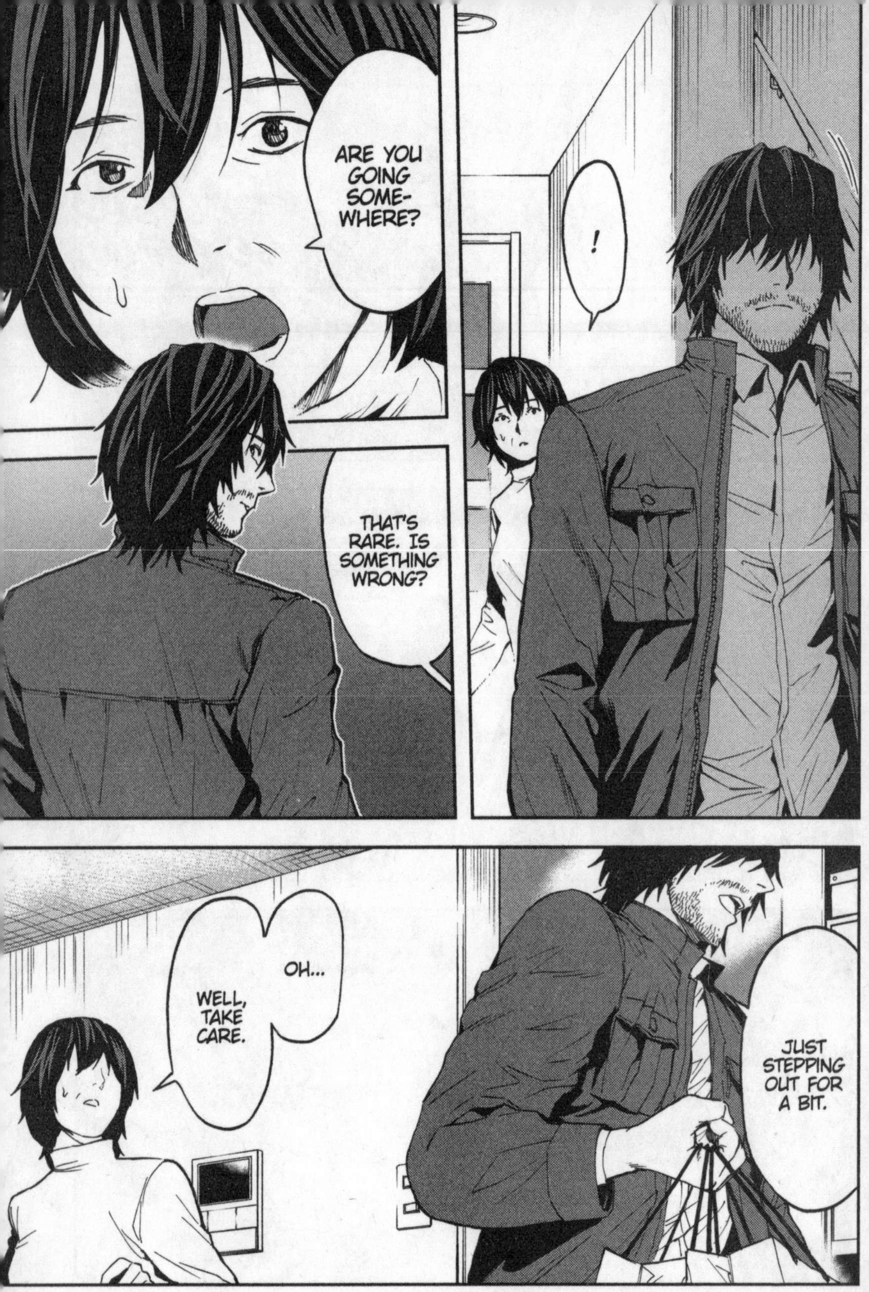
!
ARE YOU GOING SOME-WHERE?
THAT'S RARE. IS SOMETHING WRONG?
JUST STEPPING OUT FOR A BIT.
OH...
WELL, TAKE CARE.

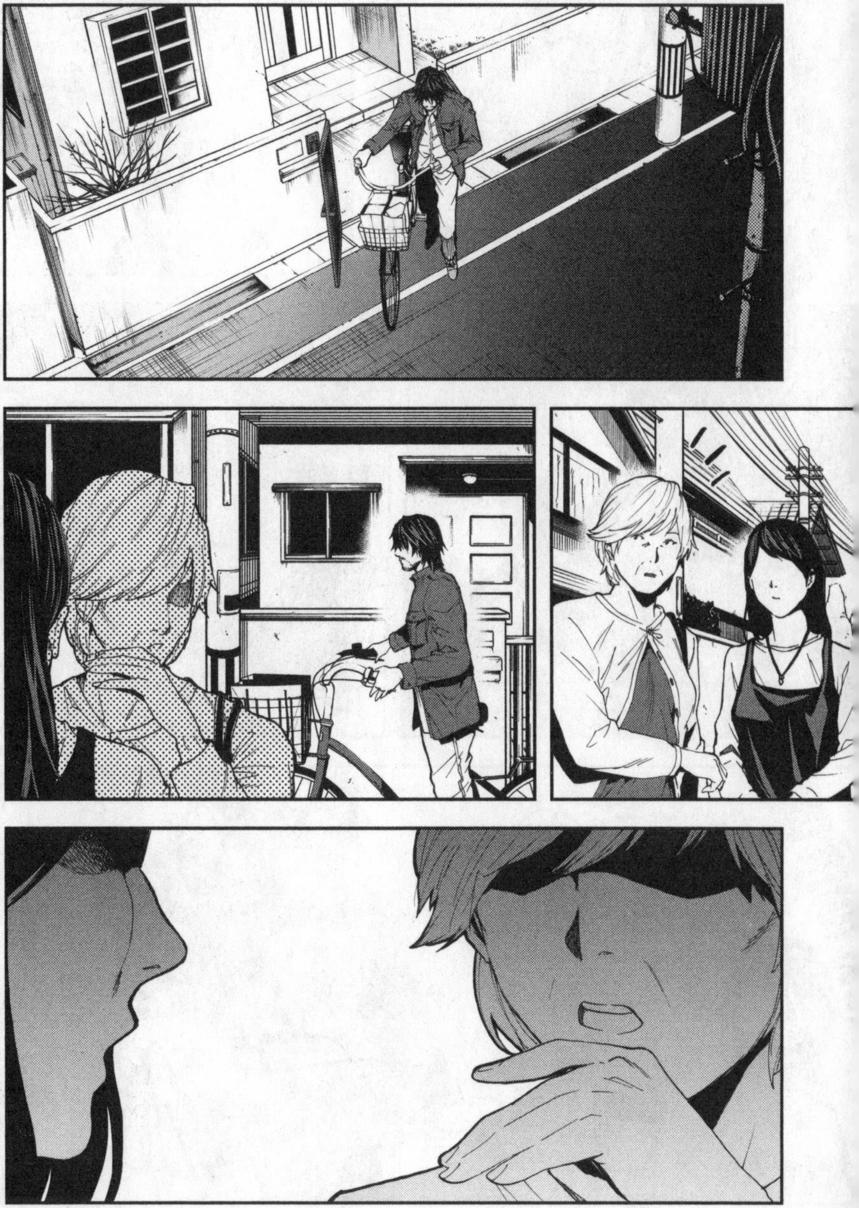

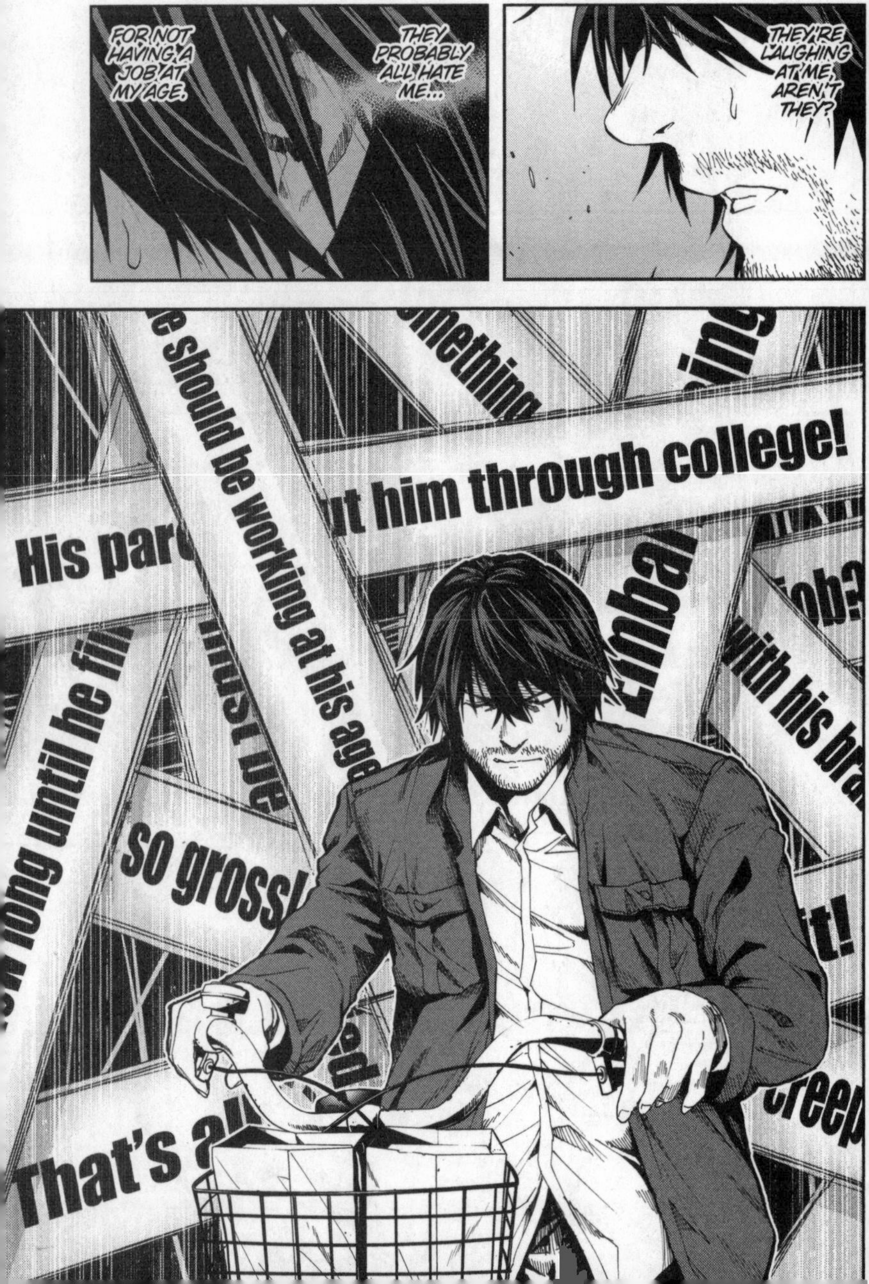
THEY'RE LAUGHING AT ME, AREN'T THEY?
THEY PROBABLY ALL HATE ME...
FOR NOT HAVING A JOB AT MY AGE.
ut him through college!
His pare
e should be working at his age
mething
Embar
Job?
with his bra
it!
creep
so gross!
until he fi
That's a

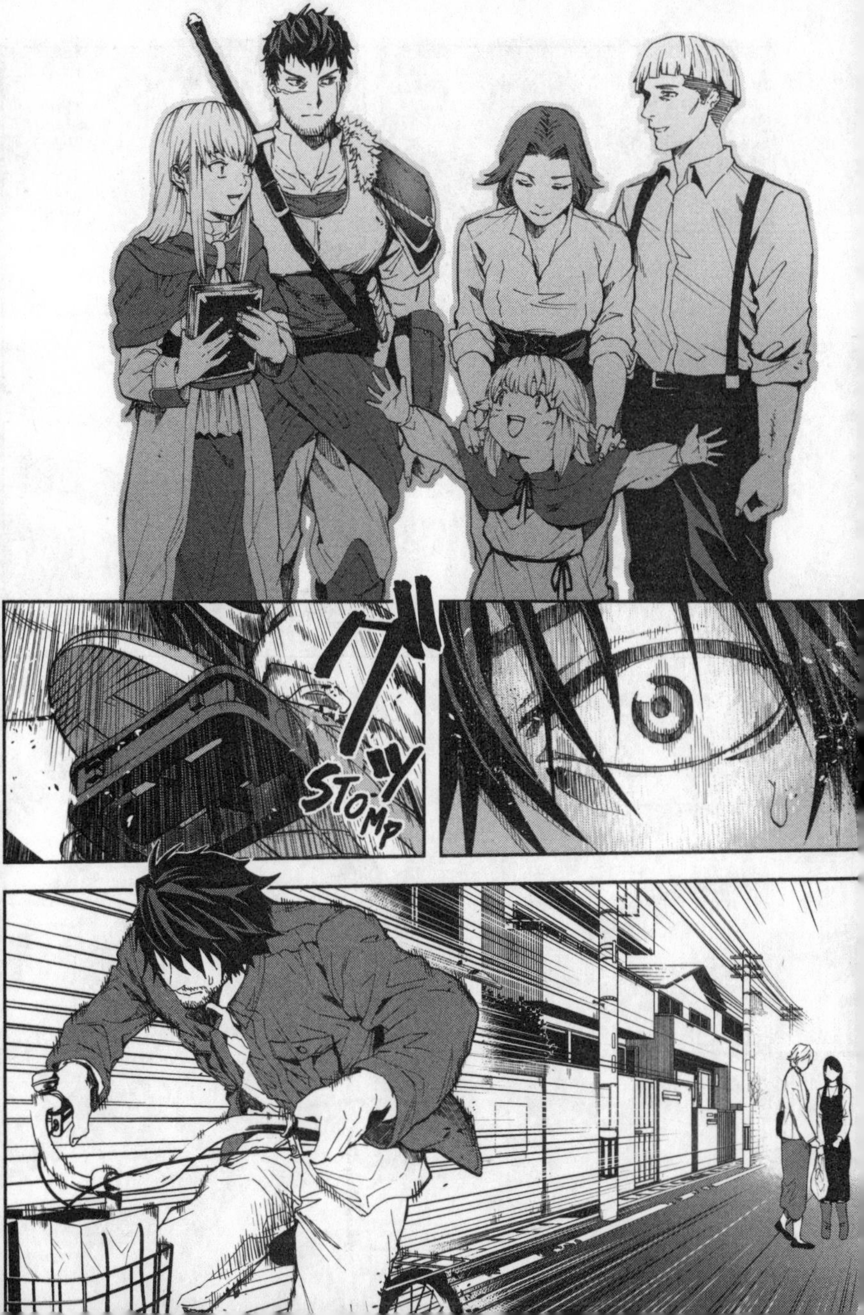
STOMP

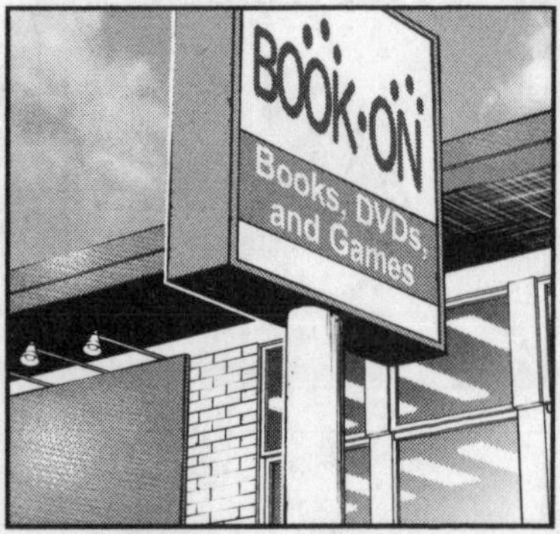
BOOK·ON
Books, DVDs, and Games
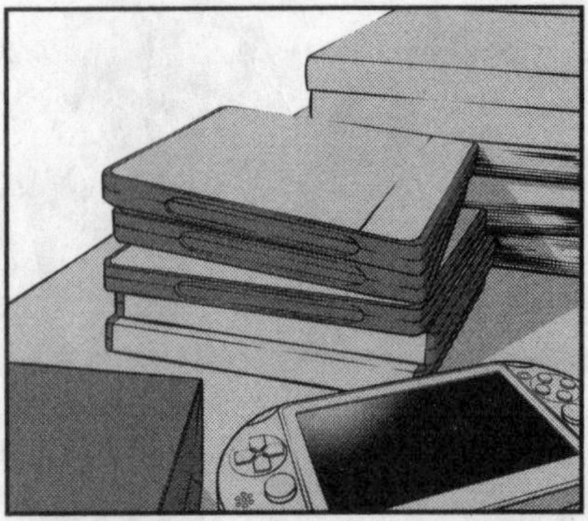
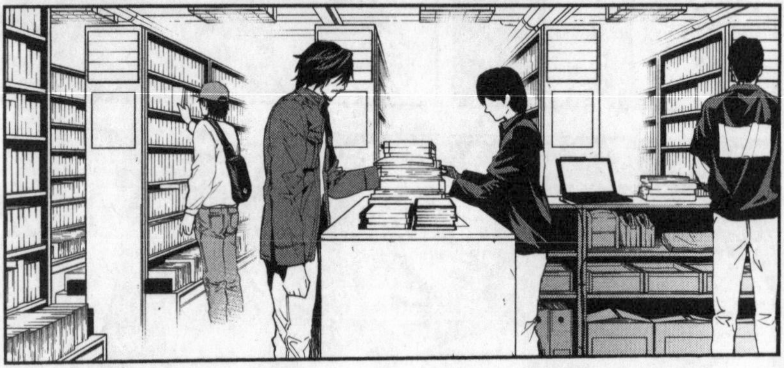
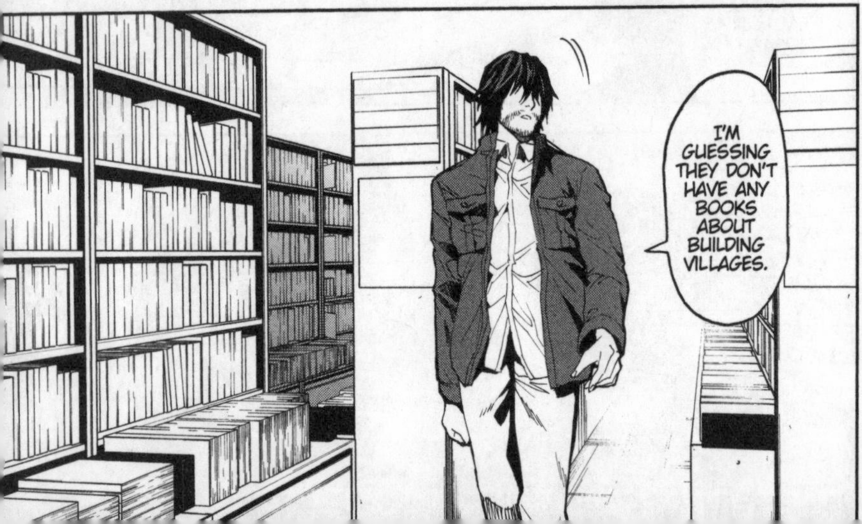
I'M GUESSING THEY DON'T HAVE ANY BOOKS ABOUT BUILDING VILLAGES.

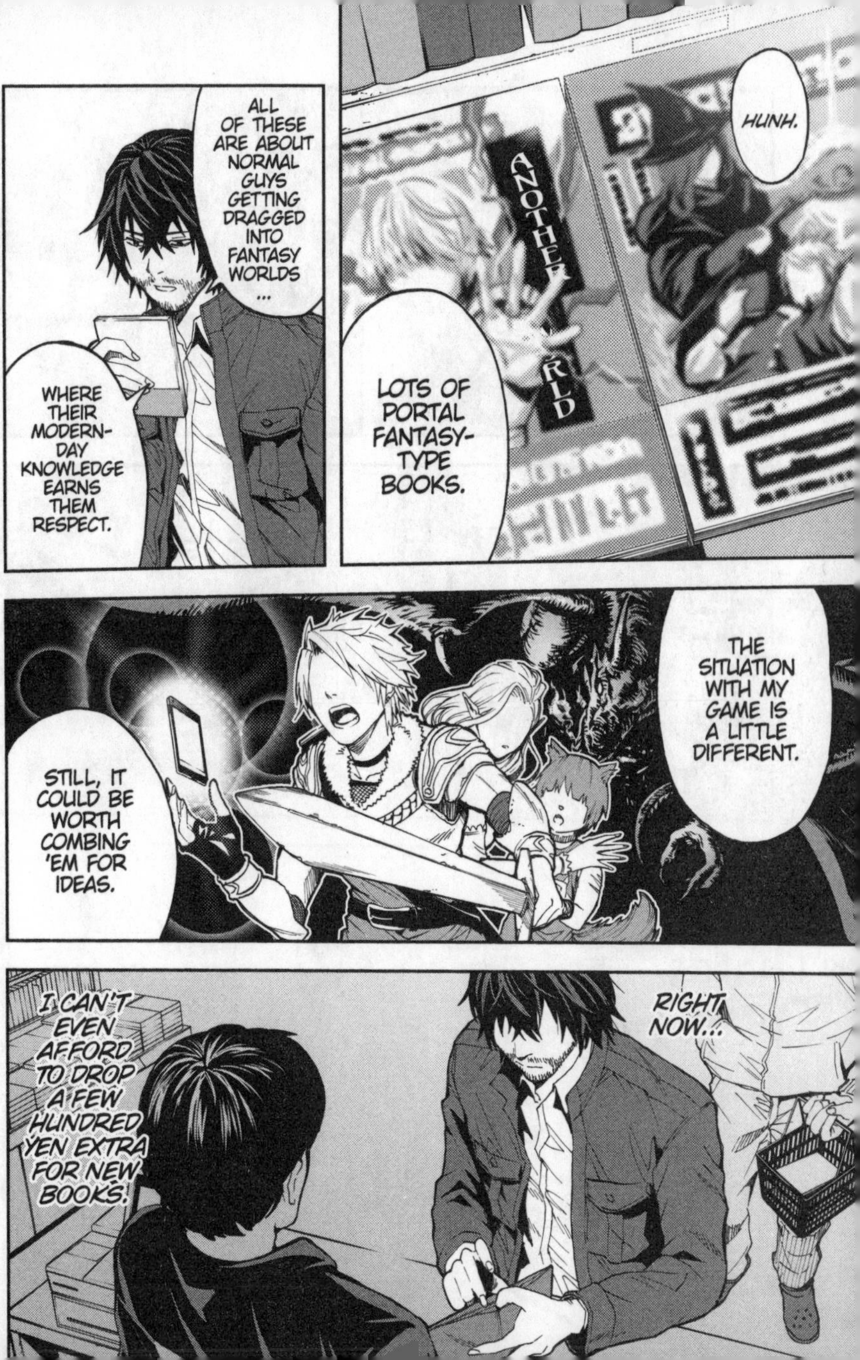
HUNH.
ANOTHER
LOTS OF PORTAL FANTASY-TYPE BOOKS.
ALL OF THESE ARE ABOUT NORMAL GUYS GETTING DRAGGED INTO FANTASY WORLDS ...
WHERE THEIR MODERN-DAY KNOWLEDGE EARNS THEM RESPECT.
THE SITUATION WITH MY GAME IS A LITTLE DIFFERENT.
STILL, IT COULD BE WORTH COMBING 'EM FOR IDEAS.
RIGHT NOW...
I CAN'T EVEN AFFORD TO DROP A FEW HUNDRED YEN EXTRA FOR NEW BOOKS!

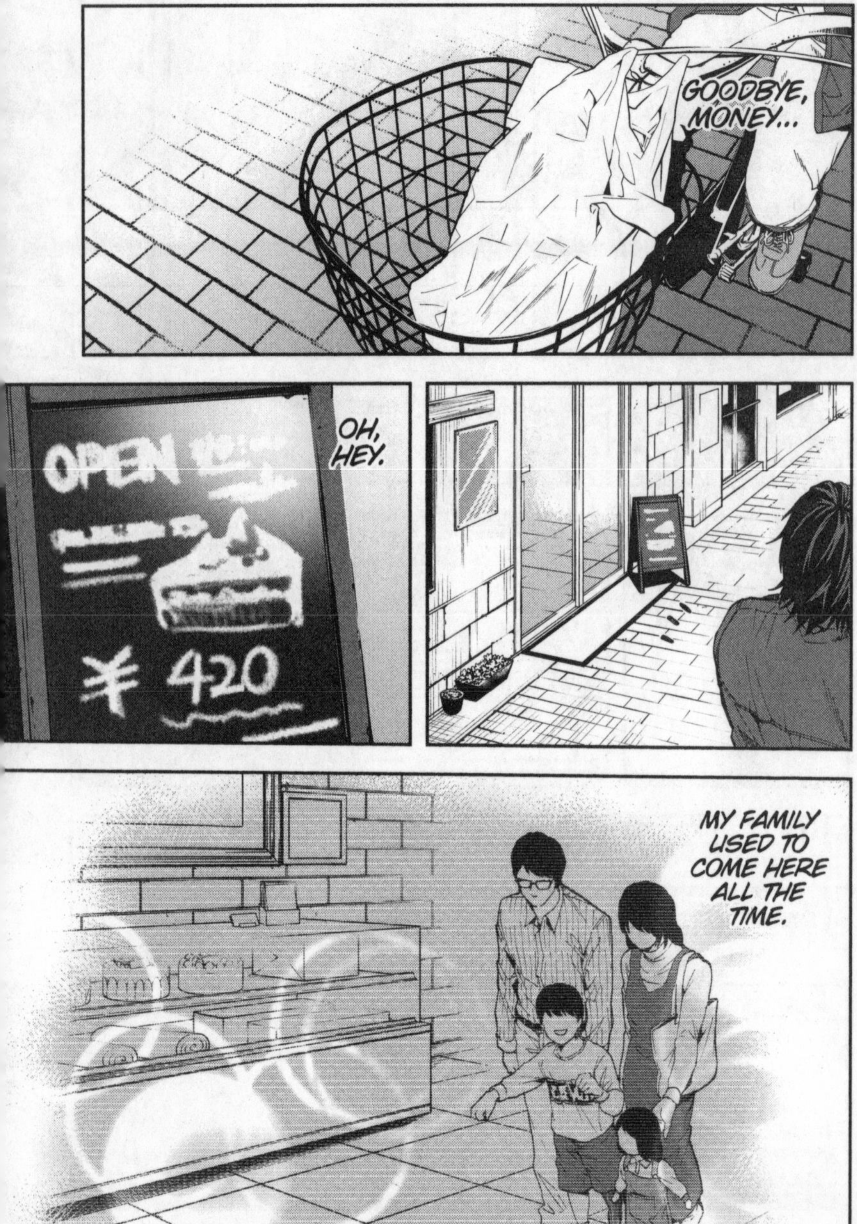
GOODBYE, MONEY...
OH, HEY.
OPEN
¥420
MY FAMILY USED TO COME HERE ALL THE TIME.

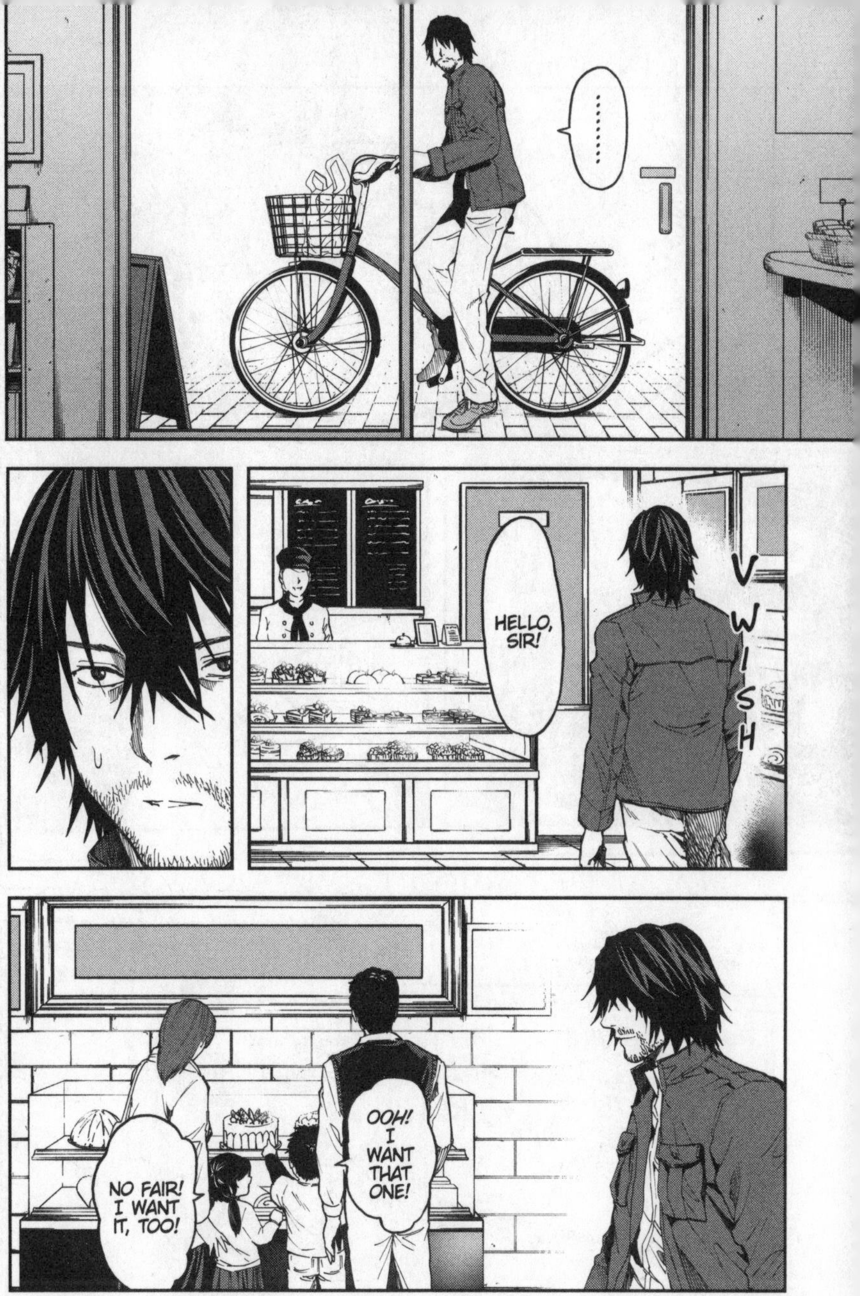
......
VWISH
HELLO, SIR!
OOH! I WANT THAT ONE!
NO FAIR! I WANT IT, TOO!

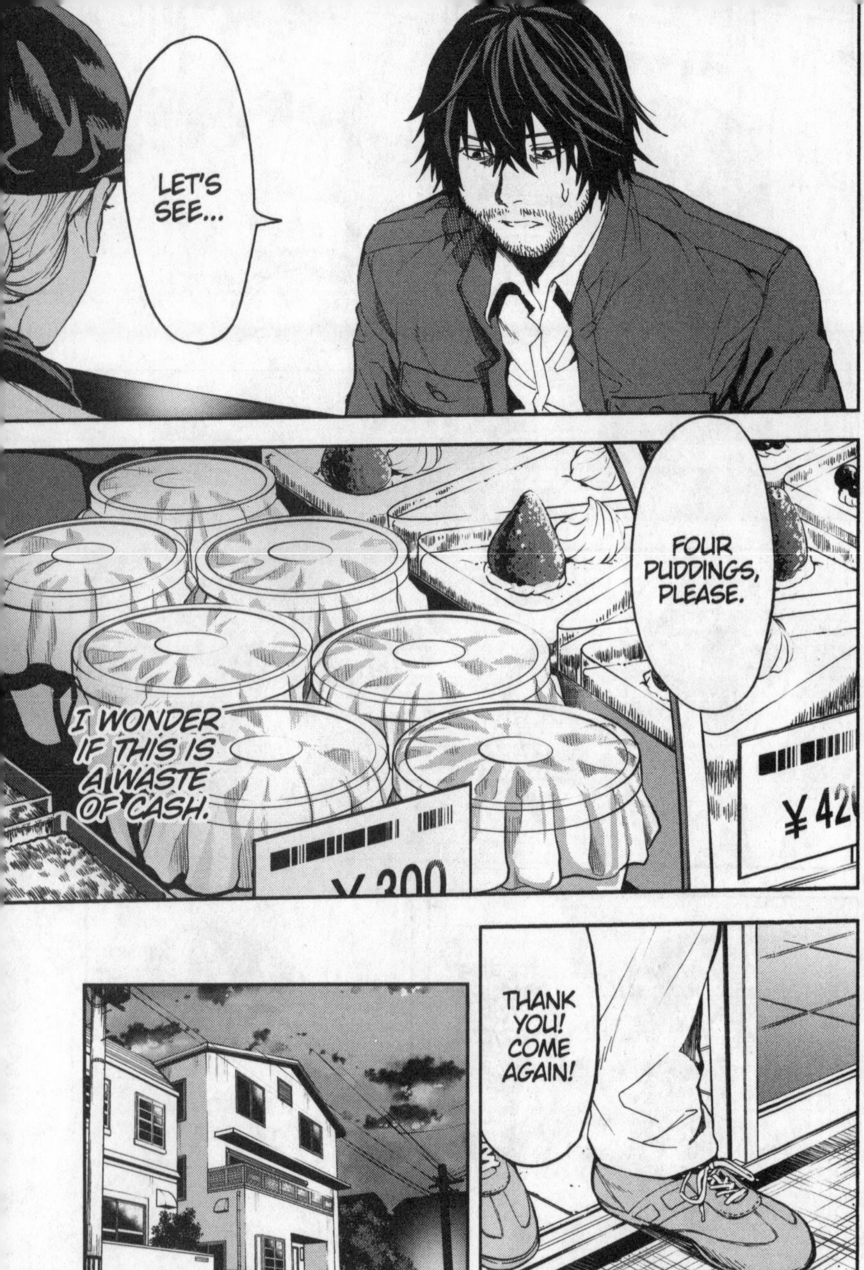
LET'S SEE...
FOUR PUDDINGS, PLEASE.
I WONDER IF THIS IS A WASTE OF CASH.
¥ 300
THANK YOU! COME AGAIN!

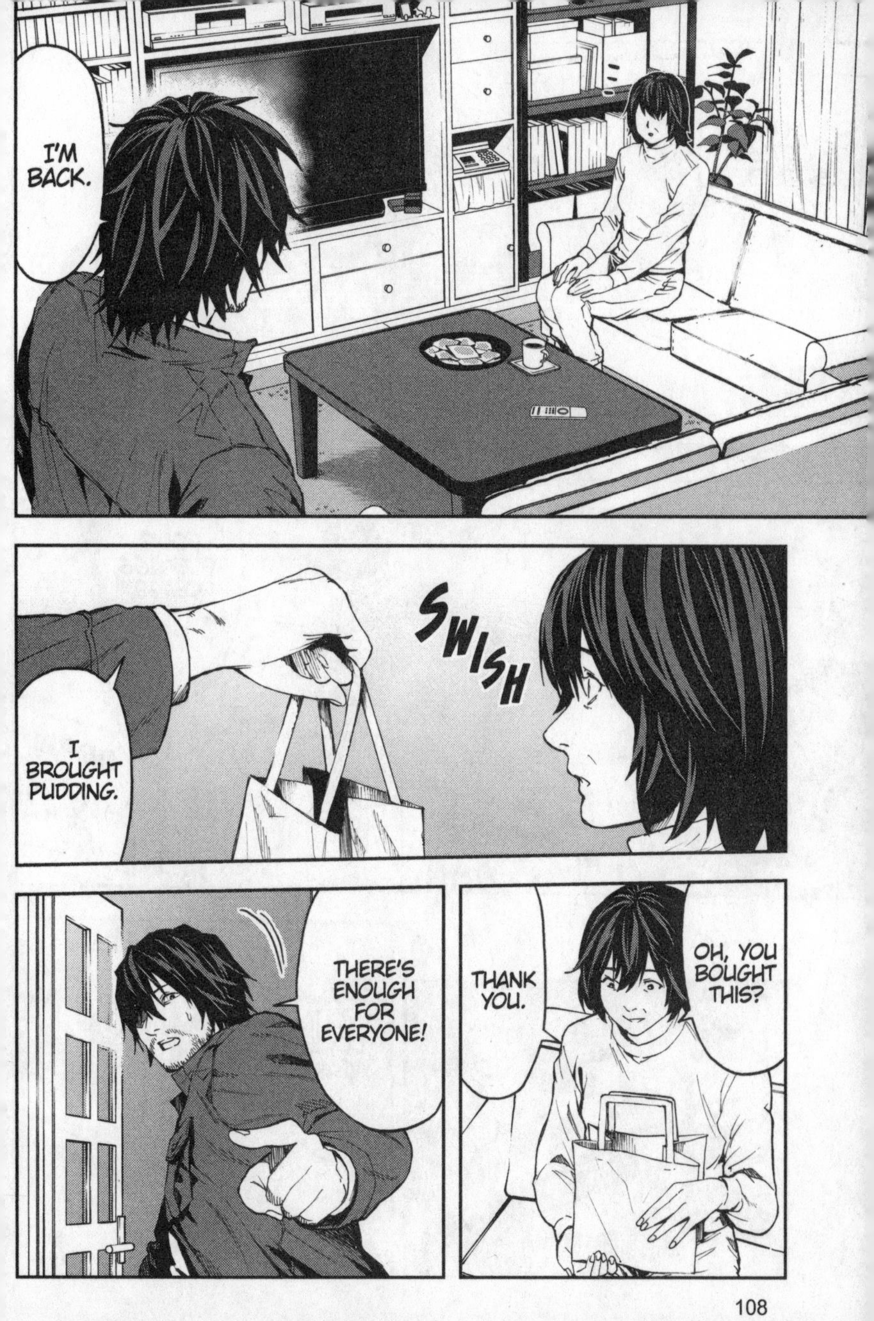
I'M BACK.
SWISH
I BROUGHT PUDDING.
OH, YOU BOUGHT THIS?
THANK YOU.
THERE'S ENOUGH FOR EVERYONE!

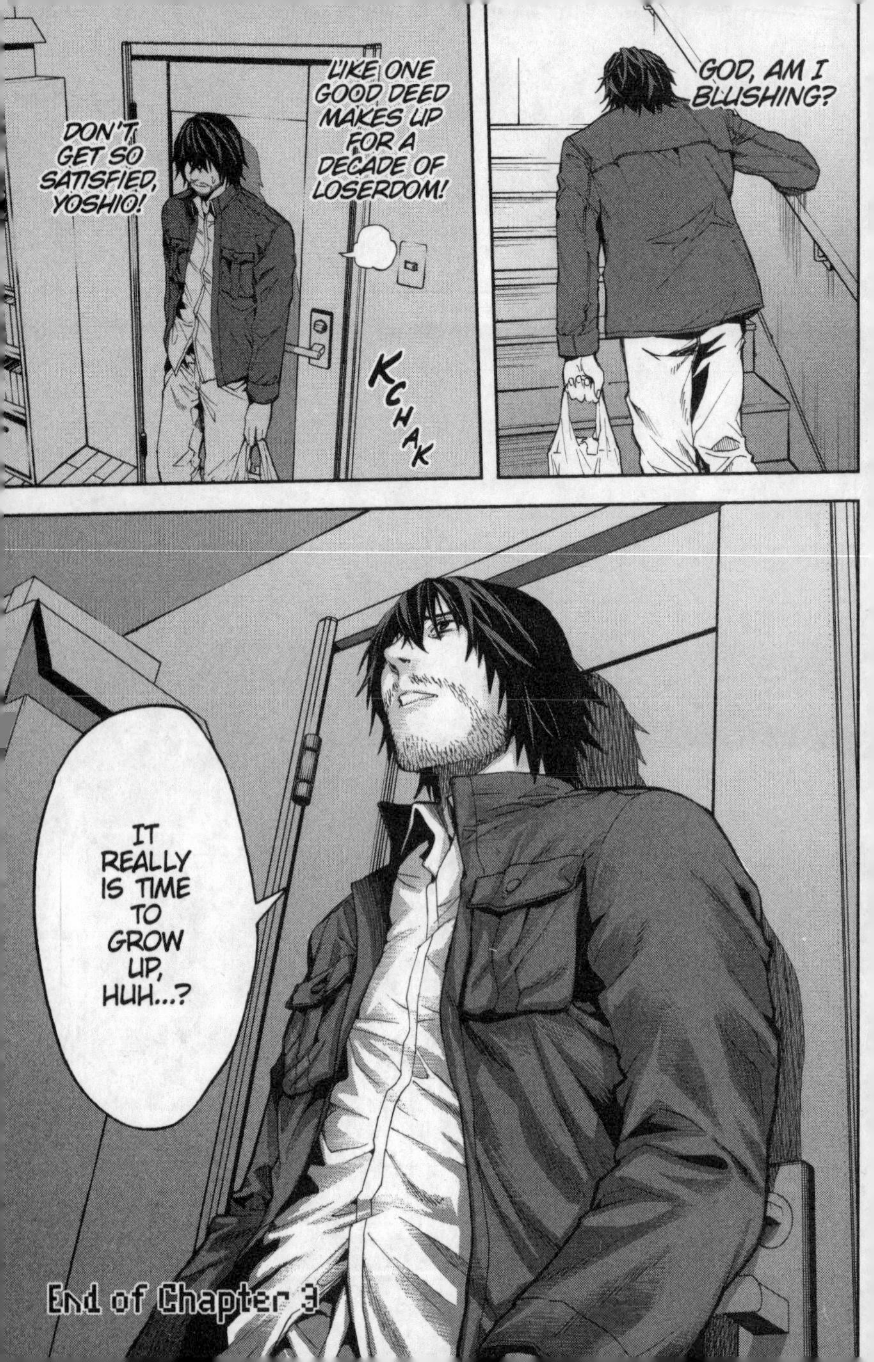
GOD, AM I BLUSHING?
DON'T GET SO SATISFIED, YOSHIO!
LIKE ONE GOOD DEED MAKES UP FOR A DECADE OF LOSERDOM!
KCHAK
IT REALLY IS TIME TO GROW UP, HUH...?
End of Chapter 3

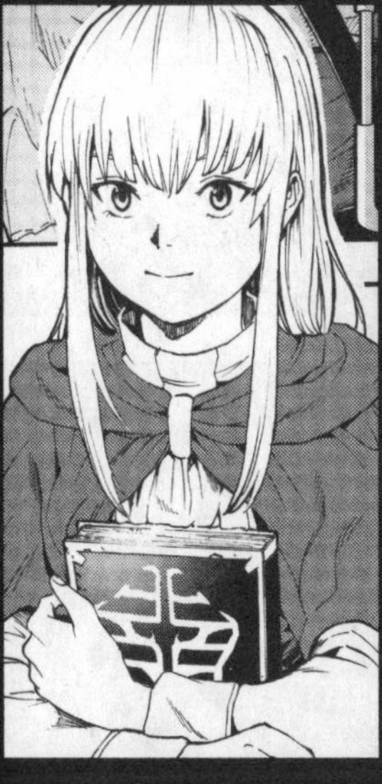

Character

Chem

▶ Gender: Female

Class: Priestess

E: Holy-Looking Robes

E: Book of Scripture

E: Brother Complex +2

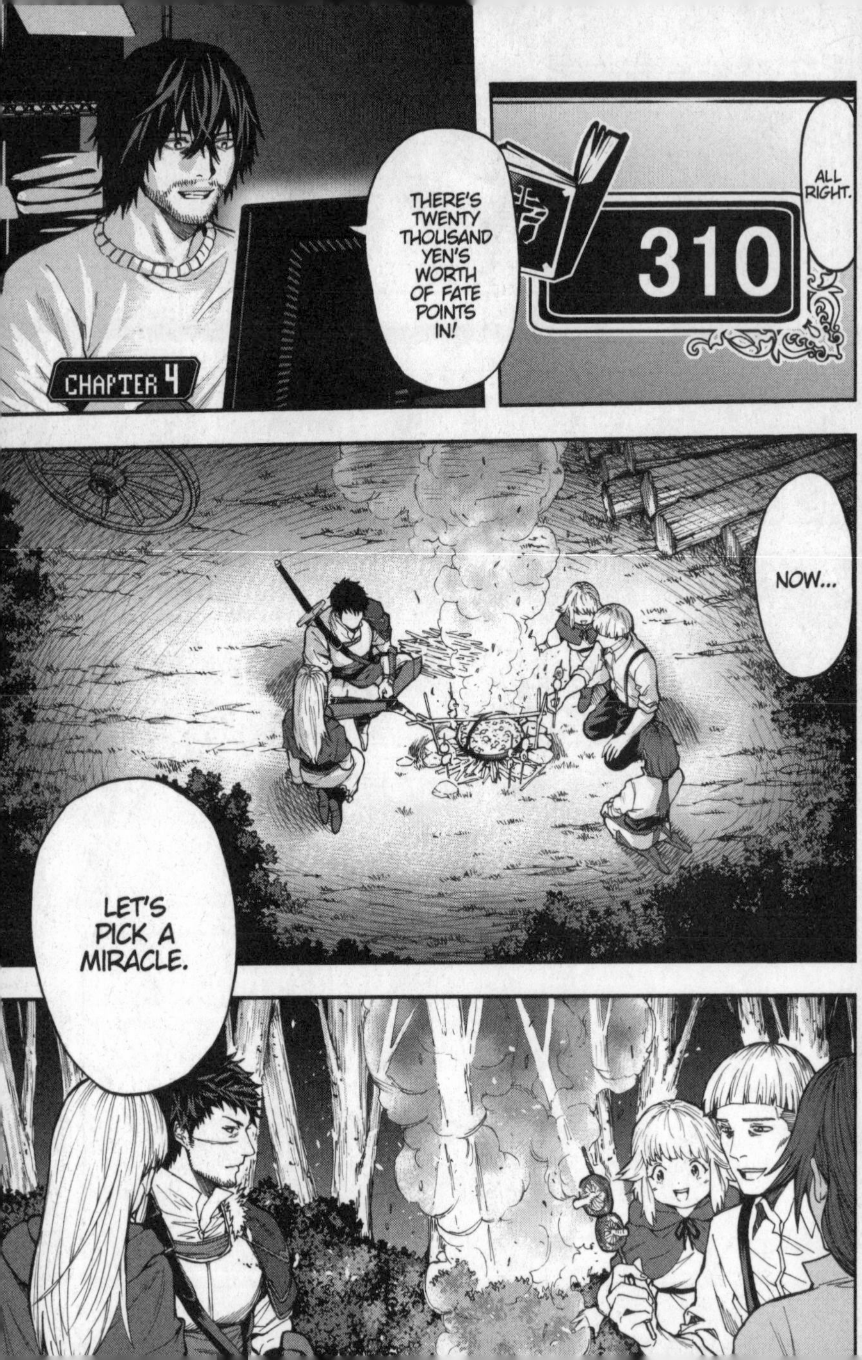
ALL RIGHT.
310
THERE'S TWENTY THOUSAND YEN'S WORTH OF FATE POINTS IN!
CHAPTER 4
NOW...
LET'S PICK A MIRACLE.

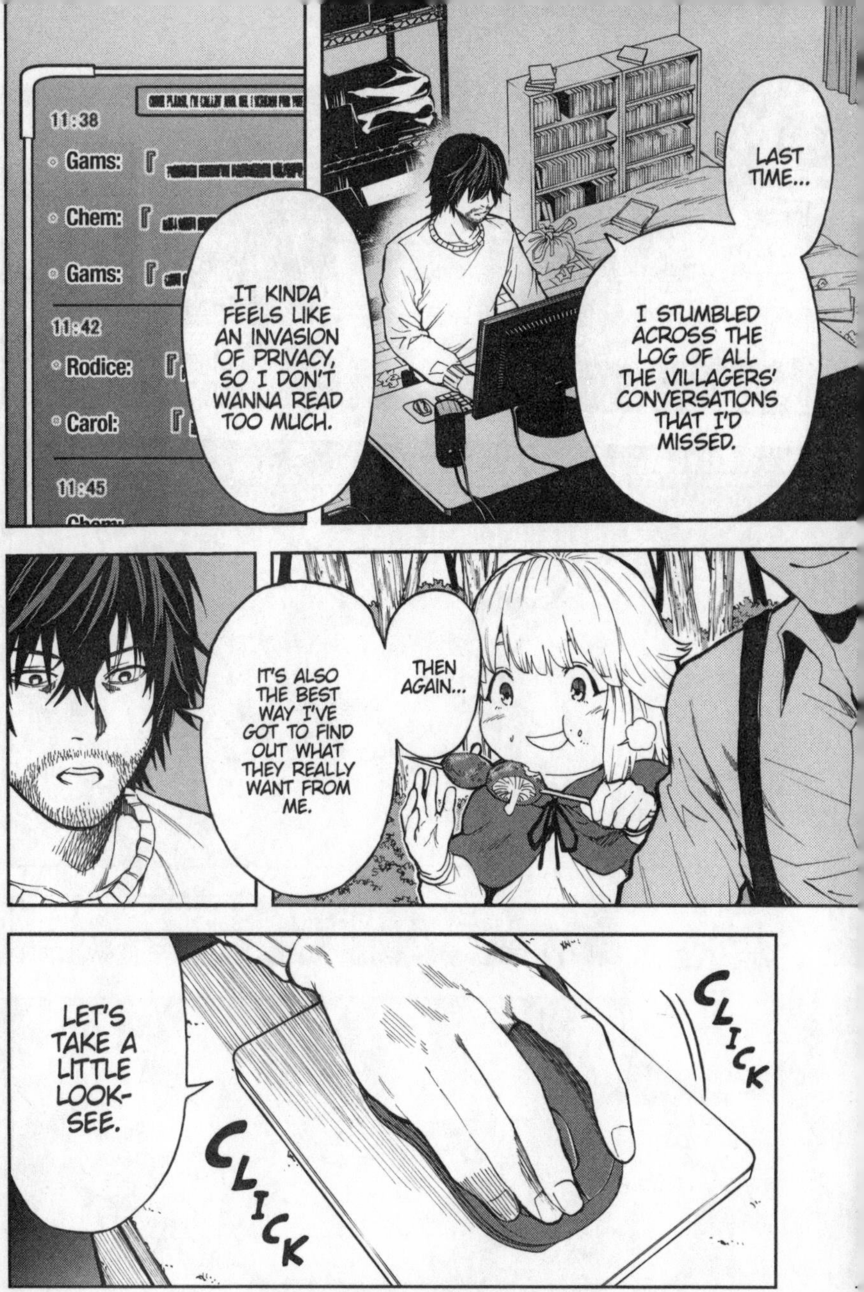
LAST TIME...
I STUMBLED ACROSS THE LOG OF ALL THE VILLAGERS' CONVERSATIONS THAT I'D MISSED.
IT KINDA FEELS LIKE AN INVASION OF PRIVACY, SO I DON'T WANNA READ TOO MUCH.
11:38
Gams:
Chem:
Gams:
11:42
Rodice:
Carol:
11:45
THEN AGAIN...
IT'S ALSO THE BEST WAY I'VE GOT TO FIND OUT WHAT THEY REALLY WANT FROM ME.
CLICK
LET'S TAKE A LITTLE LOOK-SEE.
CLICK

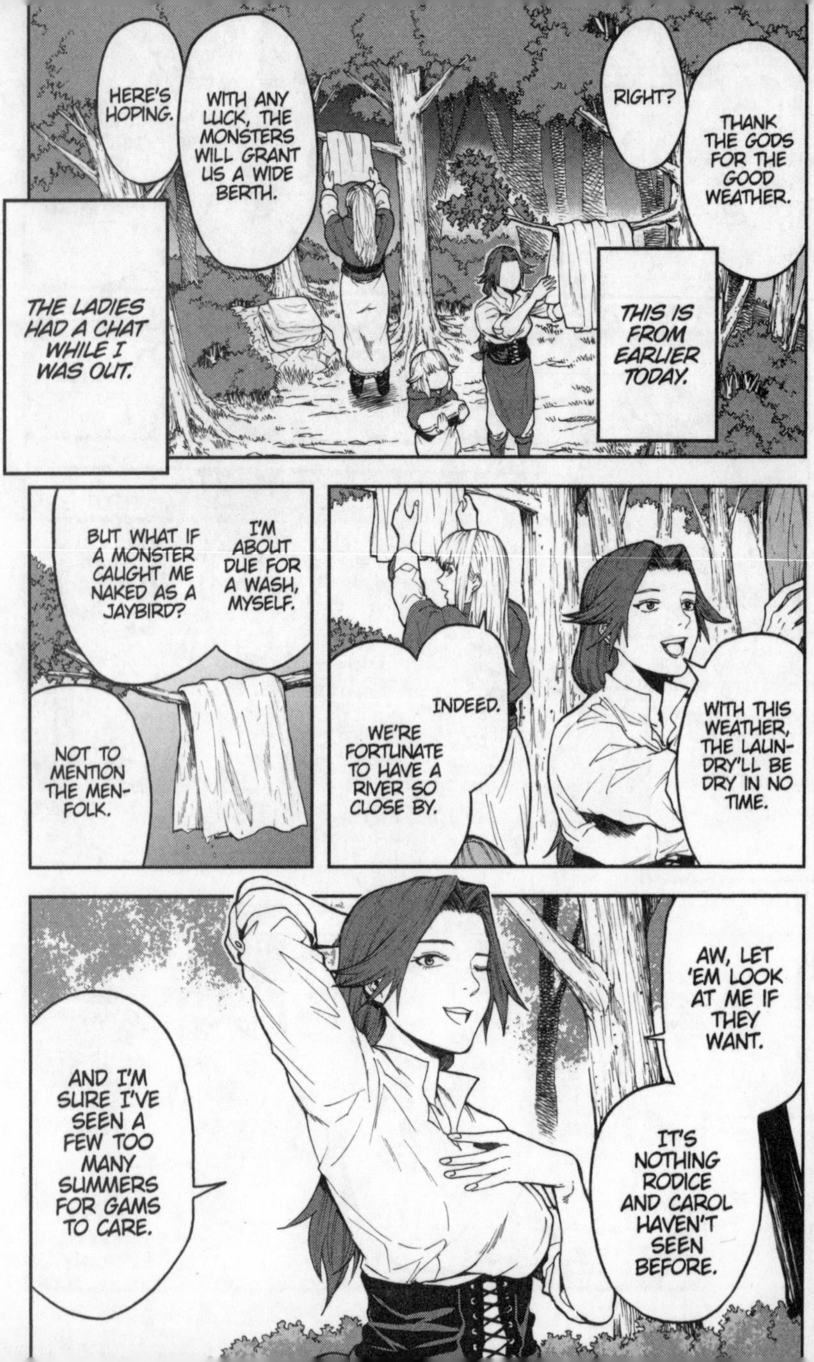
THANK THE GODS FOR THE GOOD WEATHER.
RIGHT?
WITH ANY LUCK, THE MONSTERS WILL GRANT US A WIDE BERTH.
HERE'S HOPING.
THIS IS FROM EARLIER TODAY.
THE LADIES HAD A CHAT WHILE I WAS OUT.
WITH THIS WEATHER, THE LAUNDRY'LL BE DRY IN NO TIME.
INDEED.
WE'RE FORTUNATE TO HAVE A RIVER SO CLOSE BY.
I'M ABOUT DUE FOR A WASH, MYSELF.
BUT WHAT IF A MONSTER CAUGHT ME NAKED AS A JAYBIRD?
NOT TO MENTION THE MENFOLK.
AW, LET 'EM LOOK AT ME IF THEY WANT.
IT'S NOTHING RODICE AND CAROL HAVEN'T SEEN BEFORE.
AND I'M SURE I'VE SEEN A FEW TOO MANY SUMMERS FOR GAMS TO CARE.

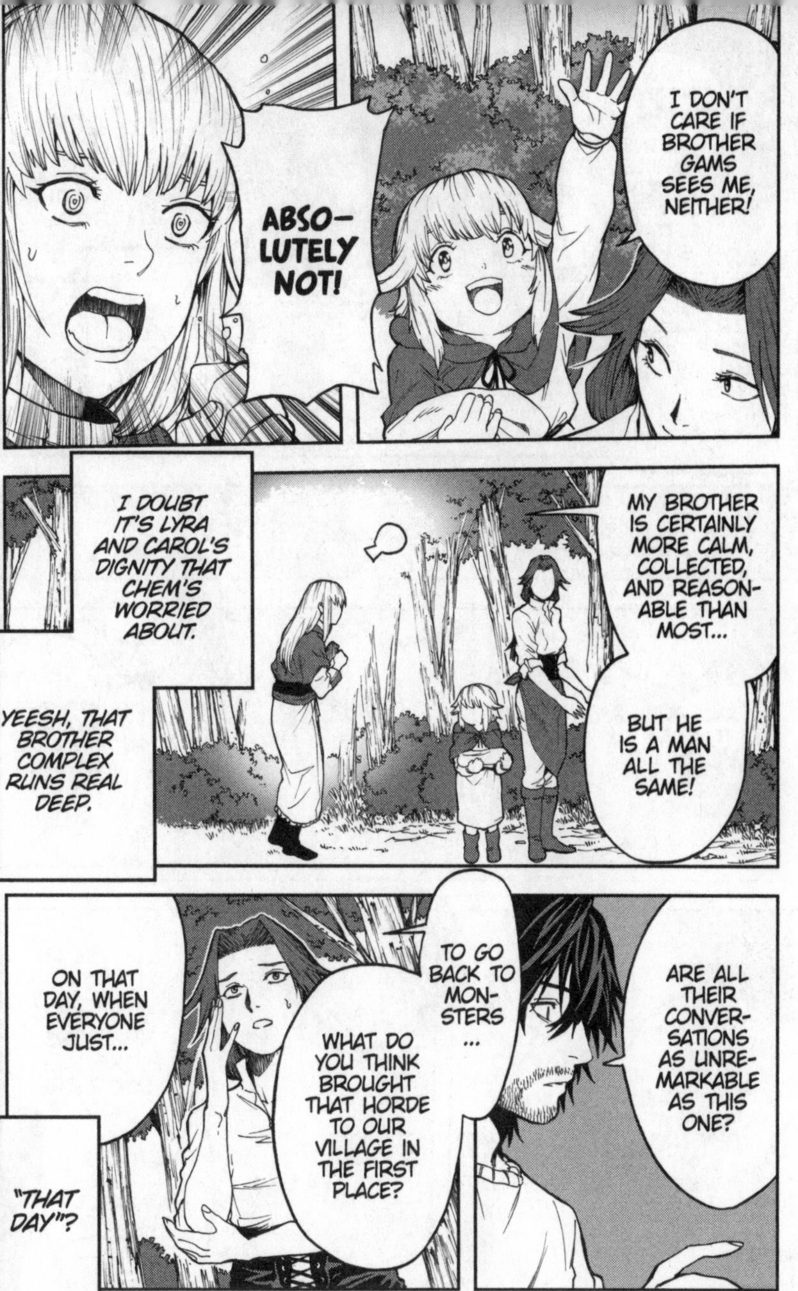
I DON'T CARE IF BROTHER GAMS SEES ME, NEITHER!
ABSO-LUTELY NOT!
MY BROTHER IS CERTAINLY MORE CALM, COLLECTED, AND REASON-ABLE THAN MOST...
BUT HE IS A MAN ALL THE SAME!
I DOUBT IT'S LYRA AND CAROL'S DIGNITY THAT CHEM'S WORRIED ABOUT.
YEESH, THAT BROTHER COMPLEX RUNS REAL DEEP.
ARE ALL THEIR CONVER-SATIONS AS UNRE-MARKABLE AS THIS ONE?
TO GO BACK TO MON-STERS ...
WHAT DO YOU THINK BROUGHT THAT HORDE TO OUR VILLAGE IN THE FIRST PLACE?
ON THAT DAY, WHEN EVERYONE JUST...
"THAT DAY"?

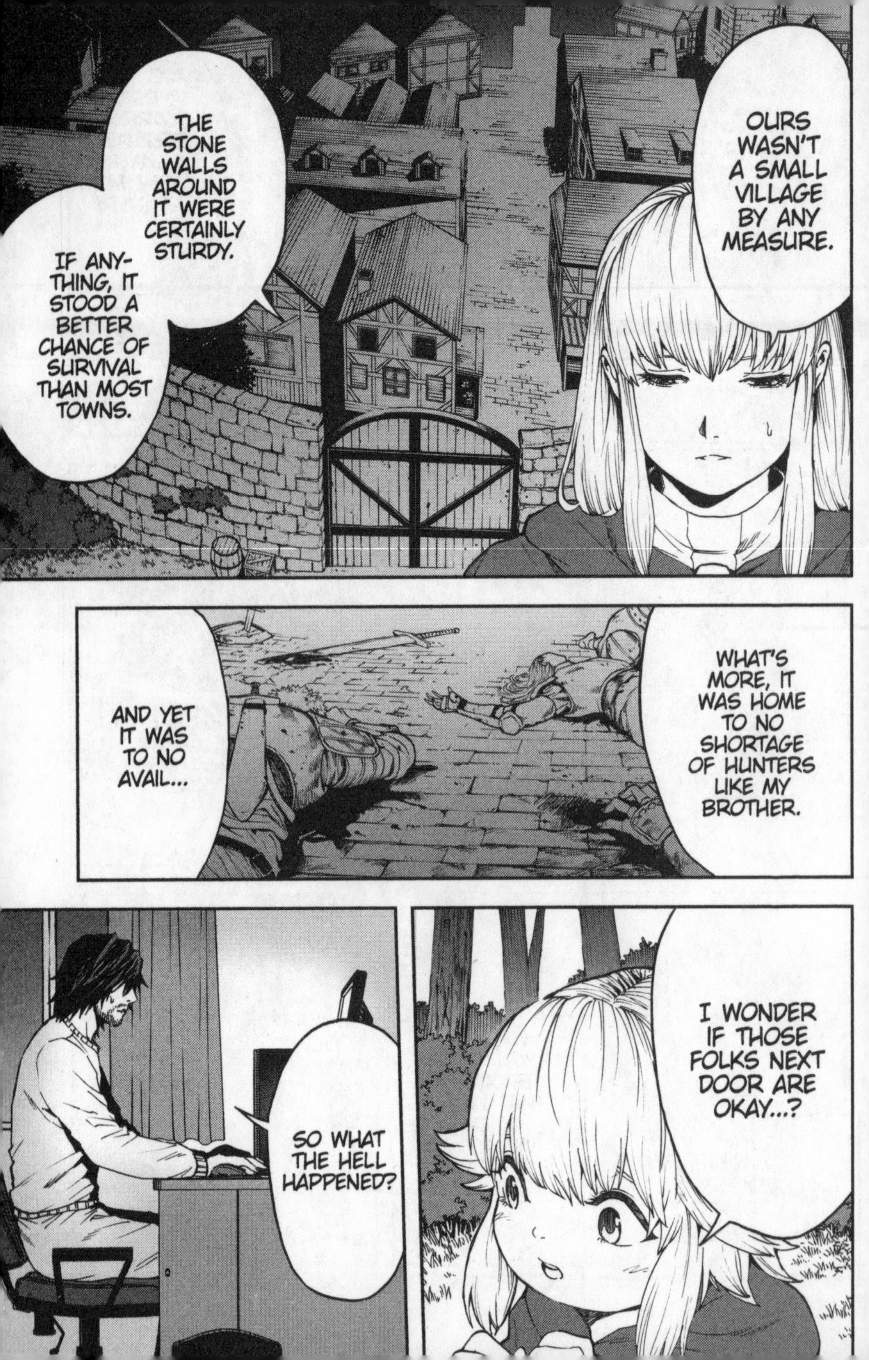

OURS WASN'T A SMALL VILLAGE BY ANY MEASURE.
THE STONE WALLS AROUND IT WERE CERTAINLY STURDY.
IF ANY-THING, IT STOOD A BETTER CHANCE OF SURVIVAL THAN MOST TOWNS.
WHAT'S MORE, IT WAS HOME TO NO SHORTAGE OF HUNTERS LIKE MY BROTHER.
AND YET IT WAS TO NO AVAIL...
I WONDER IF THOSE FOLKS NEXT DOOR ARE OKAY...?
SO WHAT THE HELL HAPPENED?

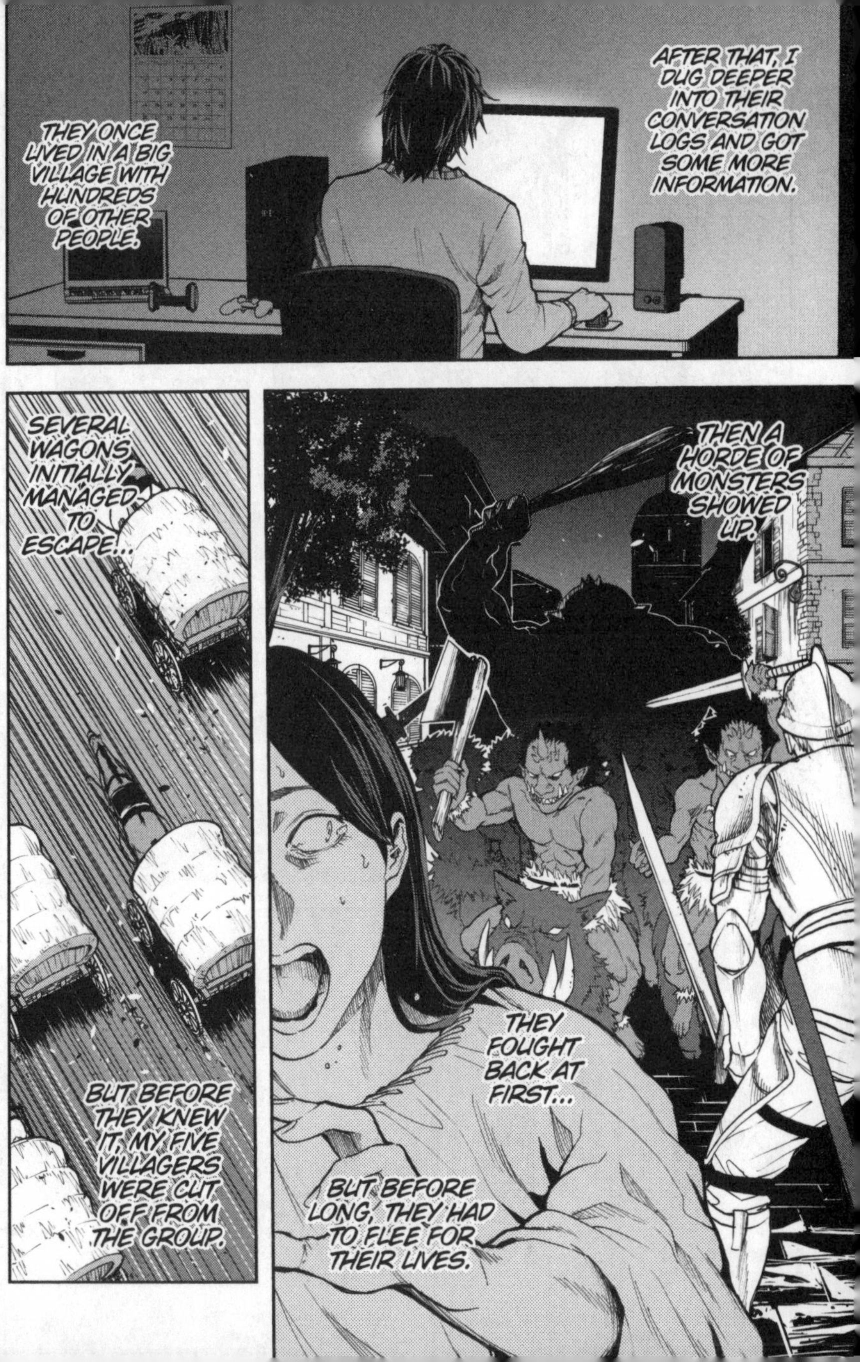
AFTER THAT, I DUG DEEPER INTO THEIR CONVERSATION LOGS AND GOT SOME MORE INFORMATION.
THEY ONCE LIVED IN A BIG VILLAGE WITH HUNDREDS OF OTHER PEOPLE.
THEN A HORDE OF MONSTERS SHOWED UP.
THEY FOUGHT BACK AT FIRST...
BUT BEFORE LONG, THEY HAD TO FLEE FOR THEIR LIVES.
SEVERAL WAGONS INITIALLY MANAGED TO ESCAPE...
BUT BEFORE THEY KNEW IT, MY FIVE VILLAGERS WERE CUT OFF FROM THE GROUP.

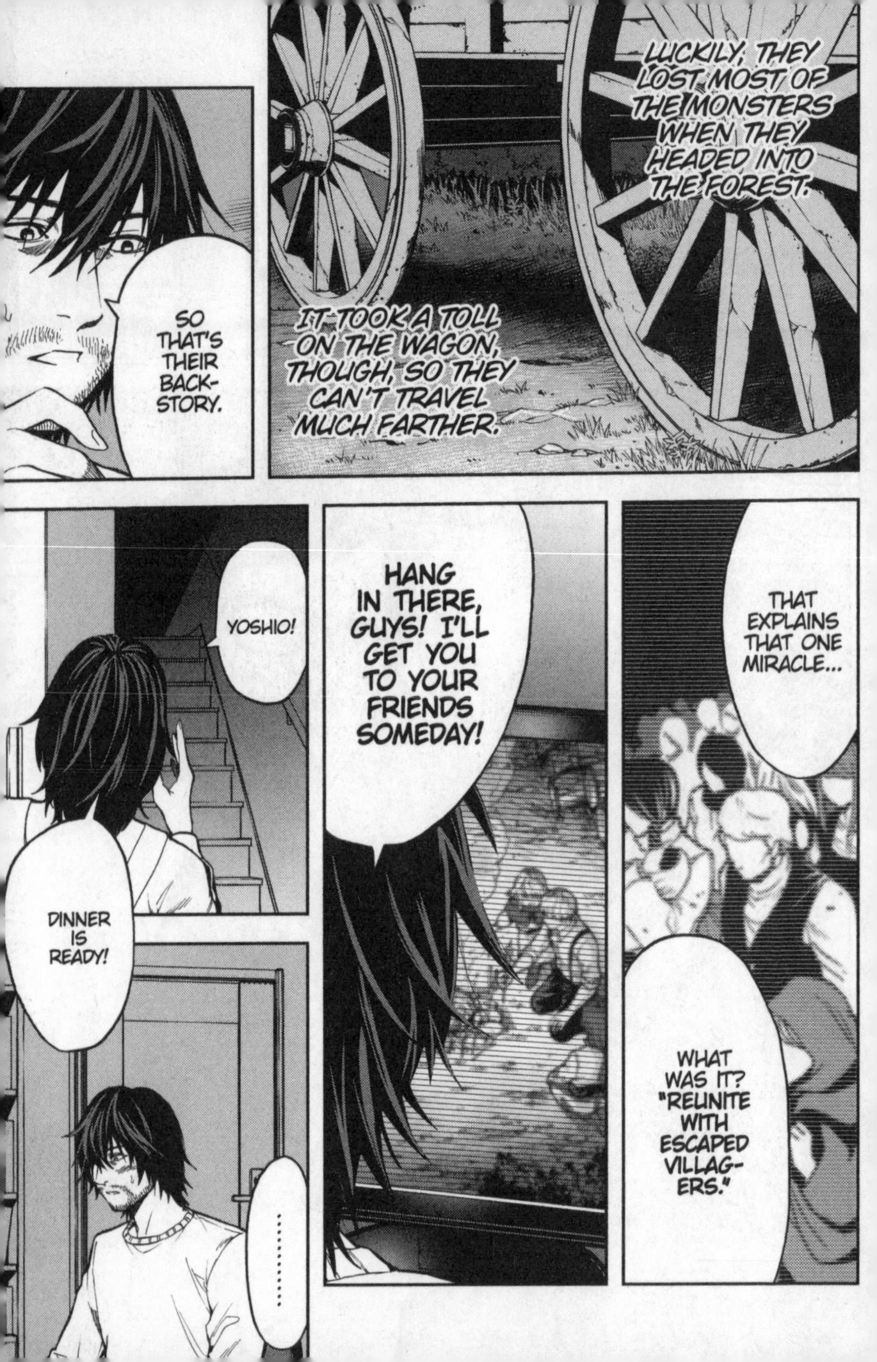
LUCKILY, THEY LOST MOST OF THE MONSTERS WHEN THEY HEADED INTO THE FOREST.
IT TOOK A TOLL ON THE WAGON, THOUGH, SO THEY CAN'T TRAVEL MUCH FARTHER.
SO THAT'S THEIR BACK-STORY.
THAT EXPLAINS THAT ONE MIRACLE...
WHAT WAS IT? "REUNITE WITH ESCAPED VILLAGERS."
HANG IN THERE, GUYS! I'LL GET YOU TO YOUR FRIENDS SOMEDAY!
YOSHIO!
DINNER IS READY!
......

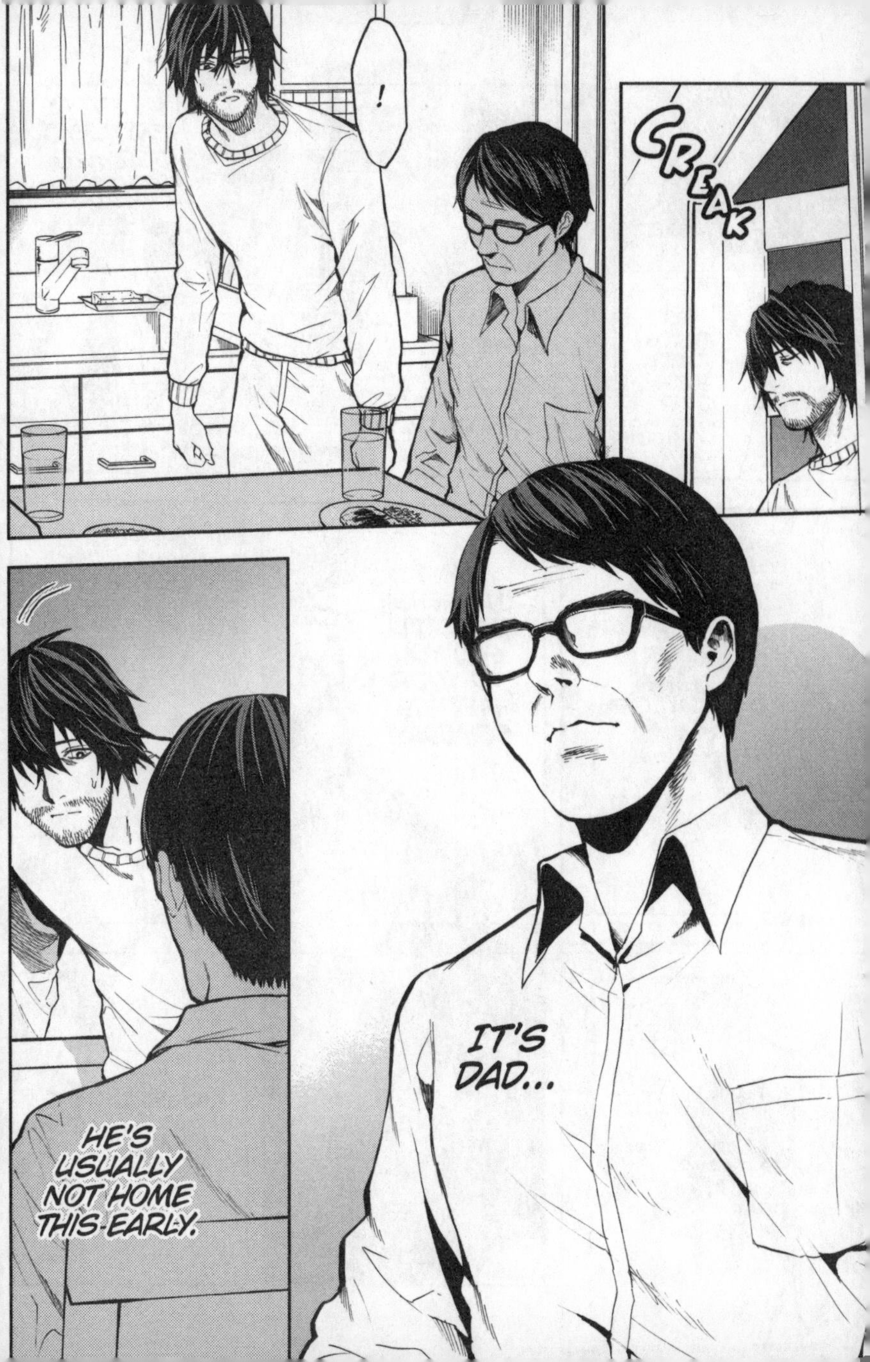
CREAK
!
IT'S DAD...
HE'S USUALLY NOT HOME THIS EARLY.

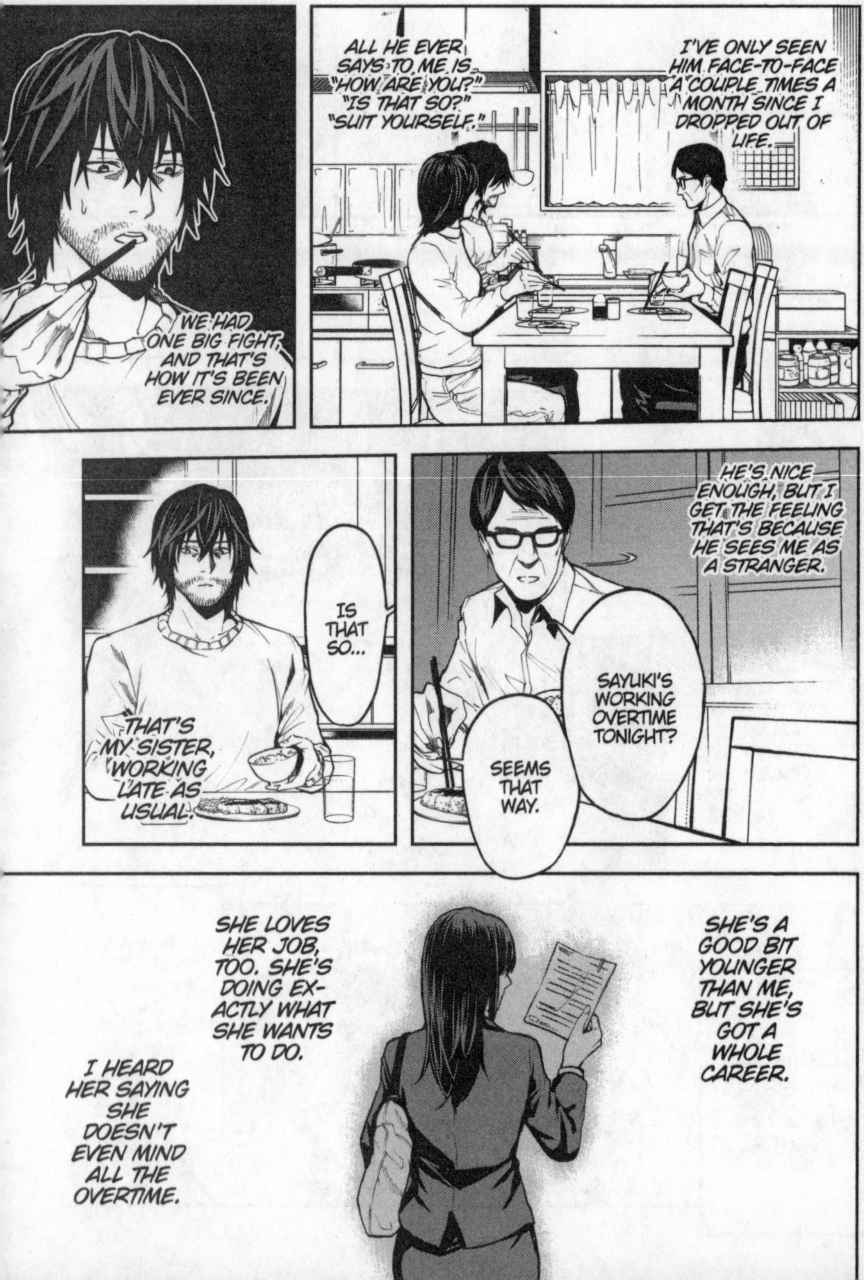
I'VE ONLY SEEN HIM FACE-TO-FACE A COUPLE TIMES A MONTH SINCE I DROPPED OUT OF LIFE.
ALL HE EVER SAYS TO ME IS "HOW ARE YOU?" "IS THAT SO?" "SUIT YOURSELF."
WE HAD ONE BIG FIGHT, AND THAT'S HOW IT'S BEEN EVER SINCE.
HE'S NICE ENOUGH, BUT I GET THE FEELING THAT'S BECAUSE HE SEES ME AS A STRANGER.
SAYUKI'S WORKING OVERTIME TONIGHT?
SEEMS THAT WAY.
IS THAT SO...
THAT'S MY SISTER, WORKING LATE AS USUAL.
SHE'S A GOOD BIT YOUNGER THAN ME, BUT SHE'S GOT A WHOLE CAREER.
SHE LOVES HER JOB, TOO. SHE'S DOING EXACTLY WHAT SHE WANTS TO DO.
I HEARD HER SAYING SHE DOESN'T EVEN MIND ALL THE OVERTIME.

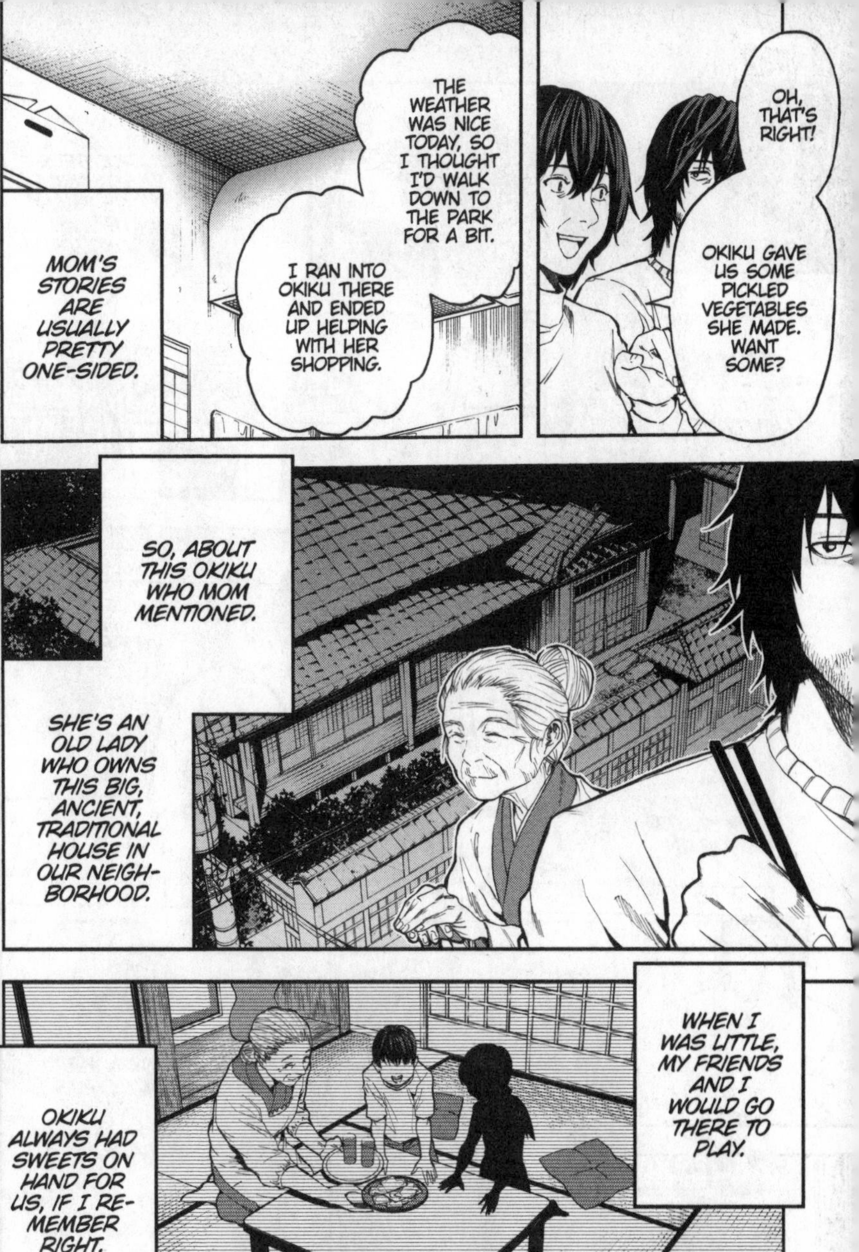
OH, THAT'S RIGHT!
OKIKU GAVE US SOME PICKLED VEGETABLES SHE MADE. WANT SOME?
THE WEATHER WAS NICE TODAY, SO I THOUGHT I'D WALK DOWN TO THE PARK FOR A BIT.
I RAN INTO OKIKU THERE AND ENDED UP HELPING WITH HER SHOPPING.
MOM'S STORIES ARE USUALLY PRETTY ONE-SIDED.
SO, ABOUT THIS OKIKU WHO MOM MENTIONED.
SHE'S AN OLD LADY WHO OWNS THIS BIG, ANCIENT, TRADITIONAL HOUSE IN OUR NEIGH-BORHOOD.
WHEN I WAS LITTLE, MY FRIENDS AND I WOULD GO THERE TO PLAY.
OKIKU ALWAYS HAD SWEETS ON HAND FOR US, IF I RE-MEMBER RIGHT.

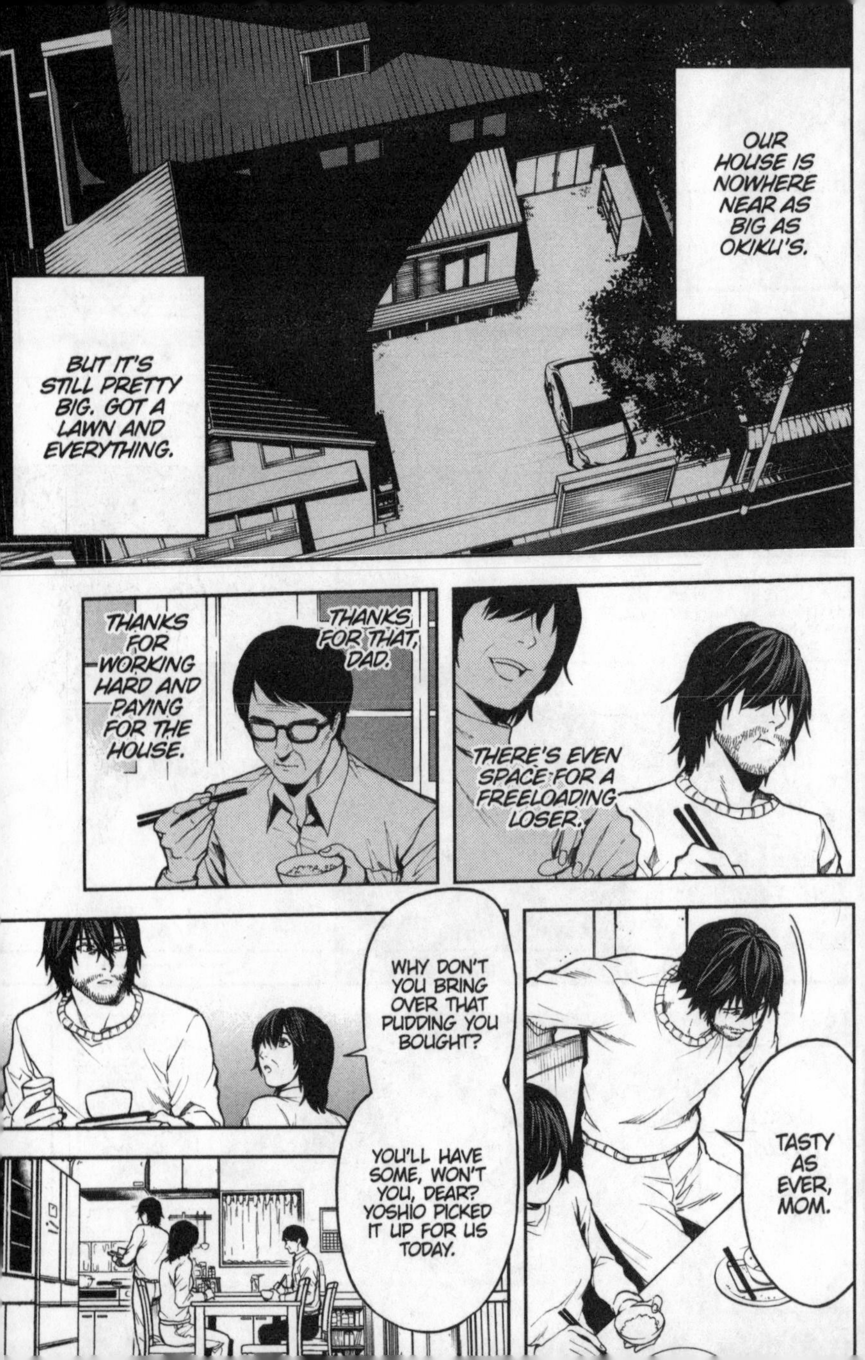
OUR HOUSE IS NOWHERE NEAR AS BIG AS OKIKU'S.
BUT IT'S STILL PRETTY BIG. GOT A LAWN AND EVERYTHING.
THERE'S EVEN SPACE FOR A FREELOADING LOSER.
THANKS FOR WORKING HARD AND PAYING FOR THE HOUSE.
THANKS FOR THAT, DAD.
TASTY AS EVER, MOM.
WHY DON'T YOU BRING OVER THAT PUDDING YOU BOUGHT?
YOU'LL HAVE SOME, WON'T YOU, DEAR? YOSHIO PICKED IT UP FOR US TODAY.

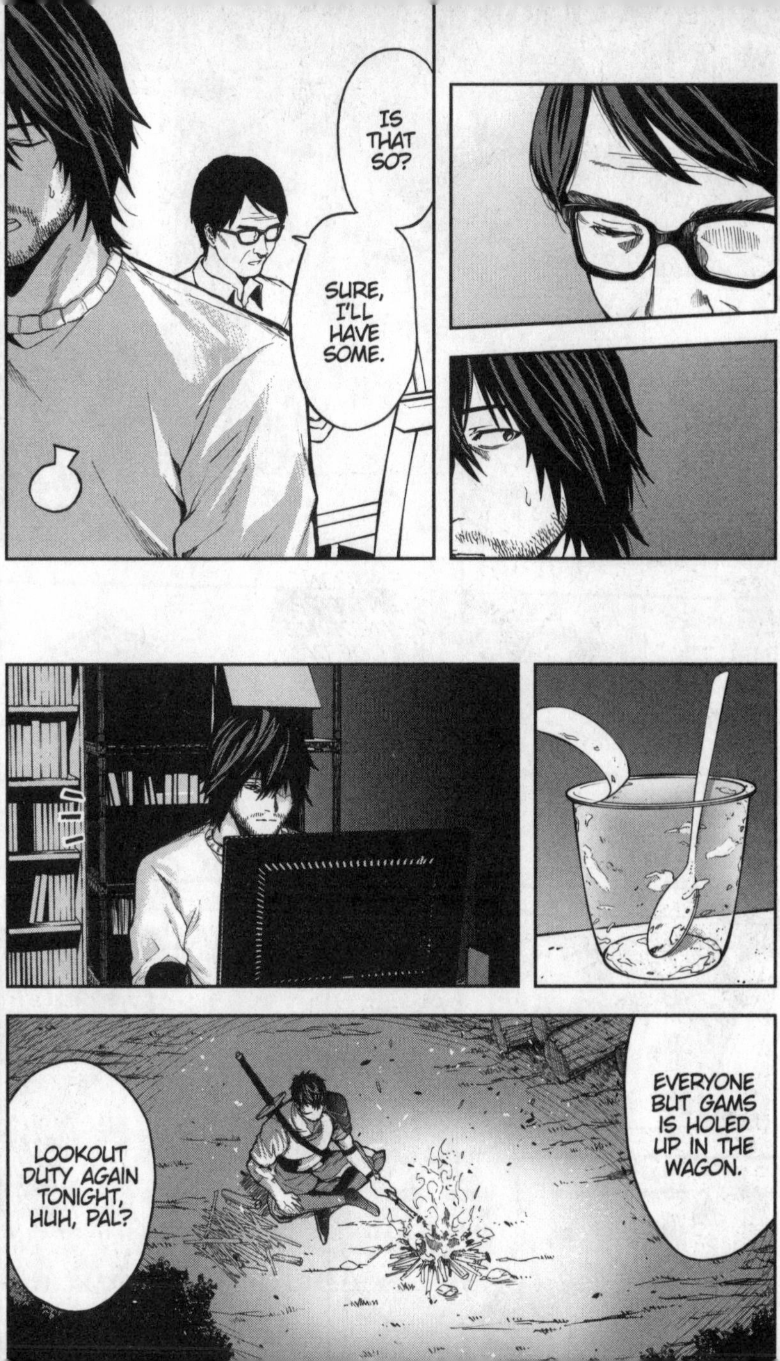
IS THAT SO?
SURE, I'LL HAVE SOME.
EVERYONE BUT GAMS IS HOLED UP IN THE WAGON.
LOOKOUT DUTY AGAIN TONIGHT, HUH, PAL?

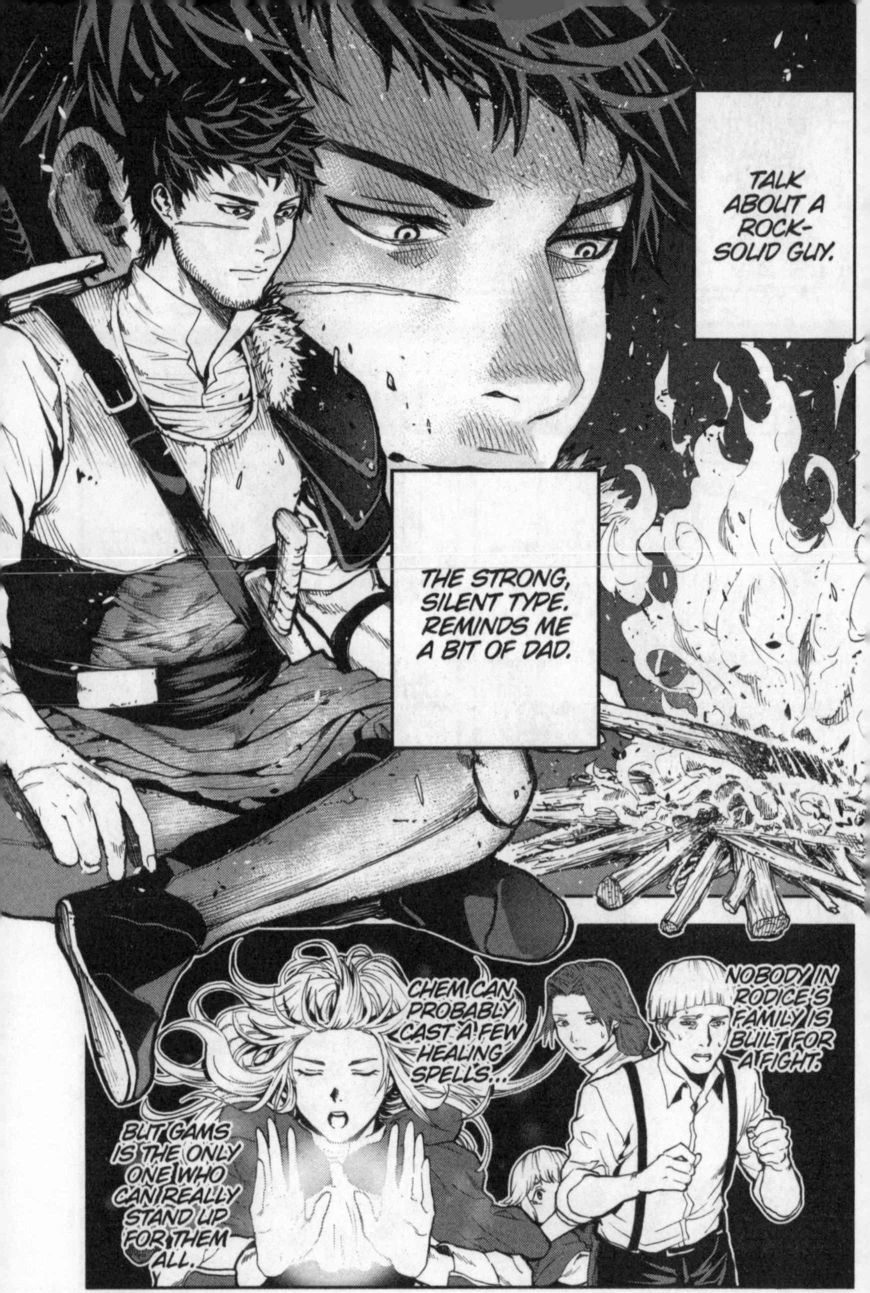
TALK ABOUT A ROCK-SOLID GUY.
THE STRONG, SILENT TYPE. REMINDS ME A BIT OF DAD.
NOBODY IN RODICE'S FAMILY IS BUILT FOR A FIGHT.
CHEM CAN PROBABLY CAST A FEW HEALING SPELLS...
BUT GAMS IS THE ONLY ONE WHO CAN REALLY STAND UP FOR THEM ALL.

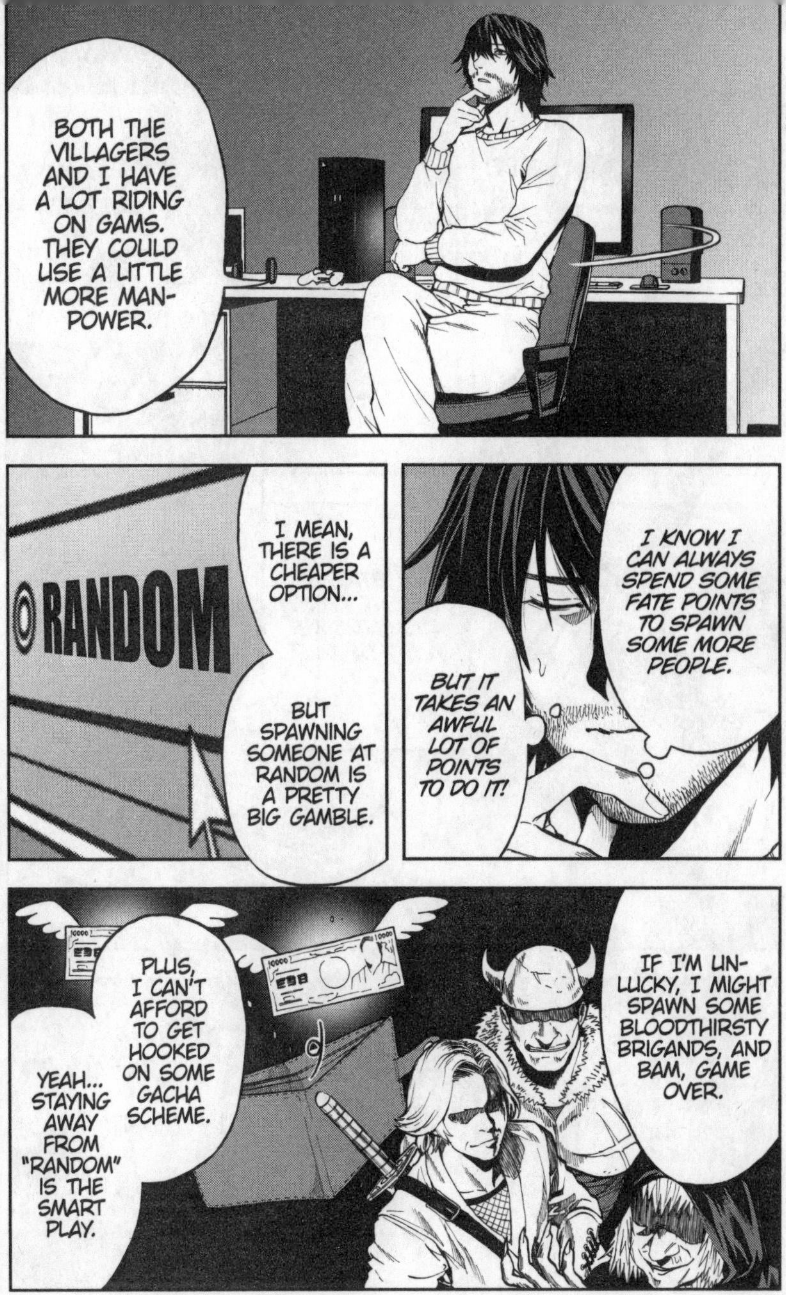
BOTH THE VILLAGERS AND I HAVE A LOT RIDING ON GAMS. THEY COULD USE A LITTLE MORE MAN-POWER.
I KNOW I CAN ALWAYS SPEND SOME FATE POINTS TO SPAWN SOME MORE PEOPLE.
BUT IT TAKES AN AWFUL LOT OF POINTS TO DO IT!
I MEAN, THERE IS A CHEAPER OPTION...
RANDOM
BUT SPAWNING SOMEONE AT RANDOM IS A PRETTY BIG GAMBLE.
IF I'M UN-LUCKY, I MIGHT SPAWN SOME BLOODTHIRSTY BRIGANDS, AND BAM, GAME OVER.
PLUS, I CAN'T AFFORD TO GET HOOKED ON SOME GACHA SCHEME.
YEAH... STAYING AWAY FROM "RANDOM" IS THE SMART PLAY.

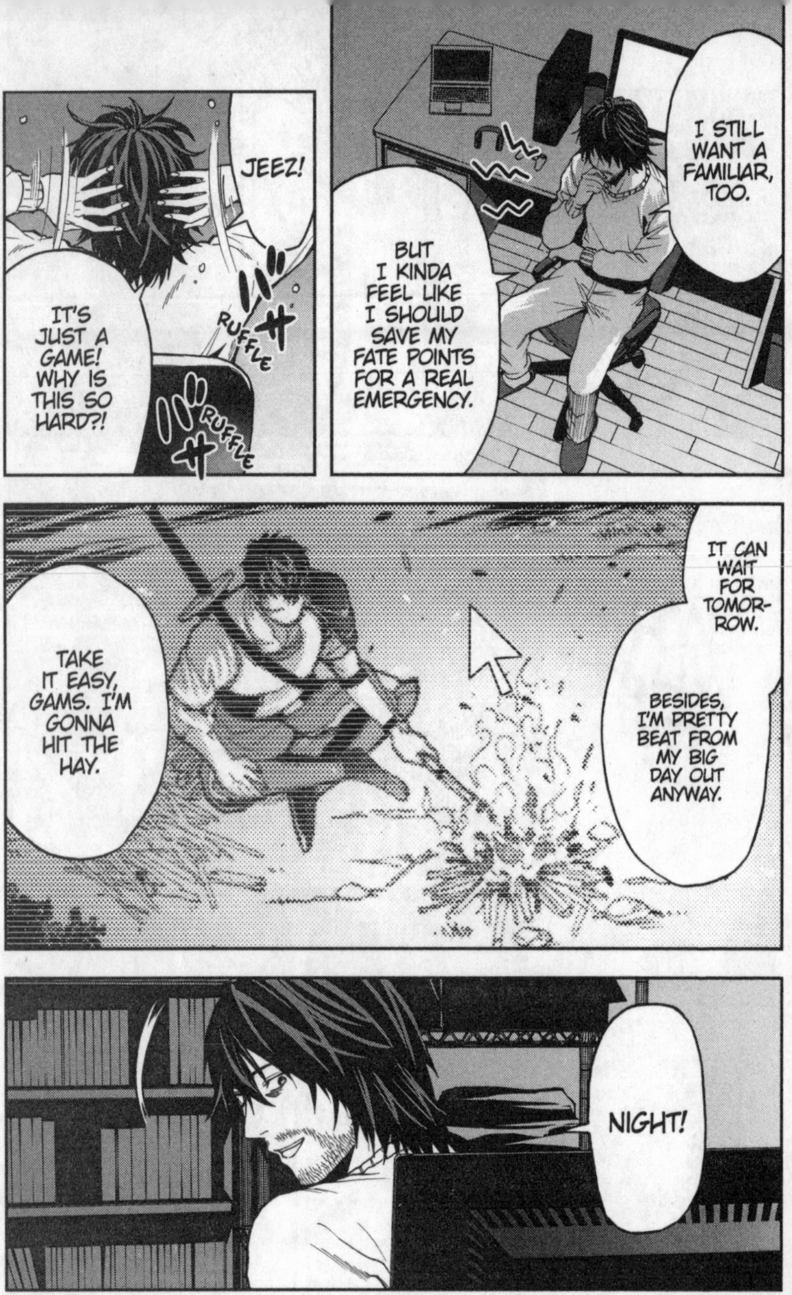
I STILL WANT A FAMILIAR, TOO.
BUT I KINDA FEEL LIKE I SHOULD SAVE MY FATE POINTS FOR A REAL EMERGENCY.
JEEZ!
IT'S JUST A GAME! WHY IS THIS SO HARD?!
RUFFLE
RUFFLE
IT CAN WAIT FOR TOMOR-ROW.
BESIDES, I'M PRETTY BEAT FROM MY BIG DAY OUT ANYWAY.
TAKE IT EASY, GAMS. I'M GONNA HIT THE HAY.
NIGHT!

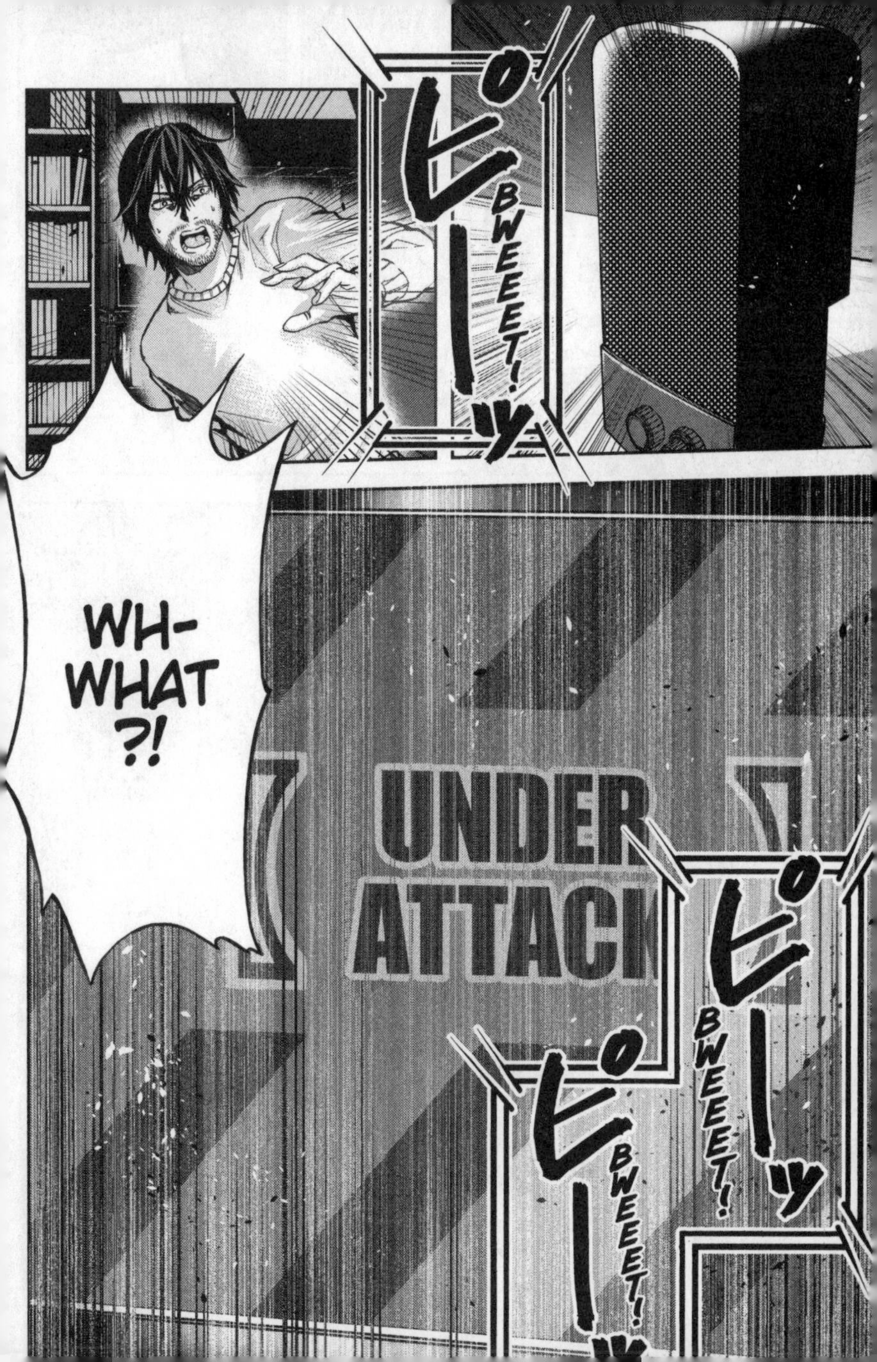
ピーッ
BWEEET!
WH-WHAT?!
UNDER
ATTAC
ピーッ
BWEEET!
ピー
BWEEET!

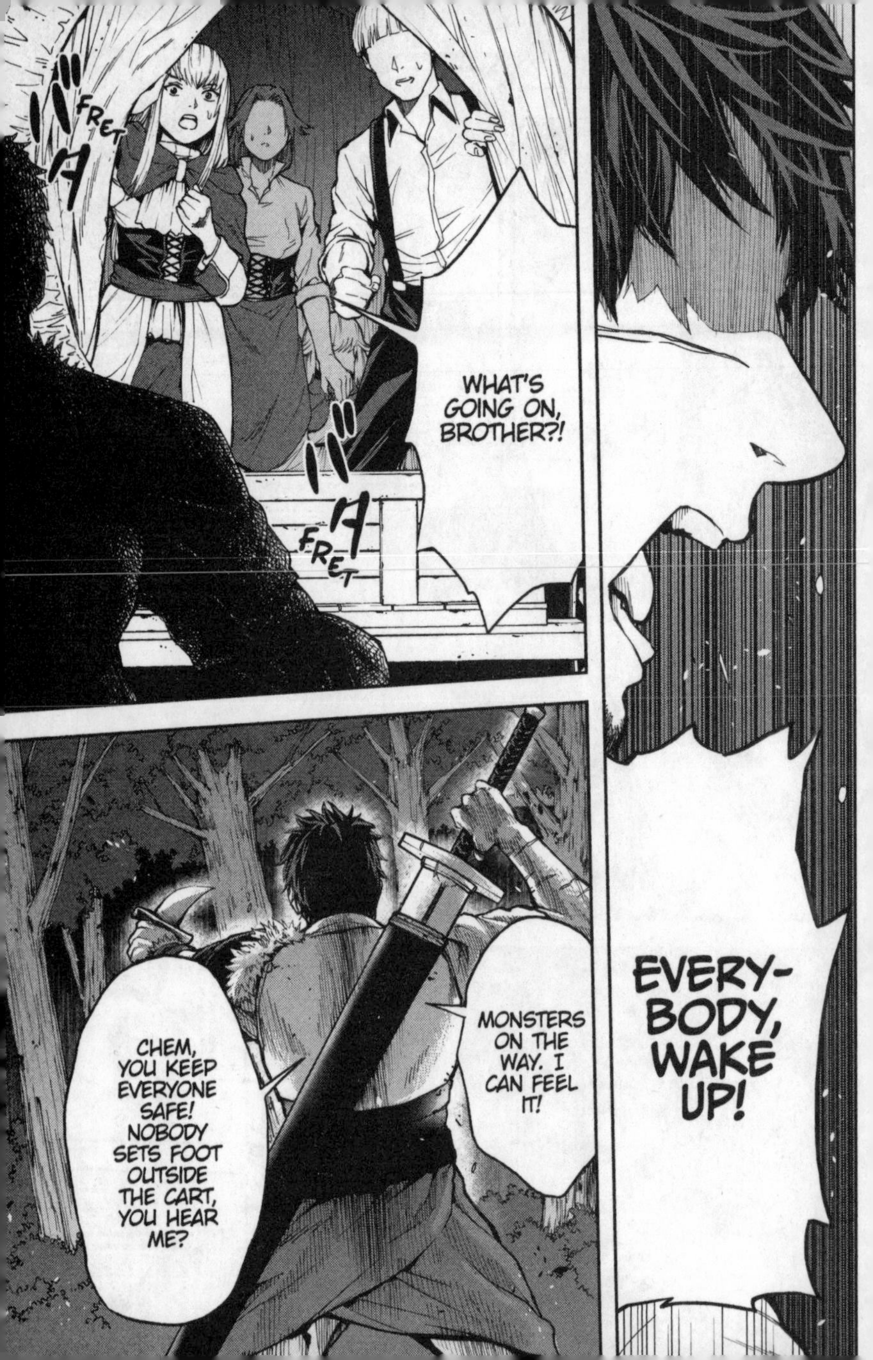
EVERY-BODY, WAKE UP!
FRET
FRET
WHAT'S GOING ON, BROTHER?!
MONSTERS ON THE WAY. I CAN FEEL IT!
CHEM, YOU KEEP EVERYONE SAFE! NOBODY SETS FOOT OUTSIDE THE CART, YOU HEAR ME?

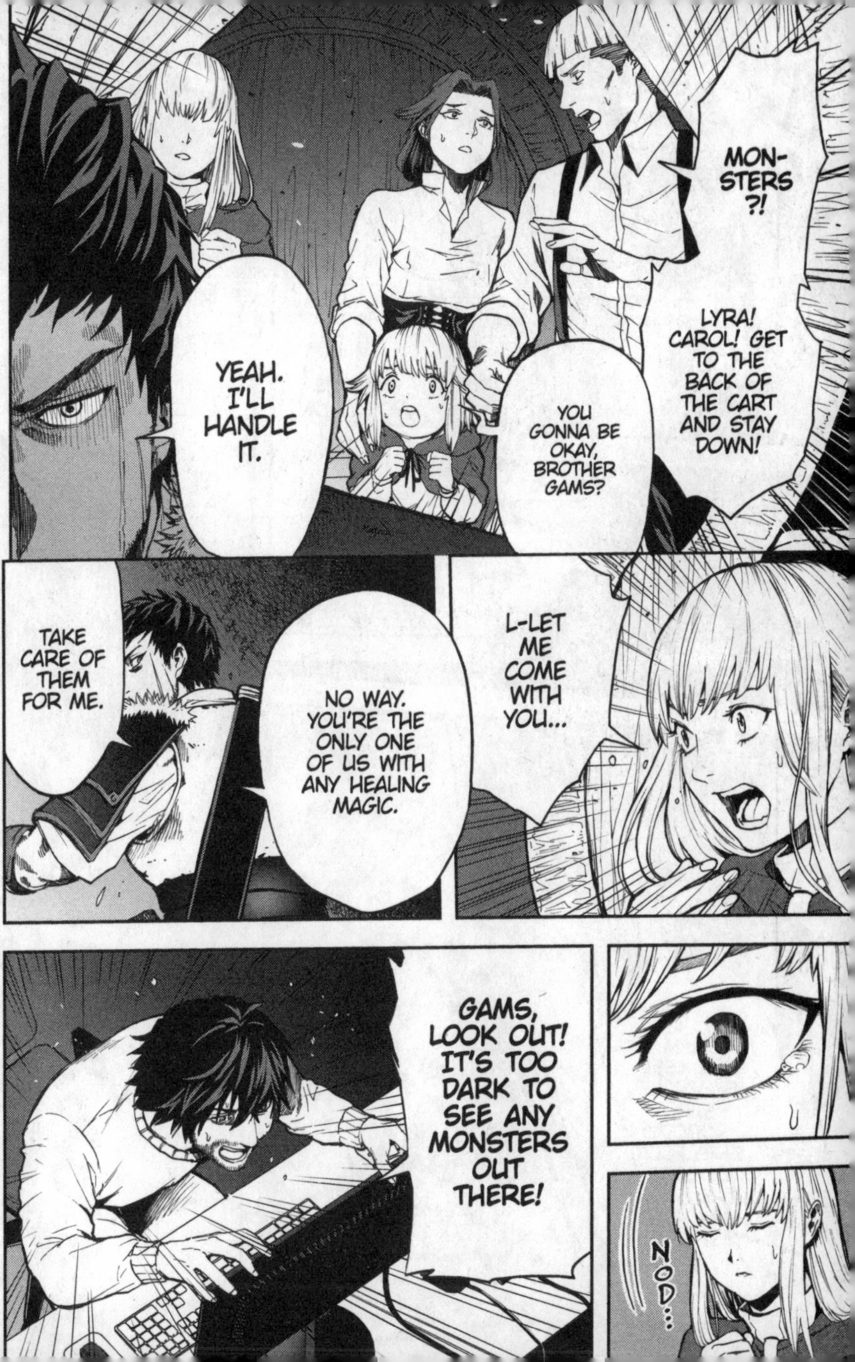
MON-STERS?!
LYRA! CAROL! GET TO THE BACK OF THE CART AND STAY DOWN!
YOU GONNA BE OKAY, BROTHER GAMS?
YEAH. I'LL HANDLE IT.
L-LET ME COME WITH YOU...
NO WAY. YOU'RE THE ONLY ONE OF US WITH ANY HEALING MAGIC.
TAKE CARE OF THEM FOR ME.
GAMS, LOOK OUT! IT'S TOO DARK TO SEE ANY MONSTERS OUT THERE!
NOD...

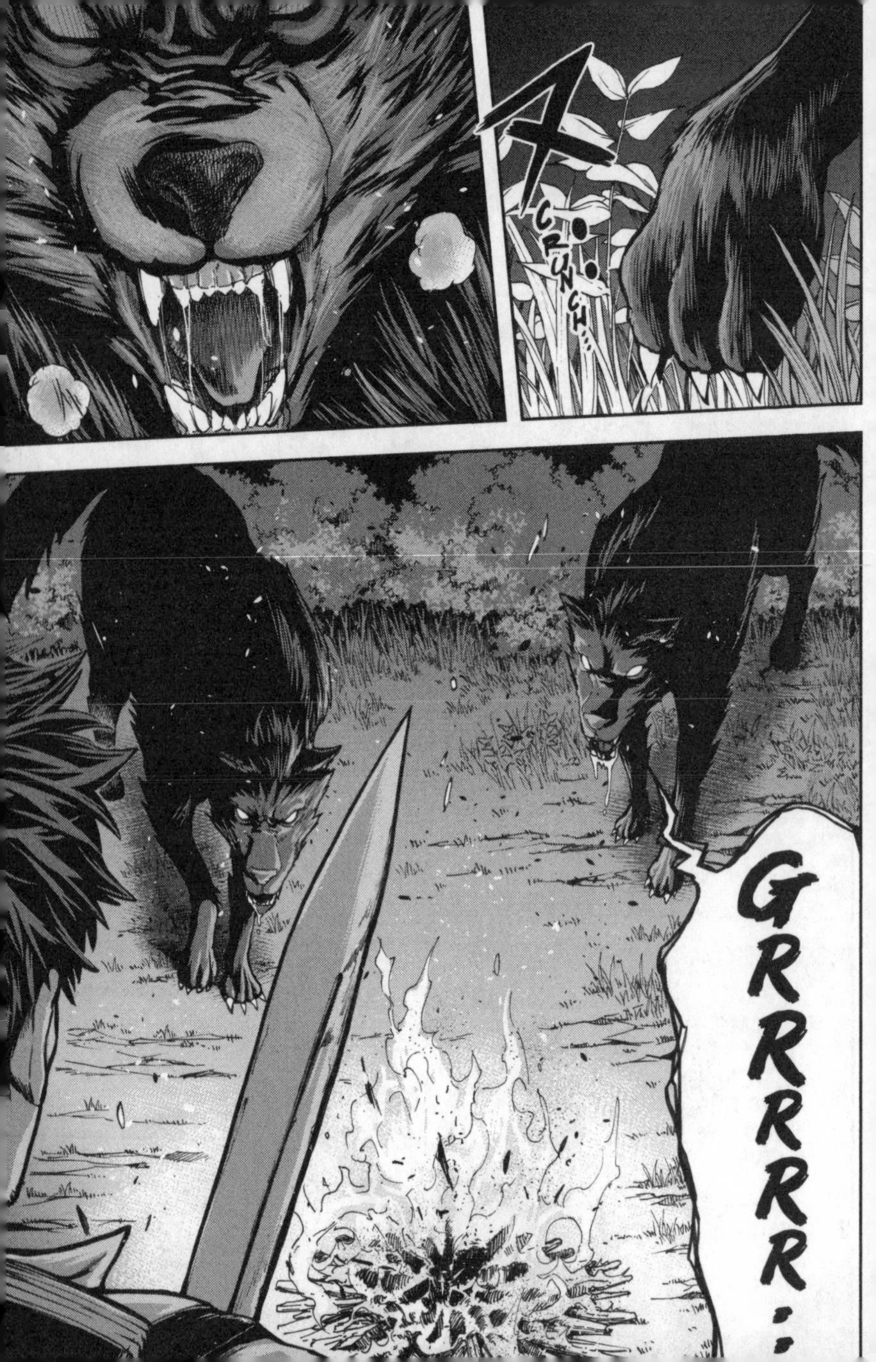
CRUNCH...
GRRRR...

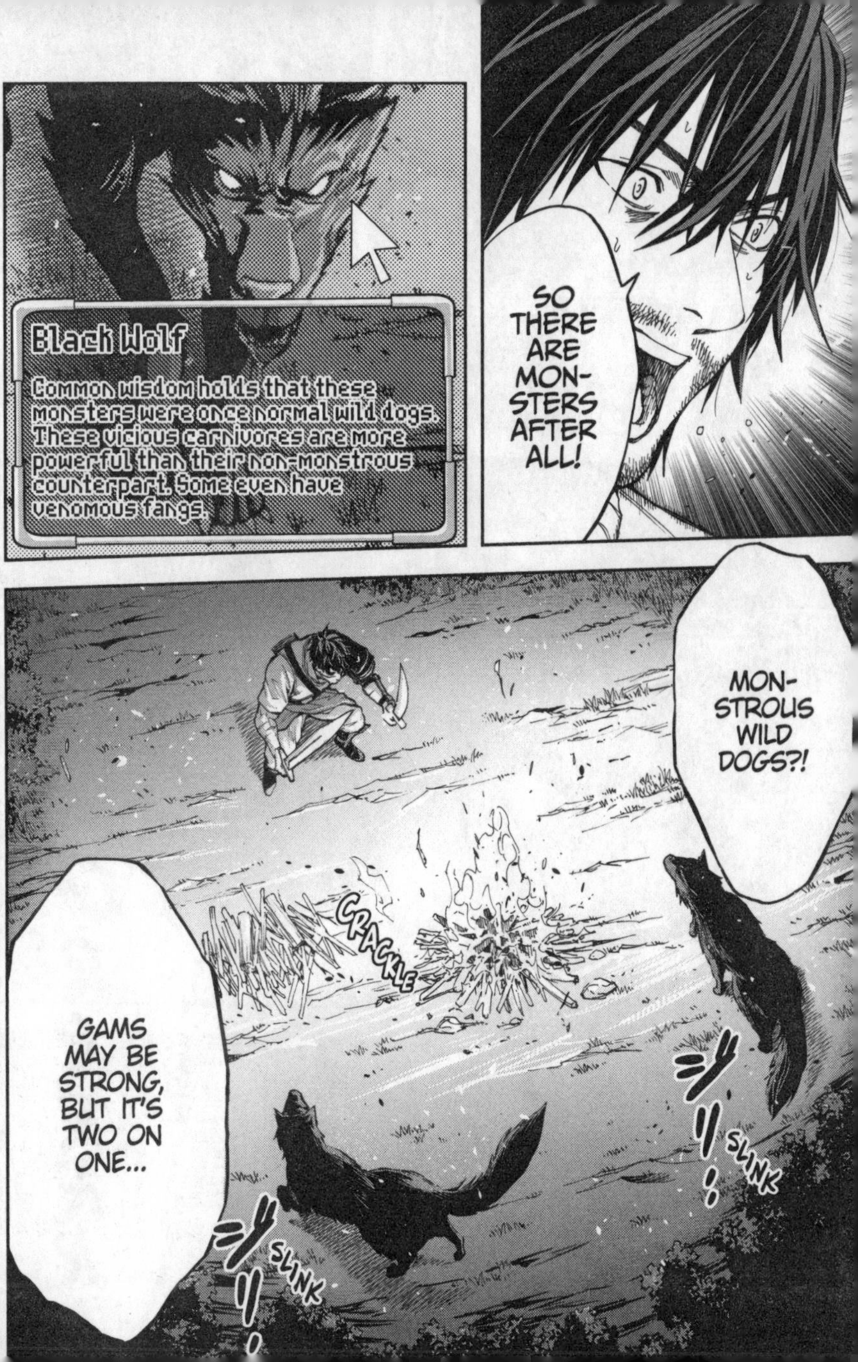
SO THERE ARE MON-STERS AFTER ALL!
Black Wolf
Common wisdom holds that these monsters were once normal wild dogs. These vicious carnivores are more powerful than their non-monstrous counterpart. Some even have venomous fangs.
MON-STROUS WILD DOGS?!
CRACKLE
GAMS MAY BE STRONG, BUT IT'S TWO ON ONE...
SLINK
SLINK

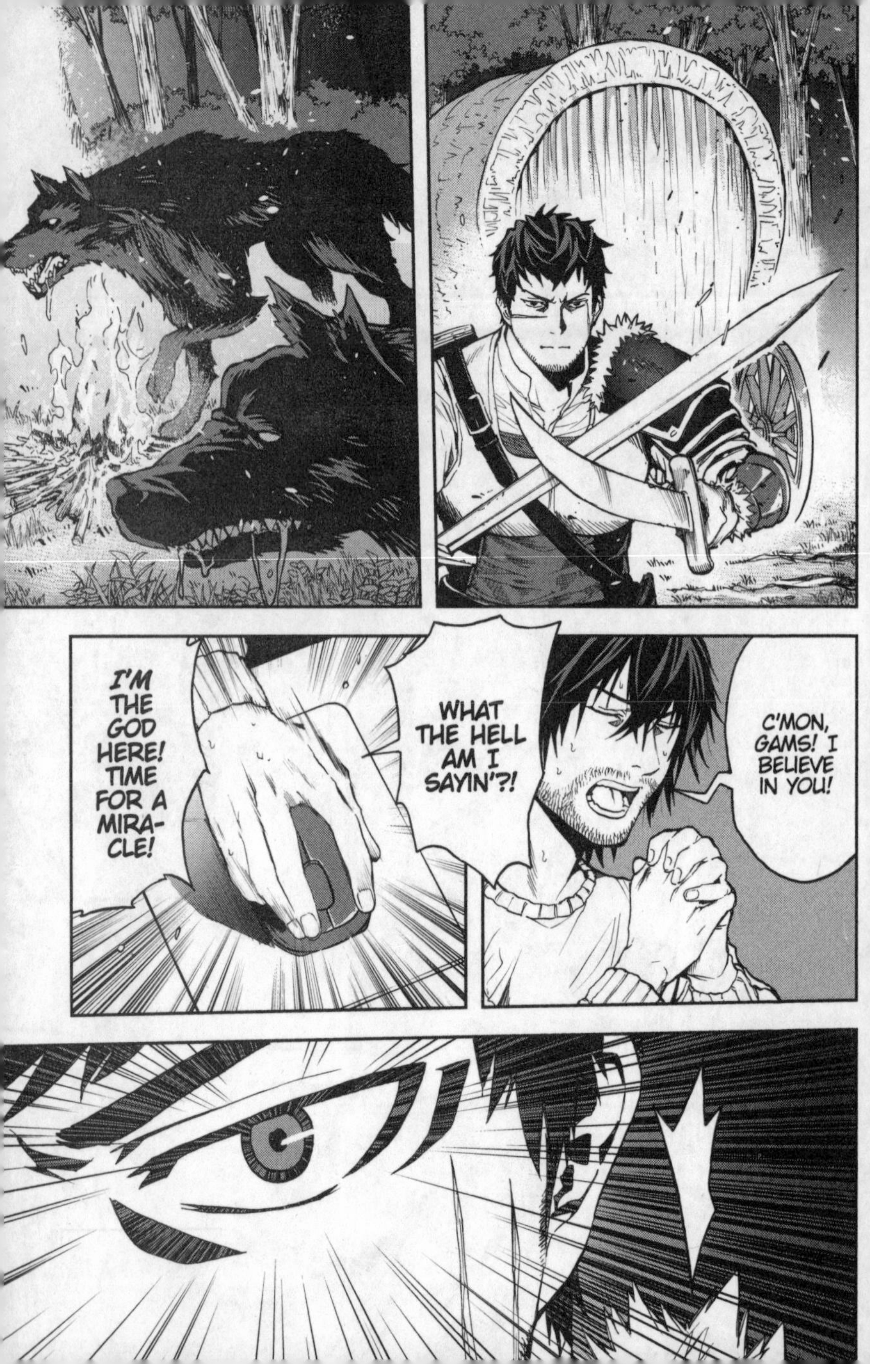
C'MON, GAMS! I BELIEVE IN YOU!
WHAT THE HELL AM I SAYIN'?!
I'M THE GOD HERE! TIME FOR A MIRA-CLE!

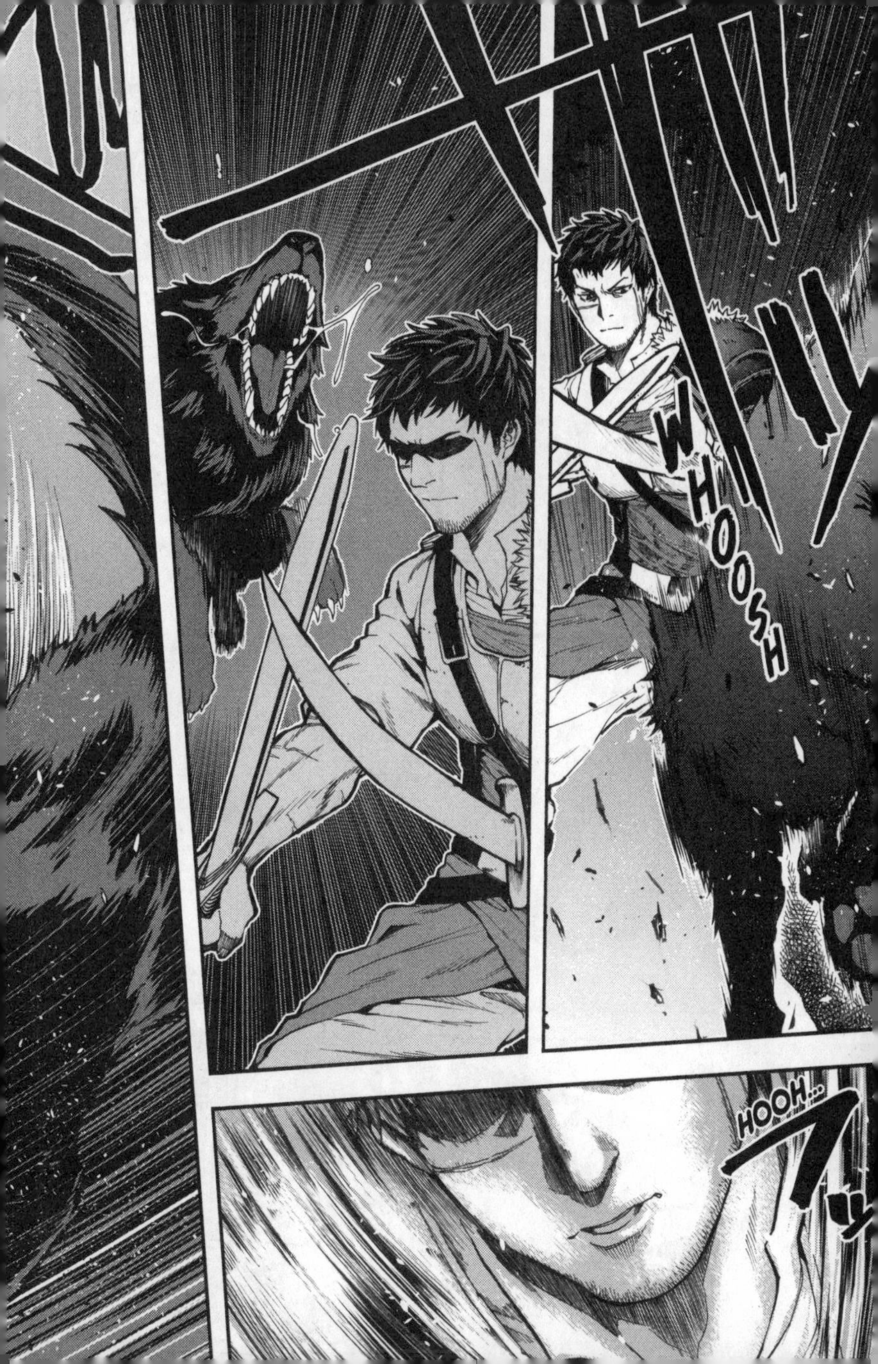
WHOOSH
HOOH...

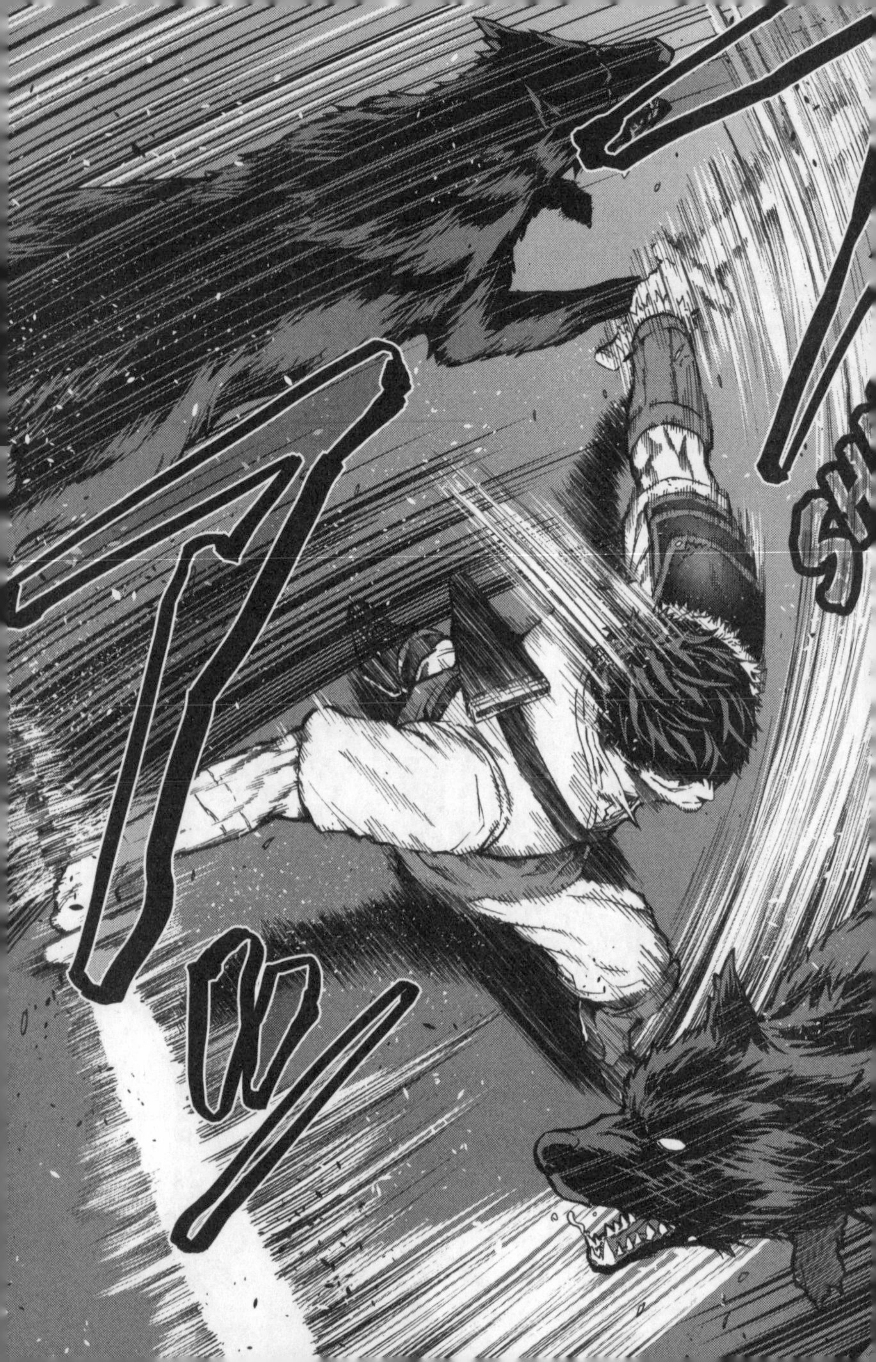

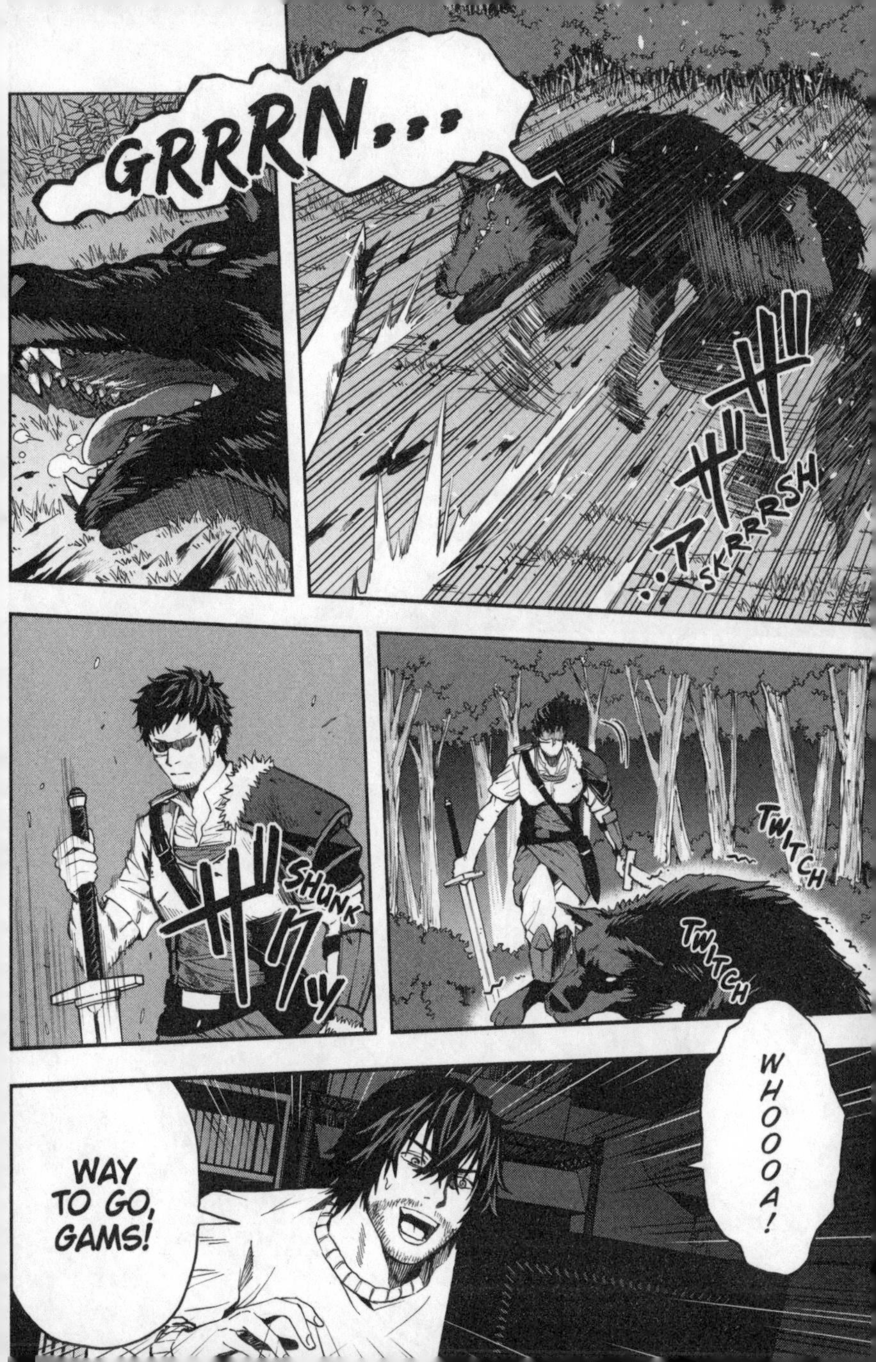
GRRRN...
SKRRRSH
TWITCH
TWITCH
SHUNK
WHOOOOA!
WAY TO GO, GAMS!

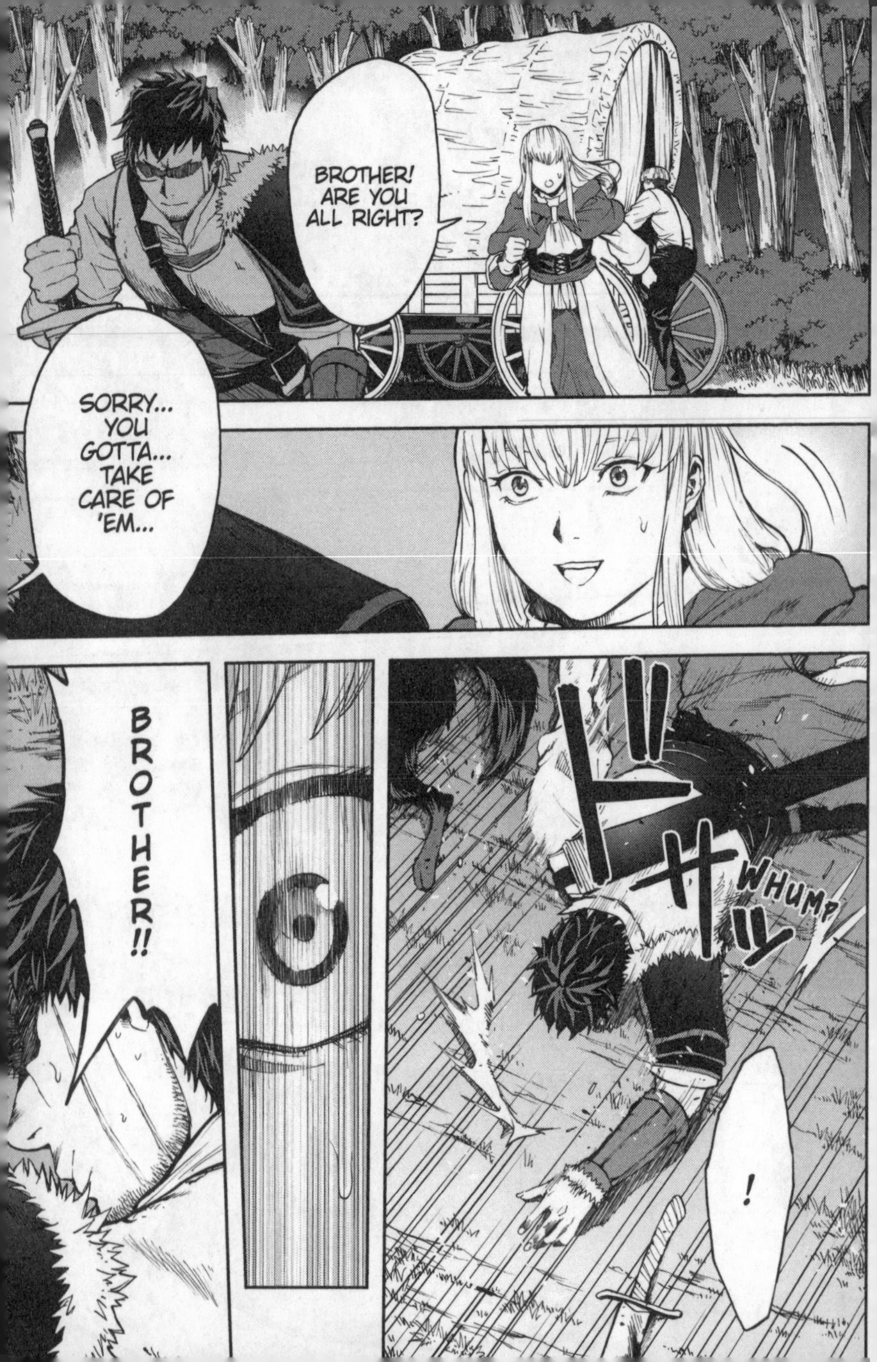
BROTHER! ARE YOU ALL RIGHT?
SORRY... YOU GOTTA... TAKE CARE OF 'EM...
!
WHUMP
BROTHER!!

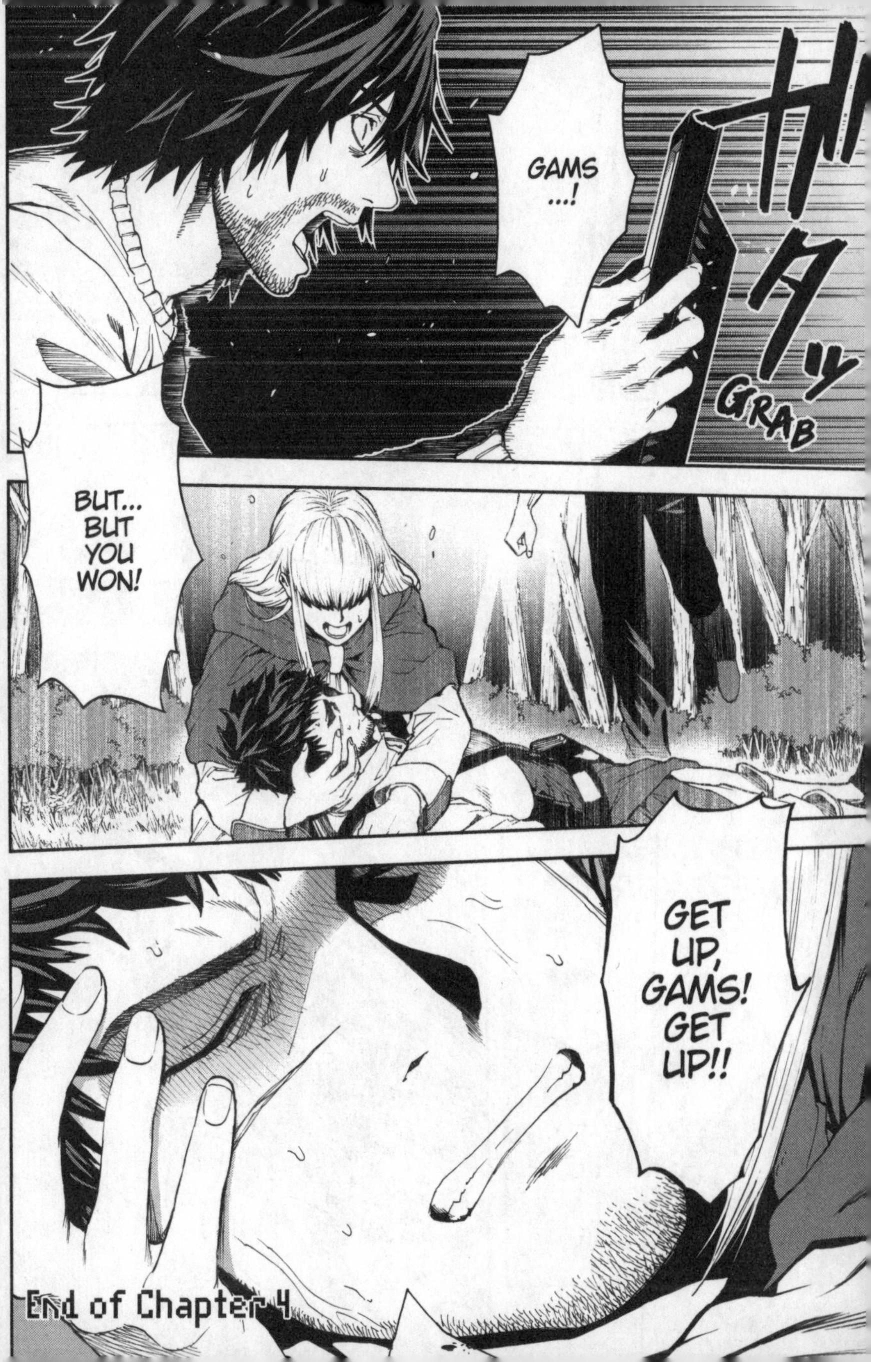
GAMS ...!
ガクッ
GRAB
BUT... BUT YOU WON!
GET UP, GAMS! GET UP!!
End of Chapter 4

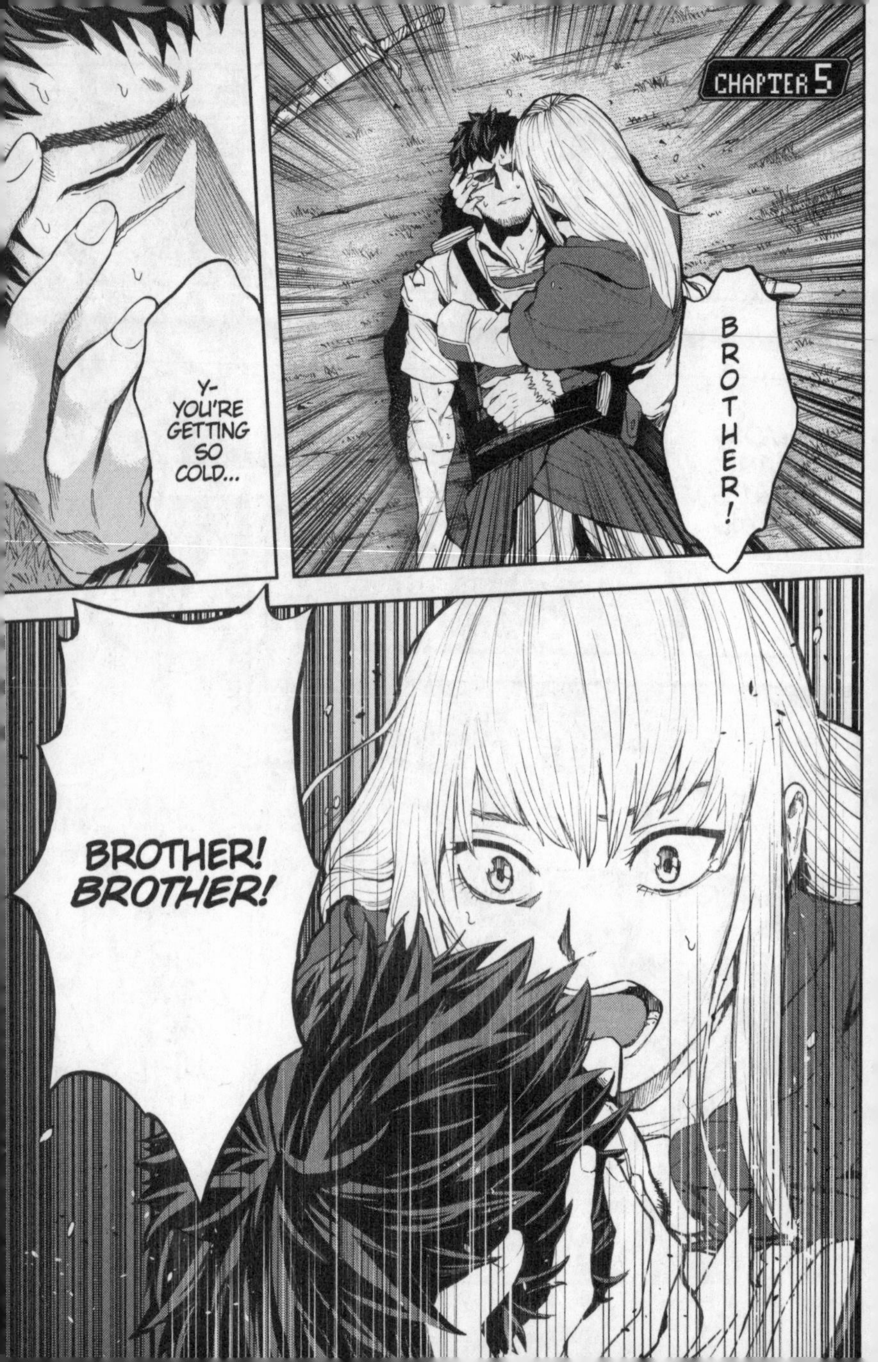
CHAPTER 5
BROTHER!
Y- YOU'RE GETTING SO COLD...
BROTHER! BROTHER!

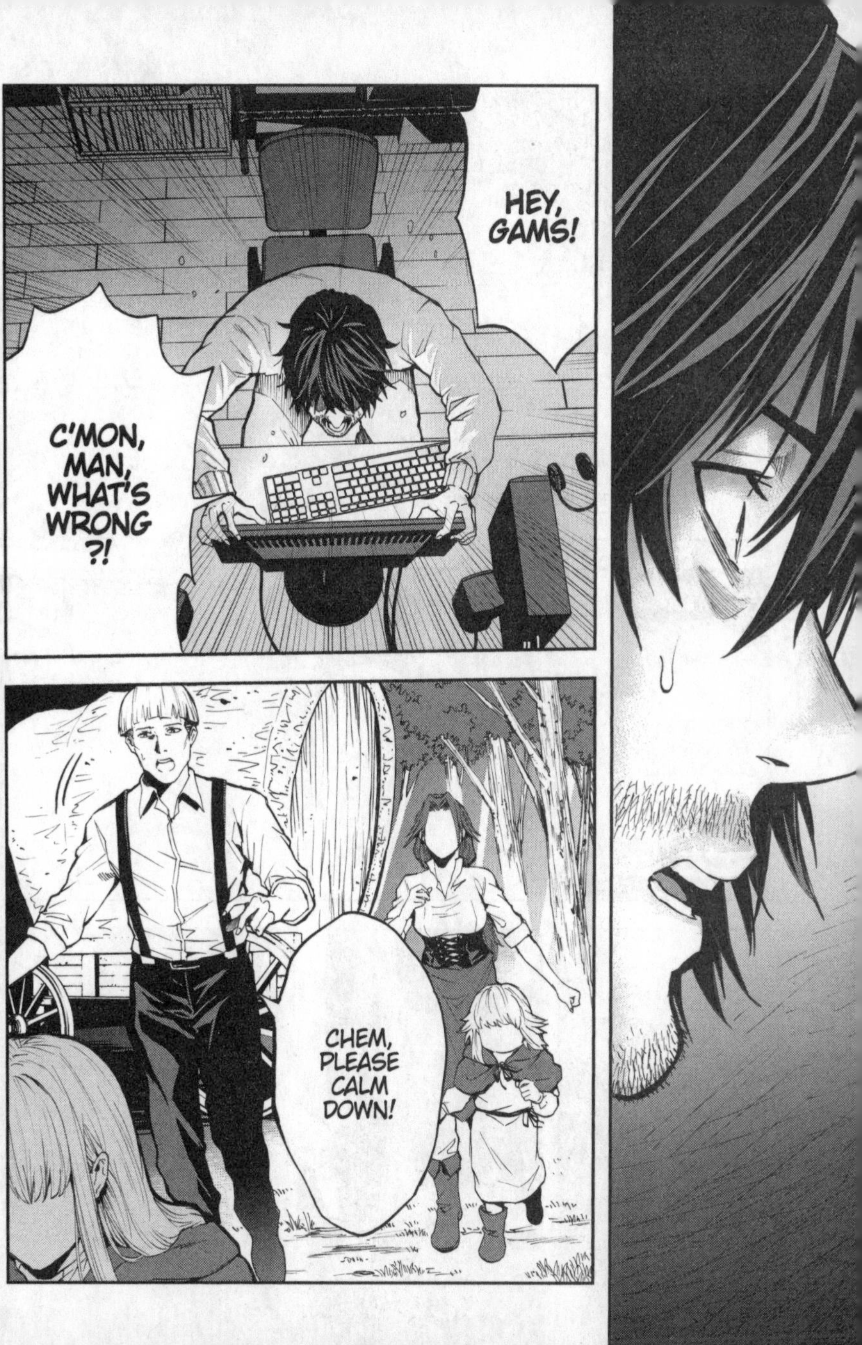
HEY, GAMS!
C'MON, MAN, WHAT'S WRONG?!
CHEM, PLEASE CALM DOWN!

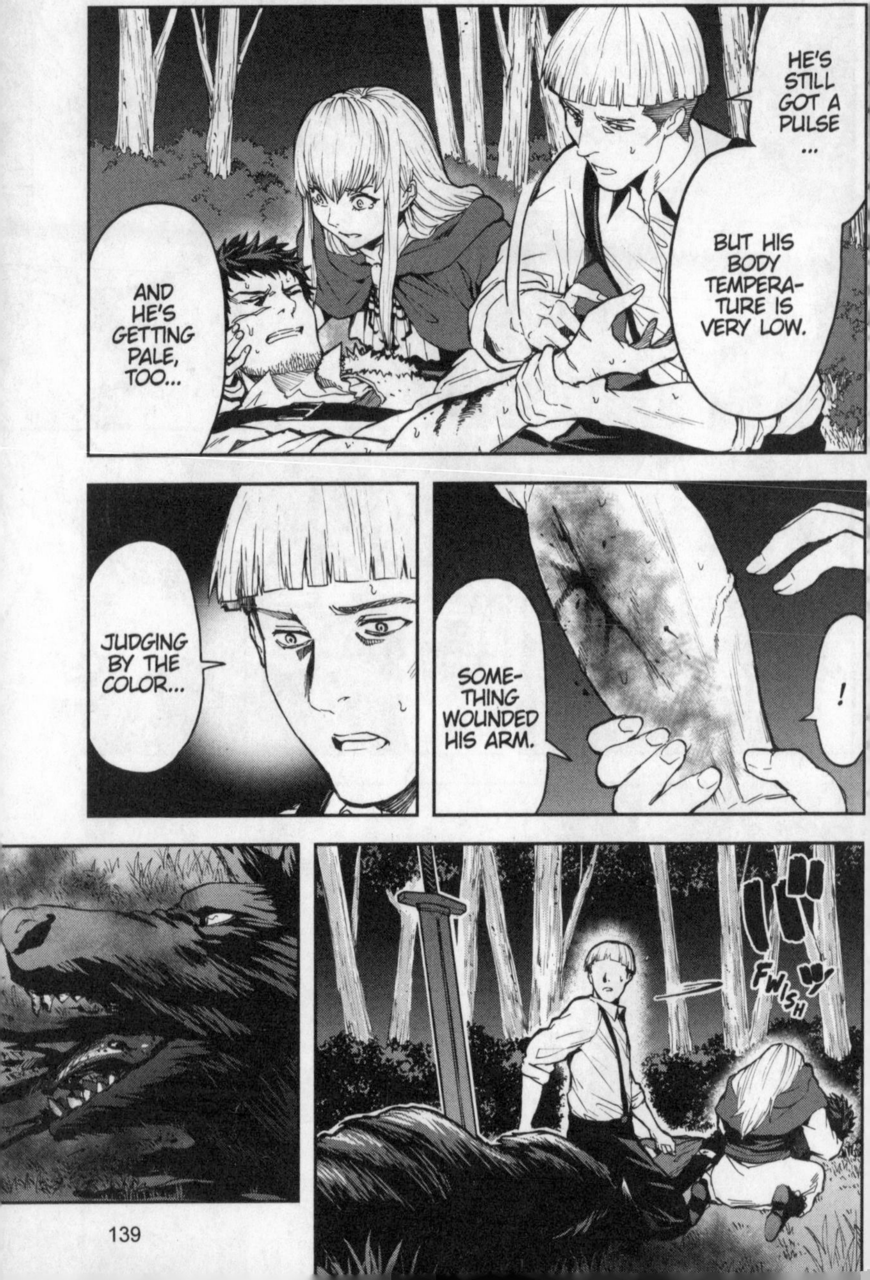
HE'S STILL GOT A PULSE ...
BUT HIS BODY TEMPERA-TURE IS VERY LOW.
AND HE'S GETTING PALE, TOO...
!
SOME-THING WOUNDED HIS ARM.
JUDGING BY THE COLOR...
FWISH

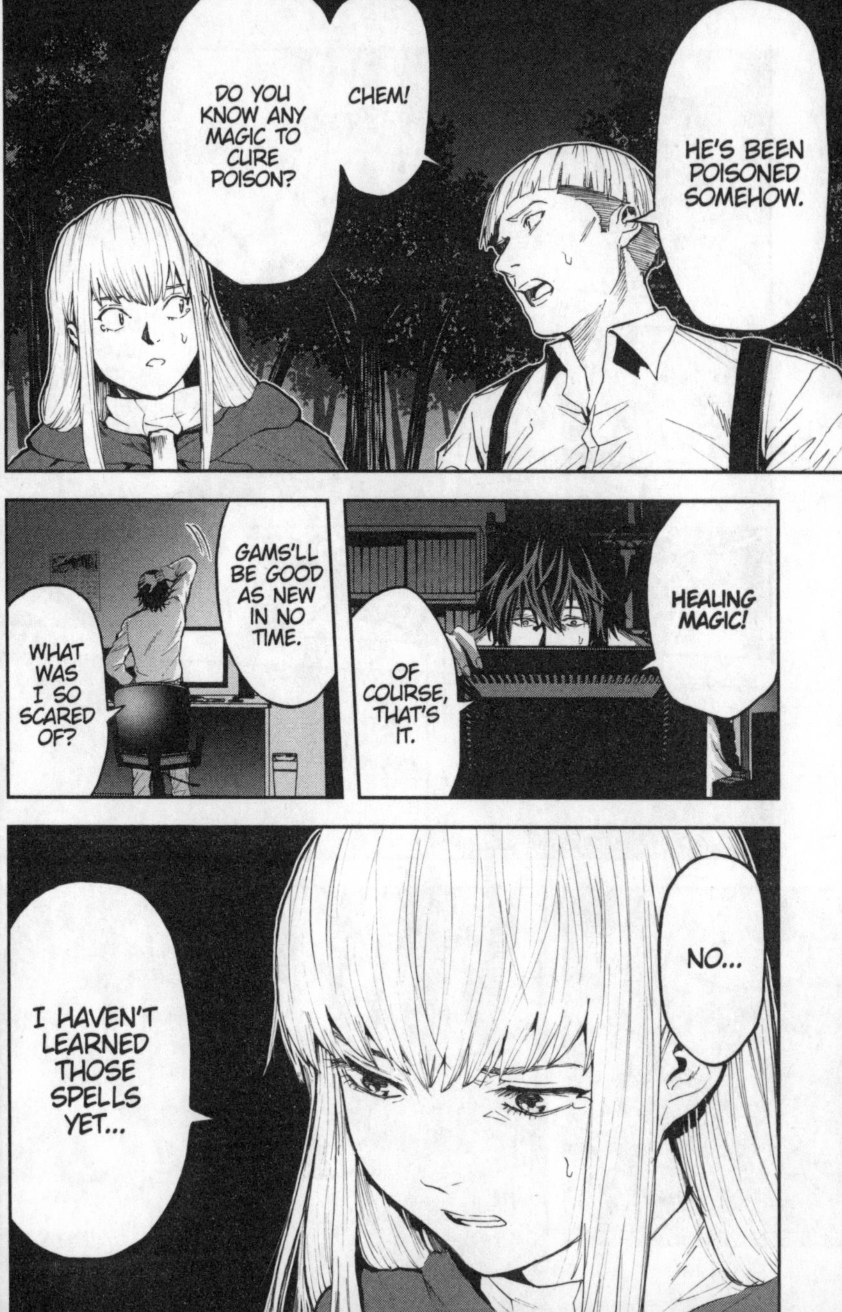
HE'S BEEN POISONED SOMEHOW.
CHEM!
DO YOU KNOW ANY MAGIC TO CURE POISON?
HEALING MAGIC!
OF COURSE, THAT'S IT.
GAMS'LL BE GOOD AS NEW IN NO TIME.
WHAT WAS I SO SCARED OF?
NO...
I HAVEN'T LEARNED THOSE SPELLS YET...

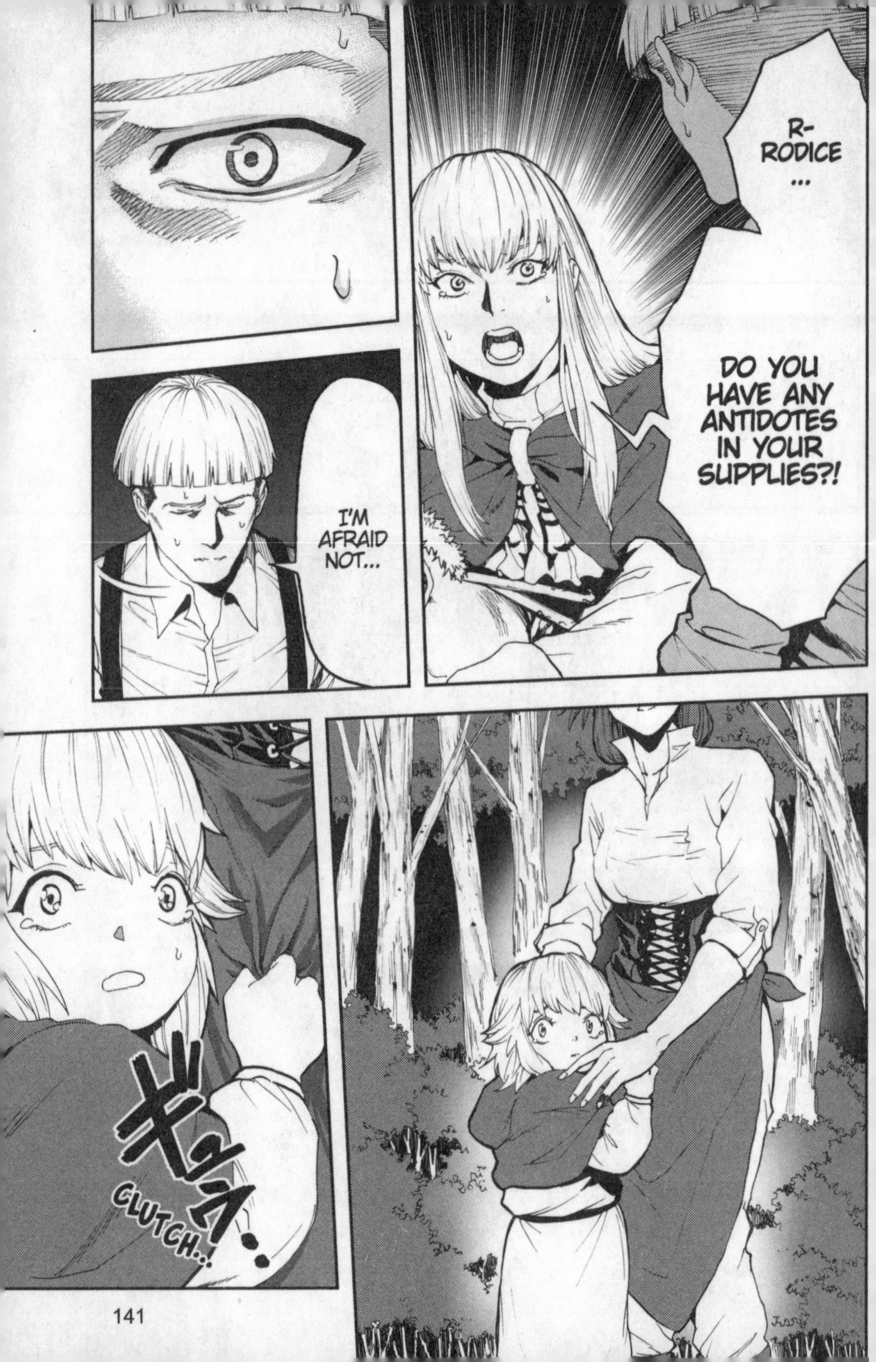
R-RODICE ...
DO YOU HAVE ANY ANTIDOTES IN YOUR SUPPLIES?!
I'M AFRAID NOT...
CLUTCH..

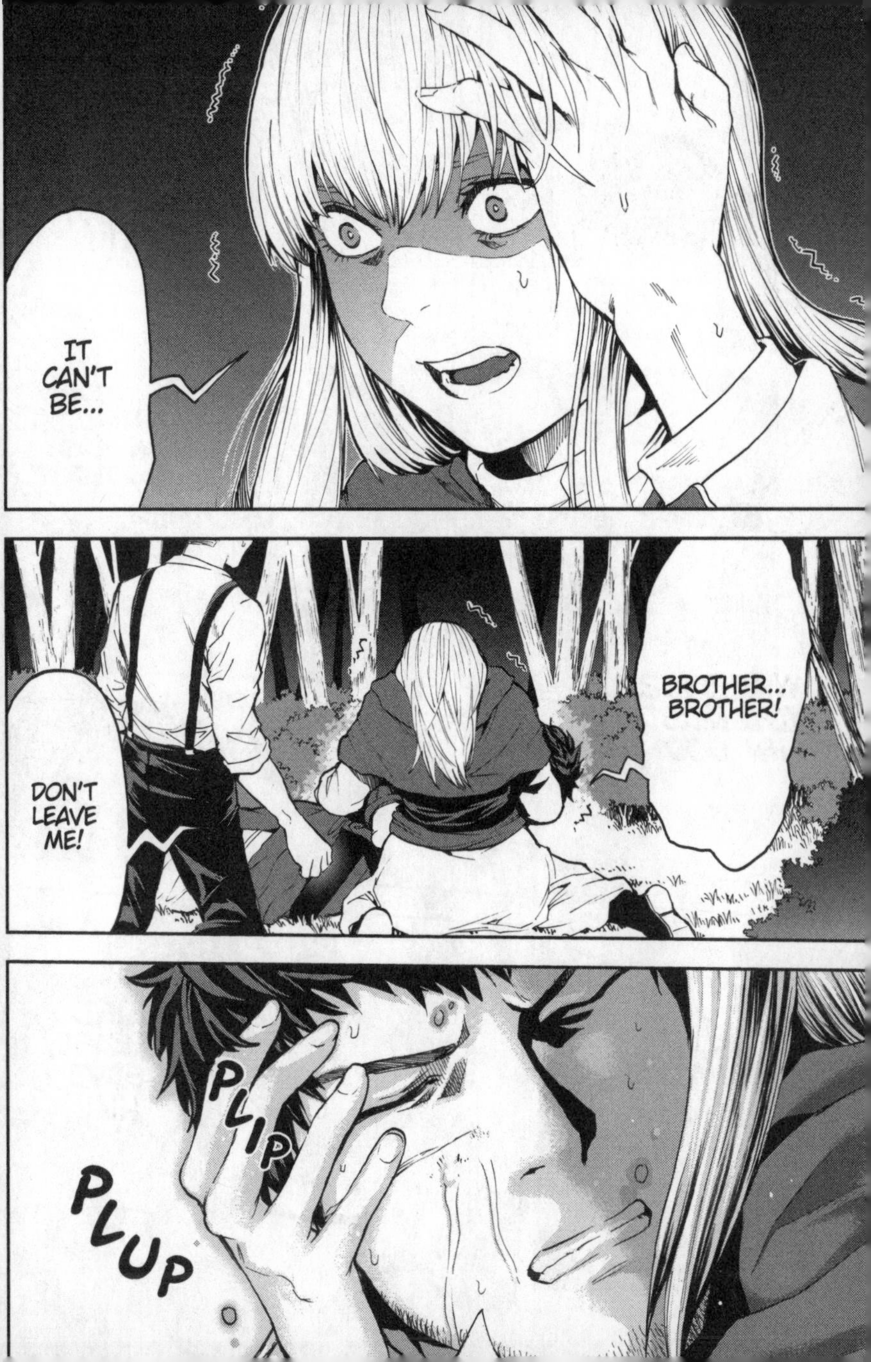
IT CAN'T BE...
BROTHER... BROTHER!
DON'T LEAVE ME!
PLIP
PLUP

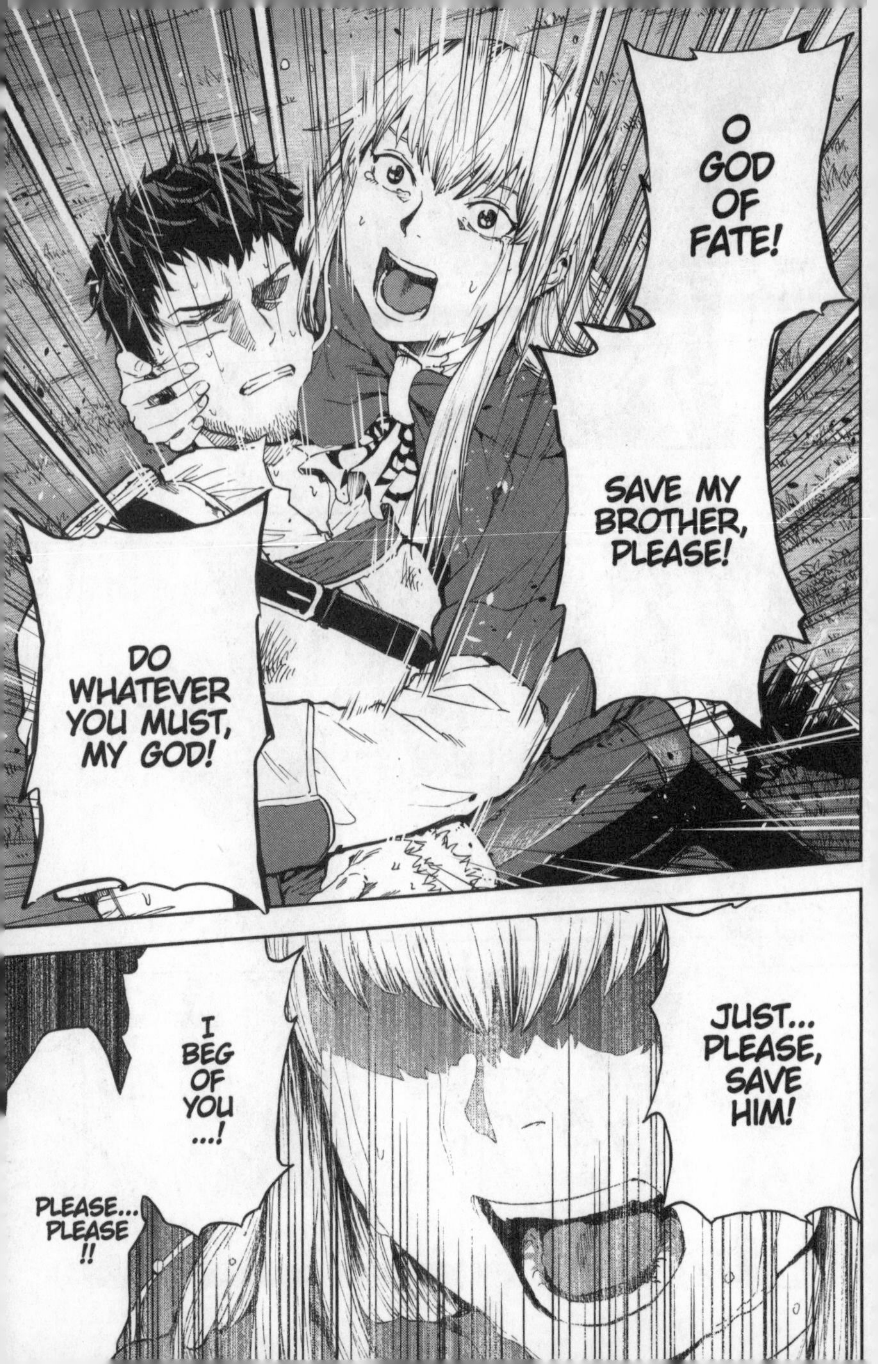
O GOD OF FATE!
SAVE MY BROTHER, PLEASE!
DO WHATEVER YOU MUST, MY GOD!
JUST... PLEASE, SAVE HIM!
I BEG OF YOU ...!
PLEASE... PLEASE !!

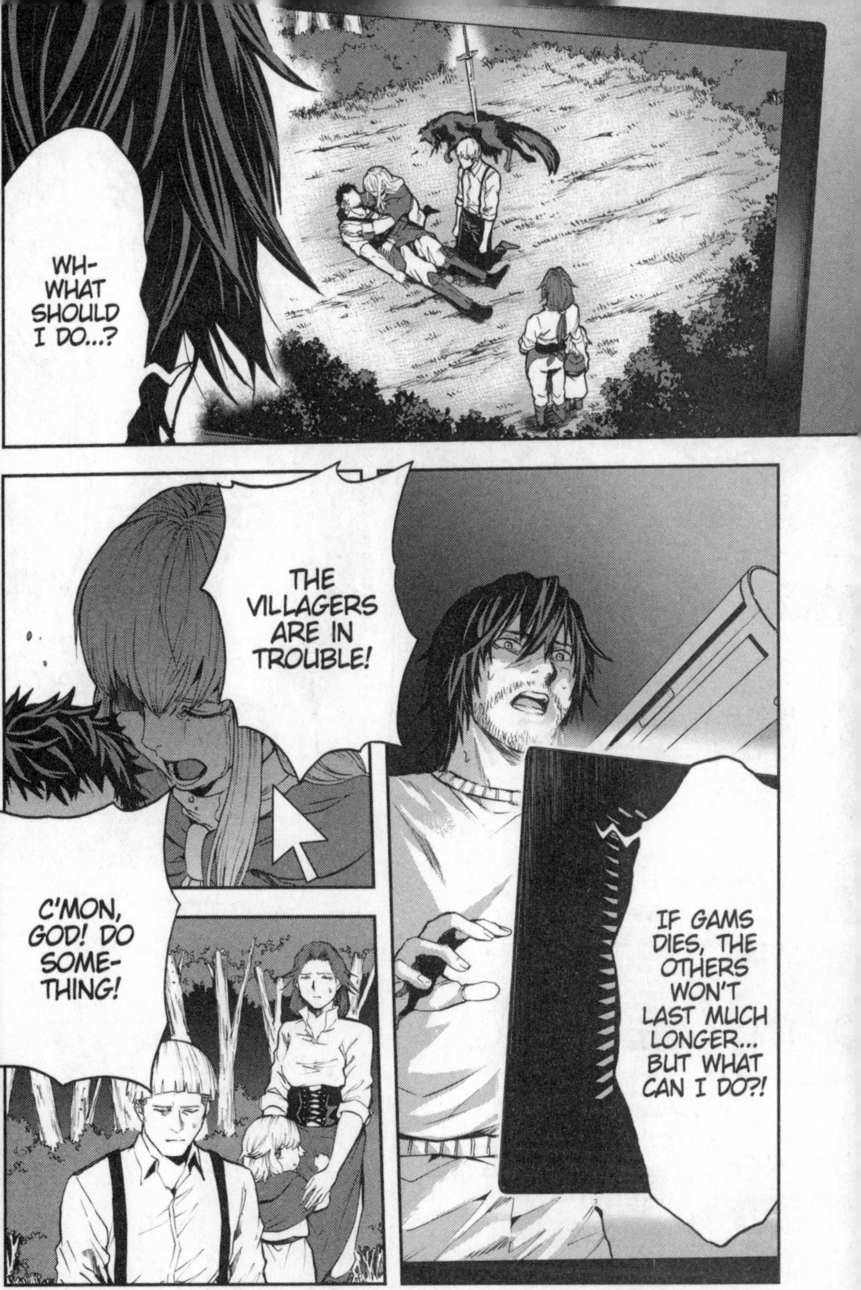
WH- WHAT SHOULD I DO...?
THE VILLAGERS ARE IN TROUBLE!
IF GAMS DIES, THE OTHERS WON'T LAST MUCH LONGER... BUT WHAT CAN I DO?!
C'MON, GOD! DO SOME-THING!

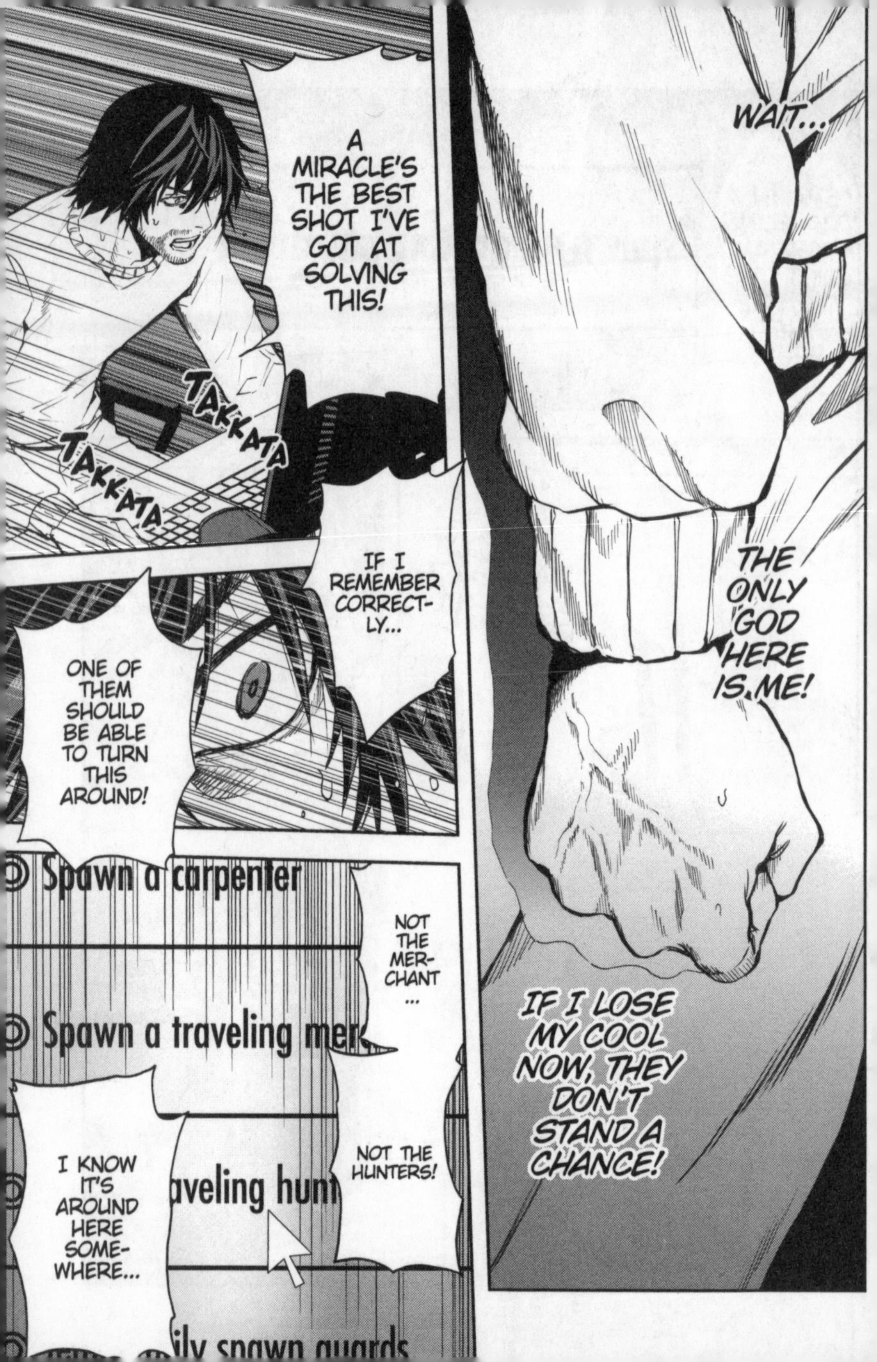
WAIT...
THE ONLY GOD HERE IS ME!
IF I LOSE MY COOL NOW, THEY DON'T STAND A CHANCE!
A MIRACLE'S THE BEST SHOT I'VE GOT AT SOLVING THIS!
TAKKATA
TAKKATA
IF I REMEMBER CORRECT-LY...
ONE OF THEM SHOULD BE ABLE TO TURN THIS AROUND!
Spawn a carpenter
NOT THE MER-CHANT ...
Spawn a traveling mer
NOT THE HUNTERS!
aveling hunt
I KNOW IT'S AROUND HERE SOME-WHERE...
ily spawn guards

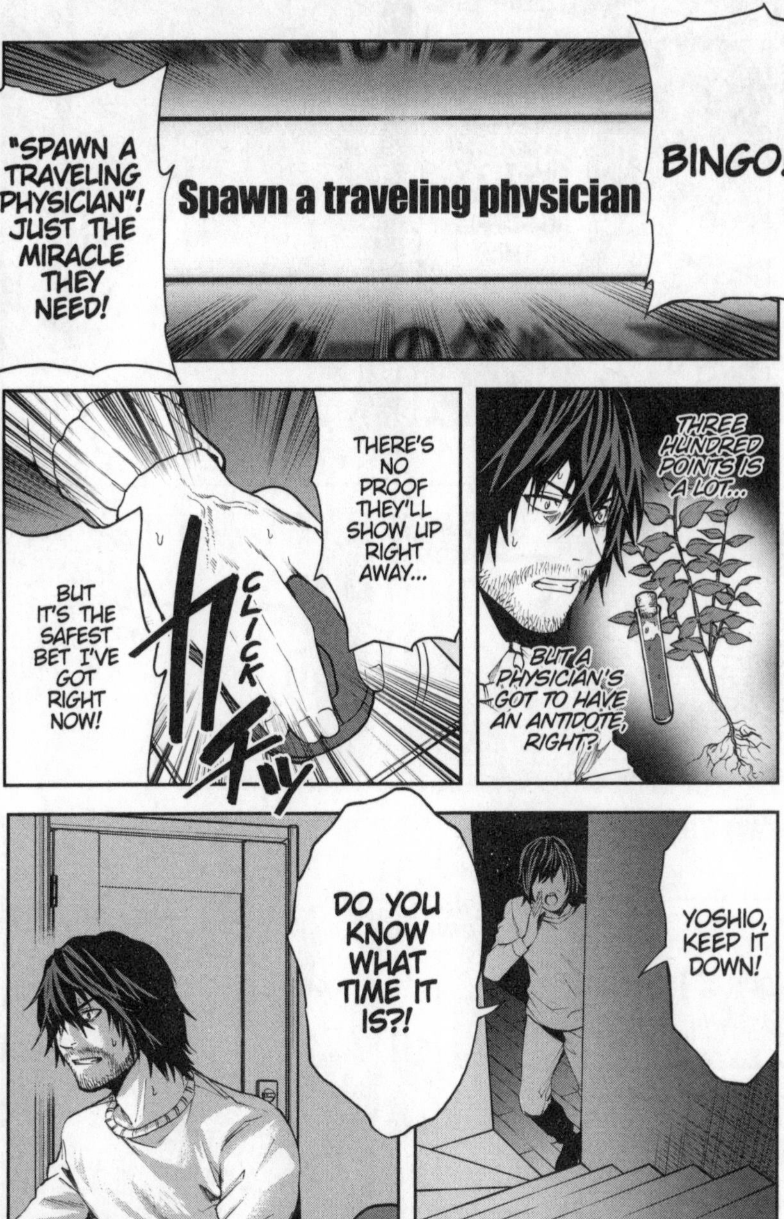
BINGO!
Spawn a traveling physician
"SPAWN A TRAVELING PHYSICIAN"! JUST THE MIRACLE THEY NEED!
THREE HUNDRED POINTS IS A LOT...
BUT A PHYSICIAN'S GOT TO HAVE AN ANTIDOTE, RIGHT?
THERE'S NO PROOF THEY'LL SHOW UP RIGHT AWAY...
BUT IT'S THE SAFEST BET I'VE GOT RIGHT NOW!
CLICK
YOSHIO, KEEP IT DOWN!
DO YOU KNOW WHAT TIME IT IS?!

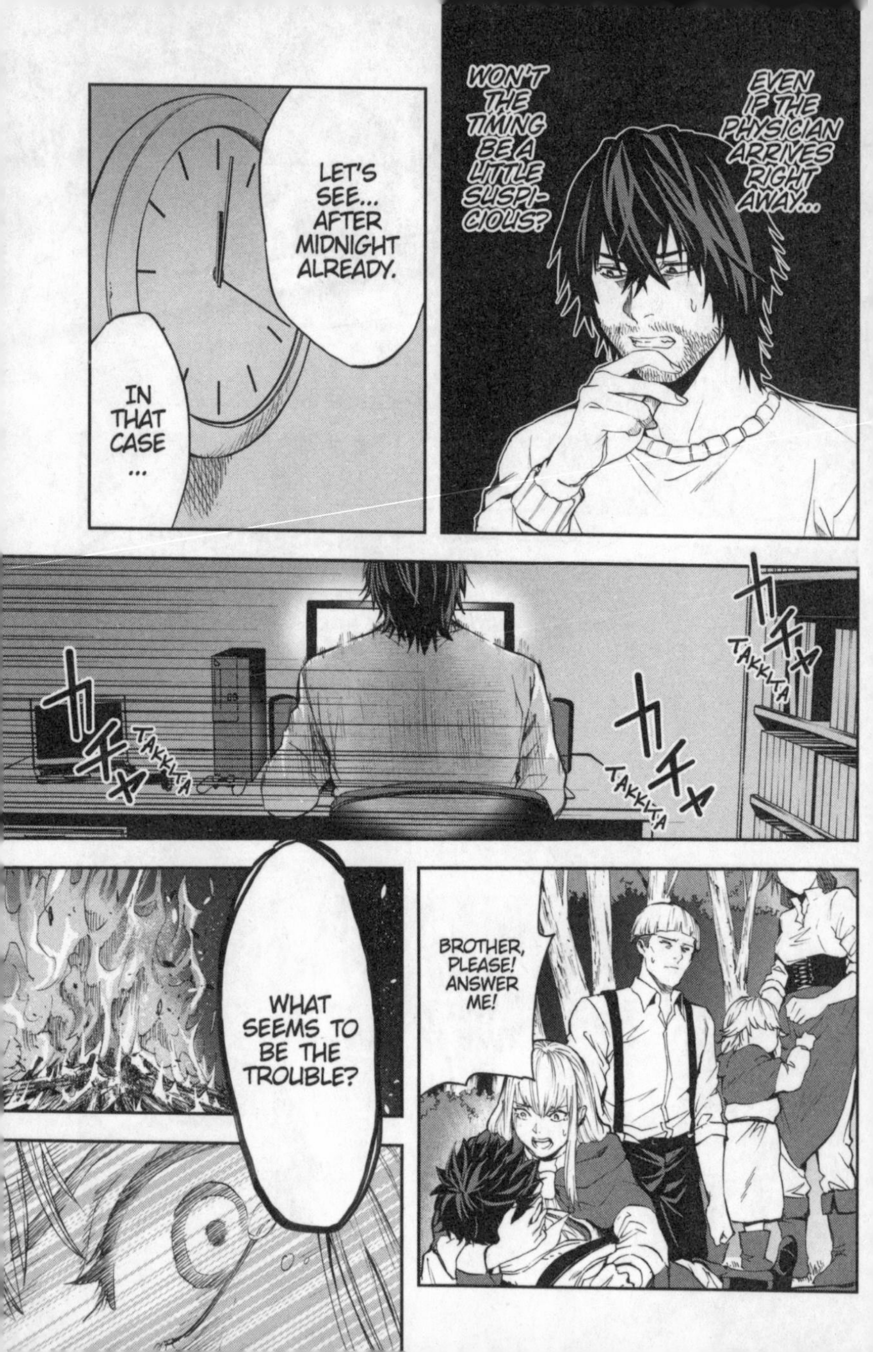
EVEN IF THE PHYSICIAN ARRIVES RIGHT AWAY...
WON'T THE TIMING BE A LITTLE SUSPICIOUS?
LET'S SEE... AFTER MIDNIGHT ALREADY.
IN THAT CASE ...
カチャ TAKKATA
カチャ TAKKATA
カチャ TAKKATA
BROTHER, PLEASE! ANSWER ME!
WHAT SEEMS TO BE THE TROUBLE?

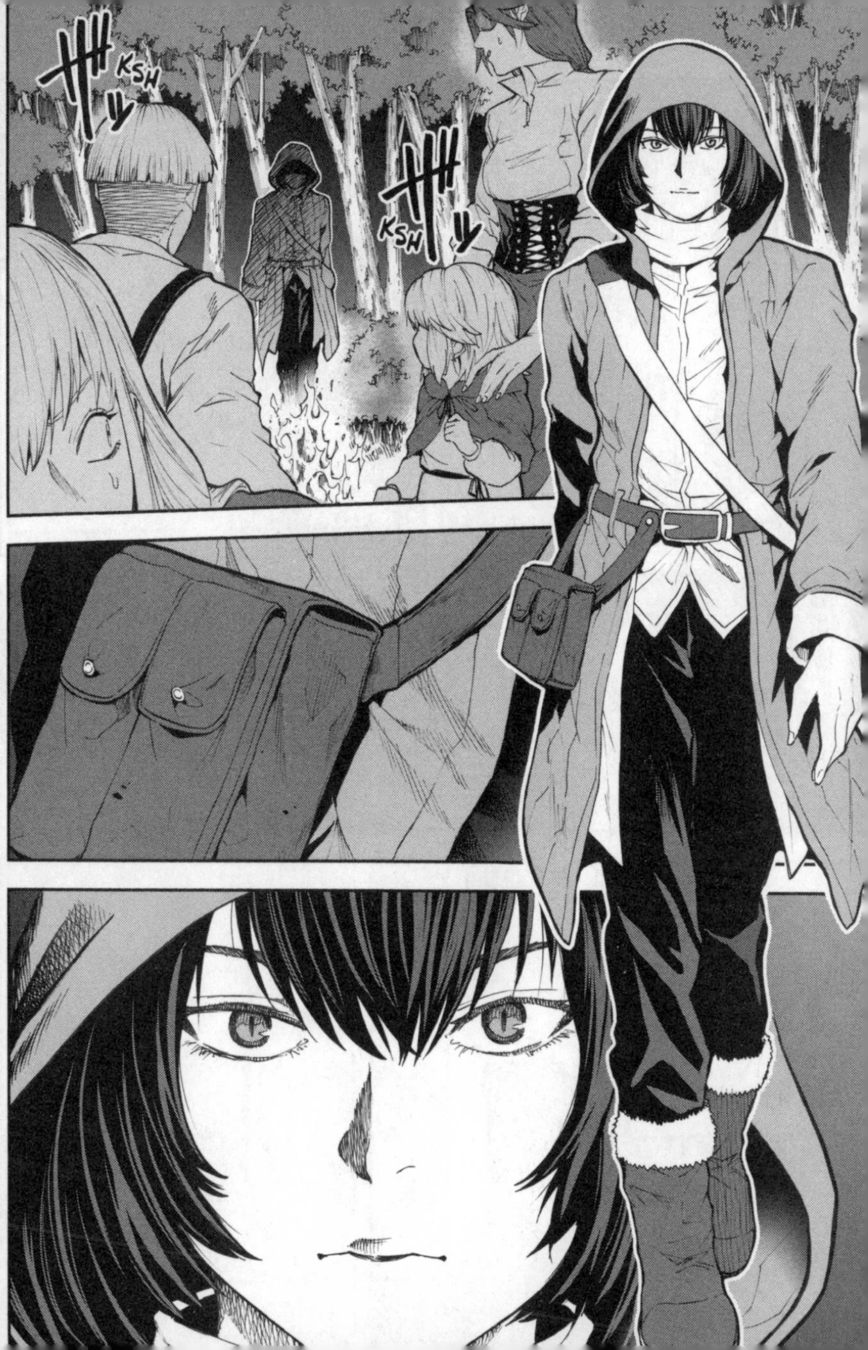
KSH
KSH

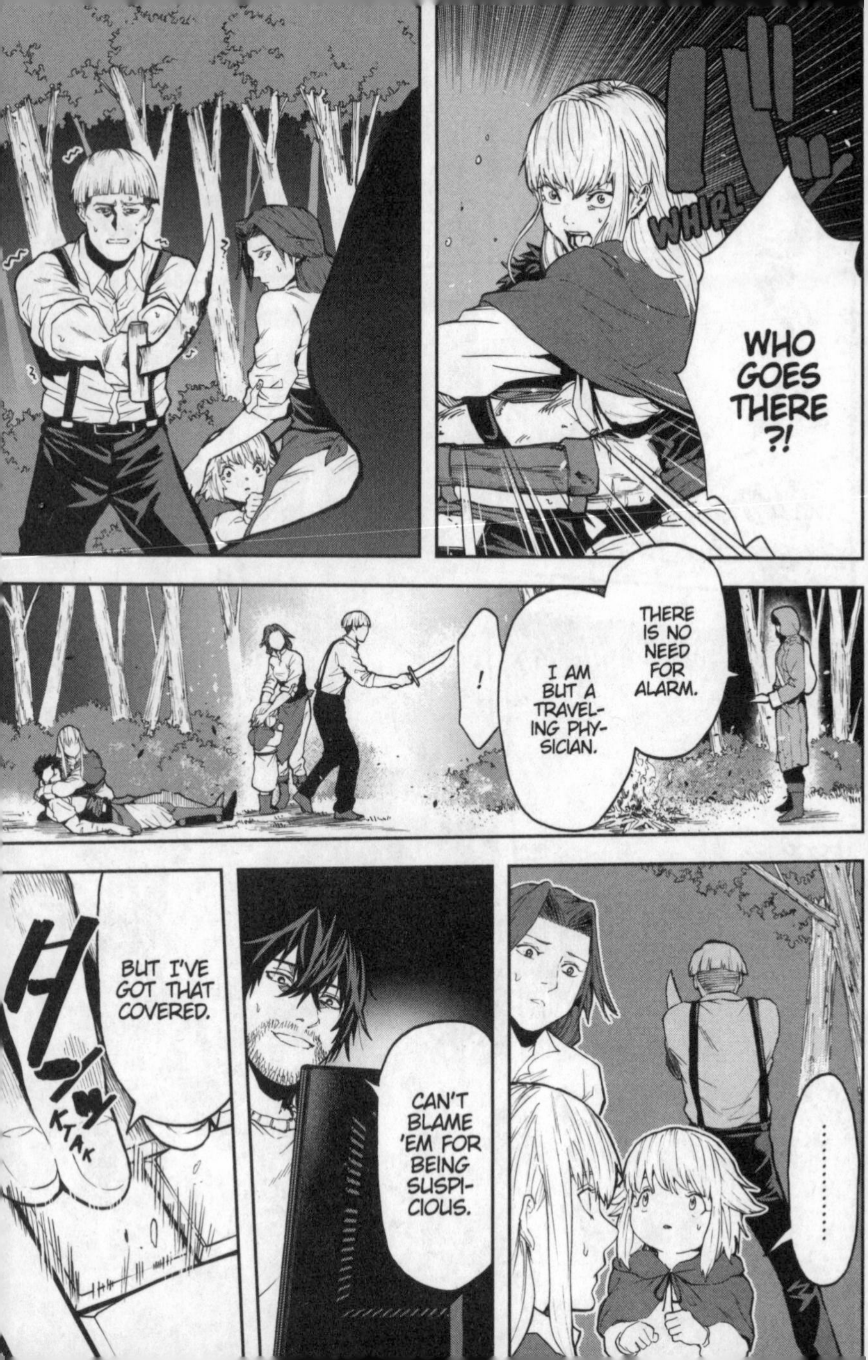
WHIRL
WHO GOES THERE?!
THERE IS NO NEED FOR ALARM. I AM BUT A TRAVELING PHYSICIAN.
!
......
CAN'T BLAME 'EM FOR BEING SUSPICIOUS.
BUT I'VE GOT THAT COVERED.
KTAK

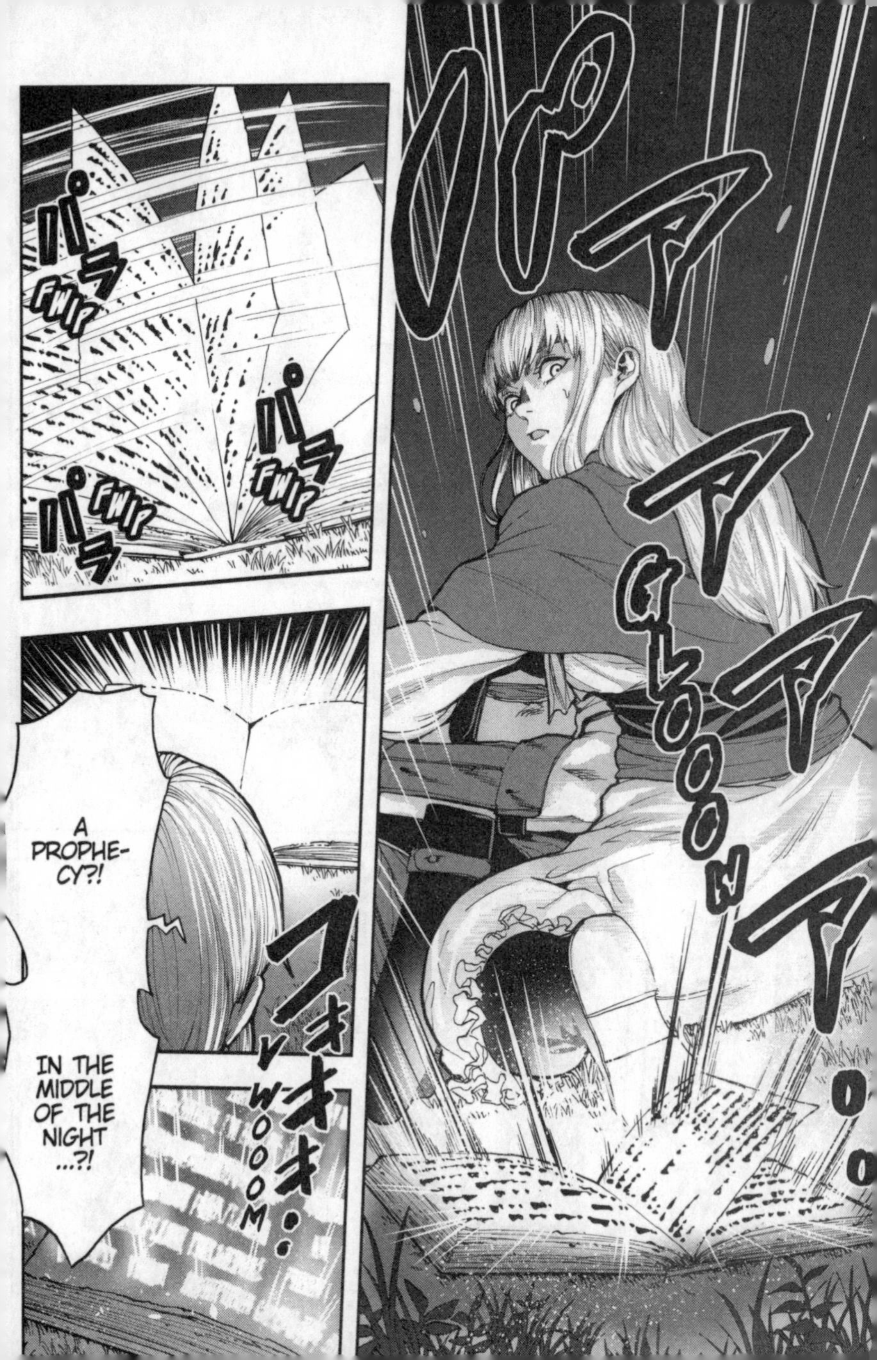
GLOOOOOW
パラ
FWIP
パラ
FWIP
パラ
FWIP
A PROPHE-CY?!
IN THE MIDDLE OF THE NIGHT ...?!
フォオ・・
VWOOOM

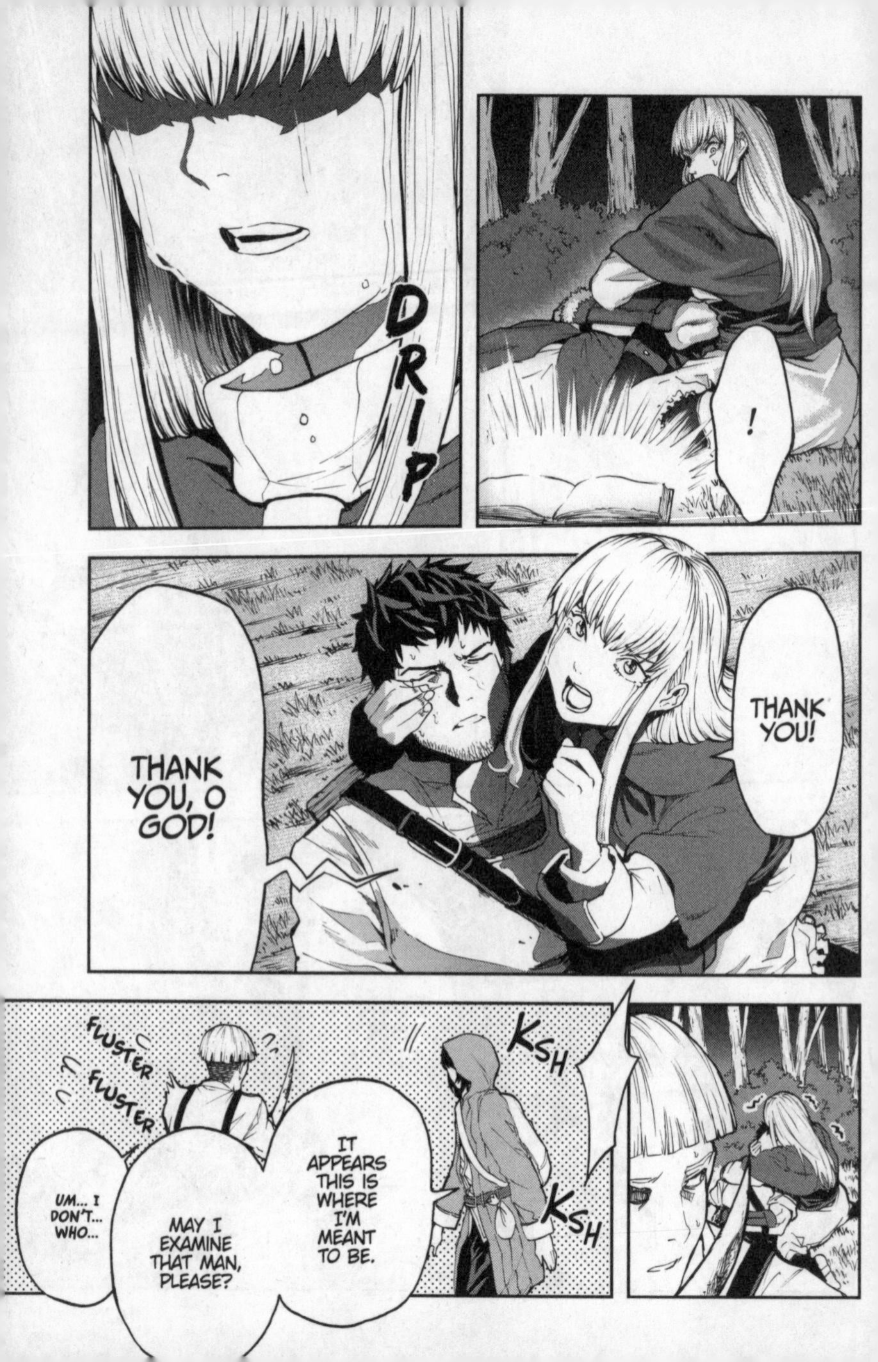
!
DRIP
THANK YOU!
THANK YOU, O GOD!
KSH
KSH
IT APPEARS THIS IS WHERE I'M MEANT TO BE.
MAY I EXAMINE THAT MAN, PLEASE?
UM... I DON'T... WHO...
FLUSTER
FLUSTER

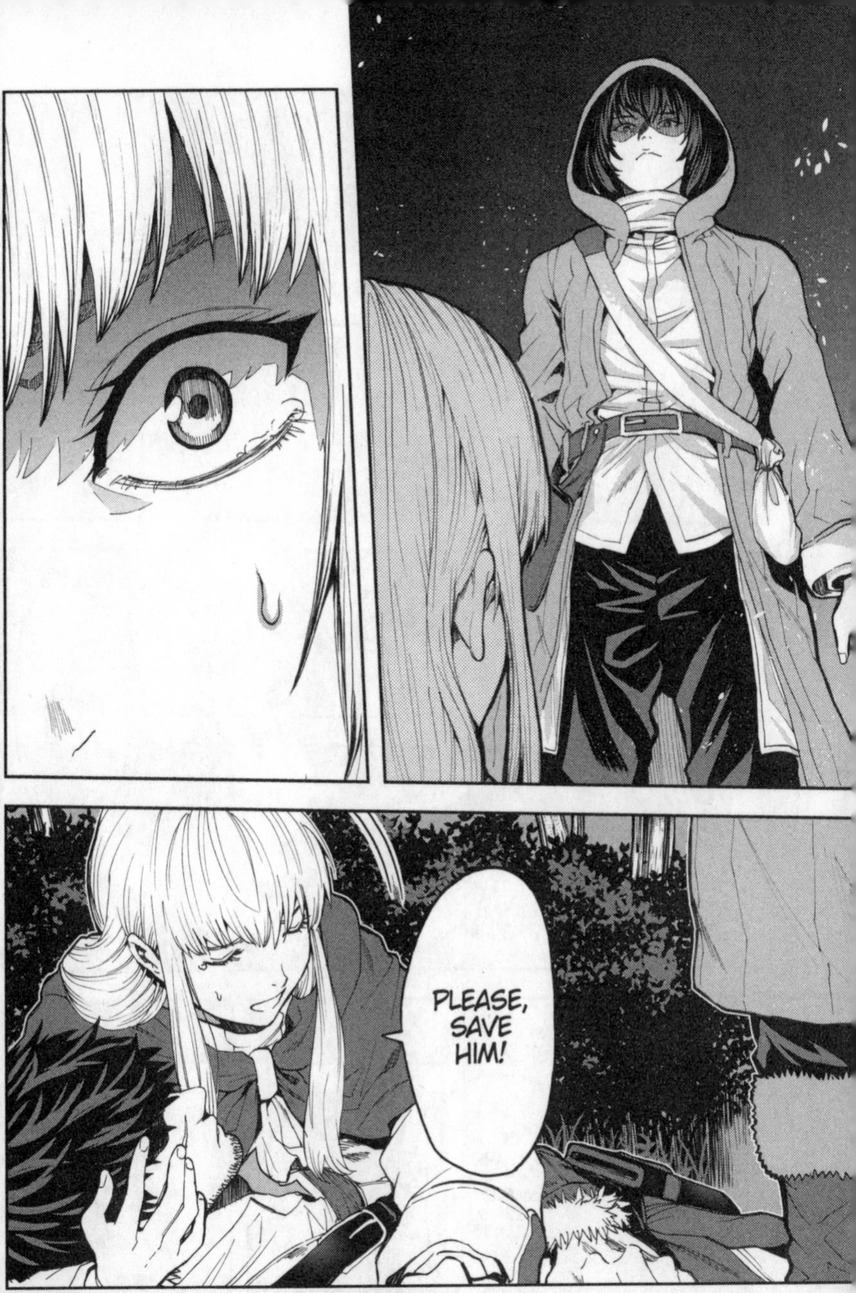
PLEASE, SAVE HIM!

PLEASE
BE OKAY,
GAMS...

RUSTLE

CLINK

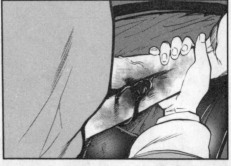

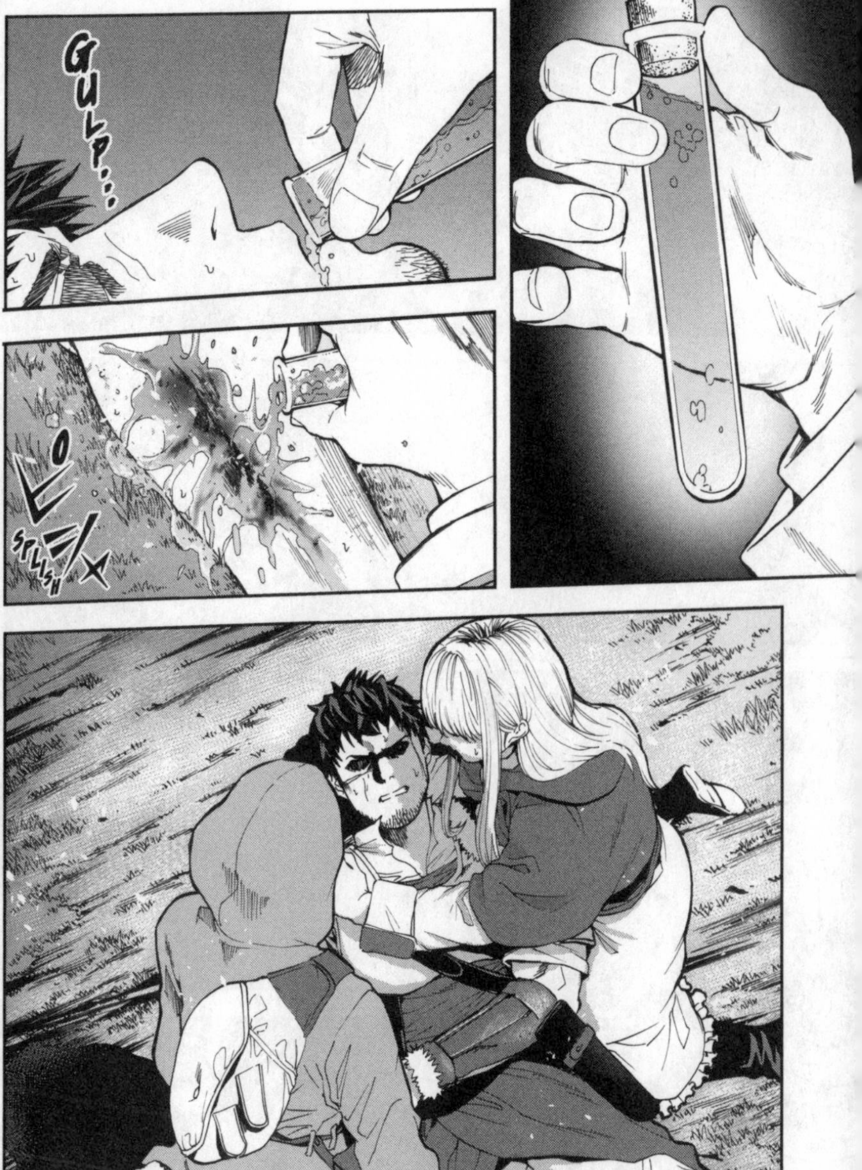
GULP...
SPLISH

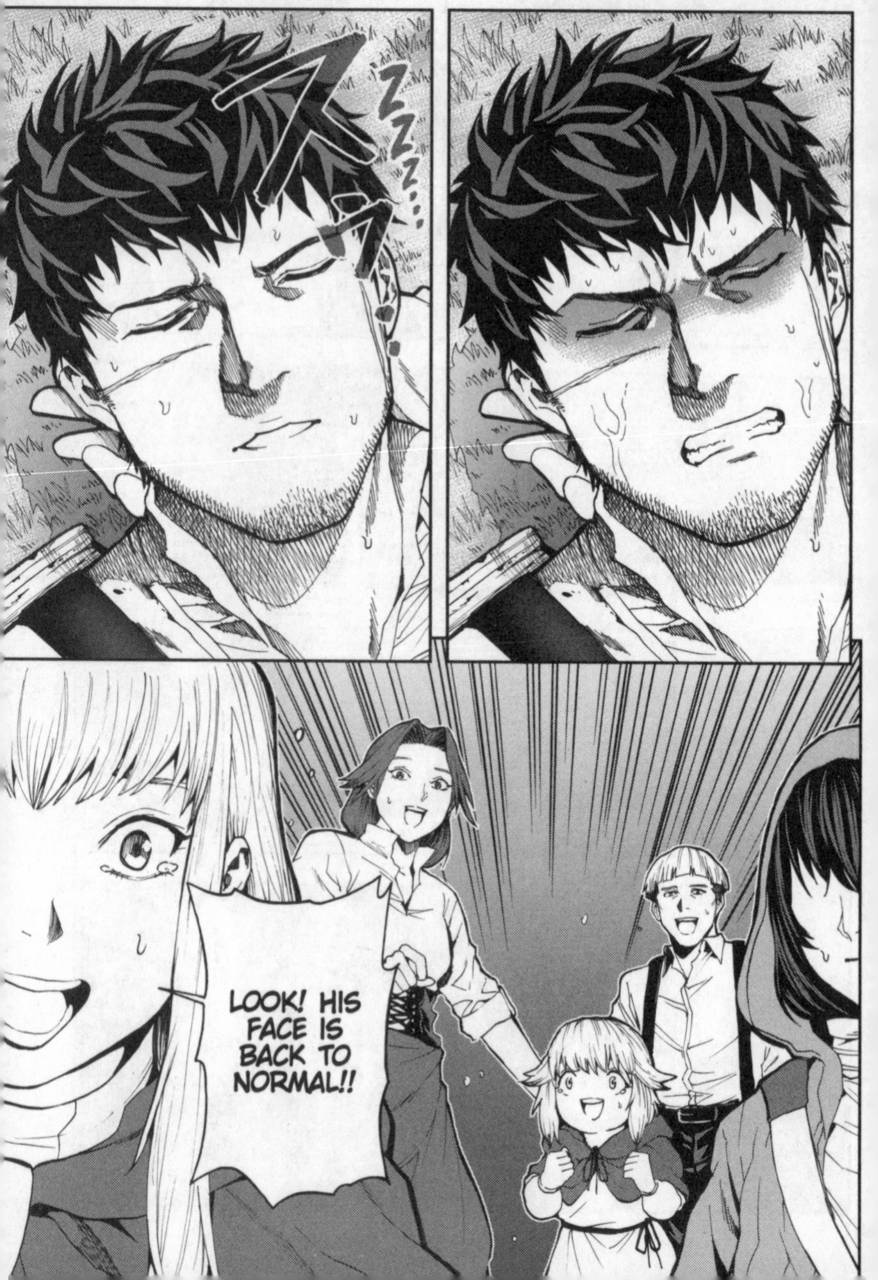
ZZZ...
LOOK! HIS FACE IS BACK TO NORMAL!!

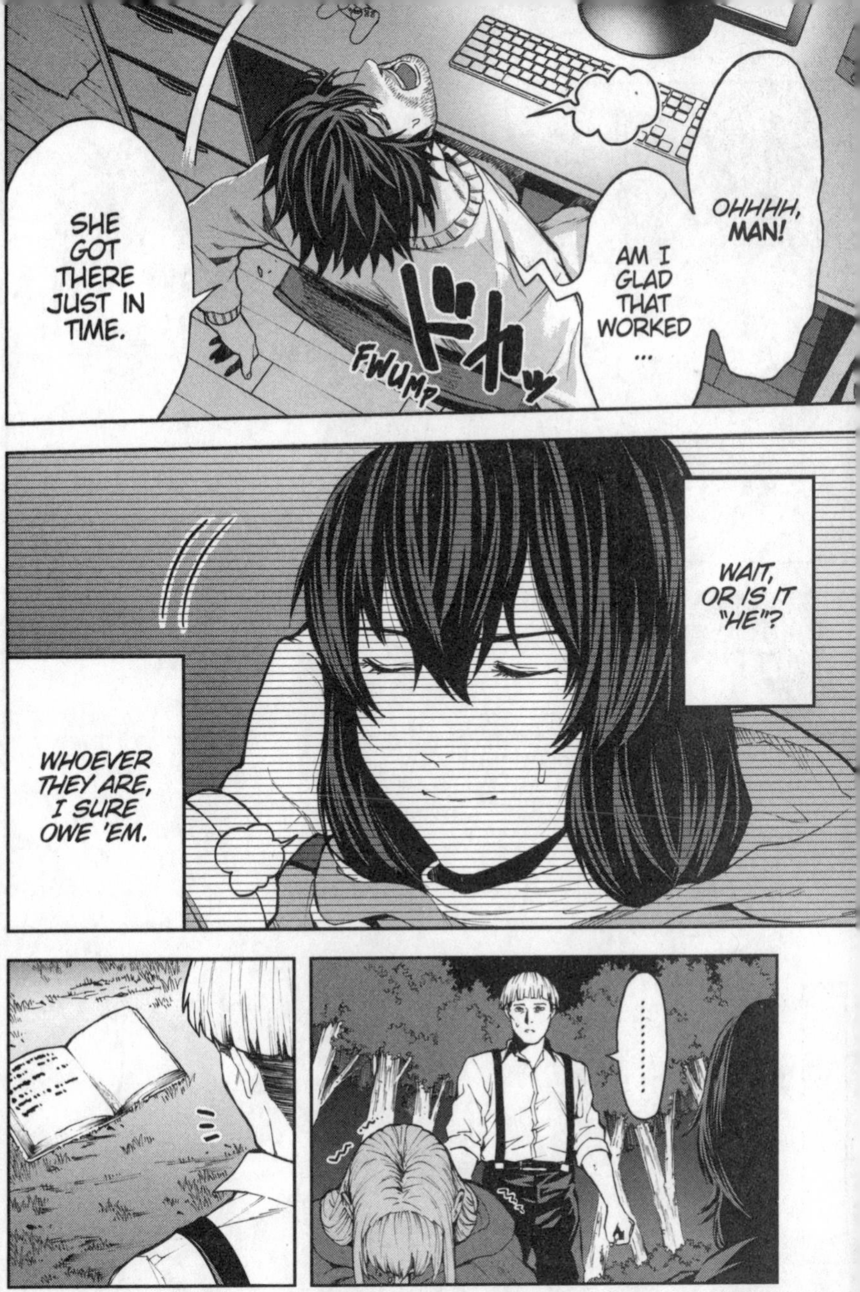
OHHHH, MAN!
AM I GLAD THAT WORKED ...
SHE GOT THERE JUST IN TIME.
ドカッ
FWUMP
WAIT, OR IS IT "HE"?
WHOEVER THEY ARE, I SURE OWE 'EM.
....

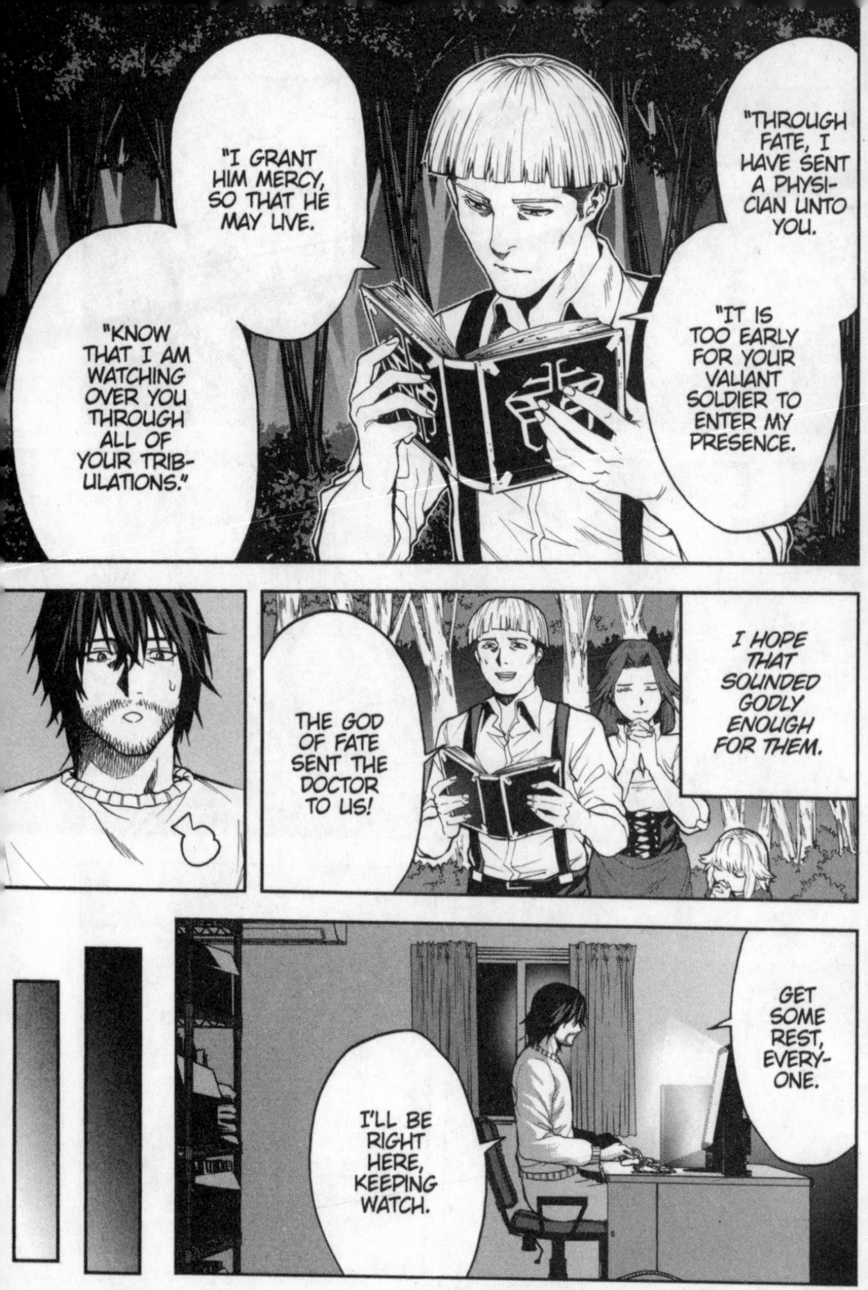
"THROUGH FATE, I HAVE SENT A PHYSICIAN UNTO YOU.
"IT IS TOO EARLY FOR YOUR VALIANT SOLDIER TO ENTER MY PRESENCE.
"I GRANT HIM MERCY, SO THAT HE MAY LIVE.
"KNOW THAT I AM WATCHING OVER YOU THROUGH ALL OF YOUR TRIBULATIONS."
I HOPE THAT SOUNDED GODLY ENOUGH FOR THEM.
THE GOD OF FATE SENT THE DOCTOR TO US!
GET SOME REST, EVERYONE.
I'LL BE RIGHT HERE, KEEPING WATCH.

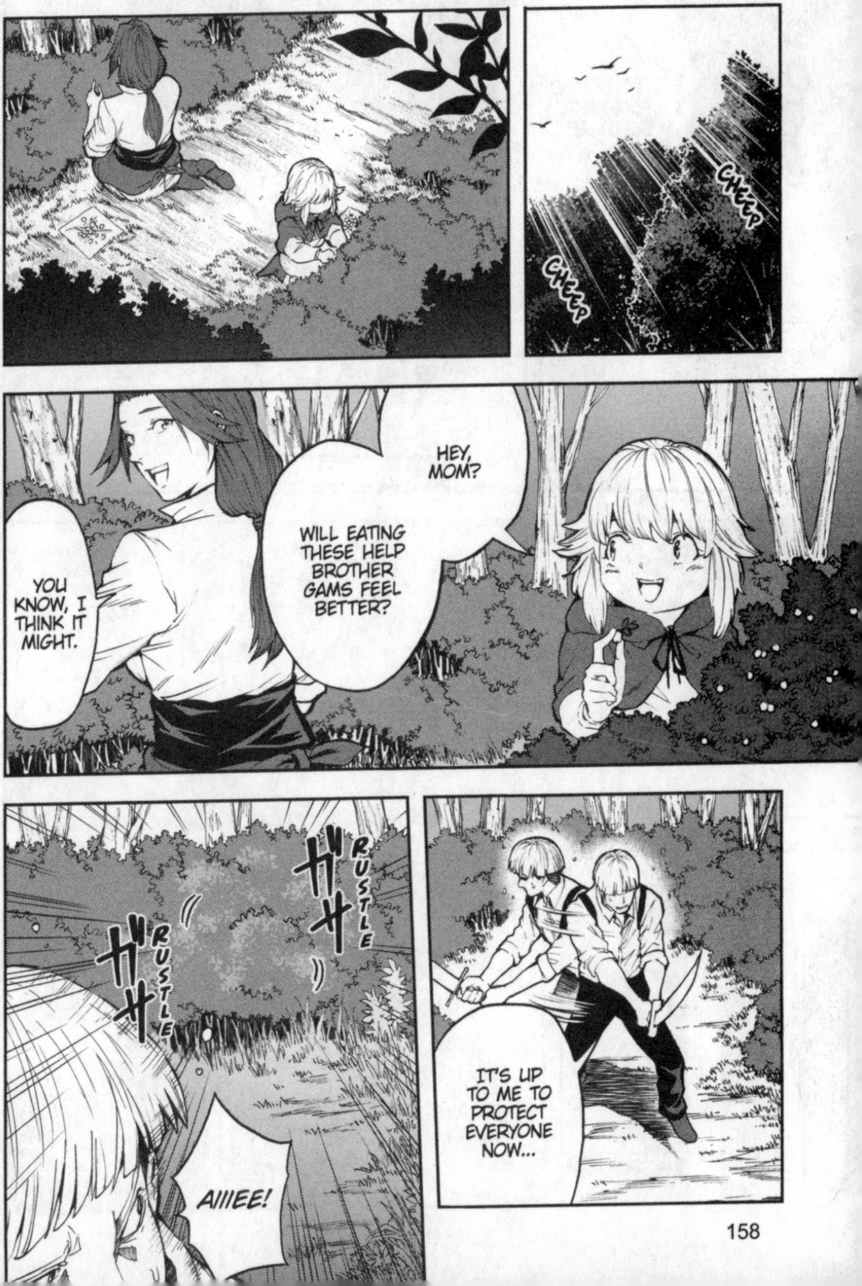
CHEEP
CHEEP
HEY, MOM?
WILL EATING THESE HELP BROTHER GAMS FEEL BETTER?
YOU KNOW, I THINK IT MIGHT.
IT'S UP TO ME TO PROTECT EVERYONE NOW...
RUSTLE
RUSTLE
AIIIEE!

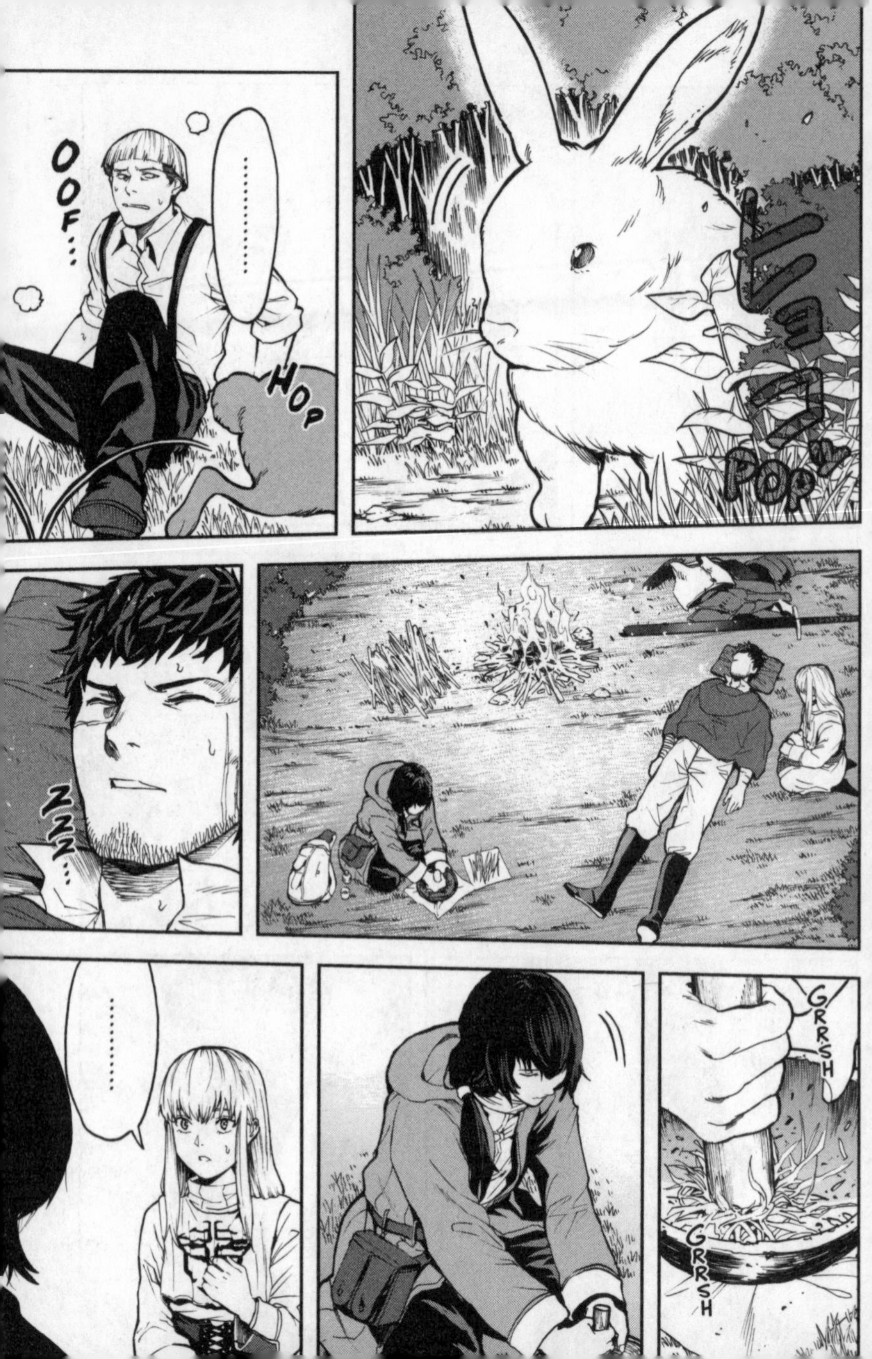
POP
......
OOF...
HOP
ZZZ...
GRRSH
GRRSH
......

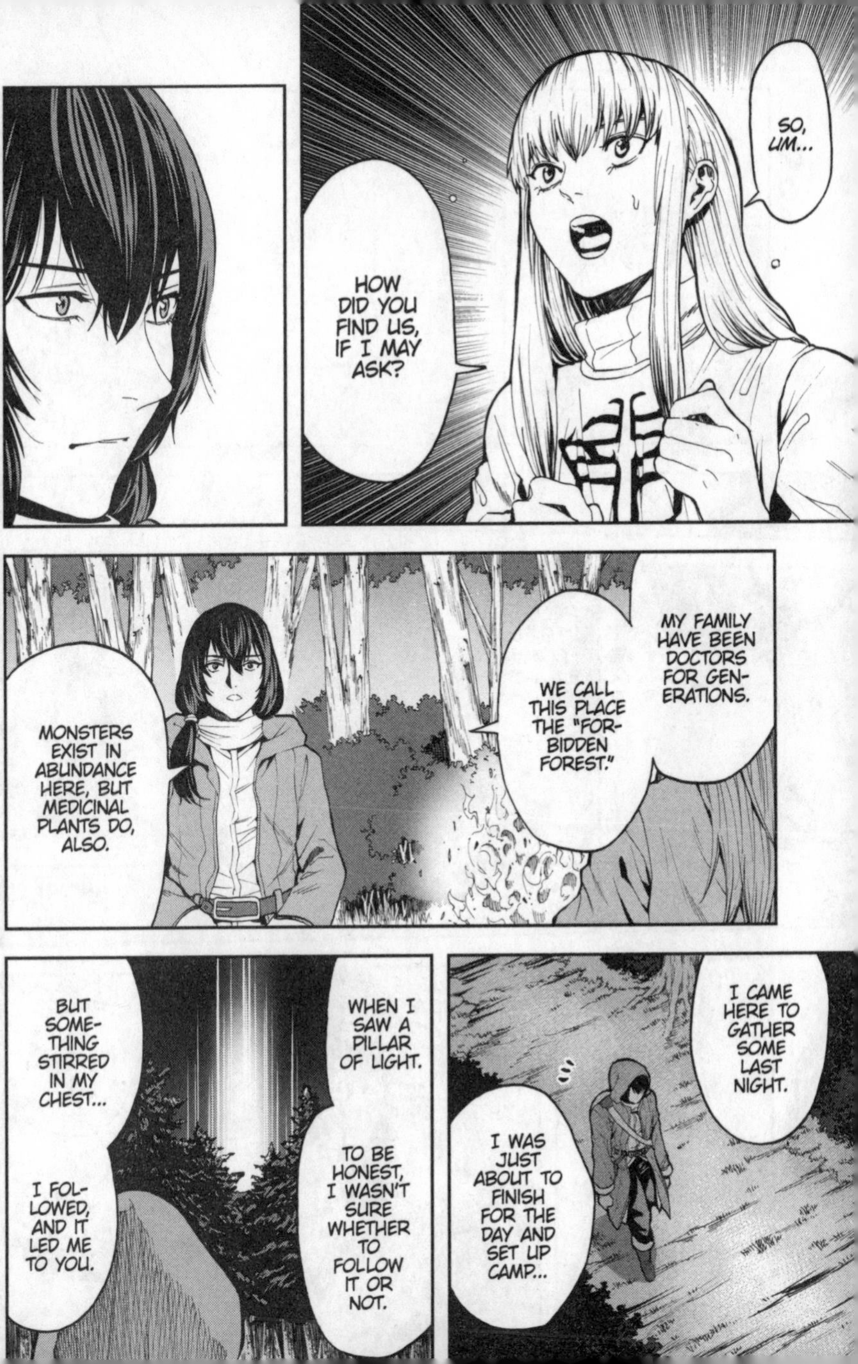
SO, UM...
HOW DID YOU FIND US, IF I MAY ASK?
MY FAMILY HAVE BEEN DOCTORS FOR GENERATIONS.
WE CALL THIS PLACE THE "FORBIDDEN FOREST."
MONSTERS EXIST IN ABUNDANCE HERE, BUT MEDICINAL PLANTS DO, ALSO.
I CAME HERE TO GATHER SOME LAST NIGHT.
I WAS JUST ABOUT TO FINISH FOR THE DAY AND SET UP CAMP...
WHEN I SAW A PILLAR OF LIGHT.
TO BE HONEST, I WASN'T SURE WHETHER TO FOLLOW IT OR NOT.
BUT SOMETHING STIRRED IN MY CHEST...
I FOLLOWED, AND IT LED ME TO YOU.

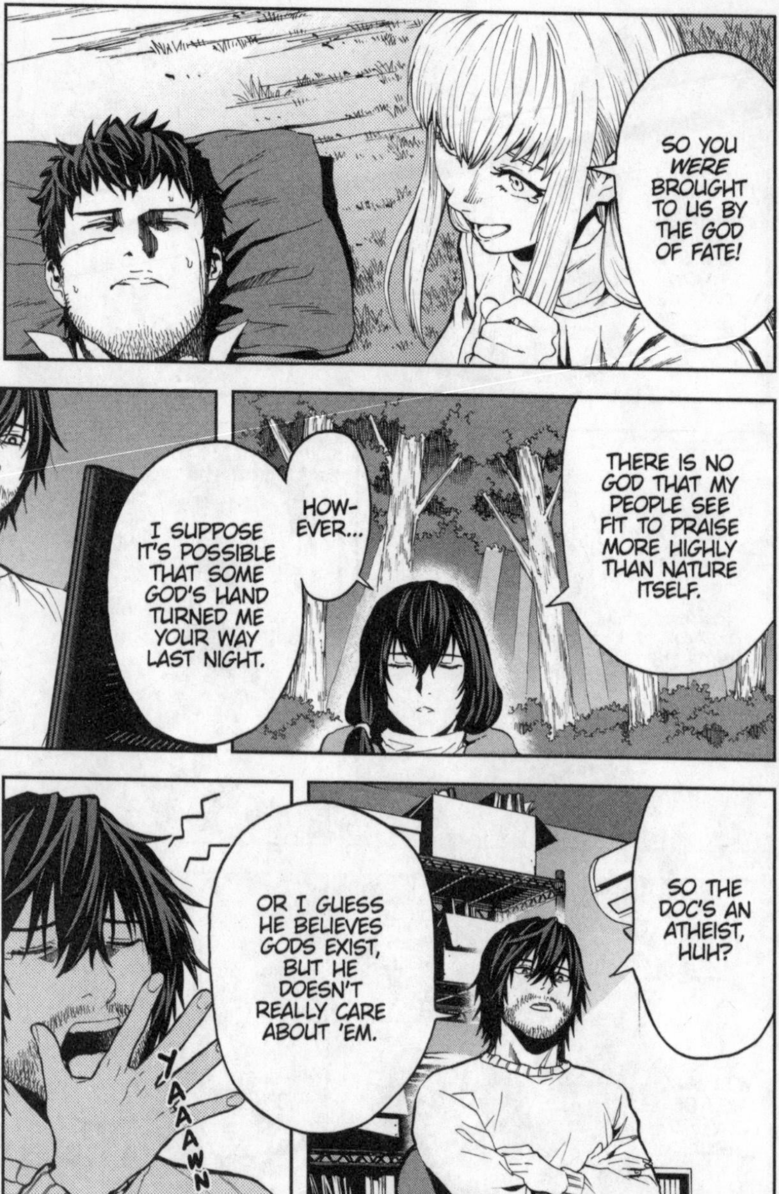
SO YOU WERE BROUGHT TO US BY THE GOD OF FATE!
THERE IS NO GOD THAT MY PEOPLE SEE FIT TO PRAISE MORE HIGHLY THAN NATURE ITSELF.
HOW-EVER...
I SUPPOSE IT'S POSSIBLE THAT SOME GOD'S HAND TURNED ME YOUR WAY LAST NIGHT.
SO THE DOC'S AN ATHEIST, HUH?
OR I GUESS HE BELIEVES GODS EXIST, BUT HE DOESN'T REALLY CARE ABOUT 'EM.
YAAAAWN

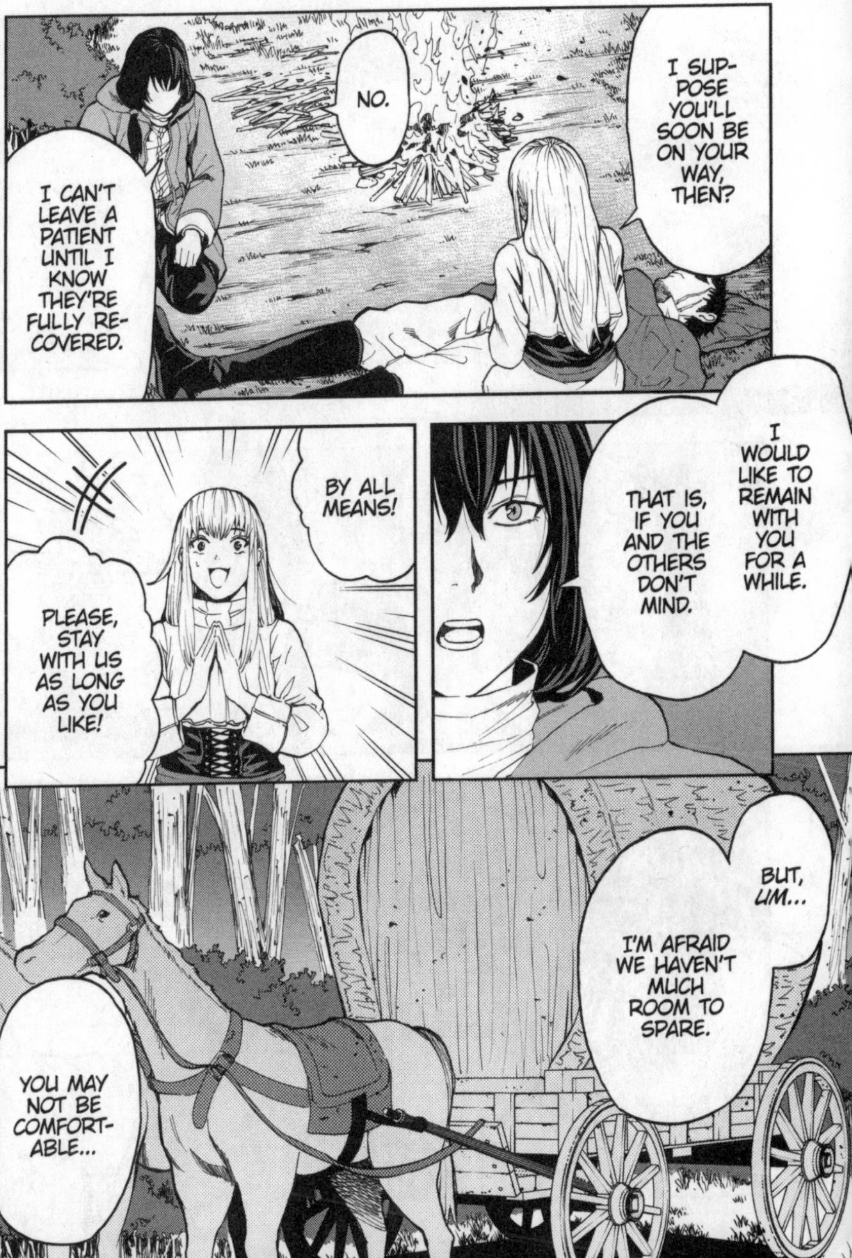
I SUPPOSE YOU'LL SOON BE ON YOUR WAY, THEN?
NO.
I CAN'T LEAVE A PATIENT UNTIL I KNOW THEY'RE FULLY RECOVERED.
I WOULD LIKE TO REMAIN WITH YOU FOR A WHILE.
THAT IS, IF YOU AND THE OTHERS DON'T MIND.
BY ALL MEANS!
PLEASE, STAY WITH US AS LONG AS YOU LIKE!
BUT, UM...
I'M AFRAID WE HAVEN'T MUCH ROOM TO SPARE.
YOU MAY NOT BE COMFORTABLE...

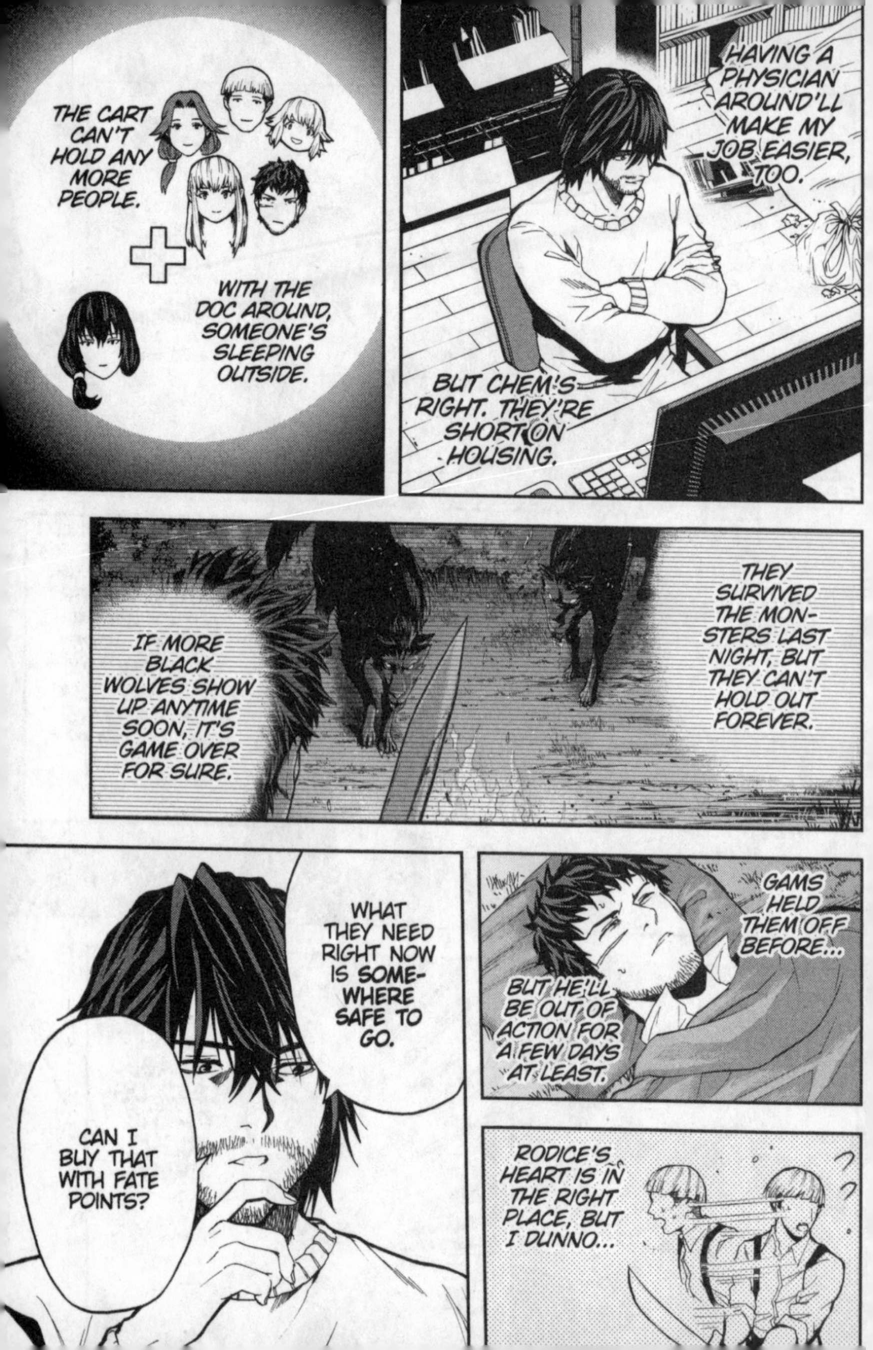
HAVING A PHYSICIAN AROUND'LL MAKE MY JOB EASIER, TOO.
BUT CHEM'S RIGHT. THEY'RE SHORT ON HOUSING.
THE CART CAN'T HOLD ANY MORE PEOPLE.
WITH THE DOC AROUND, SOMEONE'S SLEEPING OUTSIDE.
THEY SURVIVED THE MON-STERS LAST NIGHT, BUT THEY CAN'T HOLD OUT FOREVER.
IF MORE BLACK WOLVES SHOW UP ANYTIME SOON, IT'S GAME OVER FOR SURE.
GAMS HELD THEM OFF BEFORE...
BUT HE'LL BE OUT OF ACTION FOR A FEW DAYS AT LEAST.
RODICE'S HEART IS IN THE RIGHT PLACE, BUT I DUNNO...
WHAT THEY NEED RIGHT NOW IS SOME-WHERE SAFE TO GO.
CAN I BUY THAT WITH FATE POINTS?

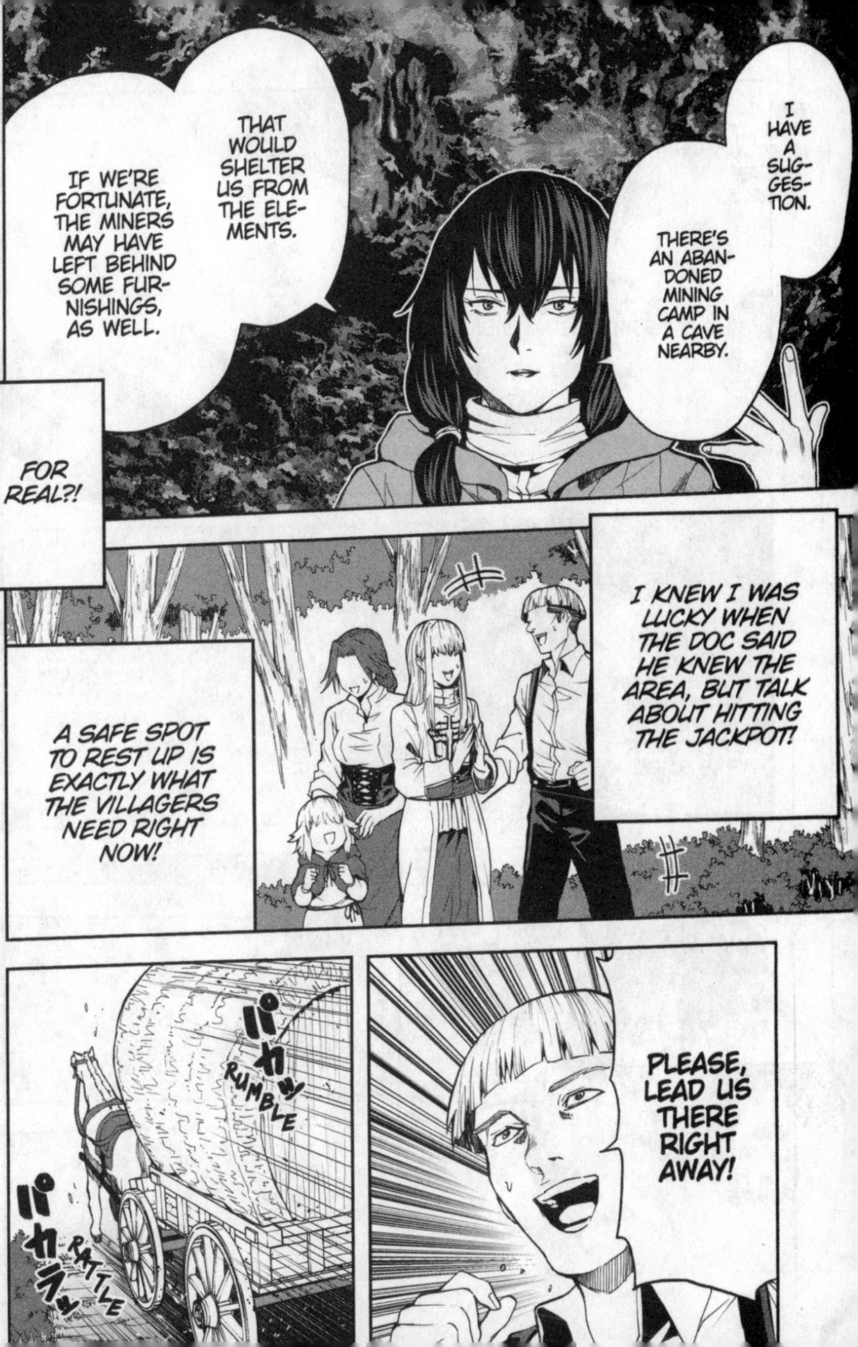
I HAVE A SUG-GES-TION.
THERE'S AN ABAN-DONED MINING CAMP IN A CAVE NEARBY.
THAT WOULD SHELTER US FROM THE ELE-MENTS.
IF WE'RE FORTUNATE, THE MINERS MAY HAVE LEFT BEHIND SOME FUR-NISHINGS, AS WELL.
FOR REAL?!
I KNEW I WAS LUCKY WHEN THE DOC SAID HE KNEW THE AREA, BUT TALK ABOUT HITTING THE JACKPOT!
A SAFE SPOT TO REST UP IS EXACTLY WHAT THE VILLAGERS NEED RIGHT NOW!
PLEASE, LEAD US THERE RIGHT AWAY!
RUMBLE
RATTLE

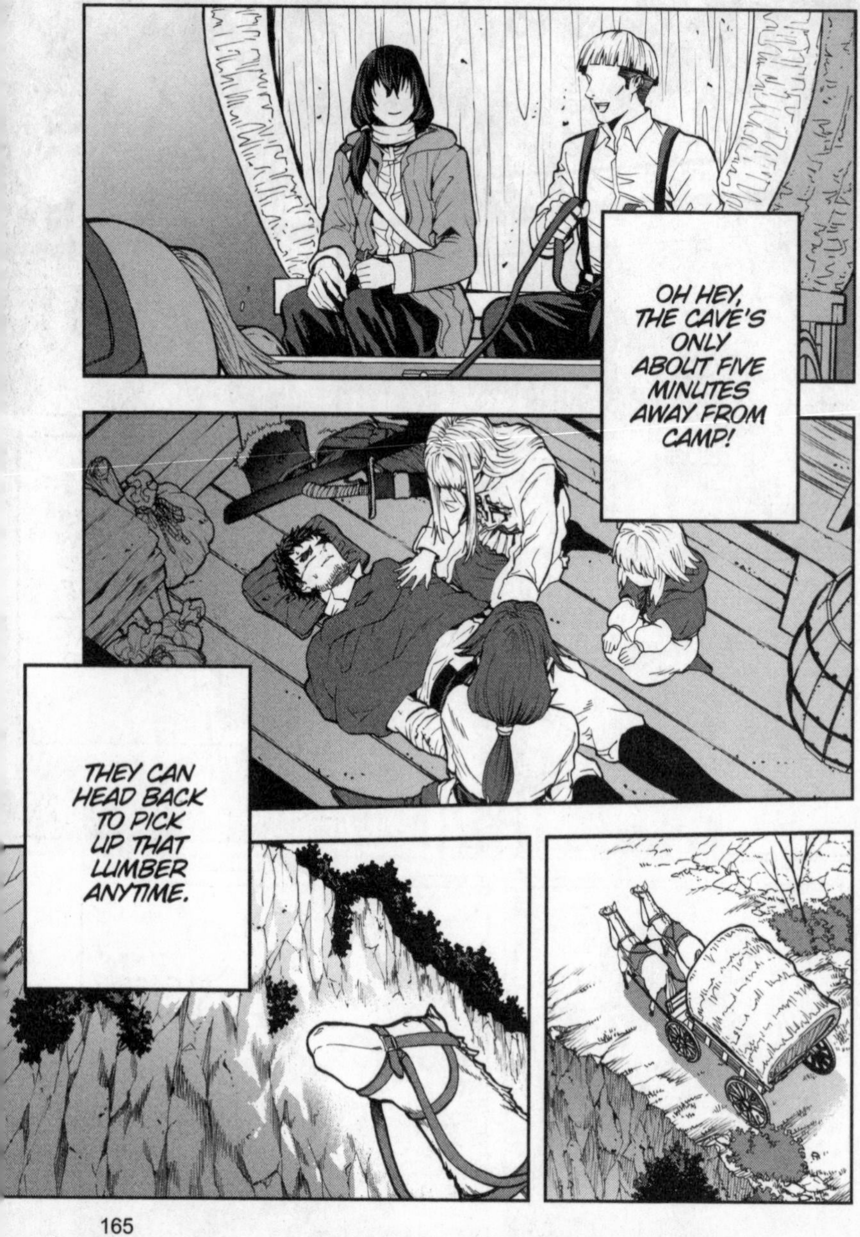
OH HEY, THE CAVE'S ONLY ABOUT FIVE MINUTES AWAY FROM CAMP!
THEY CAN HEAD BACK TO PICK UP THAT LUMBER ANYTIME.

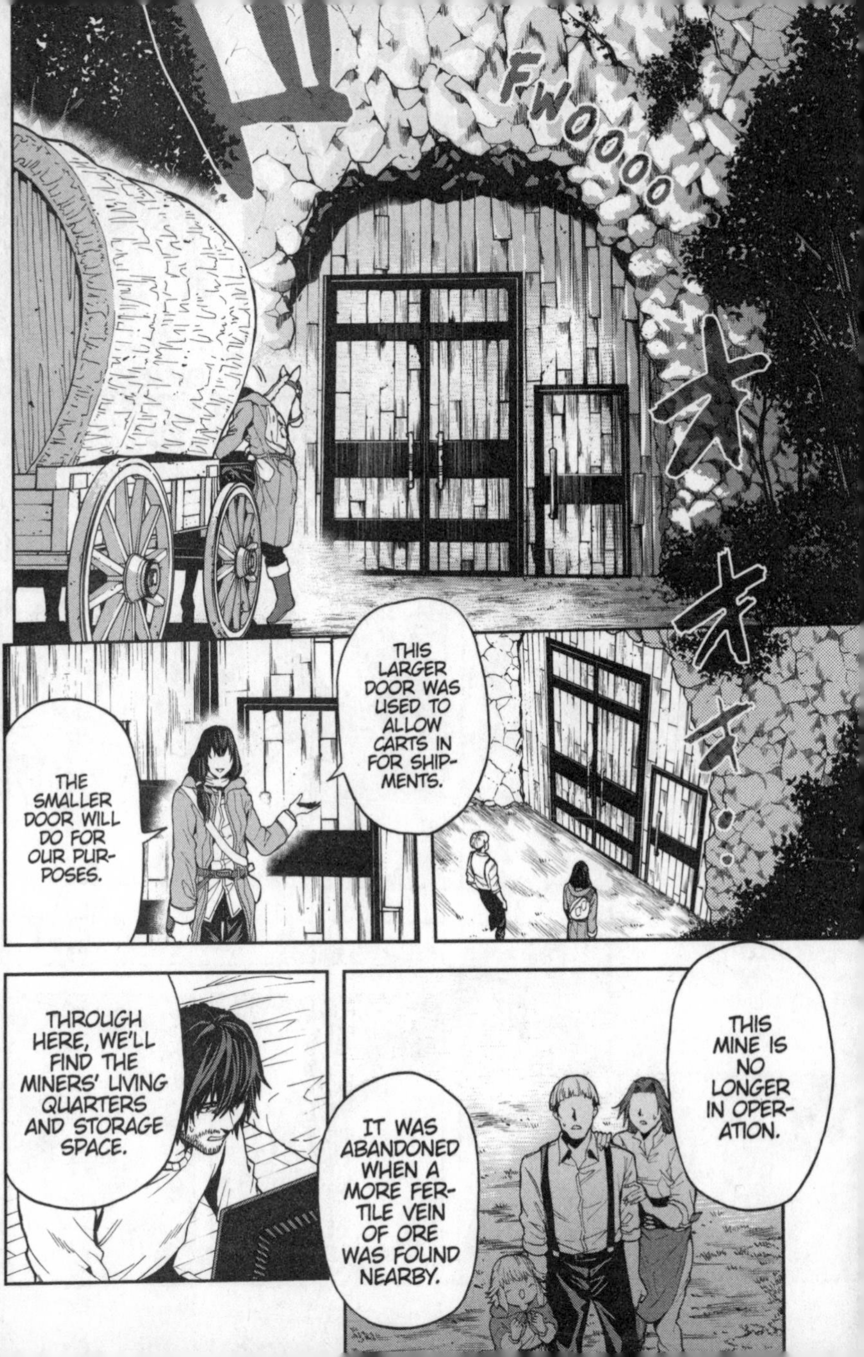
FWOOOO
THIS LARGER DOOR WAS USED TO ALLOW CARTS IN FOR SHIPMENTS.
THE SMALLER DOOR WILL DO FOR OUR PURPOSES.
THIS MINE IS NO LONGER IN OPERATION.
IT WAS ABANDONED WHEN A MORE FERTILE VEIN OF ORE WAS FOUND NEARBY.
THROUGH HERE, WE'LL FIND THE MINERS' LIVING QUARTERS AND STORAGE SPACE.

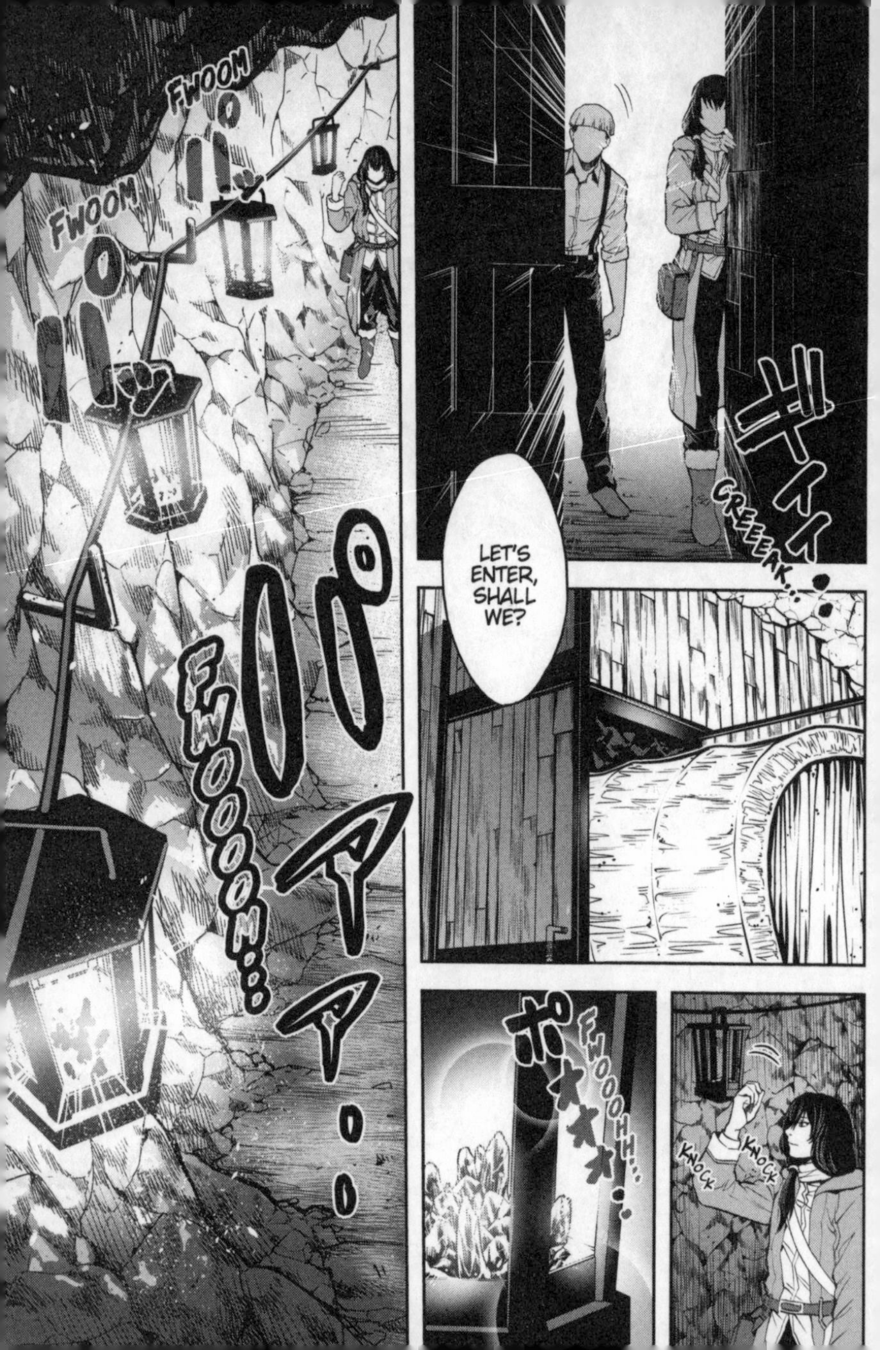
CREEEAK...
LET'S ENTER, SHALL WE?
KNOCK KNOCK
FWOOOHH...
FWOOM
FWOOM
FWOOOOOM...

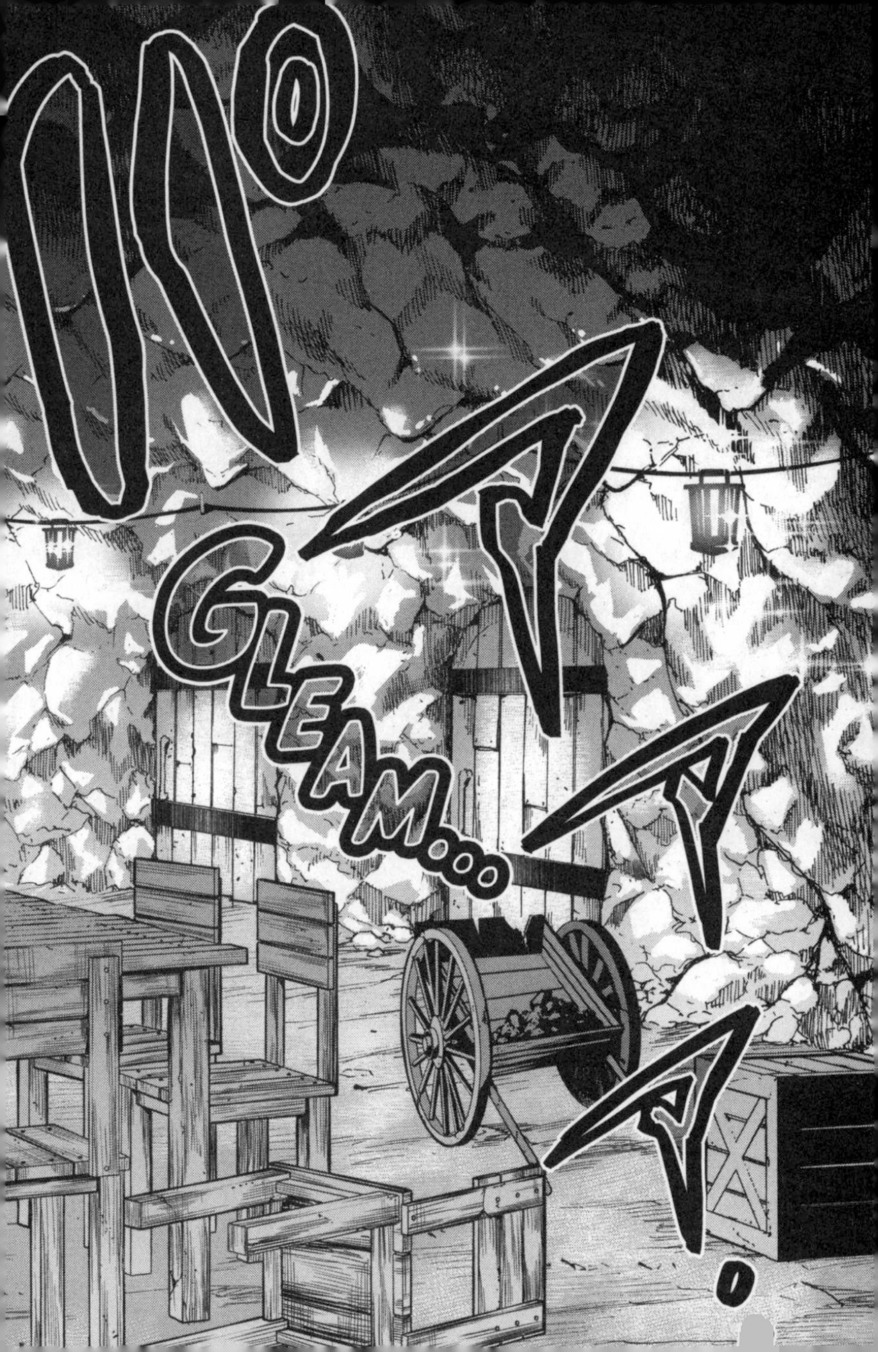

GLEAM...

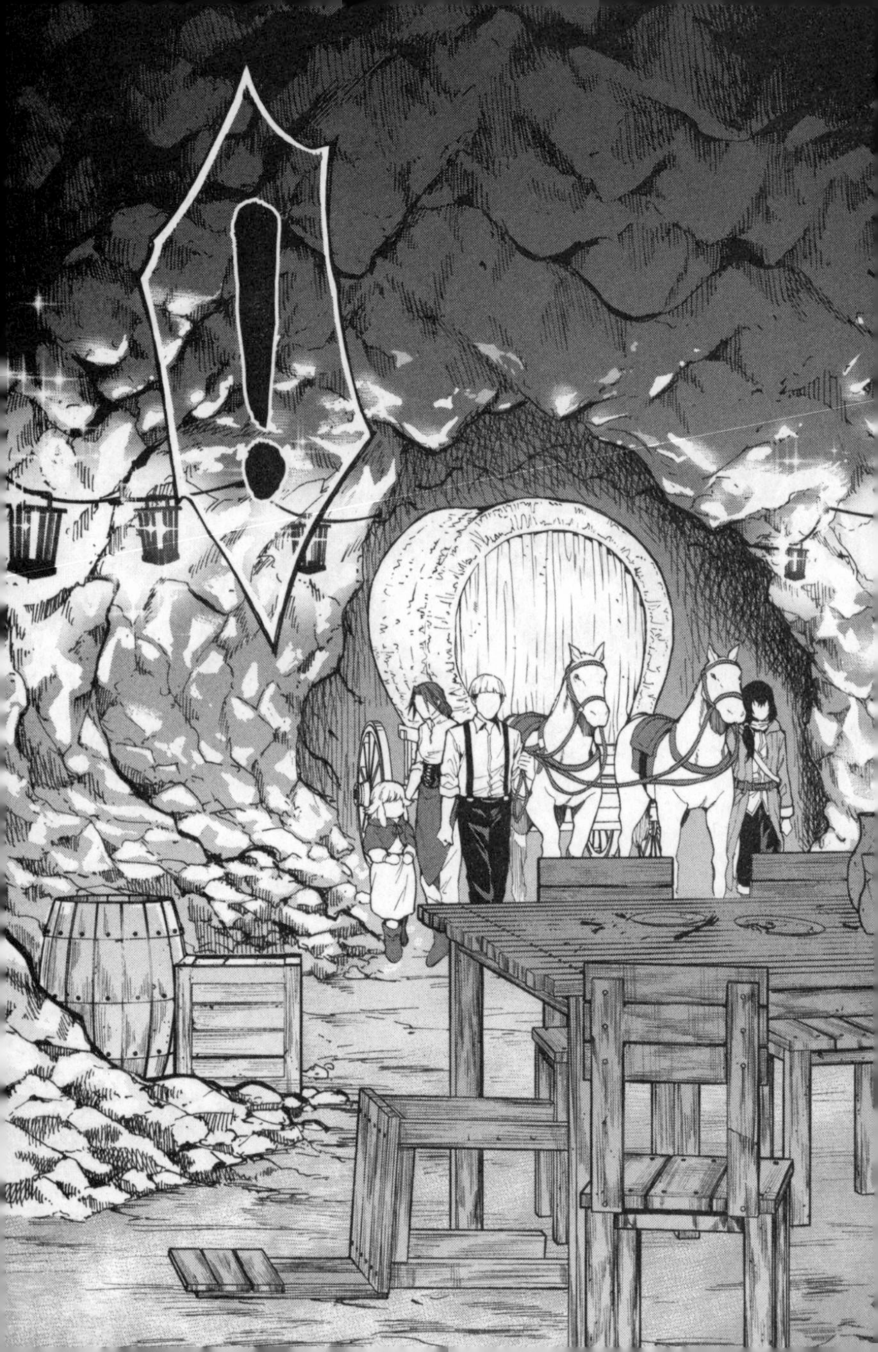
!

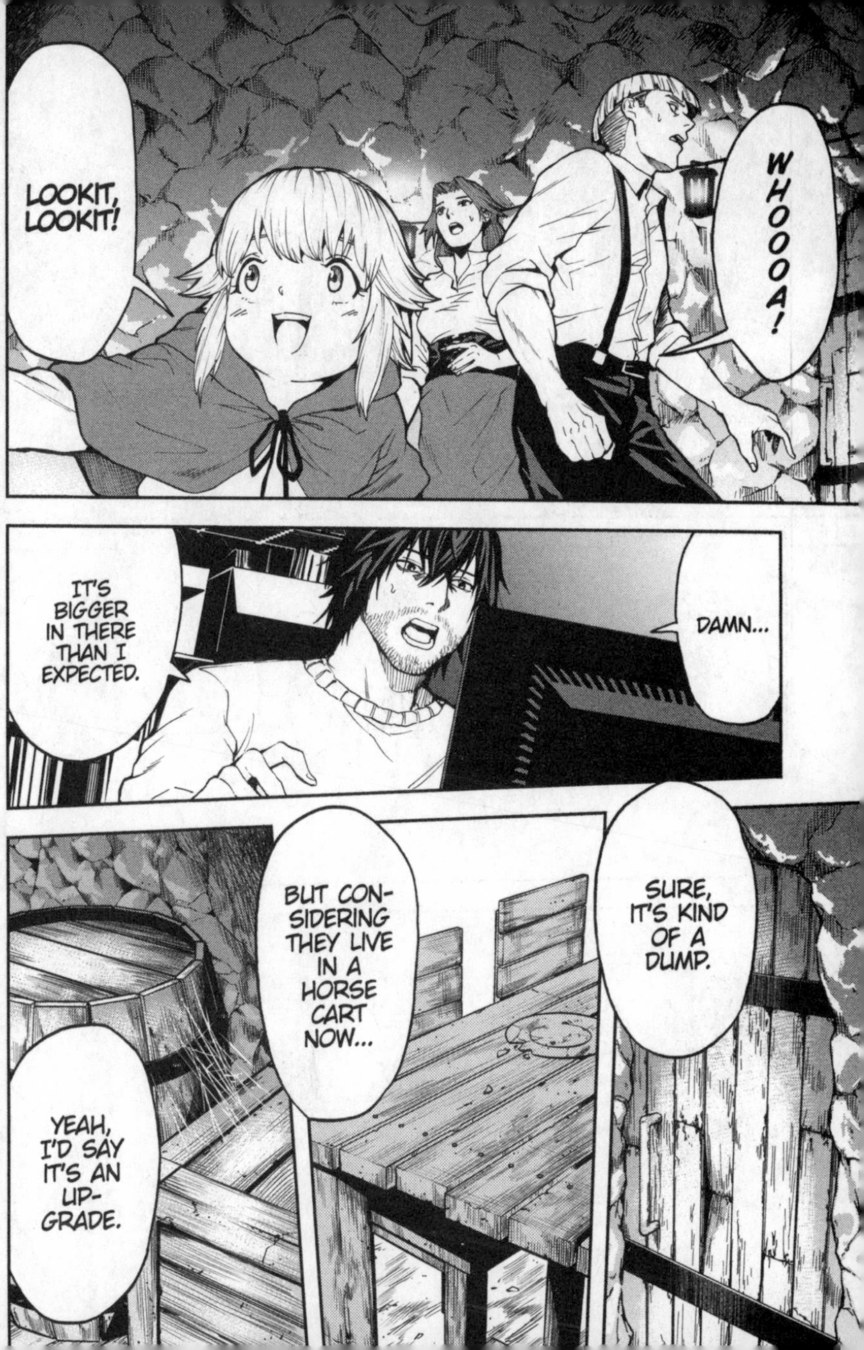
WHOOOA!
LOOKIT, LOOKIT!
DAMN...
IT'S BIGGER IN THERE THAN I EXPECTED.
SURE, IT'S KIND OF A DUMP.
BUT CONSIDERING THEY LIVE IN A HORSE CART NOW...
YEAH, I'D SAY IT'S AN UPGRADE.

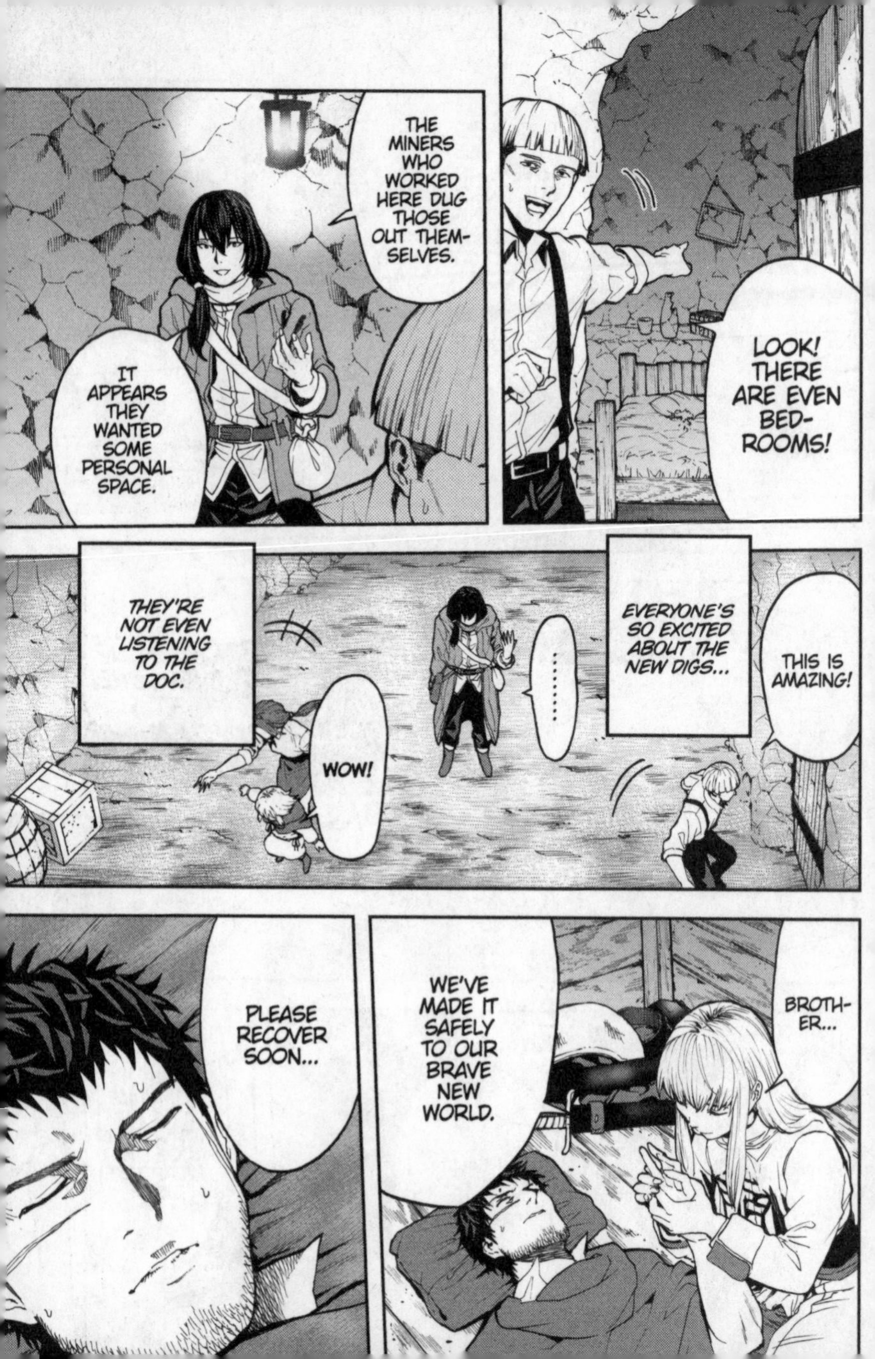
LOOK! THERE ARE EVEN BED-ROOMS!
THE MINERS WHO WORKED HERE DUG THOSE OUT THEM-SELVES.
IT APPEARS THEY WANTED SOME PERSONAL SPACE.
THIS IS AMAZING!
EVERYONE'S SO EXCITED ABOUT THE NEW DIGS...
......
THEY'RE NOT EVEN LISTENING TO THE DOC.
WOW!
BROTHER...
WE'VE MADE IT SAFELY TO OUR BRAVE NEW WORLD.
PLEASE RECOVER SOON...

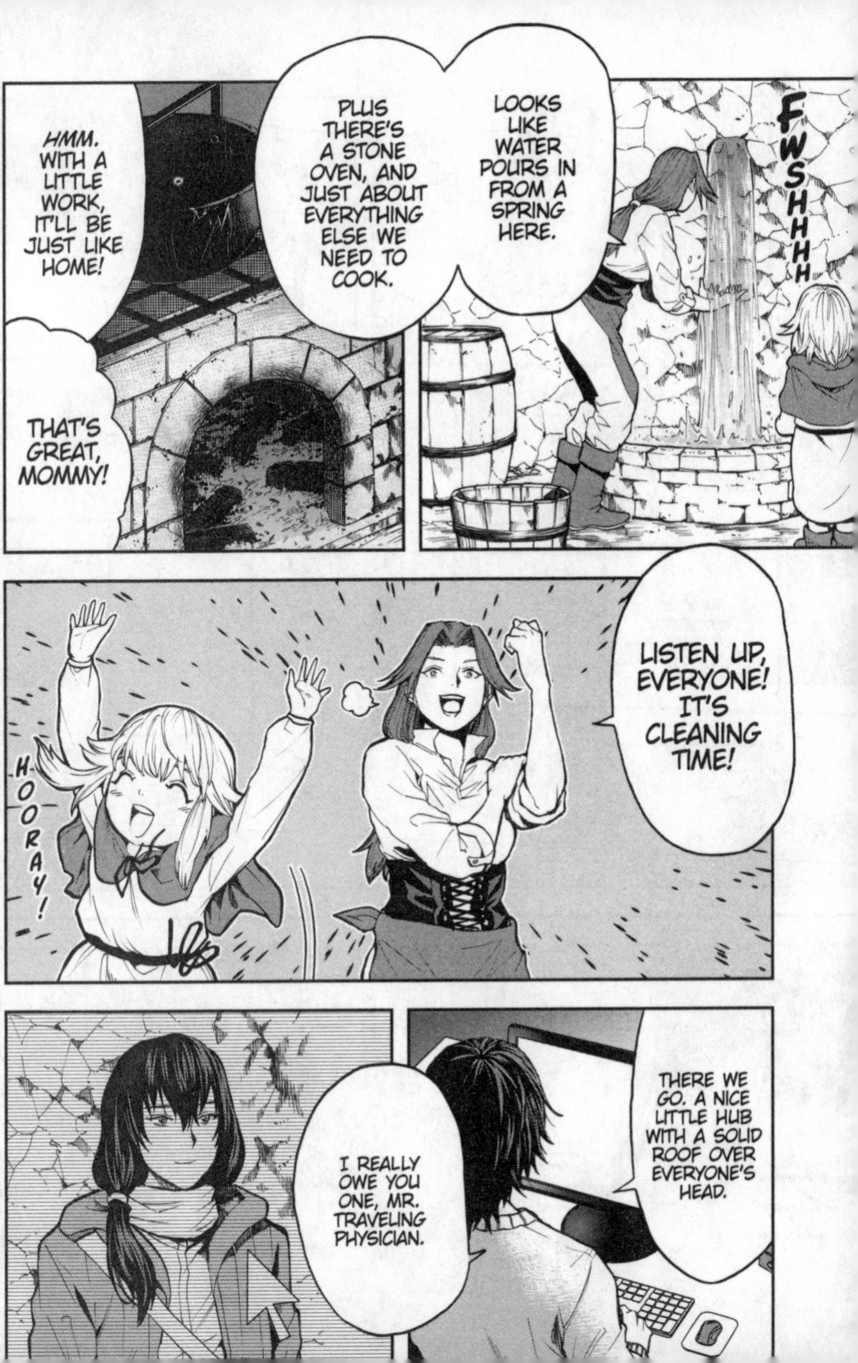

FWSHHH
LOOKS LIKE WATER POURS IN FROM A SPRING HERE.
PLUS THERE'S A STONE OVEN, AND JUST ABOUT EVERYTHING ELSE WE NEED TO COOK.
HMM. WITH A LITTLE WORK, IT'LL BE JUST LIKE HOME!
THAT'S GREAT, MOMMY!
LISTEN UP, EVERYONE! IT'S CLEANING TIME!
HOORAY!
THERE WE GO. A NICE LITTLE HUB WITH A SOLID ROOF OVER EVERYONE'S HEAD.
I REALLY OWE YOU ONE, MR. TRAVELING PHYSICIAN.

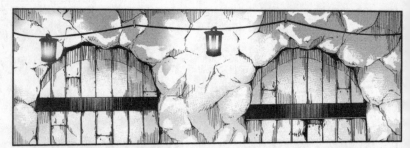

NOW, EVERYONE KEEP QUIET SO WE DON'T BOTHER GAMS, GOT IT?

LET'S GET THIS CAVE SO CLEAN, HE THINKS HE WOKE UP IN HEAVEN!

OKAY!

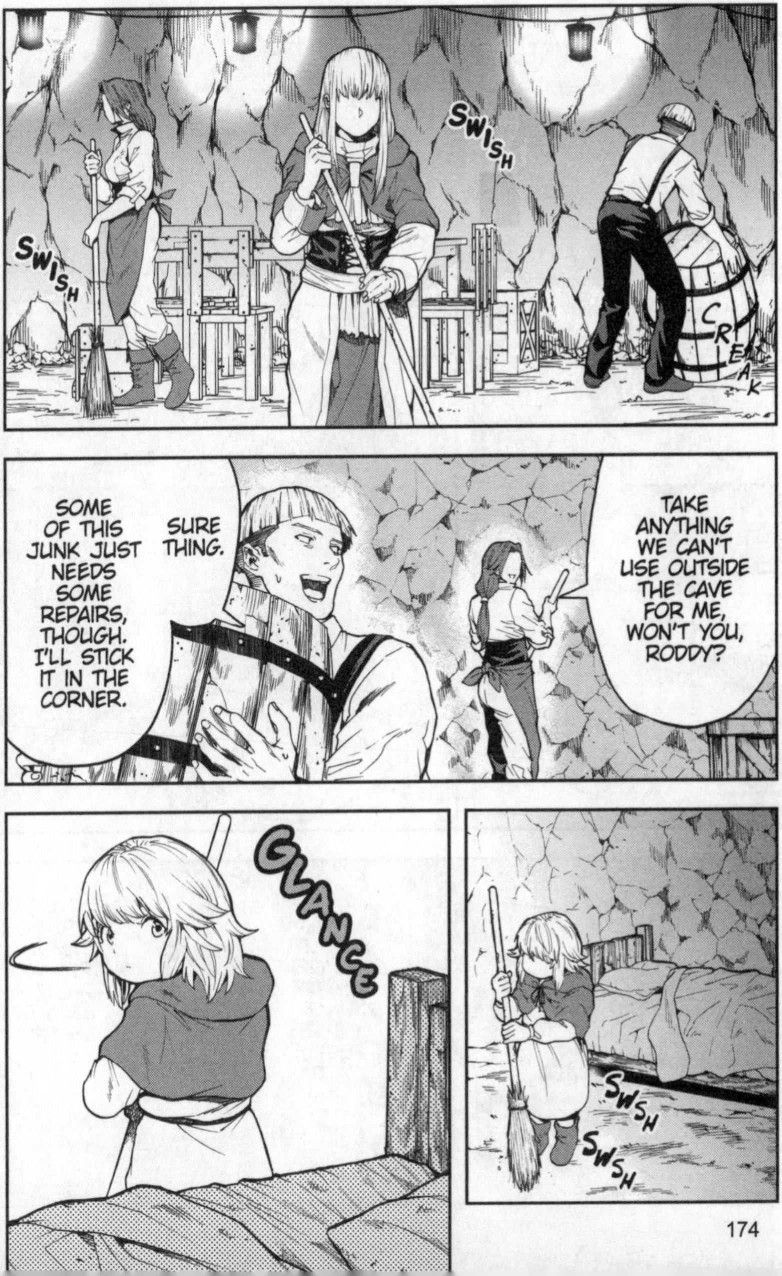
SWISH
CREAK
SWISH
TAKE ANYTHING WE CAN'T USE OUTSIDE THE CAVE FOR ME, WON'T YOU, RODDY?
SURE THING.
SOME OF THIS JUNK JUST NEEDS SOME REPAIRS, THOUGH. I'LL STICK IT IN THE CORNER.
SWSH
SWSH
GLANCE

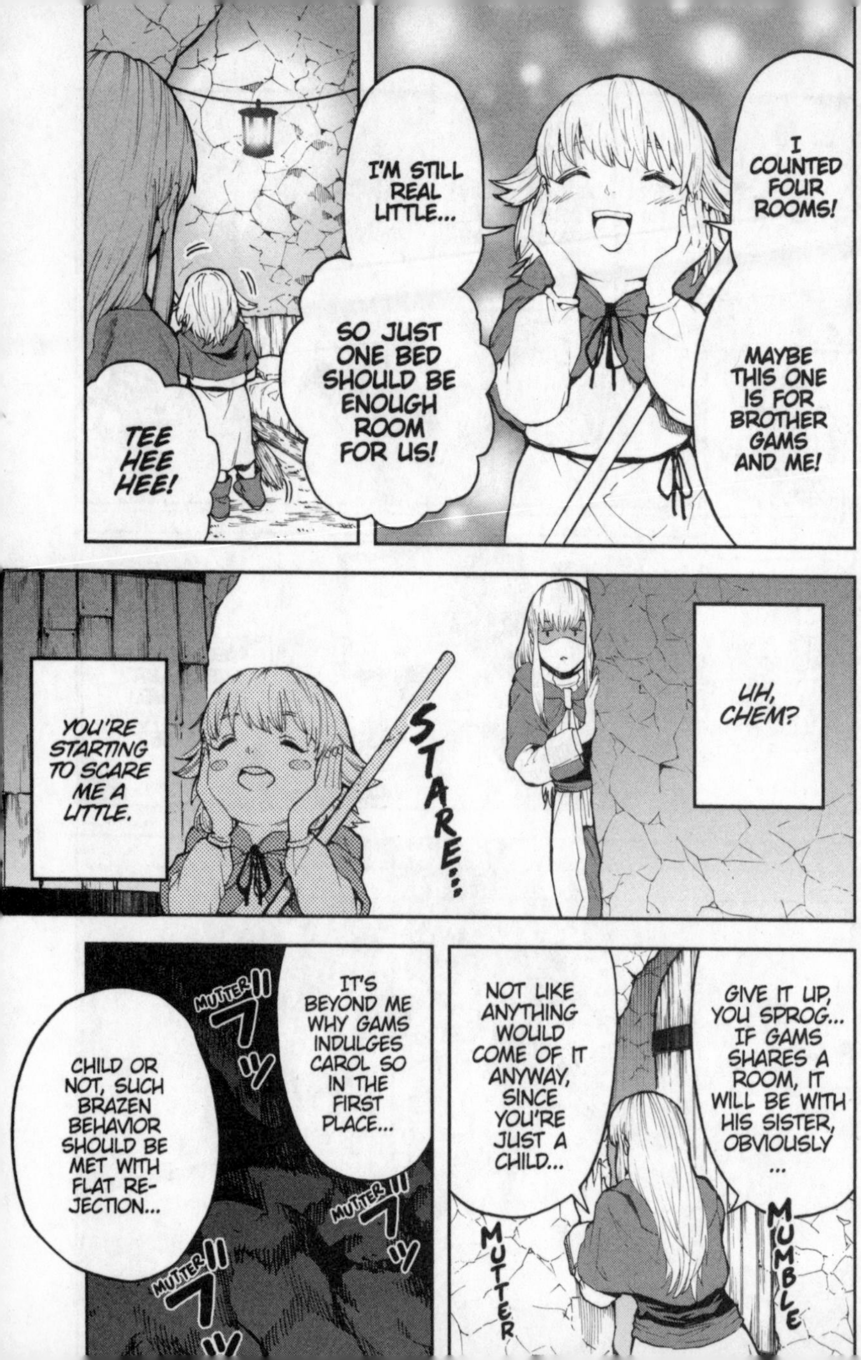
I COUNTED FOUR ROOMS!
MAYBE THIS ONE IS FOR BROTHER GAMS AND ME!
I'M STILL REAL LITTLE...
SO JUST ONE BED SHOULD BE ENOUGH ROOM FOR US!
TEE HEE HEE!
UH, CHEM?
STARE...
YOU'RE STARTING TO SCARE ME A LITTLE.
GIVE IT UP, YOU SPROG... IF GAMS SHARES A ROOM, IT WILL BE WITH HIS SISTER, OBVIOUSLY ...
MUMBLE
NOT LIKE ANYTHING WOULD COME OF IT ANYWAY, SINCE YOU'RE JUST A CHILD...
MUTTER
IT'S BEYOND ME WHY GAMS INDULGES CAROL SO IN THE FIRST PLACE...
MUTTER
CHILD OR NOT, SUCH BRAZEN BEHAVIOR SHOULD BE MET WITH FLAT REJECTION...
MUTTER
MUTTER

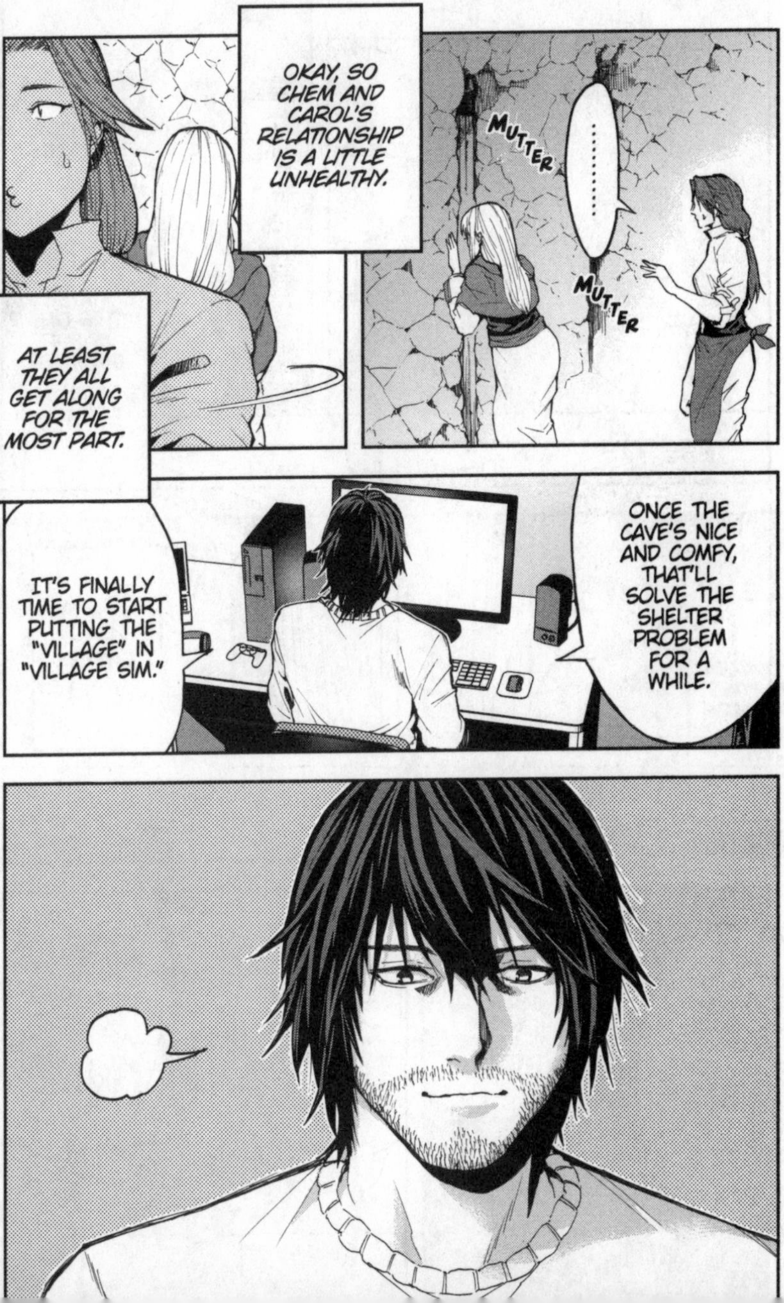
MUTTER
......
MUTTER
OKAY, SO CHEM AND CAROL'S RELATIONSHIP IS A LITTLE UNHEALTHY.
AT LEAST THEY ALL GET ALONG FOR THE MOST PART.
ONCE THE CAVE'S NICE AND COMFY, THAT'LL SOLVE THE SHELTER PROBLEM FOR A WHILE.
IT'S FINALLY TIME TO START PUTTING THE "VILLAGE" IN "VILLAGE SIM."

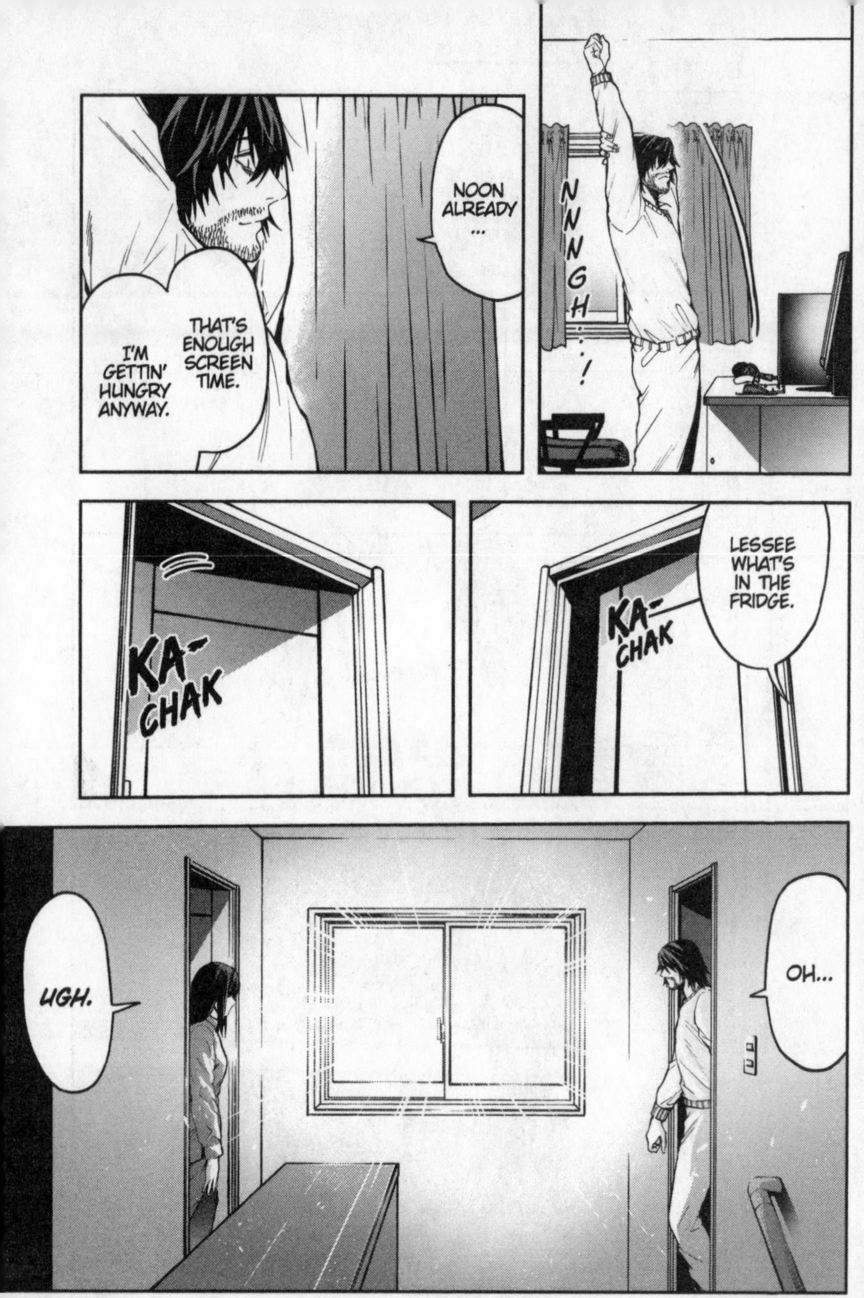
NNNGH...!
NOON ALREADY ...
THAT'S ENOUGH SCREEN TIME.
I'M GETTIN' HUNGRY ANYWAY.
LESSEE WHAT'S IN THE FRIDGE.
KA-CHAK
KA-CHAK
OH...
UGH.

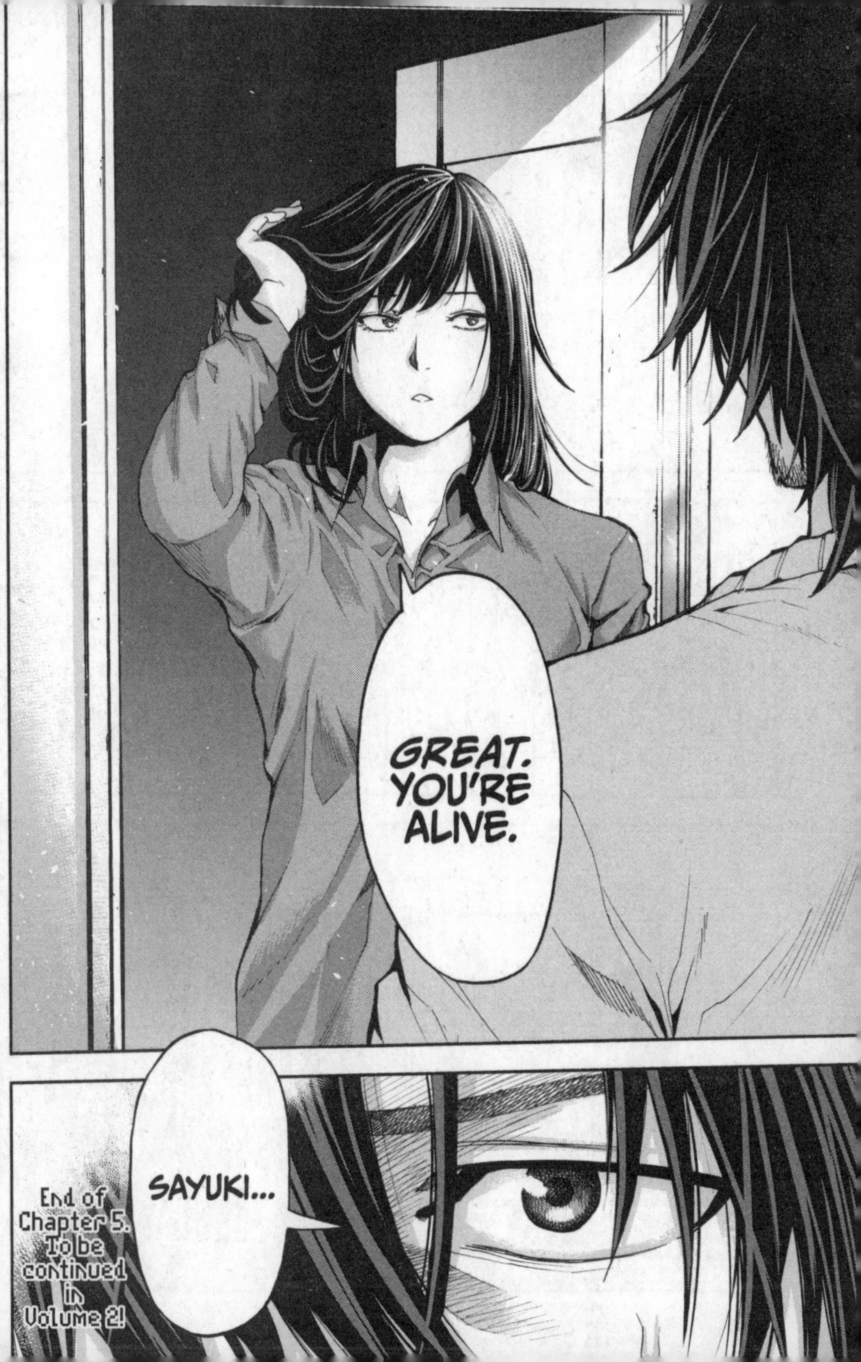
GREAT. YOU'RE ALIVE.
SAYUKI...
End of Chapter 5. To be continued in Volume 2!

THE NPCs IN THIS VILLAGE SIM GAME MUST BE REAL! ↵

SEVEN SEAS E

MW00532997

THE NPCs
SIM GAM

story by **HIRUKUMA** art by **KAZUHIKO MORITA** character design by **NAMAKO**

TRANSLATION
John Neal

LETTERING
Ochie Caraan

COVER DESIGN
Hanase Qi

LOGO DESIGN
George Panella

PROOFREADER
Brett Hallahan

COPY EDITOR
Dawn Davis

EDITOR
J.P. Sullivan

PREPRESS TECHNICIAN
Rhiannon Rasmussen-Silverstein

PRODUCTION ASSOCIATE
Christa Miesner

PRODUCTION MANAGER
Lissa Pattillo

MANAGING EDITOR
Julie Davis

ASSOCIATE PUBLISHER
Adam Arnold

PUBLISHER
Jason DeAngelis

First published in Japan in 2020 by KADOKAWA CORPORATION, Tokyo.
English translation rights arranged with KADOKAWA CORPORATION, Tokyo.

Seven Seas press and purchase enquiries can be sent to Marketing Manager Lianne Sentar at press@gomanga.com. Information regarding the distribution and purchase of digital editions is available from Digital Manager CK Russell at digital@gomanga.com.

ISBN: 978-1-64827-612-5
Printed in Canada
First Printing: September 2021
10 9 8 7 6 5 4 3 2 1

READING DIRECTIONS

This book reads from ***right to left***, Japanese style. If this is your first time reading manga, you start reading from the top right panel on each page and take it from there. If you get lost, just follow the numbered diagram here. It may seem backwards at first, but you'll get the hang of it! Have fun!!

1
2
3
4
5
6
7
8
9

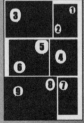

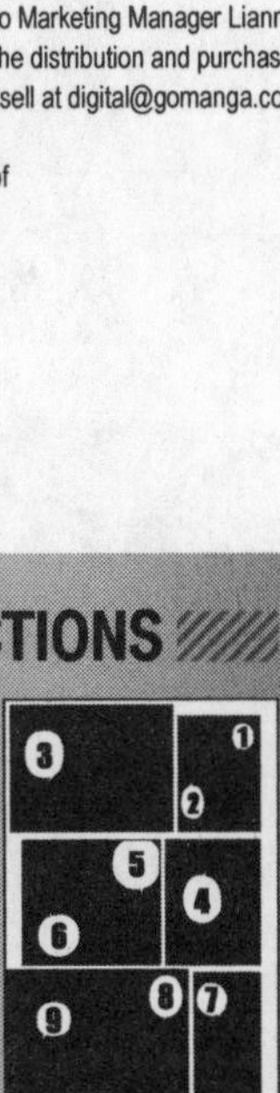

Follow us online: www.SevenSeasEntertainment.com